RACE AND SEX
DISCRIMINATION

AUSTRALIA
The Law Book Company
Brisbane . Sydney . Melbourne . Perth

CANADA
Carswell
Ottawa . Toronto . Calgary . Montreal . Vancouver

Agents:

Steimatzky's Agency Ltd., Tel Aviv;
N. M. Tripathi (Private) Ltd., Bombay;
Eastern Law House (Private) Ltd., Calcutta;
M.P.P. House, Bangalore;
Universal Book Traders, Delhi;
Aditya Books, Delhi;
MacMillan Shuppan KK, Tokyo;
Pakistan Law House, Karachi, Lahore

RACE AND SEX DISCRIMINATION

COLIN BOURN B.Sc.(Econ.)
Barrister,
Director of the International Centre for Management, Law and Industrial Relations,
Senior Lecturer in the Faculty of Law, University of Leicester

JOHN WHITMORE B.A., BCL
Practising Barrister,
formerly Legal Director, Commission for Racial Equality

SECOND EDITION

DEPARTMENT OF
PROFESSIONAL & CURRICULUM SUPPORT STUDIES

MORAY HOUSE INSTITUTE OF EDUCATION
HERIOT-WATT UNIVERSITY

LONDON
SWEET & MAXWELL
1993

First Edition
(Published as *Discrimination
and Equal Pay*) 1989
Second Edition 1993
Second impression 1994

Published in 1993 by
Sweet & Maxwell Limited of
South Quay Plaza, 183 Marsh Wall, London E14 9FT
Computerset by Wyvern Typesetting, Bristol
and printed in Great Britain by Butler and Tanner Ltd,
Frome and London

British Library Cataloguing in Publication Data

A catalogue record for this book is available
from the British Library

ISBN 0-421-472405

The index was prepared by Alex Noel-Tod

No natural forests were destroyed to make this product; only
farmed timber was used and replanted

FOREWORD

The second edition of this book is a clear and comprehensive contribution both for lawyers and others to the literature in the field of equality law, which incorporates the latest European Community developments.

A legislative framework to combat racism and sexism in certain limited fields exists in Britain albeit with various imperfections in both content and effect.

The ethos of the Single Market in the European Community, with its emphasis on the removal of barriers to the freedom of movement for goods, services, capital and people, significantly lists people last. If there is to be genuine freedom of movement, there needs also to be clarity and certainty about legal rights in employment, social security and civil liberties. The danger, against a background of growing electoral support for racist and fascist political parties, is that harmonisation of laws on race and sex discrimination in the European Community will be downwards to the most regressive and illiberal standards. In evaluating existing legislation the book considers freedom from discrimination as a fundamental right, and points the way towards further entrenchment of such rights.

The argument about how the European Community should legislate, and indeed whether the Community has the legal competence or political authority to legislate, is often deliberately clouded by those who would prefer no action at all. There is also continuing argument about the wisdom of Euro-wide anti-discrimination statutes on sex and race.

The concept of Community citizenship, if it is to have real meaning, needs both political and legal acknowledgment. The President of the European Commission, Jacques Delors, has indicated that the Commission is ready to acknowledge this. In a letter of December 17, 1992 from Mr Delors this comment was made: "Much of what the Commission does within its designated working areas more or less directly affects the fight against racism and xenophobia. Various Members of the Commission are responsible for these areas, and there is therefore a collegiate responsibility for this amongst the Commissioners."

I am sure that this book will be an important contribution to future developments in the equality field.

MEL READ
Member of the European Parliament for Leicester,
Nuneaton and North Warwickshire
May 20, 1993

PREFACE

Just four years have made the first edition of this book look very dated indeed. Equal opportunities law has developed at a rapid pace with huge changes happening all the time. There is never pause enough to make it the perfect time for a new edition. Thus, some fundamental controversies which have thrust themselves to the forefront, such as the impact of equality law on pensions, and on pregnancy and the workplace are still only part-way to being solved. We have tried to ensure that the law is up to date to the end of April 1993, but please bear in mind that changes at page-proof stage are subject to limitations.

We have taken advantage of the new edition to do some reorganisation of material. We are grateful for various suggestions by reviewers of the first edition. In particular we think you will find our treatment of the Community law background is improved. Last time we assumed a basic understanding in the reader, but then relented and added an explanatory appendix! Studying sex discrimination law can be a good way of finding out how Community law works in practice, and we are mindful of those who might wish to use the book, or parts of it, in that way, and indeed of those who may yet come to the book without any basic grounding in Community law.

We have added a chapter on public bodies (perhaps being then surprised by a Court of Appeal decision restricting judicial review proceedings where U.K. law is in apparent conflict with Community law). Also a section on maternity rights, so that the practitioner can consider the position in a text that also deals with pregnancy issues. This chapter is at the end so that we could incorporate the latest legislative material without having to re-jig pagination throughout the book. Our approach has been to set out the law as it is now and to contrast that with the position as it will be once the Pregnancy Directive is fully implemented.

The book still concentrates on the law as it stands as a text for legal practitioners, which was our original brief. Indeed there is now more material on procedural considerations than previously, possibly reflecting the fact that one of us is now back at the Bar. However there are critical reflections throughout the book on the way in which the law has developed and some pointers to the future.

As well as legal practitioners, we envisage a readership amongst personnel officers, the staff of various advisory bodies such as Racial Equality Councils and students. The number of postgraduate courses as well as undergraduate degrees which cover discrimination law is increasing.

One of the first things to understand in dealing with equal

opportunities is how value-laden all terminology is. It is hardly surprising that experts appointed by tribunals to evaluate work reveal little consistency, when the criteria traditinally used for the job evaluations were created to serve wholly different purposes. How far are tribunals, familiar with notions of reasonableness from the unfair dismissal jurisdiction, able to appreciate that what has traditionally been regarded as reasonable may actually be the cause of race or sex discrimination? In judging whether a requirement is justifiable or whether a difference is material what set of values are they to use? All this is not to express a defeatism. It is this capacity of the terminology to mean different things to different people (or perhaps more importantly to the same people at different times) which gives the subject the potential for great dynamism, except where pockets get trapped in a time-warp by *stare decisis*.

Some features of the present equal opportunities scene are very striking. Litigation, if successful, generally provides remedies for individuals not groups of people. Yet the focus of attention of those with the more advanced equal opportunity policies is increasingly on outcomes for groups. The Codes of Practice under the Acts have fallen behind, with their emphasis on procedures, and most employers are even further back. Elsewhere statutory schemes aim at making employers draw up plans, for example, under the Fair Employment legislation in Northern Ireland and the Pay Equity law in Ontario, thus in effect giving legal content to the notion of equal opportunity as opposed to merely banning discrimination. British legislation on the whole still reflects the toe-dipping efforts of the 1970s and the ripples are consequently minor.

Race discrimination law lacks the source of inspiration and change which sex discrimination law finds in Europe (witness the pensions and pregnancy issues for example). It is inevitable, therefore, that those trying to achieve change within the context of the Race Relations Act will feel the restraints of British law very keenly, as there is no alternative route. Whereas the general effect of Community law is to move freedom from sex discrimination in employment in the direction of being a basic right, freedom from race discrimination is a right which has to give way to other priorities established in the British system, wherever another statute or even a minister permits discrimination. It is odd that there should be a lower priority for ensuring freedom from racial discrimination than for ensuring freedom from sex discrimination when ethnic tensions in Europe have shown themselves both in the past and now quite capable of destroying whole societies. Putting the conditions for equality into place when society has already begun to disintegrate will be too late.

COLIN BOURN   JOHN WHITMORE
Faculty of Law   Chambers
Leicester University   21 Portland Road
                                           Leicester

April 30, 1993

CONTENTS

4 Discrimination in relation to work

5 Equal Pay

TABLE OF CASES

TABLE OF STATUTES

TABLE OF STATUTORY INSTRUMENTS

CODES OF PRACTICE

TABLE OF TREATIES AND CONVENTIONS

LEGISLATION OF THE EUROPEAN COMMUNITIES

Directives

Recommendations and Proposals

1 THE LEGAL FRAMEWORK OF EQUALITY LAW

Introduction

1.01   Race relations legislation in Great Britain consists of only one layer: the Race Relations Act 1976, as amended. Sex discrimination legislation consists of two layers: a Community layer and a subordinate national layer. Legally, Community law is supreme, but it makes more chronological and political sense to begin by describing the origins of the national law and then to turn to examine how, and by what processes, national law has been modified by Community law.

1.02   In the United Kingdom there is also the separate and more rigorous regime which attempts to ensure the fair participation of the two religious communities in Northern Ireland, but it is beyond the scope of this book to do more than compare and contrast that regime with the law on race and sex discrimination at appropriate points. There are, however, several developments in the Fair Employment (Northern Ireland) Act 1989 which merit initial attention, by way of contrast to what follows with regard to the British legislation.

Comparison between Great Britain and Northern Ireland

The Fair Employment (Northern Ireland) Act 1989   **1.03**   The Fair Employment (Northern Ireland) Act deals with religious and political discrimination and strengthens the 1976 legislation in force in the Province. It was in part a response to the threat of sanctions by United States corporations operating under the MacBride principles and to the Anglo-Irish agreement. It is useful to quote directly from the Government document "The Act at a Glance" as to the aims of the legislation:

- "active practice of fair employment by employers
- close and continuous audit of that practice by new and stronger enforcement agencies

- use of affirmative actions, and goals and timetables, to remedy under-representation
- use of criminal penalties, and economic sanctions, to ensure good employment practices"

1.04   In overall terms the main importance of the legislation for equal opportunities is that apart from dealing with discrimination in a more forceful way, with a special tribunal empowered to award compensation of up to £30,000, it gives substance to the whole idea of equal opportunities.

1.05   The main features of the legislation are:

- compulsory registration of all public employers and private employers with a workforce of more than ten employees (ss.22-26);
- compulsory monitoring of the workforces of all registered employers and the monitoring of applications for employment to all public employers and private employers of 250 or more (ss.27-30);
- compulsory reviews of recruitment, training and promotion practices to determine if fair participation in the concern is provided for the members of the two religious communities (s.31), with audit by the Fair Employment Commission under sections 32-35;
- mandatory affirmative action, and goals and timetables, as directed by the Commission under sections 36-37.

"Fair participation in the concern"   **1.06**   The concept of "fair participation in the concern" is not defined in the Act but McCrudden suggests that it will be achieved when under-representation has been eliminated.[1] Whilst the Act speaks of fair participation in the concern, McCrudden argues that regard should be had to the overall position of Catholics and Protestants, at least until a broad balance is achieved. If attention is focused only on the balance within any one concern, whilst Catholics might gain where they are under-represented, they may lose where they are over-represented, resulting in less rapid progress towards an end of under-representation at large.

1.07   As the Commission for Racial Equality say in their "Second Review of the Race Relations Act 1976":

"The whole thrust of the Northern Ireland legislation moves away from the narrow notion of eliminating discrimination to the idea of a 'more effective practice of equality of opportunity in employment', with the ultimate aim of 'fair participation' by the two communities."

[1] C. McCrudden "Affirmative Action and Fair Participation: Interpreting the Fair Employment Act 1989", *Industrial Law Journal*, Vols. 21, 3, p. 186.

The Commission also observe:

"No doubt the politics of the situation, the level of violence between the two communities, could be used to justify legislating earlier for Northern Ireland. They cannot, however, be long-term arguments against treating equal opportunities equally seriously in Britain."

Contract compliance
1.08   The Northern Ireland legislation uses not only criminal penalties but also the economic sanctions of loss of grants and contracts to punish bad practice. A useful albeit very basic system of contract compliance has been introduced.

1.09   In Britain by contrast, no attempt has ever been made to monitor compliance with equal opportunity clauses in Government contracts. Indeed, the Commission for Racial Equality once backed off from a formal investigation into this matter, rather than endanger approval of its Code of Practice in Employment. There has been a retreat from allowing local authorities to carry out contract compliance in their contracts. After the 1988 Local Government Act it was stopped altogether for sex equality and allowed only in a very restricted form for racial equality. It is a sad fact that a previous Chair of the British Equal Opportunities Commission told one of the authors that she did "not believe in contract compliance". Happily this is not the presently prevailing view. We set out in chapter 9 a brief account of contract compliance in the United States under Executive Order 11246.

1.10   The obligation placed upon employers to draw up and implement plans to deal with inequality is also a measure that can be taken with regard to equal pay, as is demonstrated by the Ontario pay equity legislation. In Ontario, employers are under a duty to post a pro-active pay equity plan, rather than simply awaiting the receipt of equal value complaints from employees.

Disabled Persons Act 1944
1.11   The other contrasting anti-discrimination regime in Britain is that in favour of the disabled. Whilst this regime, based upon the Disabled Persons Act 1944, goes beyond goals and timetables to incorporate a quota of 3 per cent. for the employment of the registered disabled by those with a workforce of 20 or more, exemptions are relatively easily obtained. The future of the 1944 Act has been seriously questioned, in particular by the 1990 consultative document "Employment and Training for People with Disabilities." Whilst the Government has since resiled from its earlier position of abolishing the quota system and substituting a voluntary code of practice, the future of this regime remains in doubt, if only because of a widespread failure to register by disabled people. The disabled fear that registration will

stigmatise them and render them less, rather than more employable, with the result that only 1 per cent. of the workforce is classified as disabled within the meaning of the Act. Not surprisingly there is a general failure by employers to engage 3 per cent. of registered disabled people. The Act does not provide a remedy for disabled persons who fail to find employment and prosecutions for the non-fulfilment of the quota are rare indeed.

The nature of anti-discrimination legislation in Britain

1.12   The anti-discrimination legislation which has been passed both in the Community and in Britain is essentially complaints based. This contrasts sharply with the Northern Ireland scheme for religious discrimination. The Northern Irish scheme is pro-active and requires employers to plan and monitor the composition of their workforces, under the general supervision of the Fair Employment Commission to ensure the fair participation of the two religious communities. Whilst the Commission for Racial Equality (CRE) has called for compulsory monitoring with regard to race in its recent review of the Race Relations Act, there is but a small chance of a legislative response to this call in the immediate future and the system is likely to continue to be primarily complaints based.

1.13   The British and Northern Irish legislation each strikes a different balance between a conception of anti-discrimination law as an individual right not to be the subject of discriminatory decisions and the use of the law as a tool to remedy social and economic disadvantage. The level of violence and social unrest in Northern Ireland has dictated a concerted attempt to eradicate the long term disadvantages suffered by the Catholic community, utilising economic, administrative and investigatory powers, in addition to litigation by individuals. Yet the Fair Employment Act defines equality of opportunity as existing where a person has the same opportunity to be considered for an hold employment on the same terms as any other person, "due allowance being made for any material difference in their suitability" (s.20(2)). Although equality of opportunity is not impugned by anything lawfully done in the pursuance of affirmative action section 20(3), it is nonetheless subject to the merit principle set out in section 20(2). Hepple, in a critical comment on the Report of the Standing Advisory Committee on Human Rights,[2] which formed the basics of the legislation, makes the point that an

[2] *Religious and Political Discrimination and Equality of Opportunity in Northern Ireland,* Standing Advisory Commission on Human Rights, HMSO Cmnd. 237 (1987) commented on by Hepple, *Oxford Journal of Legal Studies,* Vols. 10, 3, Autumn 1990, pp. 408-421.

excessive concern with merit at the point of selection may detract from the realisation that even where candidates are more or less equal, elements of prior disadvantage or discrimination may contribute to the poor showing of candidates from certain groups. "Merit" in this sense is a socially produced good; only the exceptional person is able to transcend the conditions of his or her upbringing and social experience.[3]

Real or formal equality?

1.14 In Britain the sex and race discrimination laws are primarily concerned with ensuring formal equality for individuals, less emphasis being placed on the eradication of social disadvantage. Indeed, the only elements of affirmative action which are permitted relate to training rather than to employment opportunities. Equality is thus seen as neutrality, a symmetrical application of the law which ignores the structural and social conditions which form each individual. It has frequently been asserted that anti-discrimination law incorporates a white and/or male norm by which applicants are to be judged. Fredman, reviewing European discrimination law from a feminist standpoint, observes that anti-discrimination law has often seen

> "equality as neutrality. It assumes that equality is an end in itself, rather than a mechanism for correcting disadvantage, and in doing so, it makes it impossible for the anti-discrimination principle to make real inroads into the disadvantaged position of women."[4]

Formal symmetrical equality law can be more sensitive to signs of reverse discrimination which run counter to currently accepted thinking, than it is to detecting commonly accepted practices which put woman or minorities at a disadvantage. For example, an absence of "career breaks" may do long term damage to the careers of many women but will not necessarily be perceived as a problem because such a practice does not run counter to a formal conception of equality based on typical male career patterns. Under the legislation in force on the mainland of Britain, there is no obligation to engage in monitoring or to review employment practices with a view to ensuring fair participation. A primary concern with real, rather than formal, equality would at least require, as the CRE have urged, that monitoring be made obligatory and contract

---

[3] Thus the influence of family patterns on womens' work participation is demonstrated in data from the 1989 Labour Force Survey, *Employment Gazette* 1990, pp. 619-643. See also "Ethnic Origins and the Labour Market", *Employment Gazette*, 1991, pp. 59-72 for factual data and Simon Field, "The Changing Nature of Racial Disadvantage, *New Community*, XIV 1/2 pp. 118-122 for a summary of the way in which racial factors operate in the labour market.

[4] S. Fredman, "European Community Sex Discrimination Law: a Critique," *Industrial Law Journal*, Vols. 21, 2, pp. 119-134. See also Nicola Lacey, "From individual to Group" (Hepple and Szyszczak eds, *Discrimination: the Limits of the Law*, Mansell, 1992), pp. 99-124.

compliance be more widely permitted in the public sector. These, together with a more effective framework for the exercise of the strategic investigatory powers of the Commissions, would provide the bases for a pro-active policy and complement the present emphasis of the law on formal individual equality.

1.15 The British legislation draws upon American experience, but is framed to take into account the differences which exist between the two legal systems. The main avenues for legal action under the British Acts in the U.K. are the Industrial Tribunals and County Courts, in which cases are brought at the behest of individual complainants. As Community discrimination law derived from Article 119 only concerns employment matters, cases which draw upon Community rights will normally be taken in the Industrial Tribunals, although Community discrimination law has been the basis of a number of judicial review cases in the High Court. Legal aid is not available in the industrial tribunals, although suitable cases can be assisted by the CRE or EOC. Assistance by one of the two Commissions can help to overcome the difficulties faced by an inexperienced litigant, especially one who would in other matters look to the Legal Aid Fund. Not only must the initiative come from individual litigants, but the remedies which can be awarded by the tribunals are also limited to the case in hand and are not of general application to others in similar circumstances. The difficulties faced by individual complainants in employment cases have been well documented in a survey undertaken by the EOC, which showed that even successful complainants found the experience difficult and stressful, the short term rewards limited, and in the longer term often experienced a deterioration in the relationship with their employer and even, on occasion, with fellow workers.[5] The survey showed that employers who suffered an adverse decision in an Industrial Tribunal did not necessarily modify the practice upon which the complaint had been founded, to the benefit of other workers. Complainants were shown to be very dependent on receiving skilled advice and representation, because discrimination law is a specialised field which constitutes only a small part of the workload of Industrial Tribunals.[6]

[5] Alice M. Leonard, "Pyrrhic Victories; Winning Sex Discrimination and Equal Pay Cases in the Industrial Tribunals", H.M.S.O., 1987.
[6] These difficulties illustrate the point made by Lustgarten in "Racial Equality and the Limits of the Law", M.L.R., Vol. 49 No. 1, p. 68 that essentially protective legislation, *i.e.* employment protection statutes generally and others of like kind, are relatively ineffective in promoting social change unless widely used by well supported litigants, such as has been the case with unfair dismissal. In that case many employers have improved their disciplinary practices and introduced a more professional approach, (even if there is little effective change in the extent of managerial discretion) but there are far more unfair dismissal than equal opportunity claims.

Representative and class actions

1.16　Although there is no equivalent to the American class action, the Industrial Tribunal Rules of Procedure[7] do allow for a representative action to be brought. Strictly, Rule 14(3) provides for the selection only of Industrial Tribunal representative respondents, but the Court of Appeal in *Ashmore* v. *British Coal Co*[8] held that where a dozen sample cases had been selected to be heard from a total of 1500 similarly situated applicants whose cases had been stayed, it was an abuse of process to attempt to re-open the issues in the absence of fresh evidence. Thus, provided there is some agreement, a group of applicants may concentrate their resources, or the resources of their trade union, on a few sample cases, the other complainants following the decision in those cases.

1.17　The collective aspect of discrimination is reflected in the role given to the CRE and the EOC. As well as having powers to assist individual claimants, the two Commissions can take up more widespread issues by the process of a formal investigation. These can be either of a general exploratory kind or, where there is a suspicion that discriminatory actions have taken place, against a named respondent. The use of these powers has been limited by the procedural complexities which have accrued round them, although the CRE recommends that these limitations should be repealed.[9] The Commissions also have an educational role, which has resulted is the issuing of Codes of Practice and other guidance documents under the two Acts. The purpose of the Codes is to assist in the reduction of discrimination and the promotion of equality of opportunity in employment between men and women or between racial groups. The Codes do not impose legal obligations, but are admissible and may be taken into account in any proceedings under the Acts.[10] Both Commissions have been active in commissioning research and disseminating advice about equality issues.

The national legislative framework

1.18　In considering the legislative framework of equality law it is more helpful and historically correct to take a chronological view of national anti-discrimination law, examining first equal pay, then sex discrimination and finally race relations law.

---

[7] The Industrial Tribunal (Rules of Procedure) Regs. 1985 (S.I. 1985 No. 16).

[8] [1990] I.R.L.R. 283, C.A. and *British Coal Corporation* v. *Smith*, EAT 29/91.

[9] "Second Review of the Race Relations Act," Consultative Paper, CRE, 1991.

[10] SDA 1975, s.56A(10) & RRA 1976, s.47(10).

The Equal Pay Act 1970

1.19 The movement for equal pay in Britain can be traced back as far as the 1888 Trades Union Congress (TUC), at which the first resolution in favour of this proposal was carried.[11] From that date until the call for legislation in the 1963 TUC, forty more resolutions in favour of equal pay were passed, whilst three Royal Commissions[12] and three Government Committees[13] looked into the question. As early as 1916, the Atkin Committee considered the question of equal pay in the course of its deliberations, distinguishing between situations where one sex or the other was excluded from taking up an employment, situations where both were employed but where there was a clear distinction between men's and women's work, and situations where both men and women were employed and where there was a sphere of common duties. It was only in this third situation that the Committee felt that equal pay was appropriate, by which was meant "equal pay in proportion to efficient output." Beatrice Webb, in a dissenting note, preferred the approach of a national minimum wage, combined with paying the rate for the job. She accepted that if, as has often been supposed, women were less effective as workers than men, there would be some re-allocation of work between the sexes, but she did not think that such an approach would lead to increased unemployment amongst women.

The Asquith Commission

1.20 A similar division of views occurred in the Asquith Commission, which reported in 1946. The Commission accepted the principle of equal pay in the public services, although they were not in favour of the principle being applied in the private sector. The majority of the Commission felt that existing differentials reflected, albeit not perfectly, differences in efficiency and that a move towards equal pay would be likely to lead to increased female unemployment. The minority took a broader view of the notion of equal pay and argued in a note of dissent for the acceptance of the principle of paying the rate for the job, irrespective of the sex of the worker. The Report of the Commission was accepted by the post-war Labour Government, but its implementation was delayed, because

[11] See M. Snell, P. Glucklich and M. Povall, "Equal Pay and Equal Opportunities," Research Paper No. 20, Department of Employment, 1981 and W. B. Creighton, "Working Women and the Law", Mansell, 1979 for general accounts of the history of equal pay and equal opportunities.

[12] Royal Commission on Civil Service Pay (McDonnel Commission) Cd. 7338 (1912-16), Royal Commission on the Civil Service (Tomlin Commission) Cmd. 3909 (1929-31), Royal Commission on Equal Pay (Asquith Commission) Cmd. 6937 (1944-46).

[13] The Women's Employment Committee, Cd. 9239 (1918), Report of the War Cabinet Committee on the Employment of Women in Industry (Atkin Committee) Cmd. 135, (1919) Anderson Committee on the Pay etc. of State Servants, Cmnd. 1923.

other reforms were felt to have a greater priority when only limited resources were available. In the following years there was political pressure in favour of the adoption of equal pay in the public services, which finally resulted in an agreement in 1955 that the Whitley Council would introduce equal pay in the non-industrial civil service in seven equal instalments, a process which was duly completed in 1961. The Government took the view that as a minority employer in the industrial grades it must respect the "fair relativity" principle.

1.21 The movement towards equal pay lost some of its political impetus with the granting of equal pay to non-industrial civil servants, who had been amongst its best organised advocates. But in 1961 there was a change in view by the TUC who called for the Government to ratify International Labour Organisation Convention 100, which called for the recognition of the principle of equal pay for work of equal value. The 1962 TUC recognised that this might mean the need for legislation, instead of relying on voluntary methods of reaching agreement with employers through collective bargaining, which hitherto had been its policy. "Voluntaryism" and abstention from statutory regulation of labour relations, had been the hallmark of British industrial relations for many years, although it has to be said that the unions had not been very effective in pressing employers on this issue.[14] In 1964 the Labour Government came to power, committed to legislate on equal pay and in 1970 the Equal Pay Bill was introduced. It came into force at the end of 1975, giving employers and trade unions five years to prepare for its implementation. By this time the Sex Discrimination Act had reached the statute book, with its complementary emphasis on equal opportunities. Prior to 1975 women working full-time were earning 63 per cent. of male full-time earnings, although by 1980 this figure had reached 72 per cent. The differential in earnings between women and men changed little until 1987, when an upward trend became perceptible, with the figure for 1990 being 77 per cent.[15] rising to 78 per cent. for 1991.

---

[14] Writing as long ago as 1920 Barbara Drake said: "Men trade unionists are accused of sex privilege and prejudice. . . .. A belief in the divine right of every man to his job is not peculiar to kings and capitalists, and men in organised trades are not disposed to share these advantages with a host of women competitors." Barbara Drake, *Women in Trade Unions, 1920*, reprinted in *Waged Work: A Reader* (Virago, 1987). See also the account of contemporary practice in *Women and Trade Unions*, Nicola Charles, in *Waged Work* (*supra*). Davies makes the point that the Department of Employment was concerned that an "equal value" based statute would have upset settled patterns of collective bargaining. P. L. Davies, "EEC Legislation, U.K. Legislation and Industrial Relations", in C. McCrudden (ed.), *Women, Employment & European Equality Law* (Eclipse, 1988), p. 28.

[15] Source EOC: *Women and Men in Britain 1991*, EOC, HMSO, London.

1970 Equal Pay Act

1.22 The Equal Pay Act 1970 (EqPA) was initially effective because it applied collective solutions to a collective problem. It remains true that the wages of 70 per cent. of the workforce are determined directly or indirectly by collective bargaining. Section 3 of the Equal Pay Act 1970 conferred on the Central Arbitration Committee (CAC) a power to amend collective agreements which contained terms which applied only to women and not to men. Prior to that date it had been common practice in many sectors of industry for there to be a skilled rate, an unskilled rate and a women's rate which was often less than the rate for unskilled men. In such circumstances the EqPA, s.3 gave the CAC power to amend any such non-inclusive terms, cutting out lower women's rates. At the very least the women's rate had to be brought up to the rate for unskilled men. Many employers went further than this in harmonising the pay of men and women, perhaps because the CAC took a very liberal view of its powers under section 3 to harmonise the rates of men and women, not simply eliminating the separate women's rate. Other employers simply clothed previous discriminatory practices in uni-sex language, so that although there would be no formal bar to men being in a certain grade, in practice it would contain only women. In such circumstances the CAC looked behind the formal equality of men and women and encouraged the employer to create new grades. This practice of reviewing pay structures was brought to an end in 1979 by the decision of the Divisional Court in *R. v. C.A.C. ex. p. Hymac*[16] that the CAC had no jurisdiction to hear such claims except where the employer's pay policy or collective agreement "does not on the face of it contain any provision applying specifically to men or to women". The result was a sudden collapse in applications to the CAC and an effective end to any collective jurisdiction in matters of equal pay.

1.23 Ironically the remaining equal pay jurisdiction of the CAC was removed as a result of enforcement proceedings brought against the U.K. government in 1982.[17] The E.C. Commission contended that the U.K. had not fully implemented the Equal Treatment Directive (76/207) in that it had not taken action to declare void or amend discriminatory terms in collective agreements, rules of undertakings or professional bodies. The Government responded by repealing section 3 of the 1970 Act and providing in the Sex Discrimination Act 1986 that any discriminatory provisions in collective agreements or the rules of undertakings which, if incorporated into the contracts of individuals, would be contrary to the statutory equality clause implied by the EqPA, s.1(1), were void. The result is that there is now no means of seeking the amendment of discriminatory terms in collective agreements or employers' pay structures, except the unrealistic provision

---

[16] [1979] I.R.L.R. 1979.
[17] *E E.C. Commission* v. *U.K.* [1982] I.C.R. 578.

that affected individuals may seek redress in the County Courts under the Sex Discrimination Act 1976, s.77. This major gap in current equality legislation was the subject of adverse comment by the EOC[18], which proposes that the power to review collective agreements should again be vested in the industrial tribunals or a similar "industrially literate body".

However, the Trade Union Reform and Employment Rights Act 1993 inserts new sections 4A-C in the Sex Discrimination Act 1986, in order to provide a limited right to present a complaint to an Industrial Tribunal. The purpose of such a complaint would be to declare void unlawfully discriminatory provisions in collective agreements, employers' rules and the rules of trade unions, employers associations, professional or qualifying bodies. Industrial tribunals are not, however, to be given power to amend such agreements or rules, but only to declare them void by virtue of section 77 of the Sex Discrimination Act 1975. This amendment gives effect to Articles 3–5 of the Equal Treatment Directive (76/207) and is discussed firther in chapter 4 on discrimination at work.

The Sex Discrimination Act

1.24   The history of the Sex Discrimination Act is much shorter than that of the Equal Pay Act. It owes its origins to the changing climate of opinion about the position of women in society which came about during the 1960s and more particularly during the early 1970s. This changed climate of opinion was both caused by, and reflected in, concurrent social changes, such as women's increased participation in the labour market during the period of labour shortage created by the prolonged post-war boom, the fall in the birth rate which began in the middle sixties, (itself perhaps associated with more reliable contraception and more easily available abortion), the increased rate of marital breakdown and the rise in the number of one-parent families. These developments all contributed to a changed perception of gender roles, whilst at the same time being evidence of the existence of that perception. The development of a popular feminist ideology can be traced from that era. The passage into law of the American Civil Rights Act 1964, encompassing prohibitions on both racial and sex discrimination, further stimulated interest in legislation on equal opportunities in Britain. The Labour Party set up a study group which reported in 1972, the same year in which the T.U.C. reversed its previous policy and concluded that legislation was necessary and desirable in order to achieve equal opportunities. Two Private Member's Bills on this issue were referred to a Parliamentary Select Committee, which heard a wide range of evidence, including testimony

---

[18] EOC, *Equal Pay for Men and Women; strengthening the Acts*, 1990.

from officials of the U.S. Equal Employment Opportunity
Commission and concluded in favour of legislation on sex
discrimination. The Conservative Government published a
consultative document and was in the process of preparing
legislation at the time of its defeat in the 1974 election. The
incoming Labour Government published a White Paper,
Equality for Women in 1974, and went on to introduce the
legislation which became the Sex Discrimination Act 1975.
The Sex Discrimination Act 1975 has been amended by the
Sex Discrimination Act 1986, which arose primarily from
the need to harmonise conditions as between the public and
private sectors, following the *Marshall* case on retirement
ages. Whilst the Sex Discrimination Act 1975 (SDA 1975)
was conceived only shortly before the E.C. Equal Treatment
Directive, which covers substantially the same ground, it
owes little to the Directive and was not conceived as
implementing legislation.[19] The existence of the SDA was,
however, the substantial reason why no specific
implementing legislation was considered necessary to fulfil
Britain's obligations under the Directive.

1.25   The aim of the SDA 1975 was to increase women's
access to employment opportunities at all levels. The
continuing earnings differential between men and women
can, however, be put down to three main factors, namely,

(i) the effects of horizontal and vertical occupational
segregation,
(ii) the under-valuing of the skills entailed in occupations
usually dominated by women
(iii) the lower level of human capital, in the form of
training and experience, which women on average
possess.[20]

Hakim,[21] in a review of the effects of occupational
segregation, concludes that occupational segregation has
diminished in the 1980s, with the decline in male full-time
work proceeding apace whilst the proportion of women
working full-time has risen from 33.9 per cent. in 1986 to
38.7 per cent. in 1990. The rise in women working full-time
has been accompanied by a rising level of work
commitment, with more women in top jobs, leading Hakim
to conclude that the earnings gap will continue to narrow in
the 1990s. This is predicted to come about as women
demand a more equitable return on their increased
investment in work and their career, with the re-evaluation

---

[19] P.L. Davies, "European Equality Legislation, U.K. Legislative Policy
and Industrial Relations", in *Women, Employment and European Equality
Law*, (ed.) C. McCrudden, (Eclipse, 1987), pp.23-51.
[20] See Shirley Dex, *The Sexual Division of Work* (Wheatsheaf, 1985), and in
particular chap. 5, for a review of the economic theories as to why
women and men are paid differently. For a more recent review see Jill
Rubery, *The Economics of Equal Value*, EOC, 1992.
[21] Catherine Hakim, "Explaining trends in Occupational segregation; the
Measurement, Causes and Consequences of the Sexual Division of
Labour", *European Sociological Review*, 8,2, September 1992, pp.
127-144.

of traditionally under-valued female skills, especially in areas of labour shortage. Hakim tends to discount the significance of the rise in females working part-time, arguing that the outlook and expectations of workers are shaped by their main activity, which for part-timers is less likely to be work. Perhaps it is more likely that the experiences of women working in the "case" of the employment market will increasingly diverge from that of those working at the "periphery".

Race Relations Act

1.26 The Race Relations Act 1976 takes its form from the Sex Discrimination Act; the two are substantially equivalent, except that in the one case discrimination on grounds of gender is being dealt with, whereas in the other it is discrimination on racial grounds which is proscribed. The Race Relations Act 1976 is, however, the successor to the Race Relations Acts of 1965 and 1968 and incorporates many of the lessons learned from that legislation, lessons which were also incorporated into the drafting of the Sex Discrimination Act.

Background to the legislation

The origins of legislation to combat racial discrimination lie in the post-war wave of immigration from the Caribbean and the Indian sub-continent. The prolonged post-war shortage of labour created a range of vacancies which employers found hard to fill from amongst the indigenous population, but which immigrants were willing to undertake. It was not until the end of the decade that serious questions came to be asked about the policy of unrestricted immigration from the Commonwealth. The result was the 1962 Commonwealth Immigrants Act, followed in 1968 by a further Act,[22] the effect of which was to limit the immigration of non-dependent heads of households to 8,500 a year.

1.27 Part of the response to the problems which were perceived to be associated with immigration was the adoption of a policy of integration; indeed the two were explicitly linked by Roy Hattersley in defending the 1965 White Paper: "Without integration, limitation is inexcusable; without limitation, integration is impossible."[23] The result was the 1965 Race Relations Act, which prohibited discrimination in places of public resort, such as hotels, restaurants, entertainment and public transport. There was clear evidence[24] that discrimination in other vital aspects of life remained substantial, and in 1968 a further Race Relations Act was introduced. The need to do something serious and effective about race relations was underlined by the Watts riots which took place that year in

---

[22] Commonwealth Immigrants Act 1968.
[23] Quoted by Cashmore and Troyna, *Introduction to Race Relations*, (Routledge & Kegan Paul, 1983), p. 53.
[24] W. W. Daniel, *Racial Discrimination in England* (P.E.P., 1968).

Los Angeles and subsequently in many other American cities. Under the 1968 Act, the Race Relations Board was asked to investigate complaints of discrimination across a wider field, including housing and employment, and if conciliation was ineffective, to initiate civil proceedings. Complainants only had access to the courts via the Race Relations Board, whereas the Board had no independent power to undertake investigation of racialist practices, but could only follow up complaints.

1.28   Racial discrimination has persisted in Britain despite the presence on the statute book of first the 1968 Act and then the 1976 Act. Further Political and Economic Planning (PEP) (now PSI) surveys in 1973-4[25] and in 1983-4[26] show a substantial level of discrimination in employment, which remained largely unchanged in the decade between the two surveys. Between 1984 and 1985, P.S.I. used controlled tests and found one-third of employers discriminated against Black and Asian applicants. The survey measured direct discrimination only, and the researchers estimated that nationwide there were tens of thousands of these acts of racial discrimination in recruitment each year.[27] It was against the background of further limitation of immigration in the 1971 Immigration Act, which introduced the concept of patriality, that the 1976 Act was introduced; this again illustrates efforts at integration taking place in tandem with a stricter limitation of the entry of immigrant groups from the New Commonwealth, a trend effectively continued with the 1981 British Nationality Act.

The present Act, modelled as it is on the Sex Discrimination Act, and like that Act, influenced by the American example, represents the latest stage in the policy of integrating the (now substantially British born) ethnic minority communities by providing wider and more equal opportunities.

1992 Review of the Act

1.29   There has been criticism of the effectiveness of an Act which endeavours to remedy essentially social and collective phenomena by means of individual actions.[28] The CRE has faced great difficulties in pursuing strategic investigations[29] intended to highlight the existence of what has been termed "institutional racism".[30] A second review of the Race Relations Act, published by the CRE in 1992,[31] advocates the removal of the limitations placed upon its powers to

---

[25] David Smith, *Racial Disadvantage in Britain* (P.E.P. 1977).
[26] Colin Brown, *Black and White in Britain* (Gower, 1985).
[27] Colin Brown and Pat Gay, *Racial Discrimination: 17 years after the Act*, (PSI, 1986).
[28] See Laurence Lustgarten, *Racial Equality and the Limits of the Law*, *supra*.
[29] See p. 193 *et seq*. for a discussion of the conduct of the investigative powers of the CRE & EOC.
[30] See for instance the Scarman Report (1981), Cmnd. 8427, p. 11.
[31] Second Review of the Race Relations Act 1976, CRE, 1992.

conduct formal investigations by the *Prestige* case. The Review also advocates extending legal aid to race cases heard in the Industrial Tribunals. The existing Code of Practice advocates ethnic monitoring and the adoption of positive action programmes, but these recommendations lack legal force. The Review advocates that such practices should enjoy a statutory basis and that the Government should use its economic strength to support these policy objectives. It is instructive to note that many of these reforms have already been realised in the Northern Ireland Fair Employment Act 1989 with respect to religious discrimination in the Province. The difference may be that the provision of equal opportunities with respect to the religious divide in Northern Ireland may be perceived as having a greater political salience, than do the forms of discrimination more commonly present on the mainland.

The Community framework of equality law

Equality as a fundamental right

1.30 The British Sex Discrimination and Race Relations Acts proscribe acts of discrimination based on gender or race. The non-discrimination principles embodied in these Acts do not enjoy any special status in law; the Acts are capable of amendment by the ordinary Parliamentary processes, except in so far as such amendment might be contrary to the requirements of Community law.[32] Community law has, however, recognised the elimination of discrimination based on sex as a fundamental right. The ECJ in the third *Defrenne* case sets forth the fundamental nature of the principle of equality in Community law and its place in the Community legal order.

"The Court has repeatedly stated that respect for fundamental personal human rights is one of the general principles of Community law, the observance of which it has a duty to ensure. There can be no doubt that the elimination of discrimination based on sex forms part of those fundamental rights."[33]

Anti-discrimination as a general principle of Community law

1.31 The case-law of the European Communities is replete with references to the general principles of Community law, but what are these, from whence do they originate and what

[32] See para 1.47 *et seq.* for a discussion of the supremacy of Community law.
[33] Case No. 149/77, *Defrenne* v. *Sabena*: [1978] E.C.R. 1365 at 1378.

is their significance?[34] We can see reference to such overarching principles in the Treaty, in that Article 164 provides that:

> "The Court of Justice shall ensure that in the interpretation and application of this the Treaty *the law* is observed" (emphasis added)

If "the law" were not in some sense independent of the Treaty provisions, no meaning could be attached to this provision. Article 215 provides that the Community shall, in accordance with the general principles common to the laws of the Member States, make good any damage caused by its institutions or by its servants in the performance of their duties.[35] Equally Article 173 provides for judicial review of an administrative decision[36] where there is an "infringement of this Treaty *or any rule of law relating to its application*", again presupposing some independent source of authority for such rules. The source of authority for such rules lies both in inferences drawn from specific provisions of the Treaty which are capable of generalisation to cover other related situations, and in general principles common to the law of at least some, if not all, of the Member States. This is most notable in connection with the possible violation of human rights, where in the *Internationale Handelgesellschaft*[37] case the ECJ held that:

> "(t)he protection of such rights, whilst inspired by the constitutional traditions common to the Member States, must be ensured within the framework of the structure and objectives of the Community".

The case arose from the contention that a requirement of Community law was contrary to the fundamental rights guaranteed by the German constitution, to which all German national law was subject. To avoid a head-on confrontation with the German constitutional court, in which the doctrine of the supremacy of Community law might be severely

---

[34] For a general discussion of the origin and scope of general principles in Community law see, T.C. Hartley, *The Foundations of European Community Law*, (Clarenden Press, 2nd ed., Oxford), pp. 129–153, Jean-Victor Louis, *The Community Legal Order*, (E.C. Commission, 1990). For a discussion of the application of selected principles to substantive law see A. Arnull, *General Principles of Community Law* (Leicester University Press, 1990) and for a specific treatment of the right to equality see Sacha Prechal and Noreen Burrows, *Gender Discrimination Law of the European Community*, (Dartmouth, 1990), pp. 1-23 and Evelyn Ellis, *European Sex Equality Law* (OUP, 1991), pp. 117-134.

[35] Louis (n.34 *supra*) at p. 98 argues that Art. 215 is generally agreed to be an application of a general rule that the Community is bound by general principles common to the laws of the Member States.

[36] To fall within the scope of Art. 173 the decision has to fall within strict time limits and be either addressed to a natural or legal person or in the form of a Regulation which is of direct and individual concern to her, with the result that the applicant must in practice be part of a closed and finite class, of which staff employees of the Institutions are a prime example. For further discussion of this issue see R. Greaves, *Locus standi* under Art. 173 when seeking Annulment of a Regulation, 1986, 11 EL Rev, p. 119.

[37] [1970] E.C.R. 1125.

tested, the ECJ deferred to the German constitutional position, but neatly placed this constraint as falling within the confines of Community law. Further steps were taken down this road in *Nold* V. *Commission*[38] when the ECJ held that:

> "it cannot uphold measures which are incompatible with fundamental rights recognised and protected by the constitutions of (the Member) States."

In that case, international treaties signed by the Member States for the protection of human rights[39] were also recognised as a source of such general principles. These have included the European Convention on Human Rights,[40] the European Social Charter[41] and I.L.O. Conventions No. 100[42] and 111.[43]

E.C. "general principle of equality"

1.32   The elimination of discrimination based on sex, as noted above, has been held by the ECJ in the third *Defrenne* case to form part of the corpus of fundamental human rights to be observed by Community law. The ECJ has, however, elucidated a "general principle of equality which is one of the fundamental principles of Community law. This principle requires that similar situations shall not be treated differently unless differentiation is objectively justified."[44] As Millet observes[45]:

> "Being a general principle, it is applicable in all fields and may be used not only as a guide to interpreting legislation but also to fill lacunae in legislation or even override legislative provisions which are contrary to it."

The general principle of non-discrimination on grounds of sex can be seen operating in cases brought seeking review of decisions made under the regulations governing the employment of Community staff, because being a closed group, Community staff fall within the scope of judicial review actions by natural or legal persons under either Articles 173 or 184.[46] Even though Advocate General Roemer rejected the notion of such a higher principle in Community law in *Sabbattini* v. *European Parliament*,[47] the Court itself held that the Staff Regulation which made expatriation allowances payable only to the head of a married household created an arbitrary difference between male and

---

[38] [1974] E.C.R. 491.
[39] at p. 507, para. 13.
[40] Case 36/75, *Rutili*: [1975] E.C.R. 1219.
[41] Case 149/77, *Defrenne* v. *Sabena* [1978] C.M.L.R. 312 (ground 28), Case 24/86, *Blaizot and the University of Liege* v. *Belgium*: [1989] 1 C.M.L.R.57.
[42] See A.G. VerLoren Van Thematt in Case 61/81 *E.C. Commission* v. *U.K.* [1982] C.M.L.R. 284 at p. 292.
[43] Case 149/77, *Defrenne* v. *Sabena* [1978] C.M.L.R. 312 (ground 28).
[44] *Ruckdeschel* [1977] E.C.R. 1753, para. 7, *Moullins Pont-a-Mousson* [1977] E.C.R. 1795, paras. 16-17.
[45] *Sex Equality: The Influence of Community Law in Great Britain*, pp. 219-246.
[46] See n. 36 *supra*.
[47] Cases 20/71 & 32/71[1972] C.M.L.R. 945; [1972] E.C.R. 345.

female officials and should be declared inapplicable under Article 184[48]. In that case, a female official had married and lost her allowance because she did not become the head of the household under the Regulations. A similar result was obtained in *Airola* v. *E.C. Commission*,[49] where a female official working in Italy married an Italian citizen, losing her right to an expatriation allowance because, under Italian law, she necessarily took her husband's nationality. It is perhaps notable that both these early decisions incorporate a notion of indirect discrimination, in that neither rested upon explicit differences in treatment between men and women. In *Razzouk and Beydoun* v. *E.C. Commission*,[50] a case heard after *Defrenne (No. 3)*, the Court held that:

> "in relations between the Community institutions on the one hand and their employees or those claiming under them on the other, the requirements arising from this principle (of equal treatment of the sexes) are by no means limited to those flowing from Article 119 of the Treaty or the Community directives issued in this field."

The Court went on to hold that the Commission's decisions applying the Regulations, to the effect that widowers should not enjoy the same rights to survivors' benefits as widows, were contrary to a fundamental right and inapplicable in so far as they treated surviving spouses differently according to their sex.

1.33 The other type of action in which the general principles can have play is that of questions of interpretation submitted to the European Court of Justice by the national courts under Article 177. Thus, in reviewing the derogations which are permitted from the principle of equality on grounds of public safety, the ECJ in *Johnston* v. *RUC*[51] held that such derogations could only be allowed in so far as they are appropriate and necessary, *i.e.* they must conform also to the principle of proportionality and must be reconciled with the principle of equal treatment. Equally, in the *Marshall*[52] case on retirement ages the ECJ held that "in view of the fundamental importance of the principle of equality" the exclusion of social security matters such as retirement age contained in Directive 79/7 "must be interpreted strictly."

1.34 There are no independent rights based upon the general principles, but rather as Millet suggests above, the

[48] Again *locus standi* is restricted to those to whom the decision is addressed, where it is based upon an illegal regulation.

[49] Case 21/74: [1975] E.C.R. 221. In *Van den Broeck*, [1975] E.C.R. 235 such a case was rejected because the acquisition of the spouse's nationality was not mandatory under national law.

[50] Cases 75/82 &117/82: [19840] 3 C.M.L.R. 470.

[51] Case 222/84, *Johnston* v. *RUC*: [1986] E.C.R. 1651; [1986] 3 C.M.L.R. 240; [1986] I.R.L.R. 263.

[52] Case 152/84:[1986] 1 C.M.L.R. 688; [1986] E.C.R. 723; [1986] I.R.L.R. 140.

general principles can be used as guides to interpret legislation, to fill in gaps or to override contrary provisions. The general principle of non-discrimination, as with all the principles of Community law, needs a positive law on which to operate. For example, in the third *Defrenne* case, the Belgian court was seeking an answer to the question whether the enforced retirement of air hostesses at 40 constituted discrimination contrary to Article 119 or to "a principle of Community law". The case was brought prior to the adoption of the Equal Treatment Directive, and for this reason the ECJ responded that at the time of the events then before the courts the Community had not assumed responsibility

> "for supervising and guaranteeing the observance of the principle of equality between men and women in working conditions other than remuneration."

For this reason Docksey[53] argues that the right to non-discrimination on grounds of race or religion remains incohoate. Rights to non-discrimination on grounds of nationality under Article 7 and to free movement under Article 48 relate only to nationals of Member States and do not affect the position of third country nationals, nor do they have any direct impact upon the position of members of ethnic minorities who possess Community nationality. Whilst the Charter of Fundamental Social Rights of Workers makes reference to the need for comparable treatment of non-nationals, no proposals are made with reference to racial discrimination. The Declaration on Racism and Xenophobia adopted in 1986 led to the Evrigenis Committee of Inquiry, which recommended the preparation of a draft directive on race discrimination. However, the Resolution on Racism and Xenophobia adopted by the Council and representatives of the Member States in 1990 placed primary responsibility for action with the Member States. There are, nonetheless, both economic and social arguments for a Community wide race discrimination law. The CRE has argued, by analogy with the position under Article 119, that a Member State which adopts race discrimination legislation may put itself at a competitive disadvantage, thus causing a distortion of competition within the common market. This would provide grounds for Community measures to avoid such distortion to be introduced under Articles 100, 100A or 235. Moreover, Article 8, as revised by the Maastricht Treaty, provides for Community citizenship. If ethnic minority citizens are truly to enjoy full Community citizenship, it can be argued that there is a need for harmonisation of race discrimination laws across the Community; such measures could be introduced under the new Article 8e. Note also that Title VI of the Maastricht Treaty envisages common rules on asylum, immigration controls and the rights of third country nationals, which are to be dealt with in accordance with the

[53] C.Docksey, "The Principle of Equality as a Fundamental Right under Community Law", *Industrial Law Journal*, 20, 4, pp. 258-280. at p. 261.

provisions of the European Convention on Human Rights under Article K2. Article 14 of the European Convention on Human Rights requires that the other rights and freedoms secured by the Convention shall be secured without discrimination on any ground such as sex, race, colour, religion or political affiliation etc. The renewed emphasis on subsidiarity which has developed following the signing of the Maastricht Treaty makes it hard to forecast how these powers will be used, but given the political will there is a legal basis for a Community race discrimination law.[54]

Equality or subsidiarity?

1.35   The principle of equality may conflict with other principles, such as that of proportionality, and more particularly in the current political climate, subsidiarity. Article 3 of the Maastricht Treaty provides that "any action of the Community shall not go beyond what is necessary to achieve the objectives of the Treaty" and that the Community will act "only and in so far as the objectives of the proposed action cannot be sufficiently achieved by the Member States." Just how far and in what way the principle of subsidiarity will be relied upon in judicial interpretation of the Treaty remains to be seen, but it could be seen as likely that it will be utilised to circumscribe the potential scope of social provisions which go beyond those necessary to complete the internal market. This will be more likely to limit the broader social and employment programmes which originate under Article 117 than the equality provisions which originate from Article 119, as the status of these is enhanced by their inclusion within the scope of the general principle of non-discrimination on grounds of sex or gender. The broader programmes which originate from Article 117, and which concern the improvement of living and working conditions in the course of their harmonisation, do not enjoy this status and lack the same type of internal coherence. Consequently, although these provisions may be of great value to women, particularly to those engaged in "atypical work", they may yet turn out to be seen as being limited by the principle of subsidiarity.[55] Although Lasok states:

> "given its historical and philosophical meaning, subsidiarity ought to be understood as a brake on the adventurism of the Community institutions and the ambitions of their bureaucracy, but not as an obstacle on the road mapped out by the Treaties,"[56]

[54] See Ian Forbes & Geoffrey Mead, "Measure for Measure; a comparative analysis of measures to combat racial discrimination in the Member States of the European Community," Department of Employment Research Series, No. 1 1992; Erika Szyszczak "Race Discrimination: The Limits of Market Equality," in *Discrimination; the limits of the law*, Hepple and Szyszczak eds. (Mansell, 1992), and the report of the European Parliament on Racism and Xenophobia, rapporteur Glyn Ford, AS-195/90.

[55] See Linda Dickens, "Atypical Work, its implications for sex equality," Institute of Employment Rights, 1992.

[56] See D. Lasok "Subsidiarity and the occupied field", *New Law Journal*, 142, Sept. 1992, pp. 1228-1230 at p. 1230 and see N. Emilou, "Subsidiarity; An Effective Barrier Against the Enterprise of Ambition" (1992) 17 E.L.Rev., pp. 383–407.

one must be sanguine about the possible effects of the
principle in the broader employment field.

Equal Pay under Article 119

1.36   The Equal Pay Act 1970 enacted a right to equal pay
under domestic law which has been engulfed and expanded
by rights arising from Article 119 EEC, which provides that
men and women should receive equal pay for equal work.
Article 119 forms part of the original social provisions
contained in Articles 117-120 of the Treaty of Rome. The
founders of the Community were concerned with realising
the political aim of European integration via economic
means. So-called functional integration would "spill over"
into the closer political integration which was clearly not
accessible directly. Whilst this integration was to be achieved
primarily by the creation of a common market, the broader
aims of the Community can be seen reflected in Article 2 of
the Treaty (as amended by the Single European Act 1986)
which looks forward to "a continuous and balanced
expansion, an increase in stability, an accelerated raising of
the standard of living and closer relations between the
States" via the creation of a Common Market. Whilst social
aims have always formed part of the aims of the
Community, the harmonisation of working conditions was
also dictated by the need to ensure a level playing field for
competitors within the common market. Although the
Spaak Report of 1956 took the view that the harmonisation
of social and working conditions would follow the
integration of the Market, as labour and capital flowed to
whatever region provided the most favourable terms, this
view did not entirely prevail amongst those who drafted the
Treaty. The social provisions contained in Title III represent
in part the need (as expressed in Article 117) to promote
"improved working conditions and an improved standard of
living for workers" and also a response to the fears that
French industry would be undermined without some
harmonisation of working conditions. In particular, France
had already introduced equal pay in 1957 and generally
enjoyed longer holidays than other countries in the
Community. The dual nature of Article 119 was clearly
expressed by the ECJ in the second *Defrenne*[57] case.

> "Article 119 pursues a double aim. First in the light of
> the different stages of development of social legislation in
> the Member States, the aim of Article 119 is to avoid a
> situation in which undertakings established in states
> which have actually implemented the principle of equal
> pay suffer a competitive disadvantage in intra-Community
> competition as compared with undertakings established in
> States which have not yet eliminated discrimination
> against women workers as regards pay. Secondly, this

---

[57] *Defrenne* v. *Sabena*, Case No. 43/75: [1976] E.C.R. 455; [1976] 2
C.M.L.R.98.

provision forms part of the social objectives of the community, which is not merely an economic union, but is at the same time intended, by common action, to ensure social progress and seek the constant improvement of the living and working conditions of their peoples, as is emphasised by the Preamble to the Treaty. . . This double aim which is at once economic and social, shows that the principle of equal pay forms part of the foundations of the Community."

1.37   Article 119 can be distinguished from the other social provisions of Title III by the directness of its expression, which has enabled it to give rise to directly enforceable rights for individuals. The other provisions in Title III are more programmatic, setting out broad aims to harmonise, co-ordinate and improve working conditions, including health and safety, but not giving rise to specific rights without further legislation. Once the right to equal pay was held to be directly applicable within the Member States in the second *Defrenne* case, and was elevated to the status of a fundamental right by the third *Defrenne* case, the way was open for the evolution of an autonomous jurisprudence of Community sex equality law. Little substantive progress had taken place towards equal pay in the early years of the Community, a fact attested to by the the Sullerot Report of 1972. Even prior to the renewed concerns about unemployment which followed the rise in oil prices and economic dislocation associated with the Arab-Israeli conflict of 1973, the Community had embarked upon its first Social Action Programme in January 1974. One result was the Equal Pay Directive 75/117, introduced under Article 100 as a measure directly affecting the functioning of the Common Market. This directive, intended to expedite the achievement of equal pay, first made reference to equal pay for work of equal value in Community legislation. The British legislation of equal pay and discrimination owed little to this development, having been inspired largely by internal political pressures.[58] Indeed the general view was that the 1970 Equal Pay Act went further than Article 119 with its reference only to equal pay for equal work. Subsequently British law on equal pay has been much influenced by Article 119 and the Equal Pay Directive, as discussed in the chapter on equal pay.

The Equal Treatment Directive

1.38   Shortly after the Sex Discrimination Act was passed into law, the E.C. adopted the Equal Treatment Directive 76/207 under Article 235.[59] This directive arose from the

[58] P.L.Davies, "EEC Legislation, UK Legislative Policy and Industrial Relations", in *Women, Employment and European Equality Law* (C.McCrudden ed. Eclipse Publications, 1987), p. 26.
[59] Art. 235 allows for action to be taken by the Community to achieve one

1974 Social Action Programme, which had as one of its objectives,

> "achieving equality between men and women as regards access to employment and vocational training and promotion and as regards working conditions, including pay."

The purpose of the Equal Treatment Directive is to put into effect the principle of equal treatment for men and women as regards access to employment, working conditions and social security. Article 2 of the Directive provides that the principle of equal treatment means that there 'shall be no discrimination whatsoever on grounds of sex directly or indirectly by reference in particular to marital or family status' subject to special provisions made for the protection of women, particularly as regards pregnancy and maternity and positive action in the form of measures to remove existing inequalities which affect women's opportunities. Exceptions to the principle of equal treatment are allowed where sex is a determining factor for the occupation in question. Article 3 applies these requirements to selection and promotion decisions, Article 4 provides similarly for vocational guidance and training, whilst Article 5 covers discriminatory dismissals and Article 7 victimisation. Article 6 provides that Member States must enact a right to a remedy by judicial process. Article 9 requires States to inform the Commission about measures taken to implement the Directive, which the U.K. Government considered were not necessary in view of the prior existence of the Sex Discrimination Act 1975. The Directive is broad and comprehensive in its treatment of discrimination in employment, but does not apply to non-employment situations. Decisions made under the Directive, such as the *Marshall*[60] case on retirement age, have had a profound effect upon domestic law in view of the doctrine of the supremacy of Community law.

1.39 Three other Directives also relate to sex discrimination. The Sex Discrimination (Social Security) Directive 79/9 covers matters of state social security, whilst the Sex Discrimination (Occupational Social Security) Directive 86/378 (implemented in the U.K. by the Social Security Act 1989) covers occupational pensions, although following the *Barber*[61] case the coverage of that directive has been greatly circumscribed. The Sex Discrimination (Self-employed) Directive 86/631 covers the position of self-employed women, in particular in agriculture and family businesses, a problem which perhaps bulks larger in some Community countries than in the U.K.

of its objectives where the Treaty has not otherwise provided the necessary powers. Unanimity is required in the Council of Ministers for such measures.

[60] [1986] I.R.L.R. 140, ECJ.

[61] *Barber* v. *Guardian Royal Exchange Assurance* [1990] I.R.L.R. 240, ECJ.

The direct effect of Community Law

1.40   The supremacy of Community law is essential to the very idea of the European Community; if the States could opt out of aspects of the Community legal order not to their liking there would be little left of the Community except pious hopes and aspirations.[62] Community instruments which give rise to rights which need no further legislative enactment in the Member States are usually described as being of "direct application." For example, Regulations which need no further enactment are necessarily directly applicable. All Community instruments which may be invoked directly before their national courts, are said to be of "direct effect", even though, like directives, they are required to be implemented by the Member States. Such a legislative instrument can only be said to be of direct effect until it is fully and properly implemented; after that it is necessary to rely on the national law. The use of these two terms has not always been wholly consistent, either by the Courts or by commentators.

The direct effect of Treaty provisions

1.41   In *Van Gend en Loos*,[63] a case concerning the application of Article 12 restricting the right of States to introduce import duties, the ECJ held that:

> "the Community constitutes a new legal order of international law for the benefit of which states have limited their sovereign rights, albeit within limited fields, and the subjects of which comprise not only Member States but also their nationals. Independently of the legislation of Member States, Community law therefore not only imposes obligations on individuals but is also intended to confer on them rights which become part of their legal heritage. These rights arise not only where they are expressly granted by the Treaty but also by reason of obligations which the Treaty imposes in a clearly defined way upon individuals as well as upon Member States and the institutions of the Community."

---

[62] *Amministtrazionne delle Finanze dello Stato* v. *Simmenthal* [1976] E.C.R. 629, ECJ. The ECJ held at ground 18 "(A)ny . . . legislative measures which encroach upon the field within which the Community exercises its legislative power or which are otherwise incompatible with the provisions of Community law. . .would amount to a corresponding denial of the effectiveness of obligations undertaken unconditionally and irrevocably by Member States pursuant to the Treaty and would thus imperil the very foundations of the Community." See also *Costa* v. *ENELS*, Case 6/64: [1964] E.C.R. 585; *Factortame* v. *Secretary of State for Transport* [1989] 2 All E.R. 692.

[63] [1963] E.C.R. 1.

The ECJ went on to define the characteristics of Community law which may have direct effect by reference to Article 12, holding that it was "ideally adapted to produce direct effects" because it was a

> "clear and unconditional prohibition which is not a negative but a positive prohibition", which was "not qualified by any reservations on the part of states, which would make its implications conditional upon a positive legislative measure enacted under national law."

Treaty provisions can have direct effect not only as between an individual and the State, so-called vertical direct effect, but also as between individuals, so-called horizontal direct effect. In *Walgrave*[64] the ECJ held that the Treaty provisions on free movement were horizontally effective, in that a national court may take them into account in judging the validity of a rule of a sporting organisation; in this case, the rule that pacers and cycle racers had to be of the same nationality. In the *Defrenne II* case Article 119 was held to be of direct vertical and horizontal effect, in that,

> "since Article 119 is mandatory in nature, the prohibition on discrimination between men and women applies not only to the actions of public authorities, but also extends to all agreements which are intended to regulate paid labour collectively, as well as to contracts between individuals."[65]

In *Defrenne II* the direct effect of Article 119 was limited to

> "direct and overt discrimination which may be identified solely with the aid of the criteria based on equal work and equal pay," as opposed to "indirect and disguised discrimination which can only be identified by more explicit implementing provisions of a Community or national character".[66]

The ECJ went on to hold that:

> "Among the forms of direct discrimination which may be identified solely by reference to the criteria laid down by Article 119 must be included in particular those which have their origin in legislative provisions or in collective labour agreements and which may be detected on the basis of a purely legal analysis of the situation."

Whilst this decision can be seen as delimiting the scope of direct effect to that which is clear and unconditional,[67] in its earlier case law, as regards both nationality[68] and, more hesitantly, gender equality,[69] the Court had accepted a

---

[64] Case 36/74, *Walgrave-Koch* v. *Union Cycliste Internationale* [1974] E.C.R. 1405.
[65] Note 57 at ground 39.
[66] *Ibid.*, ground 18.
[67] T.C.Hartley, *The Foundations of European Community Law* (2nd ed., Clarendon Press, 1988), p.189.
[68] Case 152/73, *Sotgiu* v. *Deutsche Bundespost* [1974] E.C.R. 153.
[69] *Sabbatini*, n.47 and *Airola*, n. 49 *supra*. See Prechal and Burrows, *Gender*

concept of indirect discrimination in the sense of the adverse impact of facially neutral criteria. Advocate General Warner pointed up this confusion in *Jenkins*,[70] a case concerned with the question as to whether it was discriminatory to pay part-time workers less than full-time workers, but the Court did not resolve the matter in its judgement, referring to the need to test whether the differential "is or is not in reality discrimination based on sex." Although Browne-Wilkinson J. (as he then was) adopted an objective view more favourable to the applicant when the case returned to the EAT, it was not until the *Bilka-Kaufhaus*[71] case that the ECJ returned unambiguously to a formulation of indirect discrimination akin to the British statutory use of the term indirect discrimination and the American usage of adverse impact discrimination. It remains true, however, that Community law will not be of direct effect where it is programmatic in the way which is manifested by Article 117, or inoperative without more detailed implementing legislation.

The direct effect of directives

1.42   Whilst Regulations are, by virtue of the second paragraph of Article 189, expressly provided to be binding in their entirety and directly applicable in the Member States, the third paragraph of Article 189 provides only that:

> "A directive shall be binding, as to the result to be achieved, upon each Member State to which it is addressed, but shall leave to the national authorities the choice of form and method."

In the labour field, with the exception of the Regulations governing free movement, harmonisation has been achieved by directive. In *Van Duyn* V. *Home Office*, a case concerning a challenge to the right of the Home Office to refuse entry into Britain by a Dutch member of the Church of Scientology, an action which was alleged to be contrary to the provisions of the relevant directive on free movement, the ECJ held that:[72]

> "If, however, by virtue of the provisions of Article 189 regulations are directly applicable and, consequently, may by their very nature have direct effects, it does not follow from this that other categories of acts can never have similar effects. It would be incompatible with the binding nature attributed to a directive by Article 189 to exclude, in principle, the possibility that the obligation which it imposes may be invoked by those concerned."

Discrimination Law of the European Community (Dartmouth, 1990), pp. 8-19 for further discussion of this issue.
[70] Case 96/80, *Jenkins* v. *Kingsgate (Clothing Productions) Co* [1981] E.C.R. 911; 2 C.M.L.R. 24.
[71] Case 170/84: [1986] E.C.R. 1607; [1986] 2 C.M.L.R. 701.
[72] Case 41/74: [1974] E.C.R. 1337 at p. 1348.

This proposition was justified by holding that the *effet utile* or "useful effect" of the directive

> "would be weakened if individuals were prevented from relying on it before their national courts and if the latter were prevented from taking it into consideration as an element of Community law"

provided, of course, that the provision in question is sufficiently clear and precise to give rise to direct effect and does not leave a significant measure of discretion to the Member States. The question arises therefore as to the position when a State has failed to implement a directive or implemented it incompletely or incorrectly. In *Ratti*,[73] the ECJ held that a Member State which has not implemented a directive may not rely on its own failure to perform its obligations. This proposition is fundamental to the ruling in *Marshall*[74] that directives are only effective against the Member States and may not be relied on as against an individual. However, the ECJ in *Marshall* held that only the State could be liable in this context, because the basis of any such action is the default of the State. This estoppel-like principle applies whether the State was acting as a public authority or only as an employer. Thus the Equal Treatment Directive was held to be only of direct *vertical* effect *i.e.* only in respect of "organs of the State".[75]

Boundaries of "the state"

1.43 As might be expected, having thus narrowed the scope of the direct effect of directives, the ECJ adopted a wide view of the boundaries of the State. In *Foster* v. *British Gas plc*[76] six employees were compulsorily retired at the age of 60 just prior to the enactment of the Sex Discrimination Act 1986. They sought to rely on Article 5(1) of the Equal

---

[73] Case 148/78, *Ratti*: [1979] E.C.R. 1629; Case 102/79: *Commission* v. *Belgium* [1980] E.C.R. 1473; Case 158/80, *Rewe*: [1981] E.C.R. 1805 and Case 8/81, *Becker*: [1982] E.C.R. 53 where at para. 24 the ECJ holds that a Member State "which has not adopted the implementing measures required by the directive within the prescribed period may not plead as against individuals, its own failure to perform the obligations which the directive entails."

[74] Case 152/84, *Marshall* v. *Southampton and South West Hants Area Health Authority* [1986] E.C.R. 723.

[75] Even though the matter was not strictly in point the Advocate General's opinion in *Marshall No. 2* supports reconsideration of the limitation of the concept of direct effects to organs of the State for three reasons. Firstly that the concept of direct effect already covers public bodies which cannot realistically be described as responsible for the default of the State in failing to implement the relevant directive, secondly that the obligation to interpret national law in conformity with directives gives rise to problems of the delimination of judicial powers and thirdly that individuals in defaulting States are still disadvantaged in comparison with individuals in States which have fully implemented the relevant directive, notwithstanding the possibility of *Francovitch* type actions.

[76] [1990] I.R.L.R. 353, ECJ. On its return from the ECJ the Lords ([1991] I.R.L.R. 268, HL) held that according to the tests set out by the ECJ the pre-privatisation British Gas Corporation was providing a public service under the control of the State under special powers contained in the Gas Act 1972.

Treatment Directive, contending that the pre-privatisation British Gas Corporation was an emanation of the State. The issue of direct effect was referred to the ECJ by the House of Lords. The Court held that where a public body, acting as such or as an employer, has been made responsible under some form of statutory authority for providing a public service under the control of the State and has been granted special powers for that purpose, it is included in any event among the bodies against which the provisions of a Directive capable of direct effect may be relied upon. Thus the direct effect of directives is confined to actions brought against organs of the State, although the boundaries of the State have been widely drawn and could include a wide variety of formally autonomous public bodies. The ECJ went on to hold that the preliminary question of whether Community measures may be relied on against certain classes of persons necessarily involves the interpretation of the Treaty and is a matter for the ECJ, whereas the national courts may decide if proceedings before them fall within one of the categories so defined.

The question remains as to where the U.K. courts will draw the boundaries of the State, a question of increasing importance in view of established Government policy to reduce the scope of the State. For example, in *Doughty* V. *Rolls Royce Ltd*[77] the Court of Appeal held that Rolls Royce was not an emanation of the State whilst it was in public ownership because, whilst it was under the control of the State, it was not providing a public service, nor was it reliant on special powers granted by the State in the same sense as the nationalised British Gas Corporation. The precise extent of the State, and therefore of the direct effect of directives, remains uncertain and a gap remains in which non-directly effective Community law finds no direct expression in the national system unless it has been fully and correctly implemented.

1.44 Whilst in the *Marshall* case the ECJ held that the Equal Treatment Directive was of direct effect, the position of the Equal Pay Directive is different, in that there has been no decision in terms that it is of direct effect. Rather the position is that in *Jenkins* the ECJ held that Article 1 of the Equal Pay Directive (which introduces the concept of equal pay for work of equal value)

> "is principally designed to facilitate the practical application of the principle of equal pay outlined in Art. 119 of the Treaty in no way alters the content or scope of that principle as defined in the Treaty."[78]

---

[77] [1992] I.R.L.R. 126, C.A.

[78] But in *Worringham* [1981] I.C.R. 558 A.G.VerLoren Van Themaat was of the opinion that the extension of the term "equal work" in Art. 119 by Art. 1 of the Directive was more a clarification than an extension of that term, relying on dicta in paras. 20 and 54 of *Defrenne (No. 2)*.

It would seem to follow that Art. 1 of the Equal Pay Directive is directly effective in the Member States, in the same way as is Article 119, but it is arguable that as the implementation of the concept of equal value relies upon the complex machinery of the Equal Pay (Amendment) Regulations, that it is not directly applicable. This dilemma arises from the observation that whilst the ECJ has held that Article 1 of the Equal Pay Directive does not extend or alter Article 119, the concept of equal value is not one which is necessarily implicit in the wording of Article 119.

1.45 In *Simmenthal*[79] the ECJ declared that "direct applicability . . . means that rules of Community law must be fully and uniformly applied in all the Member States from the date of their entry into force" by the national courts, *i.e.* the date from which they are to be implemented. In fulfilling this function the national courts must,

> "in the absence of Community rules on the subject, apply national procedural rules and time limits provided that such conditions are not less favourable than those relating to similar actions of a domestic nature nor framed so as to render virtually impossible the exercise of rights conferred by domestic law"

according to the ECJ in the Irish case of *Emmot* v. *Minister for Social Welfare.*[80] In the *Emmot* case, however, the ECJ went on to hold that time does not begin to run under national time limits until a directive has been fully and effectively transposed into national law. Only then will individuals be able to ascertain the full extent of their rights and rely on them in the national courts. Consequently, as a State may not benefit from its own default, it may not rely on national time limits in an action brought against it by an individual so long as the directive in question has not been properly transposed in to national law.[81] Following the *Emmot* ruling that the procedural conditions for bringing an action under national law must not be less favourable than those applying to claims arising under national law, the EAT in *Livingstone* v. *Hepworth Refractories*[82] held that as a COT 3 settlement made in respect of unfair dismissal proceedings could not prevent the bringing of a claim under the Sex Discrimination Act, neither could it prevent an action based

---

[79] Case 106/77, *Amministrazione delle Finanze dello Stato* v. *Simmenthal SPA:* [1978] E.C.R. 629.
[80] Case C 208/90, [1991] I.R.L.R. 387 and Case 33/76: *Rewe*, [1976] E.C.R. 1989, Case 189/82, *San Giorgio:* [1983] E.C.R. 3595.
[81] Whilst rights arising under a directive will only be of direct effect against an organ of the State, Art. 119 is both vertically and horizontally effective. It must, however, be open to question whether the rule enunciated in *Emmot* as to time running on incorrectly transposed Community rights would apply to a case brought against an individual when relying directly on Community rights, as contemplated by the Court of Appeal in *Pickstone* v. *Freeman* [1987] I.R.L.R. 218, C.A. because it is the State which has not fulfilled its obligations and not the defendant in the case.
[82] [1992] I.R.L.R. 63.

upon rights seen as arising under Article 119 following the *Barber* pensions case.[83]

The Effect of recommendations

1.46   In *Grimaldi* v. *Fonds des Maladies Professionelles*[84] the ECJ held that whilst Article 189(5) provides that recommendations have no binding force and do not in themselves confer rights on individuals upon which they may rely before national courts, such recommendations cannot be considered as lacking in legal effect[85]. The ECJ goes on to hold that:

> "National courts are bound to take Recommendations into consideration in order to decide disputes submitted to them, in particular where they clarify the interpretation of national provisions adopted in order to implement them or where they are designed to supplement Community measures."

The supremacy of Community law

1.47   In the case of conflict between rights established under Community law and those arising under national law, according to the judgement of the ECJ in *Costa* v. *Enel* it is Community law which must prevail. This doctrine of the supremacy of Community law arose from the contention that

> "the EEC Treaty has created its own legal system which, on the entry into force of the Treaty, became an integral part of the legal systems of the Member states and which their courts are bound to apply."

This situation

---

[83] Thus in *Cannon* v. *Barnsley Metropolitan Borough Council* [1992] I.R.L.R. 474 the EAT held that time limit for bringing a complaint under Art. 119 and the equality directives in respect of a discriminatory payment was six months from the date at which the discriminatory provision was rescinded by s.16(1) of the Employment Act 1989. Whilst Barnard makes the point in a note in *Industrial Law Journal*, 22. 1, at p. 54 that Knox J. is less than clear as to whether the case falls under the equality directives or Art. 119, in *Rankin* v. *British Coal Corporation* [1993] I.R.L.R. 69 the EAT in Scotland in any event extended the point to claims arising under Article 119 by concluding that a claim under Art 119 in similar circumstances made within three months of the coming into force of the Employment Act provision was timeous. See chapter 6 for further discussion of time limits.

[84] [1990] I.R.L.R. 400.

[85] See Jean-Victor Louis, "The Community Legal Order", EC, 1990 for a general view of the effects of the various Community legislative instruments and the note by E. Szyszcak in *Industrial Law Journal*, 20, 2, pp. 156-158.

"makes it impossible for the States, as a corollary, to accord precedence to a unilateral and subsequent measure over a legal system accepted by them on the basis of reciprocity . . . The obligations undertaken under the Treaty establishing the Community would not be unconditional, but merely contingent, if they could be called into question by subsequent legislative acts."[86]

European Communities Act

1.48 The principle of the supremacy of Community law is a principle of Community law which could be expected to cause difficulties for the national courts of the Member states in some circumstances, especially where the requirements of Community law appear to run counter to the fundamental provisions of national constitutions.[87] In Britain the matter is dealt with by the provisions of the European Communities Act 1972, s.2(1) of which provides as follows:

"All such rights, powers, liabilities, obligations and restrictions from time to time created by or arising by or under the Treaties, and all such remedies and procedures from time to time provided for by or under the Treaties, as in accordance with the Treaties are without further enactment to be given legal effect or used in the United Kingdom, shall be recognised and available in law, and be enforced, and allowed accordingly."

In *Coomes (Holdings) Ltd. V. Shields*[88] and in *McCarthys Ltd v. Smith*[89] the Court of Appeal accepted the supremacy of Community law. As Docksey and Fitzpatrick[90] observe, British lawyers in general and labour lawyers in particular have only really become aware of the significance of the supremacy of Community law with the *Factortame*[91] case, which had the effect of granting an interim injunction against the Crown and of disapplying a later British statute.

---

[86] Case 6/64 [1964] E.C.R. 585 at p. 593-594
[87] See Louis, *supra*, pp.139-149, for a discussion of the reception of this doctrine into the law of the Member States generally.
[88] [1978] I.R.L.R. 263
[89] Case 129/79 [1979] 3 C.M.L.R. 44, [1980] E.C.R. 1275, [1980] I.R.L.R. 209
[90] C.Docksey and B.Fitzpatrick, "The Duty of National Courts to Interpret Provisions of National Law in accordance with Community Law", *Industrial Law Journal*, 20,2, pp.113-120 at p.115
[91] Case 213/89, *R. v.Secretary of State for Transport, ex.p. Factortame* [1990] 3 W.L.R. 818 (ECJ and HL) In that case regulations made under the 1988 Merchant Fishing Act limited the right to fish under the British quota to fishing vessels registered in Britain and owned by British nationals or in the case of companies with more than 75 per cent. of the shares held by British nationals. This had a disastrous effect on certain Spanish owned vessels which had registered in Britain to take advantage of the British quota, and was arguably contrary to the relevant directly effective Article of the Treaty. The applicants sought interim relief in the form of an injunction against the Crown to disapply the Regulations whilst an Art. 177 reference was made to the ECJ on their substantive rights. The question of the seeking of such an interim injunction was referred to the ECJ which held that a rule of national law prohibiting such an injunction must be set aside, thus having the effect of disapplying a later enacted statute contrary to directly effective rights.

The supremacy of Parliament is now only likely to be preferred to the supremacy of Community law, as Lord Denning M.R put it in a potentially significant *obiter dictum* in *McCarthys*,

> "If the time should come when our Parliament deliberately passes an Act with the intention of repudiating the Treaty or any provision within it or of intentionally acting inconsistently with it and says so in express terms (then) I should have thought that it would be the duty of our courts to follow the statute of our Parliament."

1.49   The supremacy of Community law has been further emphasised by the decision in *Frankovitch and Boniface v. Republic of Italy*[92] in which the ECJ holds that Community law lays down a principle according to which a Member State is liable to make good damage to individuals caused by a breach of Community law for which it is responsible, albeit that the rights upon which the action is based are not of direct effect, provided that three conditions are met. These conditions are that the result required by the Directive includes the conferring of rights for the benefit of individuals, the content of these rights may be determined by reference to the Directive and the existence of a causal link between breach of the obligation of the State and the damage suffered by the individual.

Frankovitch arose from the failure of Italy to implement the Insolvency Directive, with the result that workers affected by insolvencies in Italy did not enjoy the rights which they were intended to enjoy under Community law. The failure to implement the Directive was established by enforcement proceedings brought by the Commission in the ECJ. Arguing from the capacity of the Community legal order to create rights in individuals both by reason of the Treaty itself and the obligations which it places upon Institutions and Member States, as established in *Costa* v. *Enels* and *Van Gend en Loos*, and the obligation placed upon national courts to give full effect to those rights,[93] the ECJ concludes that

> "The full effectiveness of Community provisions would be affected and the protection of the rights they recognise undermined if individuals were not able to recover damages when their rights were infringed by a breach of Community law attributable to a Member State."

1.50   Whilst it is for the national legal systems to determine the procedural conditions for such actions in the absence of community rules on the subject,[94] the Court held that the principle of State liability for damage is inherent in Community law. *Factortame* establishes that national

[92] Cases 6/90 &9/90, [1992] I.R.L.R. 84, ECJ.
[93] See n. 79 *supra*, *Simmenthal*
[94] See para. 1.45

procedural rules may not preclude a remedy in such a case, if these would stand in the way of the exercise of Community rights. Such a possibility complements, rather than substitutes for, rights to take action against the State arising under directly effective legislation. Where a person is working for a private employer and wishes to rely on rights arising under a Directive which has not been fully or correctly implemented (Mrs Duke in *Duke* v. *GEC Reliance*, for example, although, as Duffy comments,[95] her claim related to a period before the Directive was clarified in *Marshall*), *Frankovitch* opens the way for actions in damages against the State, provided the necessary conditions are met, even though the Directive was not directly effective between the original parties to the contract of employment. In *Frankovitch* the Advocate General observed that a judgement of the Court establishing non-implementation demonstrated a sufficiently serious breach of a superior rule of law to found liability (as required in the case law under Article 215 concerning liability to damages caused by actions of the institutions of the Community) but questions whether a judgement to this effect was actually a requirement for liability. The Advocate General commentary[96] on *Waterkeyn*[97] observed that where there are already applicable provision of Community law, individuals do not have to wait for such a judgement but may rely directly on those provisions to enforce their rights.

Indirect effect

1.51   Whilst section 2(2) provides for the making of statutory instruments to implement those Community obligations which are not directly applicable or to amplify those which are, the binding nature of directly effective Community rights is reinforced in section 2(4), which provides that "any enactment passed or to be passed. . .shall be construed and have effect subject to the foregoing provisions of this section. . .". As a matter of U.K. law it follows from the wording of section 2(4) that the U.K. courts are only obliged to interpret national law in conformity with Community law where that law is of direct effect *i.e.* that referred to in section 2(1). The logic of the section can be seen at work in *Duke* v. *GEC Reliance* (a case involving a private employer on facts similar to those found in *Foster* v. *British Gas*) in which the House of Lords rejected the contention that the Sex Discrimination Act 1975 should be construed so as to conform to the provisions of

---

[95] P.Duffy, "Damages against the State: a new remedy for failure to implement Community obligations", *European Law Review*, 1992, p. 133-138 at p.137.
[96] At para. 64.
[97] Joined Cases 314-316/82 & 83/82 [1982] E.C.R. 4337.

the subsequent Equal Treatment Directive. Templeman L.J., giving the judgment of the Court, held that:

"Of course a British court will always be willing and anxious to conclude that United Kingdom law is consistent with Community law. Where an act is passed for the purpose of giving effect to an obligation imposed by a directive or other instrument a British court will seldom encounter difficulty in concluding that the language of the Act is effective for the intended purpose. But the construction of a British Act of Parliament is a matter of judgment to be determined by the British courts and to be derived from the language of the legislation considered in the light of the circumstances prevailing at the date of enactment. . .Section 2(4) of the European Communities Act 1972 does not in my opinion enable or constrain a British court to distort the meaning of a British statute in order to enforce against an individual a Community Directive which has no direct effect between individuals. Section 2(4) applies and only applies where Community provisions are directly applicable."[98]

1.52   Nonetheless, in the *Von Colson* case the ECJ had previously held that:

"in applying national law and in particular a national law introduced to implement Directive 76/207, national courts are required to interpret their national law in the light of the wording and purposes of the directive in order to achieve the results referred to in article 189(3),"

suggesting that it is not only implementing legislation, but any national law covering the same ground, which should be construed in conformity with Community law. Reliance on this principle is not limited to cases against the State or against organisations emanating more or less from State authority, because the law applied remains national law while clarified by an interpretation in conformity with Community law, according to the opinion of the Advocate General in *Dekker* v. *VJV Centrum*.[99] In *Van Colson* the ECJ held that Article 189(3) imposes an obligation

"to achieve the results envisaged by the directive and (it is) their duty under Article 5 of the Treaty to take all appropriate measures, whether general or particular, to ensure the fulfilment of that obligation, which is binding on all the authorities of Member States, including for matters within their jurisdiction, the courts."[1]

---

[98] [1988] I.R.L.R. 118 at p. 123. and *Finnegan* v. *Clowney Youth Training Programme* [1990] 2 A.C. 407, a case concerning the Sex Discrimination (Northern Ireland) Order 1976, S.I. 1976 No. 1042, which was adopted after the Equal Treatment Directive but which was intended to implement the terms of the Sex Discrimination Act 1975 in Northern Ireland, rather than the Directive.

[99] Case 177/88, [1991] I.R.L.R. 27.

[1] Case 14/83, *Von Colson and Kamann* v. *Land Nordrhein-Westfalen* [1984] 2 C.M.L.R. 430, ground 26.

In its final ruling the Court unfortunately put the matter more shortly as an obligation "for the national court to interpret and apply the legislation adopted for the implementation of the directive in conformity with the requirements of Community law, in so far as it is given discretion to do so under national law." The passage from the *Duke* case cited above relies upon the fact that the Sex Discrimination Act was not implementing legislation, even though, at the time, the U.K. government took the view that no specific legislation was necessary because of the pre-existing Sex Discrimination Act.

1.53 The courts have, however, shown themselves willing to construe implementing legislation so as to conform with the requirements of Community law, as in the decision of the House of Lords in *Pickstone* v. *Freemans*.[2] This decision concerned the interpretation of the Equal Pay Amendment Regulations 1983 which implement the equal value aspect of the Equal Pay Directive. Article 1 of the Directive was said to enjoy both vertical and horizontal direct effect following the decision of the ECJ in the *Jenkins* case, and therefore the fact that only private persons were involved was no obstacle to the House of Lords abandoning one of the normal canons of statutory construction and looking to the intentions of Parliament in the way in which the draft of the Regulations was presented by the relevant Minister. Such a construction was held to be consistent with EEC law partly because it was plain that Parliament could not possibly have intended a failure to implement Community obligations fully and correctly. Even the need to imply words into a section of the Regulations which Lord Oliver admitted was on its face unambiguous, did not prevent a purposive construction. A similar approach marked the decision of the Lords in the transfer of undertakings case of *Litster* v. *Forth Dry Dock and Engineering Co*,[3] where a strongly purposive construction of the regulations was adopted, even though they were not of direct effect. It is, however, the intention of Parliament which is being purposively interpreted and not the Directive itself.[4]

1.54 The principle of *indirect effect* has, however, recently been extended as a matter of Community law in *Marleasing SA* v. *la Commercial International de Alimentacion SA* to encompass all relevant domestic legislation irrespective of whether it was passed to implement Community obligations and whether it was passed before or after the particular Community instrument. In *Marleasing* the ECJ held that although

---

[2] [1987] I.R.L.R. 218, C.A., [1988] I.R.L.R. 356, H.L.
[3] [1989] I.R.L.R. 161, H.L.
[4] Note the increased importance given to Parliamentary intentions by the House of Lords decision in *Pepper* v. *Hart & Others* [1993] I.R.L.R. 33.

"a Directive cannot, in itself, impose obligations on the rights of an individual and, consequently, the prescriptions of a directive cannot be invoked as such against such a person" nonetheless "in applying the national law the national court called upon to interpret it is obliged to do so wherever possible in the light of the text and of the (purpose) of the Directive in order to achieve the result envisaged by the latter and thus to conform to Article 189, third paragraph of the Treaty."[5]

Docksey and Fitzpatrick see the interpretative approach in *Marleasing* as a part of a three-pronged attack upon the limitation imposed by *Marshall* on the horizontal direct effect of directives.[6] It is to be seen alongside the extension of the boundaries of the State in *Foster* and the very wide definition of pay under Article 119, in such cases as *Barber* v. *Guardian Royal Exchange*.[7] The question has been raised as to whether the ECJ has been "running wild" in ways such as this, extending its remit beyond the bounds of established political consensus or democratic control,[8] but as de Burca[9] observes, this wide principle of interpretation poses a particular problem to the U.K. courts which have hitherto based themselves on the presumed intention of Parliament to comply with Community obligations. Yet section 3(1) of the European Communities Act 1972 provides a basis upon which the obligations contained in *Marleasing* could be accepted and reconciled with the notion of Parliamentary sovereignty, in that it provides:

"For the purposes of all legal proceedings, any question as to the meaning or effect of the Treaties, or as to the validity, meaning or effect of any Community instrument, shall be treated as a question of law (and, if not referred to the European Court) be for determination as such in accordance with the principles laid down by and any relevant decisions of the European Court."

1.55 Whether *Marleasing* imposes obligations which go so far as to forbid national courts from arriving at an interpretation not in conformity with Community law is open to question, but it would appear that they go beyond

---

[5] Case 106/89 at paras. 6 and 8.
[6] Docksey and Fitzpatrick, "The Duty of National Courts to Interpret Provisions of National Law in accordance with Community Law, I.L.J., 202, pp. 113–121.
[7] [1983] I.C.R. 521; [1983] I.R.L.R. 240; [1986] E.C.R. 703, E.A.T.
[8] The debate about about the proper powers of the European institutions has been given a sharper edge by the current concerns about "subsidiarity" and the "democratic deficit". On the role of the ECJ see H.Rasmussen, *On Law and Policy in the European Court of Justice* (Martinus Nijhoff, 1986,) "Between Self restraint and activism: A Judicial Policy for the European Court" (1988) 13 *European Law Review*, pp. 28-38 and Mauro Cappelletti, "Is the European Court of Justice "Running Wild" (1987) 12 *European Law Review*, pp. 3-17.
[9] Grainne de Burca, "Giving Effect to Community Directives" 1992 *Modern Law Review*, 55, pp. 215-241 at p. 222-223.

simply the resolving of ambiguities in the statutory wording (although in *Pickstone* v. *Freemans* and *Litster* the courts have already gone this far for implementing legislation.) Both the obligation to interpret national legislation irrespective of the natural meaning of the words and the application of the *Marleasing* interpretative principle to prior national legislation, run the risk of offending against the principle of legal certainty and the protection of legitimate expectations, a limitation acknowledged by the ECJ in *Kolpinghuis Nijmegen*.[10] Whether one might by now legitimately expect national law to be interpreted according to the wording of an existing statute or the purposes of a directive covering the same ground would appear to be a question which is open for argument.[11]

1.56 The decision of the Court of Appeal in *Marshall (No.2)*,[12] in which the respondent health authority was appealing against an award of compensation to Miss Marshall which was well in excess of the statutory limit, even without the inclusion of interest since the original date of the first action on which the damage award was based, illustrates well the difficulties which can arise for an applicant who wishes to rely on Community law rights. In *Von Colson* the ECJ had held that although Article 6 of the Directive

> "does not require any specific form of sanction for unlawful discrimination, it does entail that that sanction be such as to guarantee real and effective judicial protection. Moreover, it must have real deterrent effect on the employer. It follows that where a Member state chooses to penalise the breach of the prohibition of discrimination by the award of compensation, that compensation must in any event be adequate in relation to the damage sustained."

The majority in the Court of Appeal accepted that it was arguable that the statutory limits on compensation under the Sex Discrimination Act did not provide an adequate remedy as required by Article 6 of the Directive but held that there was no directly effective provision as to compensation upon which Miss Marshall could rely, in view of the further statement of the ECJ in the *Von Colson* case that Article 6, "does not include any unconditional and sufficiently precise obligation which, in the absence of implementing measures adopted within the prescribed time limits, may be relied on by an individual in order to obtain specific compensation

---

[10] Case 80/86 [1987] E.C.R. 3969; [1989] 2 C.M.L.R. 18, although as that case concerned a possible extension of criminal liability, it could be rationalised as concerning more the non-retroactivity of penal legislation.

[11] cf, J.Steiner, "Coming to Terms with E.C. Directives" (1990) *106 Law Quality Review*, 144-159.

[12] *Marshall* v. *Southampton and South West Hampshire Health Authority (No.2)*, [1988] I.R.L.R. 325, IT; [1989] I.R.L.R. 459, EAT; [1990] I.R.L.R. 481, C.A.

under the directive, where that is not provided under national law."[13] The majority therefore turned to the possibility of interpreting the Sex Discrimination Act so as to give effect to the purposes of the Directive but, relying on Lord Templeman's speech in *Duke*, denied that it had the "discretion" to do so as the Sex Discrimination Act was passed before the Directive rather than in contemplation of it and the statutory limit was clear and unambiguous.[14] Such an approach could be criticised as failing to go as far as the House of Lords in *Factortame* and raises the question as to how far national procedural limitations can circumscribe duties and obligations arising from Community law, albeit in this case, not directly effective Community law. In *Emmot*[15] the ECJ concluded that national time limits do not run until a directive is properly implemented and the law is therefore clear, whilst in *Cotter and McDermott* v. *Minister for Social Welfare*[16] it was said that the State could not rely on the common law rule against unjust enrichment where to do so would deny the effectiveness of Article 4(1) of Directive 76/207. The same approach may be adopted towards other procedural limitations on Community based rights, such as the statutory limit on compensation, when the ECJ pronounces upon the questions addressed to it in the second *Marshall* reference.[17] In this context there is force in the decision of the EAT in Scotland[18] that it would be incompatible with Community law to limit its effectiveness by not permitting an originating application in the Industrial Tribunals to be based on rights arising under Article 119.

---

[13] *supra* at ground 27.

[14] This result was reached notwithstanding the decision of the ECJ in *Johnston* v. *Chief Constable of Royal Ulster Constabulary* [1986] I.R.L.R. 263, that Art. 6 was directly effective at least in so far as it provided that applicants in matters of sex discrimination must have an effective judicial remedy.

[15] [1991] I.R.L.R. 387, ECS.

[16] Case 377/89 [1991] I.R.L.R. 380 & see para. 1.45.

[17] Advocate General Walter Van Gerven has rendered an opinion in *Marshall No. 2* which concludes that the imposition of a limit on compensation is not automatically contrary to the directly effective provisions of Art. 6, unless it results in the compensation not being adequate in relation to the damages sustained. The Advocate General distinguished between four elements of compensation, namely, loss of physical assets, loss of income, moral damage (injury to feelings) and damage on account of the effluxion of time *i.e.* interest and argued that if compensation is not, or is scarcely, available under each of these heads, "it cannot be said that the compensation, taken as a whole, is adequate in relation to the damage sustained" (ground 18) Thus if the statutory limit on compensation precludes the payment of interest from the date at which the injury was sustained to the date of judgement, so-called compensatory interest, the Advocate General concludes that there cannot be adequate compensation as required by Art. 6. Furthermore interest from the date of judgement to the date of conclusion of any form of appeal proceedings when the judgement is confirmed, so-called legal interest, should also be payable.

[18] *Secretary of State for Scotland and Greater Glasgow Health Board* v. *Wright and Hannah* [1991] I.R.L.R. 187 in which Lord Mayfield reviewed all the authorities on the existence of an independently justiciable right under Community law in the I.T.s.

Again a different division of the EAT in Scotland in *McKechnie* v. *U.B.M. (Building Supplies) Ltd*[19] decided that the gap between section 82(1) of the Employment Protection (Consolidation) Act 1978, which then limited redundancy claims by women to those aged only up to 60, and the directly effective right to equal pay under Article 119, was such that it could not be bridged by any interpretative device. It went on to hold that Article 119 could confer an independent right, at least where it supplemented, rather than contradicted domestic law.

1.57 In the pregnancy case of *Webb* v. *EMO Air Cargo Ltd*[20] the Court of Appeal first reached a conclusion adverse to the applicant under English law and then tested its conclusion against the case law of the ECJ, as expressed in *Dekker*[21]. Even though *Marleasing* was cited, the Court was unanimous in its conclusion, relying on *Duke*, that the construction of the relevant provision so as to conform with the interpretation of the Directive favoured by the applicants would "distort" the meaning of the Sex Discrimination Act. Again it is arguable that this is a narrow view of the "possible", perhaps influenced by an unfavourable view of the merits of the case, which may be reversed on appeal to the Lords.[22] If the Court of Appeal had first made an evaluation of the position under Community law and then had interpreted the domestic law in conformity with that view, a different result might have been obtained.[23]

The Third Action Programme on Equality

Social action programme   **1.58** As a part of the Social Action Programme based on the Charter of Fundamental Social Rights of Workers signed

[19] [1991] I.R.L.R. 283, EAT.
[20] [1990] I.R.L.R. 124, EAT; [1992] I.R.L.R. 116, C.A. For the facts see p. 2.12.
[21] *Dekker* v. *Stichting Vormingcentrum Voor Jonge Volwassen (VJV Centrum)Plus* [1991] I.R.L.R. 27, ECJ. Dekker was distinguished on the ground that it concerned the financial consequences of pregnancy related dismissals and not the case where a women was unable to perform the primary task for which she was engaged. Arnull observes, however, that "The Court of Appeal's analysis of that case was inductive in a way that is sometimes said to be characteristic of the common law: their Lordships seem to have seen the case as confined to its own particular facts rather than as laying down a general principle which might have assisted Ms Webb."
[22] Arnull (*E.L.R.*, 1992 at p. 273) comments that should the case be referred to the ECJ, the Lords may have to consider whether the domestic law is capable of being interpreted purposively to comply with whatever is then understood to be the import of the Directive. If not Arnull posits the question as to whether the Government might be exposed to a Frankovitch type action for damages at the suit of Mrs Webb!
[23] *Webb* has, however, been referred to the ECJ by the House of Lords.

by 11 of the Member countries, the European Commission was calling for:

a. a Third Community Action Programme on Equal Opportunities for Women,
b. a new directive on pregnancy (discussed in chapter 2 under *Pregnancy*),
c. a Recommendation concerning child care,
d. a Recommendation for a code of good conduct on pregnancy and maternity, including the dissemination of information intended to assist working parents, and
e. a Recommendation on Child Care Services and a Code of Good Practice to supplement it.

The proposals contained in the Third Action Programme on Equality may have more importance than is immediately apparent in view of the ECJ's dictum in *Grimaldi* that national courts are bound to take Recommendations into consideration (see para. 1.46).

1.59   The Third Action Programme on Equality attempts to clarify and improve the implementation of the existing law. In particular, guidance is to be given in a Memorandum on the criteria to be taken into account in job evaluation in the context of equal value claims, a topic on which there is still a great deal of uncertainty. The Commission will also attempt to clarify the meaning of indirect discrimination. It is proposed to amend the directive on the position of self-employed women with regard to equal treatment. The Commission reiterates that it is for the Member States to ensure that there is an adequate means of collective redress in equality cases, a significant gap in the present U.K. law. Measures are proposed to be taken to assist the re-entry of women into the labour market, including support for child care facilities, with a substantial budget of 120m ECUs to be financed out of the Structural Funds. The Commission also proposes to concern itself with the image of women in the media and their place in the decision making process by initiating studies, disseminating their results and promoting discussion of these issues.

The Third Action Programme on Equality emphasises the importance of "social dialogue" between the social partners (*i.e.* employers and trade unions) in bringing forward this issue. The Programme was adopted by a resolution of the Council on May 21, 1991, thus giving authority for continued work and development of the Programme but not committing the Council to any specific legislation in the form of directives or regulations.

The improvement of living and working conditions

1.60 Prior to Maastricht, three directives had been proposed on part-time and temporary work, which will broadly equate the terms and conditions of part-timers to those of full-timers with respect to training, health and safety, holidays and other social protections. The directives also propose that employers be obliged to consult over the introduction of large scale temporary work and that temporary work should not in general replace permanent employment. In addition, a directive is proposed on working time which will limit the extent of night work and impose mandatory rest breaks of not less than 12 hours in any 24. These proposals could be of great benefit to women.

The basis of the Social Dimension

1.61 At the Madrid Summit in June 1989, the Member States declared that:

> ". . . in the course of the construction of the single European market, social aspects should be given the same importance as the economic aspects and should accordingly be developed in a balanced fashion."

Yet prior to the Maastricht protocol there was no clear mandate for social programmes within the Community with the result that social measures need to be brought within an appropriate Treaty base; *i.e.* directed towards an improvement in health and safety under Article 118A or justified as necessary to the establishment and functioning of the common market under Article 100 or Article 100A because they reduce distortions of competition. For example, if the regulation of part-time and temporary work is more stringent in one country than another, that might give rise to unfair and distorted competition because, in the Commission's view, the differences in the cost of employing part-time workers arise largely from regulations governing social costs. The Commission argues that two of the three directives on part-time and temporary work are concerned with avoiding such distortions of competition in the market and one with health and safety.

1.62 The problem with these proposals is that Directives which, as Hepple argues,[24] *predominantly* concern the rights and interests of employed persons still require unanimity in the Council of Ministers and have to be voted under Article 100, so that they could be blocked by the U.K. or any other hostile government. Therefore, of the three directives on temporary work, one is under Article 100 (training, representation and information), one under 100A (social

---

[24] Bob Hepple, "The implementation of the Community Charter of Fundamental Social Rights" *Modern Law Review*, 53, September 1990

security benefits on the same basis as full-time workers, maximum duration of temporary contracts and pro-rata holidays) and the other under 118A (regulation of temporary work agency contracts, training and information on potential health and safety risks), to which the U.K. Government does not have fundamental objections. It is not clear at this stage whether the Article 100 or 100A proposals will survive. Objections have been raised in the Council, and not only by Britain (D.E., 1990), that the Article 100A proposals in reality concern the rights of employed persons and should be introduced on that basis, requiring unanimous voting. The position would seem to be that those directives, which are blocked by the U.K. because unanimity is required under the pre-Maastricht rules, may be acted upon by the remaining eleven under the Social Protocol, if Maastricht is ratified in its present form.

1.63   Thus the most important proposals for working women emanating from Europe may not be those which are explicitly concerned with equality, but those on working time, part-time and temporary work which, if realised, may be expected to benefit women disproportionately. Those which can supportably be described as health and safety matters, such as the pregnancy directive, are likely to be implemented regardless of the Maastricht opt-out. Those which cannot be brought within the field of health and safety, or described as measures necessary to avoid the distortion of competition but which do not preponderantly concern "the rights and interests of employed persons", however, will only be capable of realisation under the revised Social Chapter, presently contained in the Social Protocol signed only by the other eleven at Maastricht.

The implications of Maastricht for equality

Charter of the Fundamental Social Rights of Workers

1.64   It is well known that the Charter of the Fundamental Social Rights of Workers and subsequently the Social Protocol of the Maastricht Treaty, were agreed by 11 of the 12 Member States of the Community, but not by the U.K. Partly this was the culmination of a decade of de-regulation, but the British tradition is one of freedom of contract and the abstention of the State from all but an auxiliary role in labour relations. Where regulation has been traditional in Britain, as with health and safety, there has been little principled objection to the proposals contained in the Charter. The tradition of statutory regulation of health and safety matters stretching back to 1833 makes this aspect of the Charter look more natural and acceptable to British eyes. Likewise, there has been little objection to the principle of developing Community equality law and indeed it is widely accepted that Britain is ahead in Europe with respect to specific legislation on race.[25] As Wedderburn observes, the principle of equal pay contained in Article 119 and "the Directives on equal pay pay and equal treatment have never had to prove their legitimacy as corrections to distortions of competition"[26]

1.65   At Maastricht, the other 11 wished to make progress towards the implementation of the proposals contained in the Social Charter, although Britain remained adamantly opposed to any extension of Community competence in the employment sphere. In the event, the other 11 signed a Protocol to the Treaty of European Union which would allow them access to the Community Institutions in making progress towards realising the principles contained in the Social Charter. The result is that if Britain disagrees with proposals brought forward with respect to subjects which require unanimity under the pre-Maastricht rules, the other 11 are not precluded from going ahead with those proposals. What the protocol does not do is reduce or in any way alter the *acquis communitaire*, *i.e.* it does not put the clock back or undermine existing provisions such as the equality directives.

1.66   The Social Protocol consists of revised Articles 117-122, which contain both a new substantive agenda for a social Europe and new legislative processes based upon the concept of social dialogue.[27] The new Articles 117 and 118 provide a basis for more detailed Community measures to support and complement the activities of the Member States in improving living and working conditions, facilitating entry into work and increasing equality between men and women. The main change in the wording of Article 119 itself would be that equal opportunities programmes will be given a clearer and firmer legal basis, in that the anti-discrimination provisions of Article 119 shall not prevent any Member State from maintaining or adopting measures to make it easier for women to work or to compensate them for any disadvantages in their professional careers. The entirely separate protocol defining the temporal reach of the *Barber* judgement was signed by all 12 Community members. It remains uncertain as to what would be the impact on Britain of any proposals agreed upon under the Social Protocol. In view of the obligation placed upon Member States by Article 5 of the Treaty of Rome to facilitate the achievement of the Community's tasks, and the reach of Community law demonstrated in *Marleasing* and

---

[25] Second Review of the Race Relations Act, CRE, 1992.
[26] W. Wedderburn *University Dublin Law Journal*, 20, 1.
[27] See Manfred Weiss "The Significance of Maastricht for European Community Social Policy", *International Journal of Comparative Labour Law and Industrial Relations*, Spring 1992, pp. 3-14, and Barry Fitzpatrick "Community Social Law after Maastricht", *Industrial Law Journal*, 21, 3, pp. 199-213.

Frankovitch, there is a possibility that the absence of
legislative effect could be challenged in the U.K. in an
action for judicial review. Again, differential treatment
within the Community may be capable of challenge by
relying on the non-discrimination provisions of Article 7
with regard to nationality.[28] Yet it must be observed that
the renewed emphasis placed upon subsidiarity as a general
principle may circumscribe the judicial activism of the ECJ.
At the time of writing it is very unclear as to whether the
Maastricht Treaty will be ratified by all 12 Member States
and in particular by Britain. It is even less clear as to what
alternatives may arise in the further pursuit of European
unity.

1.67   The Trade Union Reform and Employment Rights
Act 1993 abolishes the Wages Councils. This is likely to
have a noticeable impact upon the relative pay of men and
women, as the majority of workers in Wages Councils
industries are low paid women. It could be argued that the
abolition of the Wages Councils is contrary to Article 5 of
the Treaty, which obliges Member States to take all
appropriate measures to ensure fulfilment of the obligations
arising out of the Treaty. One such obligation is, of course,
that of implementing the principle of equal pay under
Article 119. Furthermore in its opinion on the equitable
wage ([1992] O.J. C223/17) the Commission refers to the
need to ensure that even the low paid receive an equitable
wage and criticises economic strategies relying on the
extension or expansion of low pay. The TUC has urged the
Commission to commence infringement proceedings against
the U.K. under Article 169 in respect of this matter,
although in a climate of opinion in which greater emphasis is
being placed upon subsidiarity one must be sanguine about
the prospects for such action.

---

[28] See Catherine Barnard "A Social policy for Europe: Politicians 1,
Lawyers 0", *International Journal of Comparative Labour Law and
Industrial Relations*, Spring 1992, pp. 15-31.

2 DISCRIMINATION

What is discrimination?

2.01 If one were to describe another person as discriminating, that would be generally understood as a compliment. The inference would be that such a person has the capacity to choose, to distinguish between one option and another on the basis of a fine appreciation of the situation. Yet if one were to describe another person's conduct as discriminatory, that would normally be understood as a condemnatory or disapproving statement. What is the distinction between these two commonly understood usages of different parts of the same verb?

The essence of the matter is that those who are guilty of such discrimination have failed to distinguish between their fellow human beings as individuals. They have reacted to a whole group on the basis of the generally assumed characteristics of that group, without troubling to treat each individual on his or her merits according to the criteria which are truly relevant to the situation in hand. Such actions often spring from generalised assumptions about the characteristics of particular groups as in *Hurley* v. *Mustoe*[1] in which the employer acted on the assumption that all married women with small children were unreliable. The import of the case is not that employers must recruit women irrespective of whether or not they are reliable, but that the employer should have been prepared to assess all candidates on the grounds of their own potential reliability (amongst all their characteristics) and to choose accordingly. Reliability is relevant, whereas sex and motherhood as such are not. There was a failure to distinguish between the individuals who apply for a job (*i.e.* to discriminate in the first sense) according to criteria which are relevant to the choice which has to be made. The purpose of a job selection procedure is to select the best man or woman for the job. If choices are being made according to criteria which are not relevant to that purpose, the result must be that in practice the best person is not being selected for the job.

Discrimination **2.02** The statutes detail two basic types of discrimination-known as direct and indirect discrimination, but not so referred to in the legislation-which can form the

[1] [1981] I.C.R. 490.

basis for individual actions. In addition there is also discrimination by way of victimisation.

The elements of direct discrimination

Direct discrimination is defined in section 1(1)(a) of the Sex Discrimination Act 1975 (SDA):

"A person discriminates against a woman in any circumstances relevant to the purposes of any provision of this Act if

(a) on the ground of her sex he treats her less favourably than he treats or would treat a man."

Direct discrimination against married people is defined in similar terms in section 3(1)(a) as occurring where:

"on the ground of his or her marital status he treats that person less favourably than he treats or would treat an unmarried person of the same sex."[2]

In the Race Relations Act 1976 (RRA) direct discrimination is defined in similar terms in section (1)(a) as occurring where:

"on racial grounds he treats or would treat that other less favourably than he treats or would treat other persons."

The act complained of has to be taken on racial grounds under the Race Relations Act, s.1(1)(a). These words can encompass any actions based upon race, whether or not it is the race of the person who is affected by the action. Thus a white employee who was dismissed when he refused to obey an order to exclude young blacks from an amusement arcade in *Showboat Entertainments Centre* v. *Owens*[3] was held to have been discriminated against on racial grounds.[4] By contrast, under the Sex Discrimination Act, s.1(1)(a), the discrimination has to be based upon her sex *i.e.* the sex of the person bringing the complaint, so that a situation analogous to that in *Owens* but based on questions of gender (or marital status under s.3) would not be encompassed by the legislation.

Establishing direct discrimination

2.03 It is the ground of the alleged discriminator's actions which is important in cases of direct discrimination. It is unnecessary to show that the discriminator intended or wanted to discriminate if the effect of his actions is that women (or members of other racial groups) are treated less favourably by reason of their sex (or race). Thus in *R.* v. *Birmingham City Council ex p. E.O.C.*[5] the Council inherited a situation where more grammar school places were provided for boys than girls, and all that it was necessary to prove to

---

[2] Note that the protection on grounds of marital status applies only to protect married as against single persons and not vice versa. Neither does this provision apply to cases brought under Part III of the SDA 1975.
[3] [1984] 1 W.L.R. 384.
[4] See also Zaryzynska v. Levy I.C.R. 184, 1978 I.R.L.R. 532, E.A.T.
[5] [1988] I.R.L.R. 430, C.A., [1989] I.R.L.R. 172, H.L.

establish direct discrimination was that girls were thereby placed at a disadvantage, rather than that the Council intended to place girls at a disadvantage. Lord Goff of Chieveley put the matter as:

> "There is discrimination under the statute if there is less favourable treatment on grounds of sex, in other words if the relevant girl or girls would have received the same treatment as the boys but for their sex. The intention or motive of the defendant to discriminate, though it may be relevant so far as remedies are concerned . . . is not a necessary condition of liability: it is perfectly possible to envisage cases where the defendant had no such motive, and yet did in fact discriminate on grounds of sex. . . In the present case, whatever may have been the intention or motive of the Council, nevertheless it is because of their sex that the girls in question receive less favourable treatment than the boys and are the subject of discrimination under the Act of 1975."

The "but for" test

2.04 Thus the *Birmingham City Council* decision disposes completely of the notion that it is necessary to have an intention to discriminate for an act to constitute direct discrimination. It is the ground of the respondent's action which is important; intentions or motives are irrelevant. A married couple, Mr and Mrs James, both aged 61 went swimming at their local pool, where the wife was permitted to swim free as a pensioner but the husband was charged 75p. Mr James' claim that he had been subjected to discrimination was dismissed in the County Court. His appeal was refused in the Court of Appeal, but allowed in the House of Lords. In *James* v. *Eastleigh Borough Council* [1990] Lord Goff held that[6]

> "cases of direct discrimination under s.1(1)(a) can be considered by asking the simple question: would the complainant have received the same treatment from the defendant but for his or her sex? This simple test possesses the double virtue that, on the one hand, it embraces both the case where the treatment derives from the application of a gender based criterion and the case where it derives from the selection of the complainant because of his or her sex; and on the other hand it avoids, in most cases at least, complicated questions related to concepts such as intention, motive, reason or purpose, and the danger of confusion arising from the misuse of those elusive terms."

2.05 Lord Goff identifies the requisite intention under section 1(1)(*a*) as simply an intention to perform the relevant act of less favourable treatment. Whether or not the treatment is less favourable in the relevant sense, ie on grounds of sex or race, may derive from the application of

---

[6] [1990] I.R.L.R. 288 at p. 295, para. 39.

gender-or race-based criteria to the complainant, or from
selection of the complainant because of his or her sex or
race. On this reasoning the statutory pensionable age, being
fixed at 60 for women and 65 for men, is itself a criterion
which directly discriminates between men and women, and
it follows that any differential treatment based upon it must
equally involve discrimination on grounds of sex.

2.06   The "but for" test does not, however, dispense with
the need for the decision in question to have been taken "on
grounds of sex (or race)". A simple juxtaposition of a
woman and a man who have received different treatment, or
of two persons of different racial groups who have been
treated differently, is insufficient. Thus, in *Bullock* v. *Alice
Ottley School*[7] grounds and maintenance staff were allowed to
retire at 65, but the common retirement age for
administrative and domestic staff was 60. The EAT held
that such differential retirement ages were contrary to the
dictum of the House of Lords in *James*, but such a
comparison of domestic and grounds staff does not establish
that "but for" her sex a female domestic would have been
treated any differently to a male in similar circumstances. It
is submitted that, properly understood, the case illustrates
the fact that the "but for" test still leaves a niche for
indirect discrimination, in that direct discrimination must
still occur on the grounds of sex or race. As the Court of
Appeal emphasised, the comparison must be one of like with
like and

> "there is nothng in section 5(3) which prevents an
> employer having a variety of different retiring ages for
> different jobs, provided that in the system which he uses
> there is no direct or indirect discrimination based on
> gender. In a case of alleged direct discrimination the
> question is: would a man in the same job have been
> treated differently?"[8]

2.07   It is not necessary that the the sole reason why the
complainant experienced discriminatory treatment shall be a
racial or gender factor, according to the Court of appeal in
Owen & Briggs v. *James*,[9] a case in which a coloured
applicant was turned down for a job when race was
established as being at least an important part of the
employer's reasons, even though not the sole reason. In
Seide v. *Gillette Industries Ltd*[10] a Jewish workman was
transferred away from an anti-semitic colleague and, when
he sought to involve a new workmate in his former dispute,

---

[7] [1991] I.R.L.R. 324.
[8] [1992] I.R.L.R. 564, C.A. *per* Neill L.J. at p. 568. The Court of Appeal
  also held that whilst such a requirement was undoubtedly indirectly
  discriminatory, it was justifiable due to the difficulties experienced in
  recruiting and retaining grounds and maintenance staffs.
[9] [1982] I.R.L.R. 502.
[10] [1980] I.R.L.R. 427, EAT.

was transferred again so that he could be placed under more active management supervision. The EAT held that

> "notwithstanding that the appellant might not have been transferred had he not been Jewish . . . It does not seem to us to be sufficient merely to consider whether the fact that the person is a member of a particular racial group.. is any part of the background. . . . (T)he question which has to be asked is whether the activating cause of what happens is that the employer has treated a person less favourably than others on racial grounds."

At first sight this approach seems at variance with the "but for" test, although it would be possible to reconcile it with that test by reasoning that the complainant was moved because he attempted to involve a workmate in a personal dispute. In those circumstances a hypothetical comparison could be made between his situation and that of any other employee who attempted to involve a workmate in, say, a marital dispute, thus removing from the ambit of comparison the issue of race. In other words, it would not be true to say that "but for" his Jewishness the applicant would have been treated less favourably, if the comparison is made with a person who attempted to involve a colleague in some previous non-racial fracas.

2.08 Even if the motives and intentions of the alleged discriminator are benign they do not overcome the discriminatory effect of his actions. It is certainly highly questionable, notwithstanding the decision in *Seide* above, to move the victim of discrimination or harassment in order to avoid further difficulties or industrial unrest.[11] In *Din* v. *Carrington Viyella*[12], a Pakistani employee was not re-engaged on returning from a prolonged trip to his homeland. Just prior to his departure there had been some trouble between the applicant and his foreman which had not been resolved. The Industrial Tribunal found that the reason for not re-engaging the applicant was the employer's desire to avoid a repetition of the industrial unrest to which the previous incident had given rise. The EAT held that to seek to resolve actual or potential unrest by removing an employee against whom racial discrimination has been shown may itself be a discriminatory act, even if the employer acts from good motives. The EAT remitted the case to a freshly constituted tribunal to consider whether the potential industrial unrest, which was the proximate cause of the employer's action, was due to previous racial discrimination by a fellow employee for which the employer was responsible under section 32. Likewise, in *R.* v. *C.R.E. ex parte Westminster City Council*[13] the employer moved a black

---

[11] And in cases of sexual harassment, incompatible with the E.C. Code of Conduct on the Protection of the Dignity of Men and Women at Work.
[12] [1982] I.C.R. 256.
[13] [1985] I.C.R. 827, C.A.; affirming [1984] I.C.R. 770, E.A.T.

dustman who had been the subject of discrimination by
fellow employees, but such an action, though taken to avoid
industrial action, was held to constitute less favourable
treatment on racial grounds.

2.09   In *Grieg* v. *Community Industry*[14] a Y.T.S. trainee was
not allowed to start on her course because, following the
withdrawal of another girl, she would have been the only
female member of a group which was to be engaged upon
various building tasks. In those circumstances the employer
felt that the one remaining girl might be the subject of
unwelcome attentions from some of her fellow course
members, but such an action was nonetheless held to be
unlawful. Thus it is the reason for discriminatory acts and
not intentions and motives which are important. If the
discriminator performs an act on grounds of sex or race, his
intentions or motives are irrelevant. The House of Lords
makes clear in the *Birmingham* case that customer
preference, saving money or avoiding controversy are not
defences.

The comparison   2.10   Any comparison made between persons of different
to be made   genders, marital status or racial group must be such that the
relevant circumstances in the one case are the same, or not
materially different, in the other.[15] Even though the need to
compare like with like, to ensure that the relevant
circumstances are the same in one case as the other, has
been described as fairly obvious,[16] it has nonetheless given
rise to not inconsiderable difficulties, especially in ensuring
that the circumstances are gender-or race-neutral. For
example, in *James* v. *Eastleigh Borough Council*[17] the Court of
Appeal compared the treatment of persons of pensionable
age and concluded that there was no direct discrimination
between them. This decision was criticised by the majority
in the Lords on the ground that in comparing persons of
pensionable age, the comparison itself was gender-based, so
that the Court of Appeal was not comparing like with like.
The true comparison was between men and women age 61,
between whom the application of a gender based criterion
i.e. pensionable age, caused a discriminatory differentiation
in their treatment. The matter was put clearly by
Browne-Wilkinson J. (as he then was) in *Showboat Centre* v.
Owens[18]:

> "Although one has to compare like with like, in judging
> whether there has been discrimination you have to
> compare the treatment actually meted out with the
> treatment which would have been afforded to a man
> having all the same characteristics as the complainant

[14] [1979] I.C.R. 356.
[15] SDA 1975, s.5(3) and RRA 1976, s.3(4).
[16] *Bain* v. *Bowles and others* [1991] I.R.L.R. 356, C.A.
[17] [1990] I.R.L.R. 288; [1989] I.R.L.R. 318, C.A.
[18] [1984] I.R.L.R. 7, EAT.

except his race or his attitude to race. Only by excluding matters of race can you discover whether the differential treatment was on racial grounds."

2.11 More problematic are the decisions of the Court of Appeal in *Dhatt* v. *McDonalds Hamburgers Ltd*[19] and *Webb* v. *EMO (Air Cargo) Ltd*[20] In *Dhatt* a young man of Indian nationality who had entered the U.K. as a child with indefinite permission to stay, and who did not therefore need a work permit, applied for a job with McDonalds. The application form included the following question "If you are not a British citizen or from the EEC, do you have a permit to work in Britain? Yes/No. If yes, please provide evidence." Ultimately he was dismissed by an assistant manager who did not appreciate that the stamp in the applicant's passport "Given leave to enter the U.K. for an indefinite period" indicated that he was not subject to any restrictions as to his seeking work. The appellant claimed that comparison should be made between two young men otherwise qualified for the post, one of whom was a British or EEC national whilst the other was not. Any difference in treatment was contended to be on grounds of nationality. The Court of Appeal took the view that the appropriate comparison was not that between U.K. or EEC nationals and others, because that would not be to compare like with like; U.K. and EEC nationals do not need work permits, as other nationals normally do. The correct comparison was held to be between persons of different nationalities, each of which needed a work permit. This approach places the admittedly racially tainted factor of needing a work permit outside the ambit of comparison on the ground that it is a distinction sanctioned by Parliament in the context of immigration rules. *James* was distinguished on the ground that the adoption of pensionable age by the local authority was a voluntary act, whereas in this context even though there is no express obligation on employers to ensure that employees comply with immigration law and are free to work, there is a general obligation on employers to ensure that employees who work in their businesses are free to do so.[21] The Court of Appeal appears to have approached this question by the circuitous route of adapting the scope of comparison, perhaps because RRA, s.41, which governs conflicts between the RRA and other statutory rules, seems not to have been cited.

2.12 In *Webb*, a woman engaged as a maternity leave replacement found herself also to be pregnant and due to give birth only shortly after the woman whom she was replacing. When the pregnant maternity leave replacement

---

[19] [1991] I.R.L.R. 130, I.C.R. 238, C.A.

[20] [1992] I.R.L.R. 116, C.A.

[21] This decision has been heavily criticised by Ross in I.L.J., 20, 3, pp. 208-214, both on the ground that it takes nationality into the ground of comparison and because it ignores the operation of RRA, s.41.

was dismissed she complained under the SDA. The Court of Appeal held that rather than comparing a woman with a man *per se* when, as only women can be pregnant, any differentiation of treatment on the ground of pregnancy could only occur "but for" the sex of the woman, the correct comparison was between a pregnant woman and a man needing comparable time off for a physical condition. On this view, comparing like with like requires a comparison between two persons both of whom require substantial time off, one for pregnancy and one for some type of illness. Such an approach to the definition of the categories to be compared, which throws the emphasis on to the approach adopted by the dismissal by the employer, is arguably more faithful to the second part of Lord Goff's reasoning in the *Birmingham City Council* case quoted above, where he holds that:

> "whatever may have been the intention or motive of the Council, nevertheless it is because of their sex that the girls in question receive less favourable treatment than the boys and are the subject of discrimination under the Act of 1975."

The difficulty experienced by the Court of Appeal in applying the "but for" test in such awkward circumstances perhaps reflects the doubts expressed by Lord Lowry in his dissenting opinion in *James* where he held that what he termed the "causative" approach

> "not only gets rid of unessential and and often irrelevant mental ingredients, such as malice, prejudice, desire and motive, but also dispenses with an essential ingredient, namely, the ground on which the discriminator acts."[22]

Such difficulties led the House of Lords in *Webb* to hold that the "but for" test as formulated was not capable of application to the facts of the case. Lord Keith of Kinkel, giving the judgement of the House, based his approach on the view that Mrs Webb was not dismissed because she was pregnant but because, having been engaged as a maternity leave replacement, she was not going to be available at the time for which she had been recruited. Once the reason for dismissal is identified as unavailability at the time for which the employee has been recruited, Lord Keith took the view that there could be no material difference between such absence arising for a reason consequent upon pregnancy and absence due to a uniquely male complaint, such as, for example, a prostate operation, notwithstanding that

---

[22] Lord Lowry held that, to satisfy the test that the discriminator shall have treated the complainant less favourably *on the grounds of her sex* requires, as a matter of grammatical construction of s.1(1)(a), the adoption of a subjective approach in which the court must inevitably consider the thought processes of the discriminator to establish the ground on which he acted. This could present a formidable evidential problem of proof for complainants.

pregnancy is a normal female condition, whilst any illness is necessarily pathological.

> "The relevant circumstance for purposes of the comparison required by section 5(3) to be made is expected unavailabilty. The precise reason for the unavailability is not a relevant circumstance, and in particular it is not relevant that the reason is a condition which is capable of affecting only women, or for that matter only men."[23]

It is important to note, however, that if detrimental action is taken on the grounds of a condition which is inherently gender related such as pregnancy, this must be necessarily be directly discriminatory. Thus Lord Keith held in *Webb* that:

> There can be no doubt that in general to dismiss a woman because she is pregnant or to refuse to employ a woman of childbearing age because she may become pregnant is unlawful direct discrimination. Child-bearing and the capacity for childbearing are characteristics of the female sex, so to apply these characteristics as the criterion for dismissal or refusal to employ a gender based criterion."[24]

The House of Lords has referred the question to Luxembourg as to whether a dismissal on the grounds of prospective absence arising out of pregnancy is contrary to the Equal Treatment Directive.

2.13 In *Bain* v. *Bowles*,[25] the proprietors of "The Lady" refused to place an advertisement for a housekeeper from a single gentleman living in Tuscany in their magazine. It was the policy of the magazine not to place such advertisements for positions abroad unless there was a woman resident in the household concerned, as it was considered from experience that women who answered such advertisements might otherwise find themselves in a vulnerable position. The defendant magazine proprietors sought to argue that in any comparison to be made as to whether a like advertisement would have been accepted from a woman, the putative fate of those who might respond to the advertisement was one of the relevant circumstances. The Court of Appeal held, however, that the only relevant circumstances were those which concerned the placing of the advertisement and not subsequent events which might or might not occur, for if the motives of the defendants were to be encompassed the result would be inconsistent with *James* v. *Eastleigh Borough Council*.

2.14 The "but for" test gave rise to difficulties for the Court of Appeal in *Shomer* v. *B. & R. Residential Lettings*

---

[23] *per* Lord Keith of Kinkel at p. 230.
[24] At p. 29.
[25] [1991] I.R.L.R. 356

Ltd,[26] in which a negotiator for a residential lettings company became pregnant and, having agreed that her employment would terminate in approximately three months time, went on holiday for two weeks. Good negotiators were, it was agreed, in short supply, so Mrs Shomer was a valued employee. Just prior to her leaving for her holiday, the firm engaged a chauffeur to drive clients to appointments and as no other car was immediately available, the managing director of the firm ordered Mrs Shomer to return her company car whilst she was away on holiday. In the event she left it parked at Gatwick whilst she was away, but returned to find a notice of dismissal posted by hand through her letter box. In alleging that her dismissal was the result of her pregnancy, the appellant pointed to the fact that a replacement had been engaged to start when she left and, once the managing director had ascertained that the replacement could start within the next two weeks, her dismissal for alleged misconduct was contrived. Her claim was supported by a majority of the Industrial Tribunal members, who based themselves on *Hayes* v. *Malleable Castings* but concluded that a sick or disabled man who would had to leave in three months time would not have been dismissed. The EAT held that this decision was perverse, but the Court of Appeal preferred to base themselves on the view that the Industrial Tribunal had ignored the necessity for the comparable sick man to have committed some misconduct, or alternatively that the decision was perverse in that there was no evidence to suggest that a sick man who had committed some comparable act of misconduct would not have been dismissed. It is clear that the application of the "but for" test does not eliminate all difficulties and great care is needed to determine the appropriate ground of comparison.

Less favourable treatment

2.15 Direct discrimination occurs where a person is less favourably treated by virtue of their sex or on racial grounds. Less favourable treatment is generally associated with a narrowing of opportunities, a deprivation of choice which is experienced as a detriment. In *Jeremiah* v. *MoD*[27] Brightman L.J. put the matter as follows:

"I do not say that the mere deprivation of choice for one sex, or some differentiation in their treatment, is necessarily unlawful discrimination. The deprivation of choice, or differentiation, must be associated with a detriment. It is possible to imagine a case where one sex has a choice but the other does not, yet there is nevertheless no detriment to the latter sex and therefore no unlawful discrimination."

2.16 Likewise in *R.* v. *Birmingham City Council ex p. E.O.C.*, the House of Lords held that the loss of a chance of

[26] [19921] I.R.L.R. 317.
[27] [1979] I.R.L.R. 436, C.A. at p. 440.

something reasonably considered to be of value *i.e.* the diminished possibility of a grammar school place, constituted less favourable treatment. It was not necessary for the EOC "to show that the selective system was 'better' than non-selective education. It was enough that, by denying the girls the same opportunity as the boys, the council was depriving them of a choice, which (as the facts showed) was valued by them, or at least by their parents, and which (even though others may take a different view) was a choice obviously valued, on reasonable grounds, by many others."[28]

2.17   Under the Race Relations Act, s.1(1)(2) it is declared that to segregate a person from other persons on racial grounds is to treat him less favourably than they are treated. In *PEL Ltd.* v. *Modgill*[29] the EAT held that if there is evidence of a policy to segregate, or of the fact of segregation arising from an employer's act, there may be a breach of section 1(1)(2) but where, as in this case, a shop had been staffed entirely with Asian workers who had recommended their friends and relatives for employment, a failure to recruit non-Asian workers did not constitute less favourable treatment.[30]

Stereotyped assumptions   **2.18**   It is characteristic of discriminatory behaviour to treat all the members of a group as possessing some ascribed characteristic and then to act on the basis of that characteristic. For example, in *Alexander* v. *Home Office*[31], a West Indian prisoner whose request to work in the kitchens was refused, was described in his induction report as showing "the anti-authoritarian arrogance that seems to be common in most coloured inmates." It was found that this had the effect of not treating him as an individual but as an example of a damaging racial stereotype. Similarly, in *Hurley* v. *Mustoe*,[32] women with children were considered as a group to be unreliable. Likewise it may be thought that husbands are likely to be the breadwinners in a family[33] or that wives are more likely to follow the careers of their husbands than vice versa.[34] These are all examples of less favourable treatment based upon generalised examples about the characteristics of one sex or the other, in which the employer failed to investigate the true position of the individual in question. That is not to say that characteristics which may be generally ascribed to one sex or to a racial group may not be relevant to, say, an applicant's suitability

---

[28] *Supra* at p. 175.
[29] [1980] I.R.L.R. 142, E.A.T.
[30] It should be noted, however, that the complaints in this case arose from the segregated workers themselves. Had the complaint arisen from a rejected applicant for a job, the employer may have been held to be liable for less favourable treatment, which would not have been based upon the s.1(1)(2) definition of segregation.
[31] [1988] I.R.L.R. 190, C.A.
[32] *Supra* at para. 2.01.
[33] *Coleman* v. *Skyrail Oceanic*, [1981] I.R.L.R. 398, C.A.
[34] *Horsey* v. *Dyfed County Council* [1982] I.C.R. 755.

for a job or for promotion. What is important is that the decision should be based upon the degree to which the particular individual possesses that characteristic, rather than upon an assumption.[35]

Racial grounds and racial groups

2.19 Where section 1 of the Race Relations Act deals with direct discrimination, it refers to "racial grounds," and where it deals with indirect discrimination refers to "racial group." These expressions are defined by section 3 of the Act, though in practice those definitions have become overlaid by case law. "Racial grounds" means on the grounds of colour, race, nationality, ethnic or national origins.

"National origin"

"Nationality" was added as a ground in the 1976 Act because of the earlier House of Lords decision in *Ealing London Borough Council* v. *Race Relations Board*,[36] to the effect that "national origins" meant race as opposed to nationality, (so that discrimination against a Polish national was not under that earlier legislation unlawful). Despite the changed definition the Ealing decision continues to cause problems. It was followed by the Court of Appeal in *Tejani* v. *Superintendent Registrar for the District of Peterborough*[37] which concerned a British national born abroad. He was required to produce his passport before marriage, as were all persons coming from abroad. National origin was held to have a racial connotation and mean more than merely coming from abroad, so Mr Tejani's claim of discrimination failed. (The Tejani decision stands as a general warning to all litigants in race cases: the point on which the Court of Appeal decided the case was not one on which the parties to the appeal had chosen to argue it, but suggested by the Court itself.)

2.20 The 1976 Act does not say that the colour, race, nationality, ethnic or national origins need be that of the applicant or plaintiff. Accordingly racial discrimination can involve treating a person less favourably because of another's colour, etc. *In Zarcznska* v. *Levy9*[38] the EAT held that it was unlawful discrimination where the applicant was dismissed for serving a black customer contrary to her employer's instructions. There was a similar decision in *Showboat Entertainment Centre Ltd.* v. *Owens*.[39] Thus the legislation does not limit the racial grounds to the position of the applicant. But the same protection appears not to exist

---

[35] See also *Perera* v. *Civil Service Commission & Department of Customs & Excise* 1983 I.R.L.R. 166, C.A. on the question of proficiency in English and see *Coyne* v. *Export Credits Guarantee Department* [1981] I.R.L.R. 51, an equal pay case turning upon similar issues.
[36] [1972] A.C. 342.
[37] [1986] I.R.L.R. 502.
[38] [1978] I.R.L.R. 532.
[39] [1984] I.R.L.R. 7, EAT.

under the SDA as that legislation is differently worded in this respect.

Racial group   2.21   The Act says: "racial group" means a group of persons defined by reference to colour, race, nationality, ethnic or national origins." The section goes on to say that: "The fact that a group comprises two or more distinct racial groups does not prevent it from constituting a particular racial group for the purpose of this Act.

Whereas the word "race" has some connotation of common stock, the House of Lords in *Mandla* v. *Dowell Lee*[40] construed the meaning of "ethnic" relatively widely in a broad, cultural historic sense. Lord Fraser of Tullybelton approved a passage from the judgment of Richardson J. in the New Zealand Court of Appeal in *King-Ansell* v. *Police*[41]:

> "a group is identifiable in terms of its ethnic origins if it is a segment of the population distinguished from others by a sufficient combination of shared customs, beliefs, traditions and characteristics derived from a common or presumed common past, even if not drawn from what in biological terms is a common racial stock. It is that combination which gives them an historically determined social identity in their own eyes and in the eyes of those outside the group. They have a distinct social identity based not simply on group cohesion and solidarity but also on their belief as to their historical antecedents."

In that New Zealand case it had been held that Jews in New Zealand formed a group with common ethnic origins for the purposes of a statute under which the appellant had been convicted:

> "that with intent to excite ill-will against a group of persons in New Zealand, namely, Jews on the ground of their ethnic origins, did publish written matter, namely a pamphlet which was insulting and likely to excite ill-will against the said group of persons."

Jews were held by the New Zealand Court to be a racial group in the sense of an ethnic grouping applying Richardson J.'s criteria even though the evidence before the magistrate had been that: "there is no biological means of establishing that Jewish people are a race and that members of the Jewish People have diverse racial origins." The court also went on to say that: "The Magistrate was satisfied that Jewishness was much more than a matter of religion only."[42]

Does an ethnic group exist?   2.22   The national origins of the immigrant population of Great Britain may for many of them from day to day become less important than their religious groupings. Whilst Sikhs were held to be an ethnic group, the Birmingham Industrial

---

[40] [1983] 2 A.C. 548.
[41] [1979] 2 N.Z.L.R. 531, at p. 543.
[42] See also *Seide* v. *Gillette Industries Ltd.*, *supra* on the position of Jews.

Tribunal in *Tariq* v. *Young*[43] held that Muslims are not a racial but simply a religious group. The industrial tribunal in *Crown Suppliers* v. *Dawkins*, after hearing expert evidence accepted that Rastafarians were an ethnic group, but the EAT concluded that they were not, a view sustained in the Court of Appeal.[44]

Mandla v. *Dowell Lee*[45] is the leading case on the criteria to be applied in establishing whether an ethnic group exists. The House of Lords decided that Sikhs were a distinct ethnic group. The case was followed by the Court of Appeal in *C.R.E.* v. *Dutton*[46] who decided that Gipsies were an ethnic group. In *Mandla* at p. 562 Lord Fraser set out the position as follows:

"For a group to constitute an ethnic group in the sense of the Act of 1976, it must, in my opinion, regard itself, and be regarded by others, as a distinct community by virtue of certain characteristics. Some of these characteristics are essential; others are not essential but one or more of them will commonly be found and will help to distinguish the group from the surrounding community. The conditions which appear to me to be essential are these: (1) a long shared history, of which the group is conscious as distinguishing it from other groups, and the memory of which it keeps alive; (2) a cultural tradition of its own, including family and social customs and manners, often but not necessarily associated with religious observance. In addition to these two essential characteristics the following characteristics are, in my opinion, relevant; (3) either a common geographical origin, or descent from a number of common ancestors; (4) a common language, not necessarily peculiar to the group; (5) a common literature peculiar to the group; (6) a common religion different from that of neighbouring groups or from the general community surrounding it; (7) being a minority or being an oppressed or dominant group within a larger community, for example (say, the inhabitants of England shortly after the Norman conquest and their conquerors might both be ethnic groups.) A group defined by reference to enough of these characteristics would be capable of including converts, for example, persons who marry into the group, and of excluding apostates. Provided a person who joins the group feels himself or herself to be a member of it, and is accepted by other members, then he is, for the purposes of the Act, a member. That appears to be consistent with the words at the end of section 3(1): 'reference to a person's racial group refers to any racial group into which he falls.' In my opinion, it is possible for a person to fall into a

[43] Case No. 247738/88, EOR Discrimination Case Law Digest 2.
[44] *The Crown Suppliers (P.S.A.)* v. *Dawkins*, [1991] I.R.L.R. 327, EAT. The Guardian, Feb., 1 1993, C.A.
[45] *Supra*, n. 40.
[46] [1989] I.R.L.R. 8, C.A.

particular racial group either by birth or adherence, and it makes no difference, so far as the Act of 1976 is concerned, by which route he finds his way into the group."

In fact it was largely conceded that Sikhs met the wider definition of ethnic group, so Lord Fraser merely summarised the evidence on this point. He said[47]:

"They were originally a religious community founded about the end of the 15th Century in the Punjab by Guru Nanak, who was born in 1469. But the community is no longer purely religious in character. Their present position is summarised sufficiently for present purposes in the opinion of the learned judge in the County Court in the following passage: 'The evidence in my judgment shows that Sikhs are a distinctive and self-conscious community. They have a history going back to the 15th Century. They have a written language which a small proportion of Sikhs can read but which can be read by a much higher proportion of Sikhs than of Hindus. They were at one time politically supreme in the Punjab'."

2.23 In *CRE* v. *Dutton*[48] Nicholls L.J. summarised the state of the evidence on this issue as follows:

"On the evidence it is clear that such Gipsies are a minority, with a long-shared history and a common geographical origin. They are a people who originated in northern India. They migrated thence to Europe through Persia in medieval times. They have certain, albeit limited, customs of their own, regarding cooking and the manner of washing. They have a distinctive, traditional style of dressing, with heavy jewellery worn by the women, (although this dress is not worn all the time). They also furnish their caravans in a distinctive manner. They have a language or dialect, known as 'pogadi chib,' spoken by English Gipsies (Romany chals) and Welsh Gipsies (kale) which consists of up to one fifth of Romany words in place of English words. They do not have a common literature of their own, but they have a repertoire of folktales and music passed on from one generation to the next. No doubt, after all the centuries which have passed since the first Gipsies left the Punjab, Gipsies are no longer derived from what, in biological terms, is a common racial stock, but that of itself does not prevent them from being a racial group as widely defined in the Act. I come now to the part of the case which has caused me most difficulty. Gipsies prefer to be called 'travellers' as they think the term is less derogatory. This might suggest a wish to lose their separate distinctive identity so far as the general public is concerned. Half or more of them now live in houses like most other people.

[47] At p. 565.
[48] *Supra*, n. 46.

Have Gipsies now lost their separate, group identity, so that they are no longer a community recognisable by ethnic origins within the meaning of the Act? The judge held that they had. This is a finding of fact. Nevertheless, with respect to the judge, I do not think that there was before him any evidence justifying his conclusion that Gipsies have been absorbed into a larger group, if by that he meant that substantially all Gipsies have been so absorbed. The fact that some have been so absorbed and are indistinguishable from any ordinary member of the public, is not sufficient in itself to establish loss of what Richardson J.[49] referred to as an historically determined social identity in own eyes and in the eyes of those outside the group. There was some evidence to the contrary from Mr Mercer, upon whose testimony the judge expressed no adverse comment 'we know who are members of our community' and that 'we know we are different.' In my view the evidence was sufficient to establish that, despite their long presence in England, Gipsies have not merged wholly in the population, as have the Saxons and the Danes, and altogether lost their separate identity. They, or many of them, have retained in separateness, a self-awareness of still being Gipsies."

2.24 Following the Mandla criteria it has been held by the EAT that language is only one of a number of factors in deciding upon the existence or otherwise of an ethnic group and not decisive in itself. Accordingly, it was not possible to divide up the Welsh people into two ethnic groups comprising those who do and those who do not speak Welsh, at least on the basis of the language criteria.[50]

As section 3 of the 1976 Act recognises, a person will in fact belong to several racial groups for the purposes of the Act at the same time, and the relevant group will depend on the circumstances of the case.

On grounds of her sex

2.25 The Sex Discrimination Act 1975, s.1(1)(a) provides that discrimination occurs "if, on the ground of her sex he treats her less favourably than he treats or would treat a man." Most of the problems with this definition occur either where there is no direct comparison to be made between men and women or where the circumstances of men and women are likely to be materially different, whether for biological or socially constructed reasons.

Special concern for women

2.26 A comparable issue arises where the employer acts out of concern for the welfare of one sex, perhaps giving special

---

[49] See *King Ansell* case at p.543.
[50] *Gwynedd County Council* v. *Jones* [1986] I.C.R. 833.
[51] [1977] I.C.R. 968.

consideration to the needs of women. In *Peake* v. *Automotive Products Ltd.*[51] the employer allowed the women to leave work five minutes before the men, in order that they should not be jostled in the rush for the buses.[52] One of the able-bodied men complained that the rule was discriminatory. The Court of Appeal rejected the application on two grounds, firstly, that the rule was formulated on grounds of safety, chivalry and good administrative practice and secondly, that the wrong complained of was such a trivial nature that it came within the reach of the doctrine *de minimis non curat lex.*[53]

2.27   In the subsequent case of *Jeremiah* v. *MOD*[54] Lord Denning M.R. held that the only sound ground for his judgment in the Peake case was the *de minimis* rule *i.e.* that differentiation in the interests of chivalry, safety and good administrative practice was not an adequate justification for an otherwise discriminatory practice.[55] In *Jeremiah* men were from time to time required to work in the colour bursting shop of an ordnance factory, which was dusty and dirty work. No such requirement was made of women. It was not a sufficient justification of this rule that it was introduced out of deference to the wishes of women workers. Nor did 4p an hour obnoxious money compensate for any detrimental aspects of the work, for it is contrary to the Sex Discrimination Act, s.77 or the Race Relations Act, s.72 to attempt to contract out of the provisions of anti-discrimination law.

Pregnancy   **2.28**   The treatment of pregnancy is but the most obvious example of the fact that in making the central test of discrimination law a comparison with a similarly situated man, whether real or hypothetical, no allowance is made for the way in which either sex, or the social construction of gender, make women distinct from men. How far though does the law genuinely accommodate pregnancy and motherhood and make appropriate allowance for them? On this question the approaches adopted to date in UK and EC discrimination law divide. In *Webb* v. *EMO Air Cargo (UK) Ltd*[56] the Court of Appeal concluded that the dismissal of a pregnant woman can be, but is not necessarily, direct

---

[52] By chance one of the authors was formerly employed at the firm in question and can personally vouch for the likelihood of being trampled in the rush to leave work at the end of the day. The rule covered all women and *disabled men*. cf. *Hayes* v. *Malleable Working Men's Club (supra)*.
[53] Literally "the law does not deal with trifles."
[54] *Supra.*
[55] cf. *Page V. Freighthire (Tank Haulage) Ltd.* [1981] I.C.R. 229 in which it was held that the only exceptions to the requirement not to discriminate are those prescribed in the Acts, so that only the breach of a statutory safety requirement could justify otherwise discriminatory working practices. The Employment Act 1989 has further narrowed this exception to those safety procedures which deal with a reproductive or foetal risk (see para. 2-93).
[56] [1992] I.R.L.R. 116.

discrimination under section 1(1)(a) of the 1975 Act. Section 1(1)(a) calls for a woman to have been treated less favourably than a man would have been treated, but what is to happen when the woman is pregnant, or suffering from any other condition which is unique to women.[57] Since it is absurd to postulate a pregnant man, what approach is to be adopted? In *Turley* v. *Allders Department Store*[58] the majority of the EAT held that a dismissal on grounds of pregnancy could not be discriminatory as there is no masculine counterpart to pregnancy. The minority held that as pregnancy is a medical condition, the appropriate comparison is with a man suffering from some other medical condition, as, for example, a man who needs a hernia operation, who will require comparable time off. In the subsequent case of *Hayes* v. *Malleable Working Men's Club and Institute*[59] the EAT declined to follow the majority in *Turley*, preferring to compare a pregnant woman to a sick man and concluding that the applicant's treatment was less favourable than that which would have been accorded to a man.

2.29   Even though the EAT was endeavouring to be sympathetic to the woman and to recognise the problem associated with pregnancy, the comparison with a sick man has unfortunate connotations. Pregnancy is unique to women and a "normal" part of the lives of the great majority of women. It is not in any sense pathological, and therefore the comparison with a sick or disabled man is arguably inappropriate. An illness which necessitated as much time off as is normal for maternity leave would be relatively serious and not something which the majority of men would ever experience during their working lives. Thus, in assimilating the experience of pregnant women to that of the long-term sick or disabled man, no recognition is given to the "normality" of pregnancy and the fact that it is a usual facet of life for younger women. This difficulty has been expressed as the using of a "male norm" on which to build the concept of equality,[60] which fails to recognise the fact that the possibility of pregnancy is intrinsic to the female condition. Some employers, mainly in the banking and finance sectors which rely heavily on the services of women, have instituted a recognised pattern of "career breaks". These schemes attempt to reconcile the needs of motherhood and career and tend to "normalise" maternity but this practice is the exception rather than the rule.

---

[57] In the I.T. case of *Reynolds* v. *Mitsubishi Trust and Banking Corporation* Case no. 14003/91, DCLD 13 dismissal on grounds that the employee was to have a hystorectomy was held to be directly discriminatory.

[58] [1980] I.C.R. 66.

[59] [1985] I.C.R. 703.

[60] Sandra Fredman, "European Community Discrimination Law: A Critique", Industrial Law Journal, 21,2, pp. 119-134 and the references given therein.

2.30 Part of this difficulty is that it would seem more appropriate to treat pregnancy and maternity as a matter of employment protection law and not as a question of equality and discrimination law at all. Indeed the maternity protection regime contained in EP(C)A 1978 and discussed in chapter 10 does this. The problem has been that in lengthening the period of continuous service necessary to qualify for these rights to two years, the present administration has excluded many of the young women who are most in need of that protection. In consequence, they have needed to fall back on the SDA provisions which arguably are inappropriate.

This position willl be dramaticaly changed by the Pregnancy Directive, adopted in October 1992, and implemented in respect of dismissals by the Trade Union Reform and Employment Rights Act 1993. The amended law will provide more effective protection than hitherto in respect of pregnancy related dismissals, without being qualified by the two years service requirement to which such rights are currently subject. This is discussed in the chapter on maternity at paragraph 10.15 *et seq.*

The position in U.K. law

2.31 In judging what constitutes less favourable treatment on grounds of sex or marriage, section 5(3) of the Sex Discrimination Act requires that the comparison must be such that "the relevant circumstances in the one case are the same, or not materially different, in the other", whilst the Race Relations Act, s.3(4) requires the same to be true when comparisons are made on racial grounds. One of the difficulties under the Sex Discrimination Act is to determine what constitutes less favourable treatment when the behaviour in question has no counterpart in the other sex, such as is the case with pregnancy. At first sight it might seem uncontroversial to apply the "but for" test in *James* v. *Eastleigh Borough Council* to pregnancy cases by concluding that "but for" the fact that she is female a woman could not be dismissed or refused employment on grounds of pregnancy, but in *Webb* v. *EMO Air Cargo*[61] the Court of Appeal considered that the appropriate comparison to be made was with a sick or disabled man. *Webb* concerned a woman taken on as a maternity leave replacement who turned out to be pregnant and expecting her child quite soon after the woman whom she was replacing. Consequently Mrs Webb was dismissed. The Court could not accept her argument that since only a woman can be pregnant, and but for her sex a woman cannot be pregnant, a woman dismissed for any reason related to her pregnancy would not have been dismissed but for her sex. The notion of an inherent comparison with a man was rejected, on the ground that "it does not, of itself, provide any comparisons with the reasons why a man might be dismissed from the same

[61] See n. 56.

employment."[62] The Court of Appeal in *Webb* posited a
comparison with a man suffering from an arthritic hip, who
knew some months in advance that he would have to go into
hospital for an operation, leading Lord Justice Glidewell
(giving the judgement of the Court) to conclude that,

> "if a woman is dismissed from employment for a reason
> arising out of pregnancy, and claims that she was
> discriminated against in breach of the Act of 1975, it is
> necessary for the IT which hears her complaint to decide
> whether a man with a condition as nearly comparable as
> possible which had the same practical effect upon his
> ability to do the job would, or would not, have been
> dismissed. I therefore conclude that dismissal of a
> pregnant woman for a reason arising out of, or related to,
> her pregnancy can in law be, but is not necessarily, direct
> discrimination under s.1(1)(a)."[63]

As discussed above at paragraph 2.12 the House of Lords
based themselves firmly on the view that Ms Webb was
dismissed because of her projected absence at the time when
her services would be needed and not directly on her
grounds of her pregnancy. The Lords recognised, however,
that a dismissal or failure to employ which was based on
pregnancy would constitute the application of a gender based
criterion which would be directly discriminatory.

Hare makes the point that it is seldom that women are
dismissed because of their pregnancy as such, but rather
because of the consequences of their pregnancy in terms of
time off and the difficulty of finding a suitable temporary
replacement. He argues that it can be feasible to make a
meaningful comparison with a man who needs substantial
time off for, say, a medical condition.[64]

Thus at the present time Tribunals will need to ascertain the
reasons for such dismissals, distinguishing those which are
genuinely for an operational reason such as occurred in
Webb from those which is reality occurred by virtue of
pregnancy. The *Webb* case has been referred to the ECJ by
the House of Lords, on the question as to whether a
dismissal on grounds of putative absence such as occurred in
that case comports with the decisions of the ECJ in *Dekker*
and *Hirtz*, as to which, see below.

The Trade Union Reform and Employment Rights Act,
which in this respect will implement the Pregnancy
Directive, provides that it will be automatically unfair to
dismiss a woman who is pregnant for a reason connected
with her pregnancy or childbirth, irrespective of her length

---

[62] *per* Glidewell L.J. at p. 120.
[63] *per* Glidewell L.J. at p. 121.
[64] Ivan Hare, "Pregnancy and Sex Discrimination", *Industrial Law Journal*,
20, 2, (1991), pp. 124–130 at p. 127.

of service. This is discussed at paragraph 10.15 *et seq.* but it is important to note in this context that Ms Webb would certainly seem to have been dismissed for a reason connected with her pregnancy.[64.1]

The Community law position

2.32   Article 2.1 of the Equal Treatment Directive provides that

> "For the purposes of the following provisions, the principle of equal treatment shall mean that there shall be no discrimination whatsoever on grounds of sex whether directly or indirectly by reference in particular to marital or family status"

Article 3(1) provides that there shall be no discrimination whatsoever on grounds of sex in the conditions, including selection criteria, for access to all jobs or posts, whatever the sector or branch of activity, and to all levels of the occupational hierarchy" whilst Article 5(1) applies the principle of equal treatment to working conditions, including the conditions governing dismissal . . . without discrimination on grounds of sex."

2.33   In the *Dekker*[65] case, the complainant was a pregnant woman who was selected as the most suitable candidate for the post of training instructor in a youth centre run by the employers. The Board of the Centre refused to endorse her appointment because she was already pregnant, as she had told the selection committee at her interview, with the result that the employers would have been unable to reclaim the cost of a temporary replacement during her maternity leave from their insurers. Although there had been no male candidates for the post, Mrs Dekker claimed that her refusal of employment was discriminatory. Eventually the case was referred to the ECJ by the Dutch courts under Article 177 to ascertain whether the employer was in breach of the Equal Treatment Directive. The ECJ held that "(a)s employment can only be refused because of pregnancy to women, such a refusal is direct discrimination on grounds of sex. A refusal to employ because of the financial consequences of absence connected with must be deemed to

---

[64.1] This approach of comparing the treatment of a pregnant woman with that of a man needing substantial time off was reiterated in *Shomer* v. *B.& R. Residential Lettings Ltd* [1992] I.R.L.R. 317, C.A. (for the facts of the case see para. 2.14. in which Glidewell L.J. held that in considering whether a pregnant woman who had committed an act of serious misconduct has been treated less favourably than a man would have been, all the relevant circumstances need to be taken into account, including the effect of any hypothetical misconduct by the hypothetical man suffering from the hypothetical medical condition!).

[65] Case 177/88, *Dekker* v. *Stichting Vormingscentrum voor Jonge Volwassen (VJV-Centrum)*: [1991] I.R.L.R. 27 at para. 12.

be based principally on the fact of the pregnancy." The ECJ also held that it was not relevant that there was no male candidate for the post in question.

2.34 As Arnull observes, this is "an uncharacteristically unequivocal statement"[66] of principle by the ECJ, and one which rejects the notion of comparison with a man, whether real or hypothetical, who would need comparable amounts of time off. In examining whether the fact that there was no male candidate was significant, the ECJ goes on to argue that "the question of whether the refusal to recruit a woman constitutes direct or indirect discrimination depends on the motive for such a refusal. If this motive resides in the fact that the person concerned is pregnant, the decision is directly related to the applicant's sex . . . It is of no importance . . . that there were no male candidates." Whilst the Directive does not explicitly call for a comparison between male and female cases, as the principle of equality "requires that similar situations shall not be treated differently unless the differentiation is objectively justified,"[67] it must be taken that when the treatment of two employees are compared, any differences between men and women would not be relevant in the light of the objectives of the measure. Thus, as pregnancy can only affect women, any decision based upon it must be discriminatory as between men and women and it would not be relevant that there was no male candidate for the position. As the ECJ concluded:

> "As employment can only be refused because of pregnancy to women, such a refusal is direct discrimination on grounds of sex. A refusal to employ because of the financial consequences of absence connected with pregnancy must be deemed to be based principally on the fact of the pregnancy. Such discrimination cannot be justified by the financial detriment in the case of a pregnant woman suffered by the employer during her maternity leave."

The implication of this proposition is that direct discrimination cannot be justified under Community law, in that such justification cannot be established even if "the employer is more or less compelled not to recruit pregnant women."

2.35 Nonetheless, in the *Webb* case the Court of Appeal distinguished *Dekker* on the ground that *Dekker* was concerned with the financial consequences of pregnancy, whilst Mrs Webb's pregnancy would have physically prevented her from performing the tasks required. Yet this distinction seems at odds with the clear statement of

---

[66] E.L.Rev., (1992) at p.269.
[67] See chap. 1, n. 44.

principle quoted above, which the ECJ then applied to the facts of the *Dekker* case. The Court of Appeal also held that to follow *Dekker* when the provision in question is not of direct effect would be to distort the meaning of a pre-existing British statute contrary to the dictum of the House of Lords in *Duke* v. *Reliance Systems*. It is arguable that such a view is incompatible with the judgement of the ECJ in the *Marleasing* case, which places domestic courts under an obligation to interpret national law in the light of Community law, "wherever possible."[68]

2.36   In the *Hertz*[69] case, decided on the same day as *Dekker*, a woman had considerable time off as a result of an illness originating in pregnancy and was eventually dismissed on grounds of her non-attendance. The ECJ held that whilst it would be contrary to the terms of the Equal Treatment Directive to dismiss a woman because of her pregnancy, the question of illnesses which have their origins in pregnancy is not directly dealt with. Article 2(3), however, allows Member States to create specific rights for the protection of women, particularly as regards pregnancy and maternity, and in the view of the ECJ it "follows that during the maternity leave from which she benefits under national law, a woman is protected from dismissal because of her absence". Thus there arises a period of special protection for pregnant women from the inception of pregnancy to the completion of maternity leave, which up until now has been subject to a service qualification in the U.K.

2.37   If a comparative approach is used towards pregnancy under the Sex Discrimination Act, *Webb* raises a number of questions about the conduct of personnel policy with regard to pregnant women and those on maternity leave. First, would the claim that a man who needed time off comparable to maternity leave be sustained by evidence of the employer's practice. Second, the use of the "sick man" test demonstrates that it is arguably discriminatory to exclude pregnancy from an employer's sick pay scheme, if the treatment of pregnancy is to be equated to illness. Third, it would only be lawful to dismiss a woman who was pregnant if she has less than two years service and if her pregnancy prevents her from completing the requirements of the job. Caution needs to be exercised by employers in drawing conclusions from the *Webb* case which has been referred to the European Court of Justice in Luxembourg.[70]

---

[68] See chap. 1 for a more extended discussion of these issues.
[69] Case 179/88, *Handels-og Kontorfunktionaernes Forbund I Danmark (acting for Hertz)* v. *Dansk Arbejdgiverforening (acting for Aldi Marked K/S)*, [1991] I.R.L.R. 31.
[70] For a further discussion of the management implications of pregnancy discrimination issues, see the article by Rubenstein in EOR, 42, (1992), pp. 22-27.

2.38 The treatment of pregnancy in particular has given rise to similar cases in U.S. legislation, the Supreme Court concluding in General Electric Company v. *Gilbert*[71] that discrimination on grounds of pregnancy was not covered by Title VII of the Civil Rights Act 1964. However, the Pregnancy Disability Amendment to Title VII now prohibits discrimination based on pregnancy, but utilises a comparative approach similar to that espoused in the U.K.

2.39 The Action Programme which is intended to implement the Charter of the Fundamental Social Rights of Workers included a proposed Directive on the protection of pregnant women at work, as well as the promulgation of a code of good conduct on the protection of pregnancy and maternity. The Directive[72] was adopted in October 1992 and calls for 14 weeks paid maternity leave and protection from dismissal by reason of pregnancy from the inception of employment. The provisions of the Directive are discussed in chapter 10 on maternity.

Dress codes   **2.40** The same problem of less favourable treatment arises in relation to dress codes. In *Schmidt* v. *Austicks Bookshop Ltd.*[73] the employer required his female employees to wear skirts and to don overalls, whereas there was no comparable requirement placed upon male employees. The EAT concluded that this did not constitute discrimination, because in the absence of any comparable requirement which could be placed upon men, such a rule could not constitute less favourable treatment of women. Nonetheless, the EAT went on to hold that a more fruitful way to formulate such an issue would be to ask if there were comparable rules governing the dress of men or women, although the specific requirements under those rules might not be the same. The *Schmidt* case suggests that the way in which such problems are formulated is important.

Whilst it is necessary to compare like with like changes in fashion can lead to difficulties in matters such as, for example, the wearing of earrings by men or other items of personal jewellery. In considering whether an employer would be acting unlawfully in imposing dress rules which distinguish between men and women it is necessary to bear

---

[71] (1979) 429 US 125. Note also the decision of the London south Tribunal in *Reynolds* v. *Mitsubishi Trust and Banking Corporation* (Case no. 14003/91, EOR case digest no. 13) that a dismissal of an employee on the ground that she was to undergo an operation for a hysterectomy was on grounds of sex. The London South tribunal felt itself bound to follow the ECJ decision in *Dekker*, rather than the Court of Appeal in Webb. The Webb case was also distinguished by the Northern Ireland I.T. in *Scott* v. *McMullan and McMullan t/a Desmac Stationery*, (Case 1862/90, EOR case digest no. 13) on the basis that the facts in *Webb* were special in that the replacement was needed for a specific period.

[72] 92/85.

[73] [1978] I.C.R. 85.

in mind that the significance of specific items or styles of dress can change over time.[74]

Indirect discrimination

2.41 Discrimination is not necessarily the result of prejudice on the part of those with the power of decision making. Often the very fabric of our society constitutes what has been termed an inbuilt headwind[75] for anyone who is not a member of that group which has traditionally been expected to take part in a particular activity. For example, schools and public buildings have generally not been designed with the needs of the handicapped in mind; just to get through the door can be a major achievement, yet those who designed the buildings were not generally animated with a prejudice against the disabled; they simply failed to consider the position of the handicapped person or the effects which their plans might have upon such people. There is still little realisation that the reason that many handicapped people stay at home is the sheer difficulty of going to places planned without reference to their needs.

2.42 So it is with women, the aged, members of racial or other social minorities: their position may not have been allowed for, thus putting them at a disadvantage in any competition for valued cultural, social or economic opportunities. Thus the career pattern of managers in most private or public sector organisations does not allow for a "career break" of any length (though a few organisations are now beginning to take this requirement seriously). The absence of any such arrangements for a "career break," a negative practice so widely accepted as to be almost invisible, constitutes an inbuilt headwind against the progress of women in management. Likewise, patterns of educational qualifications or experience may be demanded for jobs which put first generation immigrants at a particular disadvantage, but which have never been critically examined to test whether they are necessary for effective job performance. Even subtle expectations about what is appropriate behaviour in a particular social setting may put newcomers or outsiders at a disadvantage.

2.43 In spite of the widespread existence of discriminatory practices[76] comparatively few tribunal cases are based on the concept of indirect discrimination, and it has not even featured to any great degree as a basis of formal EOC or CRE investigations in the employment field.[77] This may be due to ignorance or lack of will amongst applicants and their advisers, although it may be because no compensation is

---

[74] *McConomy* v. *Croft Inns* [1992] I.R.L.R. 562, NICA I.

[75] *Grigg* v. *Dukes Power Company* (1971) 401 U.S. 424, 3 FED 75.

[76] Dickens, Townley and Winchester, *Tackling Sex Discrimination through Collective Bargaining*, HMSO, 1988.

[77] McCrudden, Smith and Brown, *"Racial Justice at Work, Enforcement of the Race Relations Act in Employment"*, Policy Studies Institute, 1991.

payable in the industrial tribunals for indirect discrimination
if the respondent proves that the requirement or condition
was not applied with the intention of treating the claimant
less favourably. The EOC has proposed[78] the removal of this
limitation, which would make it more attractive to build a
case on the indirect discrimination provisions.

2.44   The Sex Discrimination Act and the Race Relations
Act provisions on indirect discrimination are aimed at the
effect of such widely accepted practices on minorities. It is
these practices which have been termed "institutional
racism",[79] by which is meant the limiting effect of socially
accepted arrangements on the aspirations of minorities.
There are parallel phenomena which operate in relation to
women, which often have the effect of keeping them out of
"men's work" and which constitute the stuff of indirect
discrimination claims under the Sex Discrimination Act. In
the social security case of *Jones* v. *Chief Adjudication
Officer*,[80] Mustill L.J. in the Court of Appeal formulated the
following approach to indirect discrimination.

1. Identify the criteria for selection;
2. Identify the relevant population, comprising all those
   who satisfy all the other criteria for selection;
3. Divide the relevant population into groups
   representing those who satisfy the criterion and those
   who do not;
4. Predict statistically what proportion of each group
   should consist of women;
5. Ascertain what are the actual male/female balances in
   the two groups;
6. Compare the actual with the predicted balances;
7. If women are found to be under-represented in the
   first group and over represented in the second, it is
   proved that the criterion is discriminatory.

It was in *Bilka-Kaufhaus GmbH* v. *Weber von Hartz*[81] that
the ECJ first formulated a clear statement of indirect
discrimination in Community law, in the United States sense
of *disparate impact* discrimination. As explained in chapter 1,

---

[78] "Equal Treatment for Men and Women: Strengthening the Acts", EOC,
1988.
[79] See the Scarman Report Cmnd 8427, 1981, at p. 11 and also Christopher
McCrudden, "Institutional Discrimination", 2 *Oxford Journal of Legal
Studies*, 303 (1982). For examples of the widely accepted and little
understood phenomenon of indirect discrimination, see J. Rosser & C.
Davies "What would we do without her? Invisible Women in N.H.S.
Administration", in *In a Man's World. Essays on Women in Male
Dominated Professions*, (Spence and Podmore eds., Tavistock
Publications, 1987); D. Spencer and A. Spencer, "Gender & The Labour
Process: the case of women and men lawyers" in *Gender and the Labour
Process*, (Knights & Willmot eds.; Gower, 1986); A. Pollert, *Girls,
Wives & Factory Lives* (Macmillan, 1981); Richard Jenkins, *Racism &
Recruitment* (Cambridge University Press, 1986).
[80] [1990] I.R.L.R. 533.
[81] [1986] I.R.L.R. 317.

indirect discrimination had acquired the connotation of "hidden or disguised" discrimination in the second *Defrenne* case and only returns to the British statutory sense of indirect discrimination, clear of imputations of intentionality, when the ECJ holds in *Bilka* that the respondent employer infringes Article 119 of the EEC Treaty when

> "it excludes part-time employees from its occupational pension scheme where that exclusion affects a much greater number of women than men, unless the enterprise shows that the exclusion is based on objectively justified factors which are unrelated to any discrimination based on sex."

Tests of indirect discrimination

2.45 The two Acts define indirect discrimination in nearly identical terms.[82] There are four tests of indirect discrimination:

1. Has a requirement or condition been applied equally to both sexes or all racial groups?
2. Is that requirement or condition one with which a considerably smaller number of women (or men) or persons of the racial group in question can comply than those of the opposite sex or persons not of that racial group?
3. Is the requirement or condition justifiable irrespective of the sex, colour, race, nationality, ethnic or national origins of the person in question?
4. Has the imposition of the requirement or condition operated to the detriment of a person who could not comply with it?

2.46 1. Is there a requirement or condition?

Unlawful indirect discrimination arises from rules or practices which are on their face neutral, but which put

---

[82] SDA, s.1: "A person discriminates against a woman in any circumstances relevant for any purposes of this Act if.(b) he applies to her a requirement or condition which he applies or would apply equally to a man but- (i) which is such that the proportion of women who can comply with it is considerably smaller than the proportion of men who can comply with it, and. (ii) which he cannot show to be justifiable irrespective of the sex of the person to whom it is applied, and. (iii) which is to her detriment because she cannot comply with it." R.R.A., s.1: "A person discriminates against another in any circumstances relevant for the purposes of any provision of this Act if. (b) he applies to that other a requirement or condition which he applies or would apply equally to persons not of the same racial group as that other but – (i) which is such that the proportions of persons of the same racial group as that other who can comply with it is considerably smaller than the proportion of persons not of that racial group who can comply with it; and (ii) which he cannot show to be justifiable irrespective of the colour, race nationality or ethnic or national origins of the person to whom it is applied; and (iii) which is to the detriment of that other because he cannot comply with it."

protected groups at a disadvantage. For example, an age limit can be an apparently neutral requirement which puts women who have or wish to have children at a disadvantage.[83] Another apparently neutral requirement which can have a disproportionate impact upon women is that of working full-time.[84] Racial minorities may have difficulty in complying with a requirement for "O" level English.[85]

2.47 All the above requirements are clear cut and act as an absolute bar on securing or continuing in employment. It is, however, commonly the case that there is no one absolute bar to gaining employment or access to some other benefit, but a selection procedure which imposes a set of inter-related requirements on which candidates are to be assessed. Whilst the EAT in *Watches of Switzerland* v. *Savell*[86] held that the need to satisfy the requirements of a promotion procedure could itself be a condition or requirement under section 1(1)(b), the application of this decision is uncertain in view of the subsequent Court of Appeal decision in *Perera* v. *Civil Service Commission and Department of Customs & Excise (No. 2)*[87]. In that case, an applicant for a post as a legal assistant had to be either a qualified solicitor or barrister and had to receive a satisfactory assessment from an interviewing board. The interviewing board was charged with having regard to a number of factors, particularly experience in the United Kingdom. The Court of Appeal held that this procedure could not constitute a requirement or condition because it was not an absolute bar to selection. Candidates could compensate for poor performance on one of the factors by excelling in some other respect, so that no one factor constituted an absolute bar and hence there could be no requirement or condition. This decision tends to reinforce managerial discretion in the balancing of criteria for selection or promotion. Absolute requirements for a job are generally of the more basic sort likely to be possessed by any serious candidate, whilst the actual selection decision will be based on a constellation of factors, one or more of which may be highly detrimental to women. As it is almost invariably the case that candidates are assessed upon a balance of criteria, it would be hard to formulate a requirement or condition which would satisfy section 1(1)(b).[88]

---

[83] See *Price* v. *Civil Service Commissioners* [1978] I.C.R. 27.
[84] See *Clarke* v. *Eley (IMI) Kynock Ltd* [1983] I.C.R. 165 *Home Office* v. *Holmes* [1983] I.C.R. 165.
[85] See *Raval* v. *DHSS* [1985] I.C.R. 685.
[86] [1983] I.R.L.R. 141.
[87] [1983] I.R.L.R. 166, C.A.
[88] Quaere: Why would the following formulation not suffice? "A requirement that to receive preferential treatment a person should possess one or more of the following characteristics". This would then make s.1(1)(b) correspond to the fact that s.1(1)(a) catches both selecting only whites and preferring whites. Rubenstein makes the point that a requirement or practice constituting an absolute ban may be a derogation

2.48   The requirement that a condition or requirement must be an absolute bar was reiterated by the Court of Appeal in *Meer* v. *London Borough of Tower Hamlets*,[89] in which the Court felt bound to follow *Perera*. In *Meer* the Authority had twelve selection criteria for applicants for the post of borough solicitor, one of which was experience in Tower Hamlets. The appellant considered this criterion discriminatory, but because it was not in itself a "must" for appointment to the post, it did not constitute a requirement. The EOC and CRE argue that any practice or policy having an adverse impact on the protected groups should be open to challenge. It is submitted that it is also implicit in the *Danfoss*[86] decision, that if it is sufficient in the context of an equal pay claim under Article 119 for women to show that there is a discrepancy in treatment for the burden of proof to be reversed, there is no need to show that this is brought about by a "requirement or condition" as opposed to a policy or practice. In the earlier case of *Clarke* v. *Eley (IMI) Kynoch Ltd.*[91] the E.A.T. emphasised that the purpose of the legislation is to eliminate established practices which have a disproportionate impact upon minorities. Consequently:

> "if the elimination of such practices is the policy lying behind the Act, although such policy cannot be used to give the words any other meaning than they naturally bear it is in our view a powerful argument against giving the words a narrower meaning thereby excluding cases which fall within the mischief which the Act was meant to deal with."[92]

2.49   Much of the mischief which this section aims at is beyond its reach, if it is only requirements or conditions which constitute an absolute bar which fall within the purview of section 1(1)(*b*). It is only if such a decision can be shown to have been based upon grounds of race or sex[93] that it would be possible to proceed successfully under section 1(1)(*a*) as an alternative. Otherwise there is very little

---

from the provisions of the Equal Treatment directive and could be attacked through that route. See M. Rubenstein, "The Equal Treatment & U.K. Law", in *Women, Employment & European Equality Law*, (C. McCrudden ed., Eclipse, 1988).

[89] [1988] I.R.L.R. 399, C.A. Balcombe L.J. questioned whether Perera was compatible with the purposes of the Act in a significant obiter, but arguing that the Court of Appeal is bound by its previous decisions preferred to leave the matter to Parliament.

[90] *Handels-Og Kontorfunktionaerens Forbund I Danmark* v. *Dansk Arbedjsgiverforening [acting for Danfoss]* [1989] I.R.L.R. 532. Neither can one see in the wording of the Directive any support for the imposition of an absolute requirement as a precondition of establishing indirect discrimination.

[91] [1983] I.C.R. 165.

[92] at p. 169 *per* Browne-Wilkinson J. It is noteworthy, that this definition of requirement or constitution has been incorporated into the provisions of the Fair Employment Bill 1989 for Northern Ireland, in spite of widespread criticism.

[93] *R.* v. *Birmingham City Council, supra.*

chance of redress for the person who feels that, though not subject to an absolute bar, his or her chances of selection for employment, promotion or some other benefit were heavily discounted by the way in which the procedure in question operated.[94] The Northern Ireland Court of Appeal held in *Briggs* v. *North Eastern Library and Education Board*[95] that there can be a "requirement" as to attendance where the nature of the job requires full-time attendance, preferring the construction of section 1(1)(*b*) by Waite J. in *Home Office* v. *Holmes*[96] to that of Wood J. in *Clymo* v. *Wandsworth London Borough Council*.[97]

2.50   2. Can a considerably smaller proportion of the protected group comply with the requirement or condition?

Indirect discrimination occurs when a requirement or condition is applied with which a considerably smaller proportion of the members of one sex or of a particular racial group can comply than would be the case for persons not of that sex or racial group.

A considerably smaller proportion

In order to establish indirect discrimination, a considerably smaller proportion of the protected group must be able to comply with the requirement in question than would be the case for non-members of that group.[98]

2.51   Perhaps the main question is to determine with whom should the protected group be compared. The Sex Discrimination Act, s.5(3)[99] provides that any comparison between men and women (or in regard to marital status) must be such that the relevant circumstances in the one case are the same, or not materially different, in the other. Thus in *Price* v. *Civil Service Commission*[1] the Industrial Tribunal considered that the appropriate pool of comparison was the whole population, but the EAT held that it was those people otherwise qualified to apply for the job. In *Kidd* v. *D.R.G.*

---

[94] *Cf.* the EAT decisions in *Enderby* v. *Frenchay Health Authority* [1991] I.R.L.R. 44 *and* *Brook* v. *London Borough of Harringey* [1992] I.R.L.R. 478 *Enderly* has been referred to the ECJ by the Court of Appeal.

[95] [1990] I.R.L.R. 181, NICA.

[96] [1984] I.R.L.R. 299, EAT.

[97] [1989] I.R.L.R. 249, EAT.

[98] Even if that proportion is nil, *i.e.* none "can comply," it was held by the EAT in *Greencroft Social Club* v. *Mullen* [1985] I.C.R. 796, that it would be contrary to the spirit of the legislation to exclude such a case, cf. the unreported case of *Wong* v. *G.L.C.* EAT 524/79.
Some American courts, in interpreting comparable legislation, have used the rule of thumb that if the proportion of the protected group which can comply with a relevant requirement is one fifth smaller than that of the larger group, that is sufficient to establish that a practice has a discriminatory effect, but no settled proportion has been accepted by the courts in Britain as constituting a "considerably smaller" proportion.

[99] s.3(4) of the R.R.A. provides similarly in comparisons between members of a particular racial group and persons not of that group.

[1] [1976] I.R.L.R. 405, IT, [1977] I.R.L.R. 291, EAT.

(*U.K.*),[2], a case in which part-timers were to be selected for
redundancy before full-timers, the EAT held that the area
for comparison, or pool, is a matter of fact for the Tribunal
in trying to match the circumstances of each case. As the
EAT acknowledged, the decisions of tribunals in
superficially similar circumstances will differ according to
their view as to what are the relevant comparisons which
have to be made.[3] Such a decision of fact is, of course, not
subject to appeal unless it is "so irrationally inappropriate as
to put it outside the range of selection for any reasonable
Tribunal," in which case "the Tribunal would have fallen
into an error of law which could be corrected in the
appellate jurisdiction."[4] Thus in *Greater Manchester Police
Authority* v. *Lea*[5] Knox J. accepted that the pool does not
have to be shown to be a statistically perfect match of the
persons who would be capable of and interested in the post
offered. Having been selected as the most suitable
candidate, Mr Lea was refused employment in accordance
with the policy of the Police Authority to refuse employment
to anyone in receipt of an occupational pension, in order to
take account of the needs of the unemployed. In this case
statistics for the whole of the economically active population,
which must have included many people neither capable of
nor interested in a vacancy such as the one in question,
showed that whereas 4.7 per cent. of men were in receipt of
an occupational pension, this was true for only 0.6 per cent.
of women. The EAT accepted that in finding the
requirement not to be in receipt of an occupational pension
was one with which a considerably smaller proportion of
men could comply than women, the Industrial Tribunal had
not come to a conclusion which no reasonable tribunal could
have reached. There is a danger, however, of incorporating
an act of discrimination into the definition of the pool of
comparison, a danger specifically highlighted by Schiemann
J. in *R.* v. *Secretary of State for Education ex.p. Schaffer*[6],
which concerned the allocation of hardship grants for
students who were lone parents, only to those who had
previously been married. Whilst the proportion of women
who were single lone parents was four times that of men, the
proportion of lone parents who were single, in the sense of
never having been married, was the same for both sexes.
The Court took the view that by choosing the latter basis of

[2] 1985 I.C.R. 405.
[3] Compare, for example, the decision in *Kidd*, with that in the *Home Office*
v. *Holmes* and *Clark & Eley* v. *IMI*.
[4] *Per* Waite J. at p. 415. In *Kidd* the pool of comparison was held to be all
those households in which the need to care for small children makes it
difficult for one or both parents to work full time. Waite J. held that a
reasonable Tribunal could conclude that it was unsafe to assume that the
burden of child care was more likely to prevent married than unmarried
women working full time in those circumstances or for married women as
against married men. Statistical proof was required of these matters in
view of the changing pattern of child rearing practices.
[5] [1990] I.R.L.R. 372, EAT.
[6] [1987] I.R.L.R. 53.

comparison, an act of discrimination was being built into the ground of comparison.[7]

2.52 The choice of the pool for comparison can be a trap for the unwary applicant. If he or she marshals the available statistics in relation to what is found by the tribunal to be an inappropriate comparison, the case may be lost. The applicant will have failed to prove that indirect discrimination has taken place, even though had the appropriate comparison been made, the statistics might have supported the complaint. Thus in *Pearse* v. *Bradford Metropolitan Council*[8] the appellant alleged that a college which restricted applications for a counselling vacancy to existing full-time members of staff, indirectly discriminated against part-timers. The appellant produced statistics showing that the ratio of full-time to part-time staff was lower for women than for men. The EAT held, however, that the appropriate comparison was not that of all full-time to part-time staff, but of full or part-time college employees otherwise qualified for this particular post, and, as the appellant advanced no figures in relation to that comparison, even though granted an adjournment in which to compile such figures, the case failed.

2.53 Where statistical proof is required, how elaborate need that be for the parties to prove their case? In *Perera*[9] the EAT accepted that there was no need to produce elaborate statistical evidence to establish that a particular practice has a disproportionate impact upon minorities. If the issue is in dispute the employer can attack the statistical evidence in rebuttal of the original contentions. Statistics may relate to the population at large, if this is the appropriate field of comparison, or to a particular workplace, or to the workforce in question. A Tribunal may, however, take into account its own knowledge and experience in examining such questions, according to the Northern Ireland Court of Appeal in *Briggs* v. *North Eastern Library and Education Board*,[10] even though the EAT in *Kidd* v DRG (UK) Ltd had felt that it needed statistical evidence to prove that married women bear a greater responsibility for child-rearing than men.[11]

Can comply **2.54** It was argued by the employer in *Price* v. *Civil Service Commission*[12] that as many women as men could comply with

---

[7] See also the Court of Appeal decision in *Jones* v. *University of Manchester* [1993] I.R.L.R. 218.
[8] EOR 21, p. 35.
[9] *Supra* at para. 2.47.
[10] *Supra* at para. 2.49.
[11] This is, however, more than an academic or even juridical point. In taking its own experience into account, a Tribunal can simply reify its own prejudices and whilst the decision in *Kidd* might seem a little far-fetched on its facts, nonetheless it avoids the trap of stereotyped thinking about family roles.
[12] *Supra* at para. 2.51.

an age limit of age 28 for applications to join the executive class of the Civil Service. There are just as many women as men below the age of 28 and if only a smaller proportion of them chose to apply, that, it was argued, was a different matter. Women had the same capacity to apply as men and therefore, in the words of the statute, the proportion of women who could comply was the same as was the case for men. This argument was rejected by Phillips J. in the EAT who stated that[13]:

> "It should not be said that a person 'can' do something merely because it is theoretically possible for him to do so; it is necessary to see whether he can do so in practice."

2.55 Such an approach recognises that in reality particular segments of the population live their lives under conditions which render it difficult or effectively impossible for them to meet a particular requirement. The same view of the capacity of Sikhs to comply with a requirement not to wear a turban was taken by the House of Lords in *Mandla* v. *Dowell Lee*[14]. Lord Fraser of Tullybelton stated[15]:

> "In the context of section 1(i)(*b*)(i) of the 1976 Act it must, in my opinion, have been intended by Parliament to be read not as meaning 'can physically,' so as to indicate a theoretical possibility, but as meaning 'can in practice' or 'can consistently with the customs and cultural conditions of the racial group'."

It was held by the EAT in *Ravall* v. *DHSS*[16], that the ability of the members of a group to comply with a requirement is to be judged at the date of the incident in question, and not at some future date. Thus the argument was rejected that whilst a smaller proportion of people of Asian origins possessed "O" level English, as there was no reason to suppose that they lacked the necessary ability, they could comply by entering the necessary examination at some future date.

2.56   3. Does the requirement or condition operate to the detriment of the complainant?

Under section 1(1)(*b*)(iii) of both Acts the complainant must also establish that the requirement or condition is to his or her detriment because he or she cannot comply with it. This sub-section is intended to establish that the complainant has locus standi *i.e.* that he or she is the victim of the alleged discrimination. In *Steel* v. *Union of Post Office Workers*[17] the

---

[13] At p. 31.
[14] [1983] I.R.L.R. 209.
[15] At p. 213.
[16] *Supra* at n. 59. See now *C.R.E.* v. *Dutton* [1989] I.R.L.R. 8, C.A. at p. 13.
[17] [1978] I.C.R. 181.

EAT held that the time to consider whether a detriment has been suffered is the time when the complainant has to comply with the requirement or condition.[18] In *Clarke* v. *Eley (IMI) Kynoch Ltd.*[19] the EAT held that it was not relevant that a complainant could have avoided a present inability to comply with a requirement if different action had been taken in the past. The employees could have avoided being selected for redundancy by electing to have worked full time at some point in the past, but were none the less held to have suffered in detriment.

Justification

2.57   4. Can the discriminator justify the requirement or condition?

An employer or other discriminator may argue that an otherwise discriminatory practice is "justifiable irrespective of the sex (colour, race, nationality, or ethnic or national origins) of the person to whom it is applied" (SDA & RRA, s.1(1)(*b*)(3)). The principal question which has arisen in the cases is what is meant by "justifiable." In the landmark case of *Steel* v. *UPW.*[20] Philips J. referred[21] to the famous judgement of the U.S. Supreme Court in *Griggs* v. *Duke Power Co.* in which it was held that[22]:

> "The Act proscribes not only overt discrimination but also practices which are fair in form, but discriminatory in operation. The touchstone is business necessity. If an employment practice which operates to exclude negroes cannot be shown to be related to job performance, the practice is prohibited."

---

[18] The issue in *Turner* v. *Labour Party* [1987] I.R.L.R. 101, C.A. was whether a divorced woman could comply with a requirement to be married in order to receive for her offspring a survivor's pension on the same terms and of the same value as would have been payable to the surviving spouse of a married member of the pension scheme. The majority of the Court of Appeal took the view that as the survivors" benefits of a pension scheme were only payable at the date of the death of the member, it could not be said that a divorced woman could not comply with that requirement before the date at which the requirement would come into operation i.e. before her death. She might not want to marry, nor could she be compelled to marry, but she could marry before then. Lord Justice Ralph Gibson, dissenting, took the view that death might occur at any time and that a member was paying contributions for present cover and not just future benefits and therefore her present incapacity to comply, not now being married, was to her detriment.

[19] [1982] I.R.L.R. 482.

[20] [1978] I.C.R. 181. In *Steel* the Post Office had had a practice of allocating postal walks (or rounds) according to the seniority of the established full-time postal workers. Prior to 1976 women had not been eligible to become established postal workers, (remaining "temporaries" no matter how long they worked there), so that even after 1976 they lacked the seniority necessary to be allocated their choice of walks, that is to pick a walk which finished near to their own homes. This was held not to be a justifiable arrangement when the case was remitted to the Industrial Tribunal. On the question as to how far women "can" join the building trades see the EAT decision in *Brooks* v. *London Borough of Haringey* [1992] I.R.L.R. 478.

[21] At p. 188.

[22] (1971) US 424, at p. 431.

2.58 It is this standard which Philips J. was seeking to adopt *i.e.* unless a practice is necessary, rather than merely convenient, it is not justifiable in this context and "for this purpose it is relevant to consider whether the employer can find some other and non-discriminatory method of achieving his objective." Subsequent cases tended to weaken this standard, perhaps reflecting the defeat in Parliament during the passage of the legislation of an amendment which would have substituted "necessary" for "justifiable." The standard adopted has been reasonably necessary[23] right and proper in the circumstances[24] reasonably necessary to the party who applies the condition,[25] acceptable to right thinking people as sound and tolerable reasons for adopting the practice in question[26] or merely of marginal advantage to the employer.[27] This series of definitions showed a consistent tendency over time for the objective standards first enunciated by Philips J. in *Steel* v. *UPW* to be weakened by the addition of subjective elements.[28]

2.59 The decision of the European Court of Justice in *Bilka-Kaufhaus GmbH* v. *Weber von Hartz*,[29] that only measures which

"correspond to a real need on the part of the undertaking, are appropriate with a view to achieving the objectives pursued and are necessary to that end",

are sufficient to justify exceptions to the principle of equal pay, reinforced the reliance on objective standards of justification. This standard was adopted by the House of Lords in the equal pay case of *Rainey* v. *Greater Glasgow Health Board*.[30] In an important *obiter dictum* the House of Lords held:

"there would not appear to be any material distinction in principle between the need to demonstrate objectively justified grounds of difference for the purpose of s.1(3) [of the Equal Pay Act] and the need to justify a requirement or condition under s.1(1)(*b*)(ii) of the Act of 1975."[31]

---

[23] *Singh* v. *Rowntree Mackintosh* [979] I.C.R. 554; E.A.T.
[24] *Panesar* v. *Nestle Co.* [1980] I.C.R. 144; C.A.
[25] *Ojutiku and Oburoni* v. *MSC* [1982] I.C.R. 661; C.A. *per* Eveleigh L.J.
[26] *Ibid. per* Stephenson L.J.
[27] *Kidd* v. *D.R.G. (U.K.) supra.*
[28] In *Clarke* v. *Eley (IMI) Kynoch Ltd.* [1983] I.C.R. 165 Browne-Wilkinson J. criticised the extent to which the *Ojutiku* formula leaves the discretion to decide such an emotive matter as racial or sex discrimination within the discretion of the tribunals. Mr. Justice Browne-Wilkinson opined that it was desirable for tribunals to receive some guidance as to how they were to balance the discriminatory effect of a requirement on the one hand with the reasons urged as a justification for imposing it on the other.
[29] [1987] I.C.R.110, [1986] I.R.L.R. 317, [1986] 2 C.M.L.R. 701.
[30] [1987] I.R.L.R. 26 and see *Greater Glasgow Health Board* v. *Carey* (1987) I.R.L.R. 484, E.A.T.
[31] *Per* Lord Keith of Kinkel at p.31.

2.60 In *Duke* v. *Reliance Systems*[32] the House of Lords held that as the Sex Discrimination Act became law prior to the Equal Treatment Directive, it was not to be interpreted as giving effect to the Directive. On this reasoning it would have been the standard enunciated by the Court of Appeal in *Ojutiku* v. *M.S.C.*[33] which constituted the standard of justification in discrimination, though not in equal pay cases. The judges of the Court of Appeal expressed this standard each in a slightly different form, thus: *Per* Eveleigh L.J.: If a person produces reasons for doing something which would be acceptable to right thinking people as sound and tolerable reasons for so doing, then he has justified his conduct.[34] *Per* Kerr L.J.: "Justifiable" implies a lower standard than the word "necessary."[35] *Per* Stephenson L.J.: The party applying the discriminatory condition must prove it to be justifiable in all the circumstances on balancing its discriminatory effect against the discriminator's need for it. But that need is what is reasonably needed by the party who applies the condition.[36]

2.61 The Court of Appeal in *Hampson* v. *Department of Education and Science*[37] adopted the test set out by Stephenson L.J. in *Ojutiku*, Balcombe L.J. stating that "justifiable" requires an objective balance between the discriminatory effect of the condition and the reasonable needs of the person who applies the condition." He went on to hold that:

> "For my part I can find no significant difference between the test adopted by Stephenson L.J. in *Ojutiku* and that adopted by the House of Lords in *Rainey*. Since neither Eveleigh L.J. nor Kerr L.J. indicated what they considered the test to be-although Kerr L.J. said what it was not-I am content to adopt Stephenson L.J.'s test as I have expressed it above, which I consider to be consistent with Rainey. It is obviously desirable that the tests of justifiability applied in all these closely related fields should be consistent with each other."[38]

The Court of Appeal in *Hampson* held that the industrial tribunals must make an adequate statement of the reasons why a requirement is justifiable, identifying the standards by which the requirement is tested. How effective is this as a reconciliation of the standards for justifiability under the Race Relations Act with those which prevail under the Equal Pay Act for a genuine material difference? The test formulated by Balcombe J., giving the judgement of the court, was that

---

[32] [1988] I.R.L.R. 118 and see *Parsons* v. *East Surrey Health Authority* [1986] I.C.R. 837, E.A.T.
[33] *Supra* at n. 118.
[34] At p. 668.
[35] At p. 670.
[36] At p. 674.
[37] [1989] I.R.L.R. 69, C.A.
[38] At p.76.

> "'justifiable' requires an objective balance to be struck between the discriminatory effect of the condition and the reasonable needs of the party who applies the condition."[39]

Certainly an objective standard is required in each case and it is not sufficient merely to adduce reasons for the conduct in question, for that would be more appropriate for direct rather than indirect discrimination. Indirect discrimination is concerned with discriminatory effect, rather than the reasons for discriminatory actions. If it is the *reasonable* needs of the discriminator that must be balanced against the discriminatory effect, there is an implicit requirement that the need itself must be objectively justified, as *Bilka* requires, by being both appropriate and necessary to meet a real need of the enterprise. This balancing of the need against the effect introduces the principle of proportionality, as stated, for example, in *Johnston* v. *The Chief Constable of the R.U.C.*,[40] in that the greater the discriminatory effect, the greater the need would have to be to justify the retention of that particular condition or requirement. The principle of proportionality was relied upon by the EAT in *Cobb* v. *Secretary of State for Employment and the Manpower Services Commission*,[41] in which it held that

> "it is for the Tribunal to decide what facts it found proved and to carry out the balancing exercise involved, taking into account all the surrounding circumstances and giving due emphasis to the degree of discrimination caused against the object or aim to be achieved the principle of proportionality. . . . (A respondent) is under no obligation to prove that there was no other possible way of achieving his objective, however expensive or administratively complicated."

2.62 In *Rinner-Kuhn* v. *FWW Spezial-Gebaudereinigung*,[42] a case concerning the exclusion of part-timers from the German equivalent of statutory sick pay, the German Government had argued that the exclusion of part-timers was justified because such workers "are not integrated in and connected with the undertaking in a way comparable to that of other workers." These arguments were dismissed as "generalised statements", not meeting the objective standards of justification enunciated in *Bilka*; *i.e.* corresponding to a real need, necessary and appropriate to achieve that end. A legislative provision which in practice gives rise to discriminatory effects may only be justified where the Member State is "in a position to establish that the means selected correspond to an objective necessary for its social policy and are appropriate and necessary to the

---

[39] Approved by the House of Lords in *Webb* v. *E.M.O. Air Cargo (UK) Ltd* [1993] I.R.L.R. 27.
[40] Case 222/84, [1986] E.C.R. 1651,3 C.M.L.R. 240, [1986] I.R.L.R. 263.
[41] [1989] I.R.L.R. 464, EAT.
[42] [1989] I.R.L.R. 493, ECJ.

attainment of that objective", as in the social security case of
Commission v. *Belgium*[43] in which the ECJ concluded that
supplements paid to those with responsibility to support a
family fulfilled a legitimate objective of social policy.

2.63   The *Bilka* definition implies that the test of whether
there is some less discriminatory way of achieving the
employer's purposes will be a strict one, otherwise it would
not be possible to say that the practice was a necessary way
of achieving the employer's objective. Nonetheless, even
though the EOC have advocated that the *Bilka* test be
written into the statute, it is still possible to plead market
forces or the pattern of collective agreements as justification
for discriminatory acts. It is submitted that the need for
statutory authority as a basis for an objective test of
justifiability was underlined by the decision of the Divisional
Court in *R.* v. *Secretary of State for Employment ex.p. EOC,*[44]
in which it was held that an assertion on behalf of the
Secretary of State that the removal of minimum hours
qualifications from redundancy and unfair dismissal
entitlements would adversely affect the employment of
women was "inherently logical" and that this was a
legitimate concern for Government social and employment
policy. Empirical evidence collected by the Department of
Employment itself does not support this contention[45] and it
is submitted that such assertions fall short of the standard of
proof demanded in *Rinner Kuhn, i.e.* demonstrating a real
policy need which it is appropriate to achieve by such
restrictions on the level and type of employment protection
afforded to part-timers and which could not be achieved in
other and less discriminatory ways.

Whilst the Court of Appeal[46] dismissed the application on
other grounds (see chapter 9) it was divided on the issue of
justifiability, Hirst L.J. concluding that the service and
hours requirements were justifiable, in particular by
reference to the increased costs and administrative
difficulties which might arise if all part-timers were to be
brought within the scope of the legislation, irrespective of
their hours and secondly by reference to the fact that the
proposed EC part-time workers directive itself incorporated
an eight hour threshold. Conversely Dillon L.J. held that
there was no evidence that the different qualifying
thresholds for employees working between eight and sixteen
hours a day were objectively justifiable.

---

[43] [1991] I.R.L.R. 393, ECJ.
[44] [1991] I.R.L.R. 493, H.C.
[45] Department of Employment Research Paper No. 83, (1991) reveals that
whereas 76 per cent. of employers questioned who employed regular
part-timers did so because the task concerned required only a limited
time, only 4 per cent. did so to avoid making national insurance
contributions etc and only 1 per cent. did so because they enjoyed lower
levels of employment protection.
[46] [1992] I.R.L.R. 10.

2.64 It has been held that it is a question of fact for the Industrial Tribunal as to whether the circumstances in any individual case meet the standards of justification then prevailing.[47] That justification must be irrespective of the sex, race or nationality etc. of the person concerned. Thus, where in *Orphanos* v. *Queen Mary College*[48] the College sought to justify the practice of charging higher fees to non-EEC students on the ground that it was not a legitimate use of public funds to subsidise the education of overseas students, the House of Lords held that this reason was so bound up with the question of the nationality of the appellant that it could not constitute a justification under section 1(*b*)(ii).

Victimisation

2.65 A separate cause of action in relation to less favourable treatment is set out in RRA, s.2 and SDA, s.4, that of victimisation. The purpose of these sections is to deter an employer from taking action against those employees who have brought proceedings under the two Acts or have given evidence against the employer in the course of such proceedings. In reality, adverse employer reaction is not uncommon, as is shown by a survey of the experiences of successful claimants undertaken by the E.O.C.[49] The existence of the section on victimisation was not effective in preventing the fact of having taken action under the sex discrimination legislation from having an adverse effect on the careers and working experience of many of the applicants who had actually been successful in the Tribunals, partly because the pressures to which they were subject were often subtle and informal.

2.66 One reason for the lack of effectiveness of the sections on victimisation is their complexity. The Race Relations Act, s.2 provides as follows:

"(1) A person (the discriminator) discriminates against another person (the person victimised) in any circumstances relevant for the purposes of any provision of this Act if he treats the person victimised less favourably than in those circumstances he treats or would treat other persons, and does so by reason that the person victimised has -

(*a*) brought proceedings against the discriminator or any other person under this Act; or

(*b*) given evidence or information in connection with proceedings brought by any person against the discriminator or any person under this Act; or

(*c*) otherwise done anything under or by reference to this

---

[47] *Panesar* v. *Nestle & Co. Ltd.* [1980] I.C.R. 144; C.A., *Cobb* v. *Secretary of State for Employment and the Manpower Services Commission* at n. 129.

[48] [1985] I.R.L.R. 349, H.L.

[49] Alice Leonard, "Pyrrhic Victories", EOC, 1986.

Act in relation to the discriminator or any other person; or

(d) alleged that the discriminator or any other person has committed an act which (whether or not the allegation so states) would amount to a contravention of this Act.

or by reason that the discriminator knows that the person victimised intends to do any of these things, or suspects that the person victimised has done, or intends to do, any of them."

The Sex Discrimination Act sets out a provision on victimisation in similar terms.

2.67 In order for the person victimised to succeed in an action under Race Relations Act, s.2 or Sex Discrimination Act, s.4 he or she must show that he or she took one of the "protected acts" set out in subsections (a)-(d) and that, in any circumstances relevant to the purposes of any provision of these Acts, the person victimised has been treated less favourably than in those circumstances the discriminator treats or would treat other persons, by reason of the person victimised having taken that action. Thus in *Cornelius* v. *University College of Swansea*[50], the appellant had complained of sexual harassment by her boss, the College accountant, and had been transferred to another post in the Arts Centre. She did not like the new job and requested a return to her previous post and when this was not forthcoming she unsuccessfully took proceedings in the Industrial Tribunal alleging discrimination. Whilst awaiting an appeal in these proceedings she again requested a transfer, and when this was refused on the ground that the College was not prepared to take any action which might seem to prejudge the results of her appeal, the appellant again took proceedings, this time under Sex Discrimination Act, s.4 alleging victimisation. The original proceedings brought by the appellant constituted a section 4(1)(a) action but the question was whether the subsequent refusal to transfer her or to hear her case under an internal grievance procedure was by reason of the proceedings which she had brought. The Court of Appeal held that this was not the case, and that the actions of the College administration were simply those which they would have taken pending the outcome of any legal proceedings and were not motivated by the fact these were proceedings under the Sex Discrimination Act. The appellant had not, therefore, been treated less favourably in those circumstances than another person would have been treated.

2.68 Somewhat similar issues arose in *Aziz* v. *Trinity Street Taxis Ltd.*[51] in which a taxi driver was expelled from the

[50] [1987] I.R.L.R. 147, C.A.
[51] [1988] I.R.L.R. 204, C.A.

company which had been set up on a co-operative basis by certain of the taxi drivers in Coventry to operate a radio control system. The driver was to be charged £1,000 to introduce a third taxi into the system, which he regarded as an arbitrary and unfair imposition. He suspected that the decision to levy such charges was racially motivated and began to consider taking action in the Industrial Tribunals. Other drivers had expressed verbal support for his point of view but because the appellant was of the opinion that they might not support him if he took action, he made secret tape recordings of their conversations. The existence of these tape recordings was revealed by an order for discovery during the Industrial Tribunal hearing. Subsequent to the hearing, the members of the company (which was limited by guarantee) voted to expel the appellant on the ground that making such recordings constituted a gross breach of trust and confidence between the members of the company.

2.69   The Court of Appeal held that making the tape recordings was an act done by reference to the Race Relations Act, which fell within section 2(1)(c), but the question was whether the expulsion was undertaken by reason of the fact that the tape recordings were made with reference to the race relations legislation or would have occurred whatever the purpose of the recordings. The comparison as to whether the person discriminated against has been treated less favourably in the relevant circumstances requires comparison to be made with persons who have not done a protected act.[52] Thus in the instant case the relevant circumstances were membership of the company and the comparison was with members who had not made such tape recordings. This led to the conclusion that the appellant had been less favourably treated. The appellant had failed to show, however, that his treatment was by reason of his having done a protected act, in that the fact that the tape recordings were made by reference to the Race Relations Act was not a relevant factor in the minds of the members who voted for his expulsion. They would have voted for the expulsion of any member who made such recordings, whatever their purpose, on the ground that this was an underhand action and a breach of trust.

2.70   Therefore a person who seeks to avail themselves of the provisions on victimisation must show:

1. that they have undertaken a protected act within the terms of the Sex Discrimination Act, s.4 or Race Relations Act, s.2, which is one of the four categories of the act specified in subsections (a)–(d), and
2. that they have been treated less favourably than other persons in the relevant circumstances, which

---

[52] It would have been simpler for the legislation to use the notion of unfavourable, rather than less favourable, treatment.

circumstances do not include the undertaking of the protected act, and

3. that the discrimination complained of is by reason of their having undertaken a protected act, rather than an act the nature of which would have brought retribution whether or not it was performed with reference to the Sex Discrimination Act or Race Relations Act.

Discriminatory practices

2.71   Whilst proceedings in respect of direct or indirect discrimination under section 1 of the Race Relations Act or the Sex Discrimination Act require there to be a victim because the discrimination must be to the detriment of the complainant, under the Race Relations Act, s.28 or the Sex Discrimination Act, s.37, the Commissions can deal with the position of an indirectly discriminatory practice found to exist in the course of a formal investigation, notwithstanding the absence of a specific victim of the discrimination.[53] The sections apply to the situation where a requirement or condition is applied which is unlawful by virtue of Parts II or III of the Acts or would do so if the requirement or condition were applied to members of the other gender or to a member of a specific racial group. Legal steps may be brought under these sections only by the Commissions in accordance with the requirements of the Sex Discrimination Act, ss.67-71 or the Race Relations Act, ss.58-62 *i.e.* in the context of a formal investigation. Under these procedures a non-discrimination notice may be issued, which could ultimately be enforced by an injunctive measure.

The liability for employees and agents

Vicarious liability

2.72   It is in the nature of things that discrimination can only occur as the result of the behaviour of individual employees and the question therefore arises as to the extent of the employer's liability for such action by employees. In this context, it is important that the Race Relations Act, s.32 and the Sex Discrimination Act, s.41 provide that:

"(1) Anything done by a person in the course of his employment shall be treated for the purposes of this Act as done by his employer as well as by him, whether or not it was done with the employer's knowledge or approval.

(2) Anything done by a person as agent for another person with the authority (whether express or implied, and whether precedent or subsequent) of that other person

---

[53] Contrast the position when an employer states an intention to discriminate directly (*e.g.* "We don't take Pakistanis.") but there is no victim. RRA, s.28 and SDA, s.37 refer back to the indirect discrimination provisions in the two Acts, and do not therefore deal with direct discrimination. See also n. 67 and the Percy Ingle investigation by the CRE.

shall be treated for the purposes of this Act (except as regards offences thereunder) as done by that other person as well as by him."

2.73 Whilst liability of the employer under Race Relations Act, s.32 and the Sex Discrimination Act, s.41 is a direct liability, the question nonetheless arises as to whether an employee who engages in some form of racial or sexual discrimination is acting within the course of his employment. The passage from the 9th edition of Salmond on Torts,[54] approved by the Privy Council in *Canadian Pacific Railway* v. *Lockhart*,[55] sets out the general principles:

"It is clear that the master is responsible for acts actually authorised by him; for liability would exist in this case, even if the relationship between the parties was merely one of agency, and not one of service at all. But a master, as opposed to the employer of an independent contractor, is liable even for the acts which he has not authorised, provided they are so connected with acts which he has authorised that they might rightly be regarded as modes . . . although improper modes . . . of doing them. In other words a master is responsible not merely for what he authorises his servant to do, but also for the way in which he does it. . . . On the other hand, if the unauthorised and wrongful act of the servant is not so connected with the authorised act as to be a mode of doing it, but is an independent act, the master is not responsible: for in such a case the servant is not acting in the course of his employment, but has gone outside it."

2.74 This passage was more recently approved and applied by the Court of Appeal in *Aldred* v. *Nacanco*[56], a case concerning vicarious liability for injury, and in the racial harassment case of *Irving* v. *The Post Office*,[57] in which a letter sorter nourished a grudge against his West Indian neighbours over a question of street parking. When the letter sorter came across a Christmas card addressed to his next door neighbours he wrote on the back of the envelope "Go back to Jamaica Sambo" and underneath it he drew a cartoon of a smiling face. When the identity of the letter sorter was discovered he was disciplined but not dismissed. Perhaps because the neighbours were not satisfied with the disciplinary penalty imposed by the Post Office (dismissal suspended for a year), they sought a declaration under the Race Relations Act that the Post Office and its servants and agents had unlawfully discriminated against them. After reviewing the authorities on vicarious liability, the Court of Appeal held that the letter sorter's action could not be regarded merely as an unauthorised way of performing the

[54] At p. 95.
[55] (1942) A.C. 591, at p. 599.
[56] [1987] I.R.L.R. 292.
[57] [1987] I.R.L.R. 289.

duties for which he was employed. His employment provided the opportunity for his misconduct, but the misconduct formed no part of the performance of his duties as a letter sorter, even though he was authorised to write on envelopes for postal purposes.

2.75 Often the fact of employment will have provided the opportunity or occasion for a discriminatory act such as racial harassment to take place, but that does not necessarily make the employer vicariously liable. It is only if the actions complained of constitute a mode of carrying out the authorised tasks that the employer will be liable. For example, in *Heasmans* v. *Clarity Cleaning Co. Ltd*[58] the defendant company were under contract to the plaintiffs to provide cleaning services. One of their cleaners, whose honesty they had no reason to doubt, ran up a £1,400 bill on the plaintiff's telephone account in three months by making a series of unauthorised international calls. Even though his employment provided the opportunity for his wrongdoing, it was held that he was not acting in the course of his employment.

2.76 Applying these principles to cases of sexual or racial harassment at work, where an employee is in a supervisory position and takes advantage of that position to engage in some form of harassment, as in *Bracebridge Engineering* v. *Darby*,[59] such abuse of authority would be sufficiently closely connected with the task of supervision as to constitute a mode of performing the duties of the post. Following the *Irving* case, it is less clear that an employee who makes unwelcome advances to a fellow employee with whom he enjoys no working relationship is doing so in the course of his employment. The conduct complained of must be sufficiently closely connected with the employment of the person in question as to constitute an improper way of performing his or her job, if it is to give rise to vicarious liability on the part of the employer.

2.77 The fact that this conduct may be unknown to the employer is not material, so long as it is taking place within the course of the employment, for the Race Relations Act, s.32 and the Sex Discrimination Act, s.41 provide that such an act shall be treated as done by the employer, whether or not it was done with the employer's knowledge or approval. However, the Race Relations Act, s.32(3) and the Sex Discrimination Act, s.41(3) provide a defence for any employer who can:

"prove that he took such steps as were reasonably practicable to prevent the employee from doing that act,

[58] [1987] I.R.L.R. 286.
[59] [1990] I.R.L.R. 3, EAT.

or from doing in his employment acts of that
description."

2.78   In *Balgobin and Francis* v. *London Borough of Tower
Hamlets*[60] a cook sexually harassed two of the female cleaners
employed in a hostel over a period of three months. As soon
as the cleaners complained, the cook was suspended whilst
the complaints against him were investigated. The
complaints were not substantiated and the employees
concerned returned to their original duties, after which there
were no further complaints of improper conduct by the
cook. Having found that the allegations had not been made
known to management, that there was proper and adequate
staff supervision and that the employers had made known
their policy of equal opportunities, the EAT upheld a
decision by the Industrial Tribunal that the employers had
established a defence under the Sex Discrimination Act,
s.41(3). The majority of the EAT took the view that it was
very difficult to see what steps in practical terms the
employers could reasonably have taken to prevent that which
occurred from occurring. The minority took the view that
the employers had taken little positive action to bring the
provisions of the equal opportunity policy to the notice of
employees or to make it clear that sexual harassment was an
offence. It is much more likely now, post the promulgation
of the E.C. Code on the Protection of Dignity of Women at
Work[61], that were the circumstances of this particular case to
be repeated, the minority view would prevail.[62] Thus an
employer who has promulgated a policy to protect the
dignity of men and women at work, and undertaken training
to bring its provisions to the notice of all concerned, would
be more likely to succeed in a defence under section 41(3).
Without that the mere absence of complaints does not mean
that a problem does not exist; it may simply indicate that
employees fear complaining or think there is no point in it.

2.79   An employer may be responsible for the consequences
of a discriminatory act performed by an employee, although
the effects of that act arise from a step taken by an
intermediary employee who may not himself be motivated
by racial considerations or considerations of gender. Thus in
Kingston v. *B.R.*[63] a transport policeman was found to have
engaged in a form of racial harassment. To avoid further
difficulties between the policeman and the employee

---

[60] [1987] I.R.L.R. 401, EAT.
[61] see chap. 4 for details of the Code.
[62] In *Coyle* v. *Cahill Motor Engineering Ltd* (Case No. 1808/87) a male
supervisor who had been previously disciplined in respect of sexual
harassment was placed in charge of a young female trainee. The
management were held not to have taken all reasonable steps to prevent
future incidents because they had at no point specifically invited the girl
in question to comment on the way she was being treated.
[63] [1984] I.R.L.R. 147; [1984] I.C.R. 781, C.A.; affirming [1982] I.R.L.R.
274, EAT.

concerned, a decision was taken by the local manager to transfer the employee to other duties. Although the manager who took the decision to transfer the employee was himself innocent of racial motivation, the employers were nonetheless liable for the consequences of an act of which the original cause was the discriminatory conduct of the policeman.

Aiding unlawful acts

2.80　A person who knowingly aids another person to do an act made unlawful by the Sex Discrimination Act or the Race Relations Act is himself to be treated as doing an unlawful act of a like description. Where a person is acting within the course of his employment so as to fall within the Race Relations Act, s.32 or the Sex Discrimination Act, s.42 (or would do but for subsection 3 of the relevant Act), he shall be deemed to be aiding the act of the employer, *i.e.* to be liable personally for the act. The Race Relations Act, s.32 and Sex Discrimination Act, s.42 make individual liability for aiding an unlawful act contingent upon the direct liability of the employer under section 31 or section 41 respectively, but this does not preclude direct action against the employee for any act rendered unlawful under Parts II, III or IV of the Acts.

2.81　Where a person relies on an assurance by the person whose act he is aiding that the act in question is not an unlawful discriminatory act, subsection 3 provides that he is not knowingly aiding that other, providing that it is reasonable for him to rely on the statement. A person who makes such a statement knowingly, or recklessly, which is in a material respect false is liable to a level 5 fine on summary conviction, under the Race Relations Act, s.32(4) or the Sex Discrimination Act, s.42(4).

Application to the Crown

2.82　Section 75(1) of the Race Relations Act applies to an act done by, or for the purposes of, a Minister of the Crown or a government department, or to an act done on behalf of the Crown by a statutory body or by a person holding a statutory office, as it applies to employment by a private person. Identical provisions occur in the Sex Discrimination Act, s.85(1). Parts II and IV of the Acts apply to service for the above purposes as they apply to employment by a private person. The Acts apply to aircraft, ships and hovercraft belonging to or possessed by the Crown, as they do to such craft when possessed by others. (Race Relations Act, s.75(4) and Sex Discrimination Act, s.85(7)).
Employment in the police is subject to the special provisions of section 16 of the Race Relations Act and section 17 of the Sex Discrimination Act.

2.83   The Sex Discrimination Act does not, however, apply to the armed forces (s.85(4)), nor to cadet forces (s.85(5)), nor to service in support of one of the armed forces. Nonetheless the EOC successfully supported a case brought by two military women who became pregnant on the grounds that their dismissal was in breach of the Equal Treatment Directive. The Race Relations Act provides that complaints under Part II of the Act shall be heard by a body constituted for that purpose under the appropriate Armed Forces Act. The Race Relations Act does not apply to rules restricting employment in the service of the Crown or certain public bodies to persons of any particular birth, nationality, descent or residence (RRA, s.75(5)). The Crown Proceedings Act 1947 applies to proceedings under Parts II-IV of the Acts as they apply to civil proceedings by or against the Crown. (RRA, s.75(6-7). SDA, s.85(8-9).

Exclusions and qualifications

2.84   The Sex Discrimination Act 1976 and the Race Relations Act apply in Great Britain, whereas the Sex Discrimination (Northern Ireland) Order 1976 and the Fair Employment legislation apply in Northern Ireland. The Sex Discrimination Act applies to women or men of any age (s.5(2)).

Acts to safeguard national security

2.85   Under the Sex Discrimination Act, s.52(1) and the Race Relations Act, s.42(1) nothing in Parts II to IV of the Acts shall render unlawful an act done for the purpose of safeguarding national security. The Sex Discrimination Act, s.52(2) provides that a certificate issued by a Minister certifying that an act was done for the purpose of national security shall be conclusive proof that it was done for that purpose. In *Johnston* v. *Chief Constable of the Royal Ulster Constabulary*[64] the Chief Constable decided that the exigencies of policing the Province meant that all police on active duty needed to be armed, so that in his view there was no longer any place for women in the full-time reserve force and the complainant's contract was not renewed. The complainant brought an action under the 1976 Northern Ireland Sex Discrimination Order, which is in the same terms as the Sex Discrimination Act 1975, but her claim under domestic legislation was impeded by a certificate issued by the Secretary of State for Northern Ireland under Article 53 of the Northern Ireland Order, (which is in the same terms as s.52 of the 1975 Act) and which was conclusive proof under the Order that the act was done for the purpose of safeguarding national security or protecting public safety or public order. The Industrial Tribunal referred a series of questions to the ECJ under Article 177, as to whether the facts of the case fell within the derogations from the principle of equal treatment which are contained in Articles 2(2) and 2(3) of the Equal Treatment Directive. The principle of equal treatment itself, as set down in Article

[64] Case 222/84: [1986] 3 C.M.L.R. 240, [1987] I.C.R. 83; ECJ.

2(1), had been held to be directly applicable in the *Marshall* case, as had its application to dismissal in Article 5(1), if and in so far as, these had not been implemented properly.[65] Article 6 requires that Member States take such measures as are necessary to enable all persons who consider themselves wronged by failure to apply to them the principle of equal treatment within the terms of the Directive, to pursue their claims by judicial process. Article 2(2) of the Equal Treatment Directive provides that a Member State may exclude from the field of application of the Directive those occupational activities where sex is a determining factor.

2.86 The ECJ approached the application of the Directive to the facts of the case along two routes. It relied firstly on the concept of indirect effect as stated in the *Von Colson* case[66], but the Court had no difficulty in holding that the application of the principle of equal treatment to access to employment in Article 3(1) and vocational training in Article 4(1) were directly applicable as against the Chief Constable, who, in spite of his constitutionally independent status, was considered to be an emanation of the State. Therefore, the applicant could rely upon the terms of the Directive "to have a derogation from that principle under national legislation set aside in so far as it exceeds the limits of the exceptions permitted by Article 2(2)." The ECJ also held that Article 6 was sufficiently precise and unconditional to be relied upon by persons who consider themselves wronged by sex discrimination, in so far as it stipulates that all such persons must have an effective judicial remedy.[67]

2.87 The ECJ first concluded that the issuing of a certificate precluding the application of claims within the ground occupied by the Directive constituted a failure to ensure effective judicial control of compliance with the terms of the Directive, as required by Article 6. The ECJ based its conclusion on the view that the requirement of effective judicial control reflects a general principle of law underlying the constitutional traditions of the Member States, which is also laid down in the European Convention of Human Rights.[68] As the Directive contains no specific reservations or qualifications to do with public safety or security, and the ECJ was of the opinion that there is no general proviso in the scheme of the Treaty to do with public safety, the next logical question was whether the facts of the case fell within the ambit of Article 2(2), in that the sex of the worker was a

---

[65] Where the requirements of a directive have been correctly implemented, it is to the the national provisions that complainants must look. See ground 51 of *Johnson*.

[66] See chap. 1.

[67] The Court held , however, that Art. 6 did not contain any unconditional and sufficiently precise obligations as to sanctions for discrimination for these to be directly effective. See the discussion of the *Marshall No. 2* case in chap. 1 for further consideration of this issue.

[68] Grounds 18-21.

determining factor. The ECJ held that it was for the national court to assess this question but stipulated that

> "the principle of proportionality must be observed. That principle requires that derogations remain within the limits of what is appropriate and necessary for achieving the aim in view and requires the principle of equal treatment to be reconciled as far as possible with the requirements of public safety which constitute the decisive factor as regards the context of the activity in question."[69]

2.88   Following *Johnston* the Sex Discrimination (Amendment) Order 1988[70] now excludes the Sex Discrimination Act, s.52(2) & (3) and Article 53 of the Northern Ireland Order (under which a Minister can issue a certificate which constitutes conclusive proof that an act was done for purposes of national security) in relation to matters of employment or vocational training *i.e.* it preserves the principle of equal treatment in employment. The parallel provision in the Race Relations Act, s.69(2), for the issue of a certificate which is conclusive proof that an act was undertaken for the purposes of national security, remains unaffected.

Acts done under statutory authority

The position under the Race Relations Act

2.89   The Race Relations Act provides in section 41(1) that:

"Nothing in Parts II to IV shall render unlawful any act of discrimination done–

(a) in pursuance of any enactment or Order in Council; or
(b) in pursuance of any instrument made under any enactment by a Minister of the Crown; or
(c) in order to comply with any condition or requirement imposed by a Minister of the Crown (whether before or after the passing of this Act) by virtue of any enactment.

References in this subsection to an enactment, Order in Council or instrument include an enactment, Order in Council or instrument passed or made after the passing of this Act."

2.90   This section was considered by the House of Lords in *Hampson* v. *Department of Education and Science*,[71] in which a teacher from Hong Kong was seeking approval of her teaching qualification to enable her to teach in a State school

---

[69] Ground 38.
[70] (S.I. 1988 No. 249).
[71] [1990] I.R.L.R. 302, H.L., 1989] I.R.L.R. 69, C.A.

in Britain. Her initial course of teacher training was of only
two years, although she had eight years later taken a further
one year course. Mrs. Hampson was refused approval under
the relevant Regulations which were made pursuant to the
Education Act 1980, as it was the practice of the Secretary
of State for Education to refuse approval for any course of
less than three years length. The Department conceded that
the action constituted indirect discrimination in that a
requirement (a three year course) was imposed with which a
smaller proportion of persons of the applicant's racial group
(Hong Kong Chinese) could comply. The Department
contended, however, that the action of the Secretary of State
was an act of discrimination in pursuance of an instrument
(the Regulations) made under an enactment (the Education
Act 1980) by a Minister of the Crown. It was argued on
behalf of the complainant that the section does not protect
administratively chosen requirements or conditions which
represent one of a variety of possible modes of doing those
acts. The majority of the Court of Appeal held, however,
that the section was apt to cover this act, albeit based upon
the exercise of a discretion by the Secretary of State as to the
actual choice made. Nourse L.J. held that the Secretary of
State was under a duty to make a decision under the
Regulations, a duty to either approve or not to approve the
particular qualification. On this view, a power to give or
withhold approval is not a power to give or withhold a
decision. The House of Lords preferred the dissenting
judgement of Balcombe L.J. in the Court of Appeal, in
which he argued that a wide interpretation of section 41
could frustrate the purposes of the Act, because the actions
of most public bodies must necessarily be derived from the
exercise of statutory powers. For this reason Lord Lowry,
giving the judgement of the Court, held that the words "in
pursuance of any instrument" are confined to acts done in
the necessary performance of an express obligation contained
in the instrument and do not also include acts done in the
exercise of a power or discretion conferred by the
instrument. Lord Lowry went on to hold that the allegedly
discriminatory act was not protected because the Secretary of
State had to set up and rely upon an administrative criterion
not found in the Regulations, namely that of three
consecutive years of training. Thus the decision was based
on administrative practice and not upon a requirement laid
down by the Regulations. He was fortified in that view by
the observation that a wide approach to the exceptions to the
Act laid down in section 41 would be capable of nullifying
and defeating the purposes of the Act as regards not simply
central but local government and many other public bodies.

2.91 The House of Lords in *Hampson* cited with approval
the decision of Wood J. in the EAT in *General Medical
Council* v. *Goba*.[72] In that case the G.M.C. had argued as a

---

[72] [988] I.R.L.R. 425, EAT.

preliminary point that section 41(*a*) provided an "umbrella" protection for all actions taken in pursuance of any statute or Order in Council. The EAT held that such a blanket protection would render nugatory those sections of the Act which deal with public bodies such as the Training Agency and that section 41 "does not provide a defence whatever the act complained of and however heinous it may be in terms of discrimination."[73] The EAT also held that only those actions reasonably necessary to comply with any requirement or condition of the statute or order were protected by section 41.

2.92 The saving in relation to acts done under statutory authority goes further in relation to nationality or place of ordinary residence or the length of time a person has been present or resident in or outside the United Kingdom, and includes not merely actions undertaken pursuant to prior legislation or statutory instruments, but also includes arrangements made with the approval of, or for the time being approved by, a Minister of the Crown (RRA, section 41(2)(*a*)) or in order to comply with any condition imposed by a Minister of the Crown. (RRA, s.41(2)(*b*)). The effect of these provisions is to exclude from the ambit of the Race Relations Act Departmental circulars and Ministerial pronouncements. In this way the structure of immigration control is removed from the ambit of the Race Relations Act's enforcement provision.

The position under the Sex Discrimination Act

2.93 Acts undertaken which are necessary to comply with the requirements of a statute passed before the Sex Discrimination Act and instruments issued under the authority of such Acts were saved by the Sex Discrimination Act 1975, s.51.[74] These provisions were considered by the EAT in *Page* v. *Freighthire (Tank Haulage) Ltd.*[75] in which it was held that acting in the interests of safety is not in itself a justification for discrimination on the grounds of sex, unless the action complained of was undertaken to comply with prior legislation, such as the Health and Safety at Work Act. The EAT went on to hold, however, that the action in question, in this case the exclusion of a woman from driving a tanker loaded with a chemical thought potentially harmful to women of reproductive age, need not be the only possible method of complying with requirements of the Health and Safety at Work Act 1974. It was said to be important to consider all the circumstances, the risks involved and the

[73] At p. 426 and see also *Savjani* v. *I.R.C.* (1981) 1 Q.B. 458, in which a narrow construction of s.41 was implicitly favoured.

[74] In *Greater London Council* v. *Farrar* [1980] I.C.R. 266, the EAT held that a licence to allow wrestling to be performed in public which imposed discriminatory conditions, was an instrument issued under an Act of a date prior to the date of the S.D.A. and it was immaterial that the licence itself was issued after the date of the S.D.A. This proviso extends to the re-enactment of a statute originally enacted prior to the date of the SDA or RRA.

measures which are reasonably necessary to eliminate the risks in question, but if the employer was in reality using such a restriction as a device to prevent the employment of women that would be a different situation.

2.94 The extent of this saving was brought into question, however, by the decision of the ECJ in *Johnston* v. *The Chief Constable of the Royal Ulster Constabulary*,[75] which concerned the non-renewal of the contract of a policewoman on the ground that henceforth all police on active duty in Northern Ireland would carry arms and that it was inappropriate for policewomen to carry arms. The case raised issues of national security, (discussed above) but also raised the question as to whether the facts of the case fell within the derogation from the principle of equal treatment which is contained in Article 2(3) of the Equal Treatment Directive. Article 2(3) provides that the principle of equal treatment shall be applied "without prejudice to provisions concerning the protection of women, particularly as regards pregnancy and maternity." Such derogations must be interpreted strictly in the view of the ECJ and Article 2(3) is intended only

> "to protect a woman's biological condition and the special relationship which exists between a woman and her child. It does not allow women to be excluded from a certain type of employment merely because public opinion demands that women be given greater protection than men against risks which affect men and women in the same way and which are unrelated to women's specific needs of protection."[76]

2.95 This decision cast doubt upon the scope of any restrictions as to the scope of work which could be undertaken by women, in so far as these did not arise from a specific reproductive concern. The result was the removal of restrictions on the conditions under which women may undertake certain types of work and consequently section 51 of the Sex Discrimination Act 1975 was amended by the Employment Act 1989.

The Employment Act 1989

2.96 The Employment Act 1989, s.1 requires that any provision of any Act passed before the Act of 1975, or any instrument made or approved under such an Act, shall be of no effect in so far as it imposes a requirement to do an act which would be rendered unlawful by any provision in Parts II (employment), III (in so far as it applies to vocational training) or IV (in so far as it relates to employment or vocational training) of the Act.[78] In any legal proceedings

---

[75] [1981] I.R.L.R. 13, EAT.
[76] See n. 64.
[77] Ground 44.
[78] s.6(2) also provides that any re-enacted legislation will be treated as if

concerning indirect discrimination, a party may argue that
s.1 of the Act does not operate in so far as the requirement
or condition in question is justifiable within subsection (b)(ii)
of sections 1 or 3 of the Act of 1975. Thus an employer,
who imposed a minimum height or weight requirement for a
job involving heavy lifting, would be able to argue that such
a requirement was justifiable and therefore he could rely on
his statutory duty not to require employees to lift weights so
heavy as to be likely to cause themselves injury. This is
complemented by section 2 which provides that the
Secretary of State may by order amend any provision of any
Act which would require the doing of an act of
discrimination within the terms of s.1 above.

2.97   Section 3 amended section 51 of the Sex
Discrimination Act 1975 to restrict the exceptions to Parts
II,III or IV, in so far as these relate to employment or
vocational training matters, to those which are necessary to
comply with a requirement of an existing statutory provision
concerning the protection of women, whether within the
ambit of the Health and Safety at Work Act 1974 or
otherwise. For this purpose, a statutory provision which has
as its object the protection of women, is one which protects
women as regards pregnancy or maternity, other risks
specifically affecting women. An existing statutory provision
means an Act passed before the Sex Discrimination Act or
an instrument made under such an Act, whether passed
before or after the Act of 1975.

2.98   The effect of the new section 51 is to render lawful
discriminatory actions based upon previous enactments only
where the purpose of those enactments is to protect women
or to comply with a relevant statutory provision as regards
the Health and Safety at Work Act 1974, in so far as that
provision has effect for the purpose of protecting women as
regards pregnancy or maternity, or in other circumstances
giving rise to risks specifically affecting women, such as
ionising radiation, working with lead etc. This much tighter
definition of the scope of protective legislation is intended to
preserve only those derogations from the principle of equal
treatment which are permitted under Article 2(3). The
amended provisions will ensure that women are excluded
only from those forms of employment which are deleterious
to them as regards pregnancy, maternity or reproductive
matters more generally. It can be observed that the
construction placed upon "necessary" in *Page* v. *Freighthire
(Tank Haulage) Ltd.*[79] did, however, already reflect this
concern that health and safety legislation is not used as a
pretext to exclude women from employment.

contained in an Act prior to 1975. S.6 (1)enables the Secretary of State
to make an order as appropriate to disapply the provision of s.1 in any
case where he considers that provision would otherwise apply.
[79] *Supra* at n. 75.

2.99 The 1989 Act, s.9 repeals the restrictions on the employment of women underground, or on heavy work or on the supervision of winding apparatus under the Mines and Quarries Act 1954. Likewise, the restrictions on the employment of women in the cleaning of machinery are repealed, as are a variety of other restrictions on the employment of women listed in Schedule 2 of the Act. Otherwise, the amended section 51 is subject to section 4 of the 1989 Act, which renders lawful an act of discrimination, if it was necessary for a person to do it to comply with a requirement of any of the remaining provisions concerned with the protection of women at work specified in Schedule 1 of the Act.[80]

Power to amend certain provisions of the Acts

2.100 The Secretary of State may, by an order which has been laid before Parliament, amend section 9 of the Race Relations Act, which provides an exception for seamen recruited abroad. In spite of a great reduction in the number of seamen recruited in the Indian sub-continent, no such order has as yet been made. Orders may also be made to render lawful acts which are unlawful by selected sections of the Race Relations Act. No such orders have been made to date. Neither have any orders been made in respect of the similar powers to amend the statute contained in the Sex Discrimination Act, s.80.

[80] Factory and Workshop Act 1901, s.61, as set out in Sched. 5 to the Factories Act 1961; Public Health Act 1936, s.205; Factories Act 1961 ss.74, 128 and 131; S.R. & O. 1907 No. 17, 3 (Manufacture of paints and colours); S.R. & O. 1925 No. 752,10. (Lead smelting, manufacture of red or orange lead and flaked litharge); S.R. & O. 1922 No. 329 (Indiarubber Regulations); S.R. & O. 1925 No. 28.1. (II) (Electric Accumulator Regs); (S.I. 1950 No. 65), 6(i) to (vi) (Pottery (Health and Welfare) Regs); (S.I. 1985 No. 1333), Parts IV and V of Sched. 1 (Ionising Radiation Regs); (S.I. 1985 No. 1643), Art. 208 (Air Navigation Order, in so far as it relates to pregnancy); (S.I. 1980 No. 1248) Para. 118 (Code of Practice relating to the Control of Lead at Work Regs); (S.I. 1938 No. 808) Part X so far as relating to gynaecological conditions, and Part XI of the Merchant Shipping Notice No. M. 1331 (issued for the purposes of Reg. 7 of (S.I. 1983 No. 2426) the Merchant Shipping (Medical Examination) Regs.

3 PROOF OF DISCRIMINATION

Characteristics of Direct Discrimination

3.01   In this chapter we deal with matters relating primarily to proof of direct discrimination. Some direct discrimination has overt features and proof is straightforward, but most is predominantly covert and proof is problematical.

Overt discrimination, in the sense of discrimination where the discriminatory ground is made manifest, is more common than may be imagined. The blatant discriminator, who knows full well he or she is discriminating in making decisions and is prepared to let the victim know it too, may be, nowadays, the exceptional case. (But overt sexual harassment may be quite widespread). There, however, are cases where the discriminator relies on supposed white or male solidarity and expresses his discriminatory reasoning in the presence of another person, who then blows the whistle on him, and becomes the principal witness against him. There are also cases where the discriminator, believing that what he is doing is lawful because he himself is not prejudiced, acknowledges the discrimination (*e.g.* "I'm not prejudiced but I cannot appoint a black/woman foreman, because the shopfloor staff would not accept it.") to the victim or somebody else, and indeed sometimes in response to questionnaires under the Acts, only to find that he has in fact admitted a breach of the law.

3.02   Certain unlawful acts under the legislation, it should be noted, necessarily consist of overt discrimination, witting or unwitting. For example, instructions or pressure to discriminate. The main evidence in these cases will usually be that of the person who was on the receiving end of the instructions or pressure, and the cases will stand or fall according to whether the person is believed and what construction the court or tribunal places upon what is proved to have been said. Unlawful advertisements are a special case of overt discrimination. Except in these particular cases where the nature of the unlawfulness so requires, proof of an overt manifestation of a discriminatory ground is not a necessary feature of a discrimination case. Clearly, however, where that manifestation is present, proving discrimination is far less problematical than where it is not.

3.03 Proving *covert* discrimination generally involves overcoming several obstacles.[1]

The true ground of the alleged discriminator's decision is in his or her mind at the time of his decision. Proof of a state of mind is necessarily difficult. The alleged discriminator's own evidence as to state of mind is likely to be unreliable. There will generally be a wish to avoid liability. Even where there is an attempt to be totally honest in denying discriminatory grounds for the decision, he or she may be unaware of the discriminatory influences affecting the decision. Discrimination occurs not only because of views which are so outrageous that persons holding them are aware that they are racist or sexist. Persons may make unfounded assumptions about the reactions of others to black people or women; they may have unfavourably stereotyped views of the characteristics of black people or women; they may unconsciously prefer a person of their own race or sex because they feel more comfortable with such a person.

Further, the documentary evidence which would assist in proving that a discriminatory ground was the substantial cause of less favourable treatment is likely to be in the control of the alleged discriminator. Examples are notes relating to decisions concerning the Applicant and others and documents such as references which were relied on.

3.04 The statements of law and discussion which follow concern attempts to find solutions to these difficulties, and the working out of the problems in relation to: the treatment of the burden of proof; the questionnaire procedure; the discovery rules; and testing. Each of these topics will be dealt with in turn. There will be reference throughout to a typical characteristic of much discrimination. There will often have been other opportunities for the alleged discriminator to have discriminated either against the same complainant or against others. What use can be made of evidence relating to these other instances?

3.05 If a coin which is tossed one hundred times comes down 95 times heads, and 5 times tails, one could be pretty certain that something was wrong, without being able to say on which particular extra occasions it should have come down tails, or indeed even exactly how many extra times it should have come down tails. All that one can say is that over a large number of instances one could have expected the number of heads and the number of tails to be roughly

---

[1] For an account of these difficulties see Alice Leonard, Judging Inequality, Cobden Trust, 1987. See also the excellent article, "Proof of Discrimination in the United Kingdom and the United States" by Steven L. Willborn, 1986, *Civil Justice Quarterly* 321 (but written before *Singh v. WMPTE*).

the same. The reasoning in a discrimination case is much the same. The following quotation from a tribunal case illustrates the process:

> "The table shows that despite about one quarter of the workforce being from members of ethnic minorities, only one has been promoted into a supervisory position. We find that the statistical evidence, given that it represents a pattern of at least 16 years duration, is logically probative of the impression held by the Asian Community in Derby that Derby City Transport was not a workplace within which Asians were able to achieve promotion, if they sought it. There was evidence before us that many did apply, and whilst we were bound to accept that many were rejected for reasons other than race, some were not."[2]

The relevance of evidence arising from ethnic monitoring of decision-making is generally that it has a supporting role in a case from which an inference may be drawn. The law on admissibility is looked at below and there is also a further look at the monitoring process and its advantages at the end of this chapter.

3.06   Such monitoring data may play more than a supportive role where a Commission serves a non-discrimination notice in an investigation. Here the evidence on which the Commission wholly relies may be an analysis of a large number of instances of decision-making.[3] The analysis reveals such disparities in the decisions in favour of the different sexes or races at the receiving end that, in the absence of any satisfactory explanation, it is possible to infer sex or race discrimination on the balance of probabilities. Here the evidence is central to the finding of discrimination. It appears to be the case that a Commission can find discrimination on this basis even though it cannot with certainty point to an individual case of discrimination.

The argument would be that the Commission accepts that it might, on close examination, be possible to explain away on non-discriminatory grounds a small part of the disparity, but that the disparity is so great between decisions in favour of one sex or race as compared with those of another that it is not going to be possible to explain it all away, and it is enough for the Commission's purposes to be satisfied that the person "is committing, or has committed" unlawful acts.

Codes of practice   **3.07**   The assumption of both the RRA and SDA is that there are steps which can be taken by employers to prevent

---

[2] *Joshi and Whittaker* v. *Derby City Transport and Booker* 20017/91 & 20021/91 Nottingham Tribunal.
[3] See for the example the CRE's formal investigation into Hackney LBC.

racial discrimination occuring. The Acts provide for the making of codes of practice by the Commissions and state that the codes

> "may include such practical guidance as the Commission think fit as to what steps it is reasonably practicable for employers to take for the purpose of preventing their employees from doing in the course of their employment acts made unlawful by this Act."[4]

An employer can avoid liability by showing that such steps have been taken. Tribunals are bound to take into account a provision in a code if it appears relevant to a question in the proceedings.[5] It should ensue that if an applicant proves a failure to follow a relevant part of the code Tribunals could well see this as making it more likely that discrimination will have occurred. On the whole, however, we have been struck by how little reference there is in the case law to the codes. We have decided to deal with the essential features of the codes in the context of proof of discrimination to try to redress the balance.

The standard of proof

3.08   Discrimination cases are civil cases. (Do not be misled by the statement of one of the Law Lords in *Mandla* v. *Lee*[6] who wrongly said they were criminal). Accordingly, the standard of proof is no higher than the balance of probabilities. Tribunals are therefore able to find sex or racial discrimination even when they are unsure about it if the Applicant has established that it more probably happened than not. Perhaps there is a need for tribunals to be reminded on appeal that certainty is not required. The success rate in discrimination cases is low. In 1985 the CRE said in the Review of the Act:

> "The probability is that tribunals are dismissing cases involving genuine discrimination."[7]

If they are correct, is it that many tribunals are unfamiliar with the subject-matter? Or is it that tribunals regard discrimination as extremely serious and so in practice, whatever they say, find discrimination only when they are sure that it exists precisely because they think it so serious?

The burden of proof

3.09   The burden of proof is distributed as follows in discrimination cases:

1. In direct discrimination cases it falls upon the party alleging discrimination.
2. In an indirect discrimination case it falls upon the

---

[4] s. 32 (3), RRA and s. 41 (3), SDA.
[5] s. 47 (10), RRA and s. 56A (10), SDA.
[6] [1983] 2 A.C. 548.
[7] CRE "Review of the Race Relations Act 1976 -proposals for change" 1985. Similar views were stated in the 1992 Review.

party alleging discrimination, except as to the question of justifiability where the burden is upon the party attempting to justify the requirement or condition.

3. Where a party alleges that the case falls within one of the exceptions to the Acts, that party assumes the burden of establishing that this is so.

4. Where a non-discrimination notice has been issued in a formal investigation conducted by one of the Commissions, the burden falls upon the party alleging that a Commission requirement is unreasonable (because it is based on an incorrect finding of fact or some other reason).

The United Kingdom Government has blocked a proposed E.C. Directive modifying the burden of proof in sex discrimination and equal pay cases.[8] Both CRE and EOC have recommended that in circumstances consistent with direct racial or sex discrimination or victimisation the evidential burden of establishing an innocent explanation should shift to the respondent.[9] The Northern Ireland courts seem to have reached that position already.[10]

Treatment of the burden of proof

3.10 We have set out above where, formally, the burden of proof lies, but it is impossible to understand the position in discrimination cases without taking into account the gloss which case-law has put upon this topic. Although the burden of proof is on the individual alleging discrimination it has been recognised that explanation for the respondent's behaviour is best looked for from the respondent. At the same time, notions of burdens shifting to the respondent were rejected as unduly complicating the matter for industrial tribunals.

3.11 We wish that we could set the matter out simply by reference solely to recent Court of Appeal authority, see page 107 for the *China Centre* case, but in practice earlier EAT authority is still referred to in the Tribunals and it is as well to run through the background of this a central issue of discrimination law. Quotations from the cases are self-explanatory for the most part.

In *Khanna* v. *Ministry of Defence* Browne-Wilkinson J said:

"The right course in this case was for the Industrial Tribunal to take into account the fact that direct evidence of discrimination is seldom going to be available and that accordingly in these cases the affirmative evidence of discrimination will normally consist of inferences to be

---

[8] Without U.K. opposition the proposal would have gone through. But see the *Danfoss* case [1989] I.R.L.R. 532 ECJ.

[9] Proposals made by the CRE in 1985 and again in 1992, and by the EOC in 1988.

[10] See *Dorman* v. *Belfast City Council* [1990] I.R.L.R. 179 N.I. C.A.

drawn from the primary facts. If the primary facts indicate that there has been discrimination of some kind, the employer is called on to give an explanation and, failing clear specific explanation being given by an employer to the satisfaction of the Industrial Tribunal, an inference of unlawful discrimination from the primary facts will mean the complaint succeeds."[11]

In *Chattopadhyay* v. *Headmaster of Holloway School* Browne-Wilkinson J. again presiding in the EAT said:

"the law has been established that if an applicant shows that he has been treated less favourably than others in circumstances which are consistent with that treatment being based on racial grounds, the Industrial Tribunal should draw an inference that such treatment was on racial grounds, unless the respondent can satisfy the Industrial Tribunal that there is an innocent explanation."[12]

3.12 It may be appropriate to draw inferences both of race and sex discrimination as happened in the case of *Noone* v. *South West Thames Regional Health Authority*.[13] The EAT rejected an appeal against liability, where the Khanna principle had been applied to the case of failure to short-list an Asian origin woman for the post of consultant microbiologist, despite her qualifications. Inferences of both race and sex discrimination had been drawn by the Industrial Tribunal and were upheld by the EAT.

The question of when the primary facts will be such that it is appropriate to raise an inference of discrimination needing a satisfactory answer has been left vague. In most cases it does not matter because no shifting of the burden occurs, and it has been held that it is not normally appropriate to dismiss a complainant's case without hearing the respondent's evidence unless the case is exceptional or frivolous.[14] Accordingly, what the cases amount to is not the definition of a turning point (and quite possibly the courts do not wish to focus attention on such an artificial matter), but a way of analysing the whole of the evidence received in the case. Do the circumstances call for explanation? Did we get an explanation? Are we satisfied with it? What is the inference to be drawn?

3.13 Where the employer has appointed an apparently less well qualified person instead of the applicant, and that person is of a different race or sex, the tribunals will no doubt take the view that an explanation is called for.

---

[11] [1981] I.R.L.R. 331, at p. 333 and compare the Northern Ireland case *Wallace* v. *South Eastern Education & Library Board* [1980] I.R.L.R. 193.
[12] [1982] I.C.R. 132, at p. 137 and [1981] I.R.L.R. 487.
[13] Referred to in the report of *North West Thames RHA* v. *Noone* [1987] I.R.L.R. 357 and [1977] I.R.L.R. 225.
[14] See *Oxford* v. *DHSS* [1977] I.C.R. 884, EAT.

However, the trickier situation is where there are equally well qualified persons. In *Saunders* v. *Richmond-upon-Thames LBC*[15] qualifications were found to be roughly the same and the EAT took the view that an inference of discrimination was inappropriate. The position may be different, however, if the complainant is able to demonstrate a pattern of decisions by the employer against women or black persons.[16] In these circumstances it may be reasonable to infer discrimination even though the person appointed is equally well qualified, because the decision between equally well qualified people must be based on some criterion, and failing an explanation of that criterion it looks as though sex or race is being used as the determining factor.

3.14 In *Noone* v. *North West Thames Regional Health Authority*,[17], the Court of Appeal held that where there is a finding that a black candidate for a post has not been selected despite superior qualifications, usually the proper inference will be that the discrimination was on racial grounds if the employer fails to provide a satisfactory explanation.

Dr Noone was of Sri Lankan origin and had applied for a post as consultant microbiologist with the respondents. She had superior qualifications, greater experience and more publications than the successful applicant but was not appointed. The industrial tribunal found discrimination on the grounds of race: the interview procedure amounted in their view to "little more than a sham," and the decision was so subjective as virtually to be arbitrary. The EAT allowed an appeal against liability by the health authority. There was evidence entitling a conclusion that the decision of the appointments panel was unsatisfactory and unreasonable indeed revealing personal bias, but the EAT found no positive evidence that that was attributable to race, and therefore nothing to justify an inference that the discrimination was on the prohibited ground. The Court of Appeal restored the tribunal's finding on liability. Lord Justice May said:

> "In these cases of alleged racial discrimination it is always for the complainant to make out his or her case. It is not often that there is direct evidence of racial discrimination, and these complaints more often than not have to be dealt with on the basis of what are the proper inferences to be drawn from the primary facts. For myself I would have thought that it was almost common sense that, if there is a finding of discrimination and of a difference in race and

[15] 1978 I.C.R. 75.
[16] See *West Midlands Passenger Transport Executive* v. *Singh* [1988] 2 All E.R. 873, [1988] 1 W.L.R. CA 730, [1988] I.R.L.R. 186, [1988] I.C.R. 614.
[17] [1988] I.R.L.R. 195.

then an inadequate or unsatisfactory explanation by the employer for the discrimination, usually the legitimate inference will be that the discrimination was on racial grounds."

He went on:

"If there is no evidence or material from which an Industrial Tribunal can draw the inference of racial discrimination then, of course, they should not do so. On the other hand, one must not forget that it is the Industrial Tribunal who see and hear the persons actually involved. Perhaps more than in most cases the assessment by the Industrial Tribunal of the thinking of the person or persons against whom the allegation of racial discrimination is made is most important. As is well known, appeals lie from an Industrial Tribunal to the Employment Appeal Tribunal only on a point of law, and it is only when the latter is satisfied that there was no material upon which the former could reach the conclusion they did that the Appeal Tribunal should entertain the appeal . . . I do not find the Employment Appeal Tribunal's reasoning on this aspect of the case convincing. If in the circumstances of the instant case the discrimination is held to have been based on a personal bias or personal prejudice, it seems to be only a very small step to go on and conclude that the discrimination was racial."[18]

3.15 The *Noone* position that where there is a difference in race, less favourable treatment of the applicant, and an unsatisfactory explanation by the respondent, then *"usually"* the legitimate inference will be racial discrimination, appeared to represent some backtracking from the *Khanna* and *Chattopadhyay* position that in those circumstances the tribunal *"should"* infer racial discrimination.

3.16 Shortly after the Noone case in the Court of Appeal, the EAT in fact held in *Barking and Dagenham London Borough Council* v. *Camara*[19] that the *Khanna* and *Chattopadhyay* formulations were wrong in law. Instead, an industrial tribunal having found the primary facts should make such findings as it thought *"fair"*, having regard to the difficulty of putting forward a case of discrimination, and thereafter, bearing in mind the burden of proof on the applicant, decide whether discrimination had been established. An appeal was allowed against a finding of discrimination based on the industrial tribunal's understanding that they *"should"* draw an inference of racial

[18] at p. 198.
[19] [1988] I.C.R. 865, and see also a further attempt to restate the law in *British Gas* v. *Sharma* [1991] I.R.L.R. 101 which the CRE describes as the EAT being reluctant to bow to the view of the Court of Appeal in *Baker* v. *Cornwall CC* in their consultative document for the 2nd Review of the RRA.

discrimination when the primary facts had established a difference in race, less favourable treatment and there was an unsatisfactory explanation for that treatment. The case was remitted for rehearing. The *Camara* decision was, in our view inconsistent with the restatement of *Khanna* in *West Midlands Passenger Transport Executive* v. *Singh*[20] and the Court of Appeal has twice looked at the whole question again.

The *China* Centre guidelines

3.17 In *Baker* v. *Cornwall County Council*,[21] the Court of Appeal held that if discrimination takes place in circumstances which are consistent with the treatment being based on grounds of sex or race, the tribunal *"should be prepared"* to draw the inference that the discrimination was on such grounds unless the employer satisfies the tribunal that there was some innocent explanation. In *King* v. *The Great Britain-China Centre* Neill L.J. stated the following:

"(1) It is for the applicant who complains of racial discrimination to make out his or her case. Thus if the applicant does not prove the case on the balance of probabilities he or she will fail.

(2) It is important to bear in mind that it is unusual to find direct evidence of racial discrimination. Few employers will be prepared to admit such discrimination even to themselves. In some cases the discrimination will not be ill-intentioned but merely based on an assumption "he or she would not have fitted in".

(3) The outcome of the case will therefore usually depend on what inferences it is proper to draw from the primary facts found by the Tribunal. These inferences can include, in appropriate cases, any inferences that it is just and equitable to draw in accordance with s.65(2)(b) of the 1976 Act from an evasive or equivocal reply to a questionnaire.

(4) Though there will be some cases where, for example, the non-selection of the applicant for a post or promotion is clearly not on racial grounds, a finding of discrimination and a finding of different race will often point to the possibility of racial discrimination. In such circumstances the Tribunal will look to the employer for an explanation. If no explanation is then put forward, or if the Tribunal considers the explanation to be inadequate or unsatisfactory, it will be legitimate for the Tribunal to infer that the discrimination was on racial grounds. This is not a matter of law but, as May LJ put it in Noone, "almost common sense".

(5) It is unnecessary and unhelpful to introduce the concept of a shifting evidential burden of proof. At the conclusion of all the evidence the Tribunal should make

---

[20] [1988] I.R.L.R. 186.
[21] [1990] I.R.L.R. 194 C.A.

findings as to the primary facts and draw such inferences as they consider proper from those facts. They should then reach a conclusion on the balance of probabilities, bearing in mind both the difficulties which face a person who complains of unlawful discrimination and the fact that it is for the complainant to prove his or her case."[22]

3.18 In the hands of tribunal panels experienced in discrimination cases, the *China Centre* formulation is capable of producing a just result. However, in the hands of tribunal panels unfamiliar with the subtle ways in which discrimination occurs, and too ready to accept at face value assertions by employers relating to nebulous matters such as "wrong personality", "lack of leadership qualities," in the face of the contrary evidence of qualifications, experience, and references, injustice may well still occur.

3.19 It is often the case that an applicant will be able to point to failures on the part of respondents to follow their own procedures. In the case of *Qureshi* v. *London Borough of Newham*,[23] which involved failure to follow equal opportunity procedures, the Court of Appeal held that an employer's incompetence does not, without more, become discrimination merely because the person affected by it is from an ethnic minority. If there is overt racism it would be different. In practice, the effect of this decision is to relieve the employer of the necessity to demonstrate similar incompetence also in the case of men or white applicants.

3.20 To avoid having the wool pulled over their eyes however, a tribunal would do well to consider whether they are indeed looking at an incident of incompetence or something else. Suppose the Applicant seems to have attracted a whole series of supposedly incompetent acts on the part of the respondents. The tribunal would need to bear in mind that although, following *Qureshi*, incompetence without more is not discrimination, nevertheless they should be working within the *China Centre* framework and asking whether they are satisfied with the Respondent's explanation for less favourable treatment. If they reach the conclusion that the series of incidents looks more like a series of responses targeted at the Applicant than part of a general pattern of incompetence they would be free to draw the appropriate inference.

3.21 Indeed it is always wise for the tribunal to look at what has happened in the round as well as at each incident that makes up the whole picture, because explanations which individually seem satisfactory on balance may seem far-fetched when viewed together.

[22] [1991] I.R.L.R. 513 at p.518.
[23] [1991] I.R.L.R. 264.

The questionnaire procedure

3.22 Both the Sex Discrimination Act and the Race Relations Act and orders made thereunder make provision for the service of a questionnaire on a potential or actual respondent (in a tribunal case within 21 days of the commencement of proceedings or thereafter with leave; the county court position is different, see chapter 7):

> "With a view to helping a person ('the person aggrieved') who considers s/he may have been discriminated against in contravention of this Act to decide whether to institute proceedings and, if he does so, to formulate and present his/her case in the most effective manner, the Secretary of State shall by order prescribe
>
> (a) forms by which the person aggrieved may question the respondent on his reasons for doing any relevant act, or on any other matter which is or may be relevant; and
> (b) forms by which the respondent may if he so wishes reply to any questions . . .".

A person aggrieved may question a (proposed) respondent without using the prescribed forms.[24]

3.23 In practice, the length of time taken to respond to the questionnaire means that tribunal proceedings (the time limit is three months) are often commenced only to be withdrawn when the respondent provides what the aggrieved person regards as a satisfactory explanation for his act or decision. Sometimes tribunals underestimate the importance of the questionnaire procedure and list cases for hearing before the complainant has received the response to the questionnaire. Quite often the answers to the questionnaire will satisfy an Applicant and he or she will withdraw the case.

3.24 The question and any reply are admissible in evidence, subject in the case of court proceedings to applying prior to the hearing for a determination as to admissibility. In theory there is a considerable incentive for a respondent to give a prompt and full reply to the questionnaire because the Act says:

> "if it appears to the court or tribunal that the respondent deliberately, and without reasonable excuse, omitted to reply within a reasonable period or that his reply is evasive or equivocal, the court or tribunal may draw any inference from that fact that it considers just and equitable to draw, including an inference that he committed an unlawful act."[25]

3.25 In practice, tribunals are reluctant to draw inferences except in extreme circumstances, as in *Virdee* v. *EEC*

[24] SDA, s. 74, RRA, s. 65.
[25] SDA, s. 74(2)(*b*), RRA s. 65(2)(*b*).

Quarries Ltd[26] where the answer completely evaded all the questions save a partial answer to one. The statute says "may draw any inference . . . that it considers just and equitable to draw." If it is just and equitable to draw an inference, it is difficult to see what else the court or tribunal might take into account in deciding whether to draw an inference. In the *China Centre* case, referred to above an inference of racial discrimination was drawn from the questionnaire response taken together with other material.[27]

3.26 It is unclear whether the questionnaire procedure under section 74 of the Sex Discrimination Act applies also to proceedings under the equal pay legislation, although there is no good reason why a similar procedure should not apply.

The Commissions do not have the power to use the questionnaire procedure in cases where only they have the right to bring proceedings since the power is limited to persons who believe they may have been discriminated *"against"*.

In practice, an individual can often get assistance from the Commissions in drafting an appropriate questionnaire under their discretionary power to provide assistance.

3.27 Since under the discovery rules (see below) it is not possible to order a party to create a schedule of evidence where the documents are not already in existence, the questionnaire procedure may sometimes be used to achieve this. Thus the EAT in *Carrington* v. *Helix Lighting Ltd.* suggested the use of a supplementary questionnaire served with leave of the Tribunal to get data on ethnic make-up of the workforce, where documents relating to ethnic monitoring were not already in existence.[28]

The questionnaire procedure can also be used, for example, to probe for reasons for the prospective (or actual) Respondent's acting or not acting in certain ways and what criteria if any have been applied in making decisions, or to find out how others have been treated in similar circumstances, or indeed what other comparators there might be, or to get the Respondent to say what documents exist.

3.28 It is surprising how often at trial the Respondent's case does differ from replies to the questionnaire so as to provide fertile ground for cross-examination. Lack of consistency in the explanation put forward by the

---

[26] [1978] I.R.L.R. 295, I.T.
[27] [1991] I.R.L.R. 513 at p.516.
[28] [1990] I.R.L.R. 6 at p.9 and [1990] I.C.R. 125.

Respondent is likely to lead to the tribunal not being satisfied with the explanation. Conversely, too detailed and thorough a questionnaire on some matters can simply alert a respondent in advance to areas of difficulty, giving ample opportunity to invent answers thus making cross-examination more difficult. Thus we have heard some advocates express the view that questions about the Commissions' Codes of Practice are best left for cross-examination, since putting them in the questionnaire may prompt a mastery of the relevant code which would not otherwise have existed.

The discovery rules

3.29   In *British Library* v. *Palyza and Mukherjee* Nolan J. in the EAT said

> "that Parliament has seen fit to place upon the complainant of racial or sexual discrimination the burden of proving his or her case, notwithstanding that the bulk of the relevant evidence is likely to be in the possession of the respondent to the complaint. The procedure of discovery is designed to offset the probative disadvantage which the complainant would otherwise suffer."[29]

Whereas the questionnaire procedure is available before as well as after proceedings are commenced, discovery of documents is a process applicable only after proceedings have been commenced. The parties on discovery can be made to disclose all documents necessary for fairly disposing of the issue in dispute. The House of Lords set out the principles in relation to two cases which reached them at the same time, one under the Sex Discrimination Act, the other under the Race Relations Act: *Science Research Council* v. *Nasse, Leyland Cars* v. *Vyas*:[30]

1. the information necessary to prove discrimination cases is normally in the possession of the respondents so making discovery essential if the case is to be fairly decided;
2. confidentiality of the material is not, of itself, a reason for refusing discovery, but is a factor to be considered. In the case of confidential documents the Court or tribunal should examine them to see whether disclosure really is necessary, and if so to consider whether it is possible fairly to preserve confidence by covering up irrelevant parts;
3. the test in both the courts and tribunals is whether discovery is necessary for fairly disposing of the proceedings or for saving costs.

---

[29] [1984] I.C.R. 504 at p. 507 and [1984] I.R.L.R. 306.
[30] [1979] I.C.R. 921, [1980] A.C. 1028. But note that public interest immunity might apply, see *Halford* v. *Sharples* [1992] 3 All E.R. 624, C.A. (police complaints and disciplinary files).

3.30 In discrimination cases, discovery and inspection is frequently sought of material for the purposes of comparing the complainant's case with that of other persons, especially those who have been treated more favourably than the complainant. This material is often viewed as confidential by the authors and by the employer from whom it is sought: for example references, and other assessments of the people concerned. If discovery is necessary for fairly disposing of the proceedings, discovery must be ordered notwithstanding the documents' confidentiality. In deciding whether discovery is necessary for that reason the tribunal should first inspect the documents and consider whether justice could be done by taking special measures, such as covering up confidential but irrelevant parts of the documents, substituting anonymous references for specific names, or, in rare cases, a hearing *in camera*. In both the *Nasse* and *Vyas* cases discovery which had been ordered of confidential documents without such inspection was held to be wrong.

3.31 Lord Salmon commented on the relationship between the questionnaire procedures under the Acts and the right to discovery and inspection:

"I do not think that the importance to the complainant of the right to claim an order for inspection of the relevant documents is diminished by the statutory machinery which exists to allow the complainant and indeed the industrial tribunal to question the employer and at an early stage to obtain answers relating to whether the employer has unlawfully discriminated against his employee. It is, no doubt, possible that the answers, if reliable, might establish or negative the alleged unlawful discrimination and therefore make inspection of any documents unnecessary. On the other hand, there is the danger that the answers may be exiguous or unreliable and misleading. The only way of testing the accuracy of the employer's answers may often be by comparing them with the reports and records in their possession. The statutory machinery for obtaining early information from the employers was not, in my view, intended to be a substitute for, but an addition to the complainant's rights of discovery and inspection of documents."[31]

3.32 Generally, where it is necessary for fairly disposing of the case information relating to comparators such as a statement of the sex or race as the case may be, qualifications, and description of work experience, is revealed only in anonymous form without the names or addresses of those concerned. Often a list form is used with the comparators being referred to as A, B, C, D etc, but if a

[31] at p. 933 in the I.C.R. version.

complainant seeks verification, the tribunal system may provide the means of verification.[32]

Discovery and the fairness test

3.33   Discovery, even though relevant, will not be granted if it is oppressive. It will fail the fairness test. In *West Midlands Passenger Transport Executive* v. *Singh*[33] the Court of Appeal suggested two ways in which a discovery claim might be oppressive: it may require the provision of material not readily to hand, which can only be made available with difficulty and at great expense: or the effect of discovery may be to require the party ordered to make discovery to embark on a course which will add unreasonably to the length and cost of the hearing.

In *Selvarajan* v. *Inner London Education Authority*,[34] a lecturer claiming racial discrimination after the Race Relations Act 1976 came into force sought discovery of documents relating to various occasions between 1961 and 1976 during his employment when he had failed to obtain various jobs. His case was that there was continuing discrimination. The Industrial Tribunal had limited discovery to events after 1973, but the EAT could see no logic in this cut-off date. The events going back to 1961 could be probative, so the EAT held, of the allegation of discrimination after the Act. Thus the issue was whether there was oppression or unfairness. Because of the limited nature of the documents sought, and further safeguards which were available, the EAT held there was none. The application was limited to the application forms of the candidates who were appointed, and of the applicant, minutes of appointment and minutes of governors' meetings on certain dates, and the applicant's own file. As regards matters prior to 1971, however, it was left open to the respondents to apply to the tribunal that the applicant should not be allowed to go into those matters if a lapse of time meant explanations and so forth were unobtainable.

3.34   Discovery in the *Selvarajan* case related to previous incidents concerning the complainant himself, but an applicant may seek discovery of evidence relating to the treatment of others to establish a discriminatory pattern into which the applicant's case fits. The law here was established by the Court of Appeal in *West Midlands Passenger Transport Executive* v. *Singh*. Balcombe L.J. stated the issue as follows:

> "The issue is whether evidence that a particular employer

---

[32] See *Oxford* v. *DHSS* [1977] I.R.L.R. 225, EAT; [1977] I.C.R. 884 EAT. and *Williams* v. *Dyfed County Council* [1986] I.C.R. 449, EAT.
[33] [1988] I.R.L.R. 186.
[34] [1980] I.R.L.R. 313, EAT; there is no relevant distinction between hostility pointing to a racialist attitude before the act complained of and such hostility shown afterwards, and evidence relating to both is admissible, see *Chattopadhay* [1981] I.R.L.R. 487, EAT.

has or has not appointed any or many coloured applicants in the past is material to the question whether he has discriminated on racial grounds against a particular complainant; and whether discovery devoted to ascertaining the percentage of successful coloured applicants with successful white applicants should be ordered."[35]

3.35 The Court went on to observe that in considering the relevance of the material sought to be adduced, it was to be noted that cases based on racial discrimination had a number of special features:

1. that the law had established that if the applicant could show that he had been treated less favourably than others in circumstances consistent with that treatment being based on racial grounds, an Industrial Tribunal should infer that such treatment was on racial grounds, unless the employer could show the contrary;
2. that evidence adduced in such cases was not required to show decisively that the employer had acted on racial grounds, but was required to tend to prove the case;
3. since discrimination involved an individual not being treated on his own merits, but as receiving unfavourable treatment because he was a member of a particular group, statistical evidence might establish a discernible pattern which might give rise to an inference of discrimination against the group;
4. if a practice were being operated against a group, in the absence of a satisfactory explanation, it was reasonable to infer that the complainant, as a member of the group had himself been treated less favourably on the ground of race;
5. there was an approved practice in such cases for employers to provide evidence of a non-discriminatory attitude which could be accepted as having probative force, and in consequence, any evidence of a discriminatory attitude on their part would also have probative effect;
6. Suitability of candidates for posts was rarely measured objectively, and if there was evidence of a high percentage rate of failure to achieve promotion by members of a particular racial group, that fact might indicate a condition of unconscious racial attitude by employers.[36]

The Court was satisfied that the statistical material was relevant to the issues. Having decided that the discovery was relevant, the test of whether the discovery was necessary for fairly disposing of the case was applied, but there was no evidence to suggest oppression.

[35] [1988] I.R.L.R. 186.
[36] at p. 188.

Testing	**3.36**	In this section we discuss providing similar fact evidence by artificially creating applications made in similar circumstances.

Suppose a black person applies for a job and is told that the job has gone, but disbelieves that explanation. One option open to him is, as soon as possible, to get white friends to make comparable applications to that employer citing the same qualifications. Sometimes a local community relations council can arrange such a test. If it is established by the testing that the job is still open to the white applicant, the inference that the employer's statement to the complainant that the job had gone was a pretextual reason given for a racially discriminatory decision is strong.

3.37	The CRE commonly uses "testing" evidence of this sort in cases supported by it of the sort outlined above. Other examples are cases of refusal of entry to a nightclub, or of a drink in a public house. In these situations the number of reasons other than race which can be offered by way of explanation are limited. In both cases age, dress or behaviour may be cited and therefore it is essential for the testers to be of the same age, wear comparable clothes and to behave similarly. In the case of a nightclub, whether or not the person is a member is also likely to be relevant. These precautions serve to narrow the alleged discriminator's scope for pretextual explanations.

3.38	In recent years courts and tribunals have been happy to accept supporting evidence of the testing kind. It may or may not be backed up by evidence relating to the way other genuine applicants/customers were treated. However, it is one thing artificially to create a situation for the purposes of comparison. It may be quite another thing artificially to create a complainant/plaintiff in a case by putting forward a person who is not genuinely interested in a job or the provision of a service, certainly if there is any attempt to claim damages for loss or injury to feelings.

3.39	Where there is a contemporaneous test using a comparator, the evidence would be admitted by direct reference to section 3(4) of the Race Relations Act 1976 (or the equivalent provision SDA, s.5(3) as the case may be). (Subs. 3(4) RRA reads "A comparison of the case of a person of a particular racial group with that of a person not of that group under section 1(1) must be such that the relevant circumstances in the one case are the same, or not materially different in the other." That the relevant circumstances have been artificially created would appear to be immaterial for this purpose.) However if the tests are not contemporaneous, since the surrounding circumstances may have changed, it is better to consider the evidence as relevant by virtue of the third special feature listed in *West*

Midlands Passenger Transport Executive v. *Singh*[37] and provide both black and white comparable testers on the new occasion.

3.40 In any event it should be added that testing depends for its efficacy on the simple nature of the situation. In more complex situations where the number of comparable features which have to be controlled increases, it is decreasingly useful as a tool. This is particularly so where the actual presentation of people is called for. It may be possible to test certain complex situations if, for example, the test takes the form of a comparable written application form. An Industrial Tribunal found racial discrimination against an applicant for solicitors' articles who was of Sri Lankan origin where she reapplied using an English sounding name. She was rejected on her application under her real name Dharani Thiruppathy, but invited for interview under the name Jane Thorpe. It did not amount to a perfect test because there were some small differences other than race in the two application forms, but the rejection rate for ethnic minority candidates was much higher than for white candidates and the Tribunal found racial discrimination.[38]

3.41 In some types of situations testing may be decreasingly useful as the nature of discrimination changes in society. If discrimination takes the form not of a complete ban on women or members of ethnic minorities, but instead acceptance of only those who are way above their male or white counterparts who are being accepted with lower qualifications, then the level at which the qualifications are pitched in the test becomes all-important. If high, then all the applicants male, female, white and ethnic minority will be accepted. If low, then all the female and ethnic minority applicants will be rejected. The Commissions will need to bear this in mind if they carry out wide-scale testing as part of formal investigations. Indeed, it may well be that the investigations would only give a true picture if matched testers were used at several different levels of qualification in respect of each potential discriminator.[39]

Codes of Practice **3.42** In this edition of the book we have decided to put material relating to the Codes of Practice and monitoring alongside material on proof of discrimination. We are conscious that the future of equal opportunities may well lie in giving legal content to the concept of equal opportunity in

---

[37] [1988] I.R.L.R. 186.

[38] *Thiruppathy* v. *Steggles Palmer* Equal Opportunities Review Discrimination *Case Law Digest* No. 8 1991, p. 7.

[39] With hindsight it is quite possible to see that the CRE's formal investigation "Sorry It's Gone" may well have been bedevilled by these factors. The testers all had a high level of "respectability" in their appearance and story-lines.

its own right as a positive matter and creating specific associated duties such as that to monitor, rather than concentrating wholly on avoiding racial discrimination. That is really the way Northern Ireland law on religious discrimination has gone.[40] Dealing with the material on the codes and monitoring in this chapter should not be seen as blinkering ourselves to that possibility, but rather as a way of drawing attention to its relevance to proof.

The employment codes

3.43 On the status and general purpose of the Employment Codes produced by the EOC and CRE under the relevant legislation the Acts say:

> "A failure on the part of any person to observe any provision of a code of practice shall not of itself render him liable to any proceedings; but in any proceedings under this Act before an industrial tribunal any code of practice issued under this section shall be admissible in evidence, and if any provision of such a code appears to the tribunal to be relevant to any question arising in the proceedings it shall be taken into account in determining that question."[41]

3.44 There is a defence for an employer to prove that he took such steps as were reasonably practicable from doing the act in question or acts of that description, and the Acts contemplate guidance on the appropriate steps as being one of the functions of the Codes.[42]

3.45 Both Codes recommend that equal opportunity policies should be monitored.[43] In the basic discrimination legislation, there was no power in the Commissions to produce Codes outside the area of employment with the same status, but the CRE has now been given power in the field of housing to make codes (See chapter 8). Recommendations to carry out *monitoring* of the operation of equal opportunity policies are included in the Codes. The CRE has also produced a "quasi-code" in education with just such recommendations (having been refused a code-making power in that area, although oddly the Secretary of State then endorsed the "quasi-code").[44]

CRE employment code

3.46 The CRE Employment Code says:

> "In order to ensure that an equal opportunity policy is

---

[40] See Fair Employment (Northern Ireland) Act 1989.
[41] RRA, s. 47 (10) and SDA, s. 56A (10).
[42] RRA, s. 32 (3) and SDA, s.41 (3).
[43] CRE Employment Code paras. 1.4f and 1.33 to 1.42; EOC Code paras. 37 to 40.
[44] Code of Practice for the elimination of racial discrimination in education, CRE 1989; there is a separate version for Scotland.

fully effective, the following action by employers is recommended:

(a) allocating overall responsibility for the policy to a member of senior management;

(b) discussing and, where appropriate, agreeing with the trade unions or employee representatives the policy's contents and implementation;

(c) ensuring that the policy is known to all employees and if possible to all job applicants;

(d) providing training and guidance for supervisory staff and other relevant decision makers (such as personnel and line managers, foremen, gatekeepers and receptionists) to ensure that they understand their position in law and under company policy;

(e) examining and regularly reviewing existing procedures and criteria and changing them where they find that they are actually or potentially discriminatory;

(f) making an initial analysis of the workforce and regularly monitoring the application of policy with the aid of analysis of the ethnic origins of the workforce and of job applicants."[45]

3.47　There was nothing very new about these recommendations. It will be seen that the essential features of what is stated would need but slight modification to be appropriate as a *management programme* for the personnel aspects of, say, a car manufacturing company introducing a new model on a new production line (allocating responsibility for policy; getting agreement on implementation; ensuring everyone knows what is happening; providing proper training; keeping procedures under review; and keeping a check on production figures, hours worked etc. The various parts of the programme would be interrelated. If, for example, production figures were below expectations, this would lead to an enquiry as to the cause, procedures would be checked, as would the sufficiency of training, guidance etc., if procedures were found to be faulty, and ultimately if the matter was not put right, responsibility would be laid at the door of a particular manager.)

3.48　Whilst some Tribunals patiently listen to questions about the codes from the applicant's representative, others are dismissive and succeed in implying that the Codes really are not all that important. Yet in any other context they would probably accept the simple proposition that things are likely to go wrong in the absence of proper management. Just as an employer can show in defence that he has taken steps to avoid discrimination, so an employee should be able to rely on a failure to take such steps as making it more

---

[45] CRE code para. 1.4.

likely that discrimination did occur. Because of the *Qureshi* case (see above at page 108) failure to follow an equal opportunity policy will not, without more, prove racial discrimination, but that does not mean it is irrelevant to proof.

3.49 To take an example, specific recommendations in the CRE Code say that staff responsible for shortlisting, interviewing and selecting candidates should be clearly informed of selection criteria and for the need for their consistent application; given guidance or training on the effect which generalised assumptions and prejudices about race can have on selection decisions; made aware of the possible misunderstandings that can occur in interviews between persons of different cultural background; and wherever possible, shortlisting and interviewing should not be done alone but should at least be checked at a more senior level. If a completely untrained and unguided person acts alone to make an employment decision involving persons from different races and has no selection criteria established to be applied and no monitoring has ever been done of such decisions, does not this make racial discrimination likely?

Monitoring **3.50** The Codes recommend monitoring on the basis of sex, or on the basis of ethnic origin[46] in situations such as appointments to jobs, or recipients of a service, or admission to educational courses. There is one immediate and obvious difference between monitoring on the basis of sex and monitoring on the basis of ethnic origin. It is that records have traditionally been kept in such a way that it has been possible to distinguish male from female. This applies to personnel records, housing department records and education records. The same is not true of ethnic origin records. Where those same records did contain comments about ethnicity it was usually haphazard and sometimes with malevolent intent or effect. Thus systematic ethnic monitoring has had to be introduced.

3.51 Most discrimination these days is covert and indeed it is often, though by no means always, unintentional. Most managements, when first asked to carry out monitoring, will at first respond by saying: "We don't need to because we do not discriminate and nobody has ever proved that we have." That discrimination will not have been established by litigation would not be surprising. Relatively few individual cases have succeeded, and for the very good reason that it is often not difficult in an isolated instance to advance plausible

---

[46] See "Jobs and Racial Equality" a booklet by Mary Coussey and John Whitmore (1987) British Institute of Management. Also Mary Coussey and Hilary Jackson "Making Equal Opportunities Work" (Pitman Publishing 1992). These two authors had considerable experience of monitoring in practice, having dealt with the civil service from the Cabinet Office, and Coussey is the Employment Director of the CRE.

reasons for decisions unconnected with sex or race. However, when large numbers of similar decisions are looked at and analysed, a common discovery is that these reasons, plausible in the individual case, start to look highly implausible when multiplied as explanations for wide disparities in male/female, or white/black success rates.

Comparisons 3.52 Monitoring data can be used to make the following types of comparison:

1. to compare the proportion of black people/women in the appropriate labour market with their proportion as applicants for particular jobs as employees; with adaptations the same can be applied to potential recipients of services/candidates applying for services, education places;
2. to compare the proportion of black people/women in grades, jobs and departments and branches in similar areas; the same can be done in the case of recipients of housing from a local authority (*e.g.* are black people predominantly in inferior quality housing; or to educational courses (*e.g.* are women predominantly, on certain types of courses?);
3. to compare the application and success rates of blacks/women whites/men for vacancies and promotion: the same can be done in the case of recipients of housing from local authorities (*e.g.* are black people on a waiting list less successful than white people?); or to admission to, say, a university: are black people/women less successful than white people/men?).

Disparities and barriers 3.53 Disparities in any of these comparisons may indicate where there are barriers to equal opportunities. The points at which more than minor disparities appear are those where reasons should be sought. It is here that an understanding of the various hurdles in the way of equal opportunity is crucial, because without such an appreciation the identification of particular hurdles present in the circumstances under review will be very difficult. The removal of one barrier may lead to another being created. Suppose that an all-white workforce is reproducing itself by reliance upon word-of-mouth recruiting. If open advertising of jobs is substituted as a practice, it may well be found that black applicants are disproportionately rejected upon receipt of written applications, or at interview because those responsible for selection still feel happier with persons in their own image; and this will need proper training and guidance, and criteria that are as objective as possible.

Numerical targets differentiated from quotas 3.54 In ordinary business management understanding of the techniques, procedures, etc. necessary to achieve an objective is very important, but in practice targets are set in numerical terms *e.g.* to achieve a production or sales of so many cars per week. That gives both management and managed a measure of performance against which judgments can be made. The target will be based upon what can reasonably be expected to be achieved if things are running smoothly. If the target is not reached, questions will be asked about whether things are running smoothly.

3.55   Numerical target-setting is in fact implicit in certain of the voluntary provisions of the Sex Discrimination Act 1975 and the Race Relations Act 1976: those permitting positive action with regard to training and encouragement to take up particular work (see chapter 4). The statutory conditions in which they may apply relate to underrepresentation; and it follows that the provisions cease to apply when that state of underrepresentation is at an end. An employer applying section 38 of the Race Relations Act 1976 should therefore be thinking something like "when the numbers of black workers in this work reach such and such a number we shall no longer need or be able to use these provisions." This point is mentioned to illustrate the contention that setting numerical targets is consistent with the overall aims of the two pieces of legislation.[47]

3.56   The Codes of Practice do not, however, deal with target-setting and, arguably, need updating in this respect. In contrast, the Department of Employment's guide "Ten Point Plan for Employers"[48] is more realistic and advocates action plans which include targets.

3.57   The argument for setting numerical targets goes beyond the case where special positive action provisions apply. Indeed they are then more relevant to proof of discrimination. If, for example, it is possible to estimate what would be the likely numbers of black persons or women taken on as employees in a given period assuming that equal opportunities are being provided, there is a management case for setting that figure as a target against which to measure whether equal opportunities are being provided.

3.58   Care must be taken, however, to ensure that the target is not regarded as a fixed quota which must be reached willy nilly and not exceeded. A quota will be unlawful. Targets are lawful so long as it is understood that they are to be achieved by lawful means. That is to say that (except in those rare cases which form exceptions to the general principles of the legislation) decisions must not be taken on the prohibited grounds of sex, marital status, or

---

[47] see also SDA, s. 48.
[48] "Equal Opportunities-Ten Point Plan for Employers" Department of Employment 1992. This guide is highly recommended.

race. Failure to reach targets will lead to questions as to whether discriminatory decisions are being made preventing the appointment of blacks or women, as the case may be; or whether there are unnecessary barriers being placed in their way. Where very small numbers are concerned, it is probably unwise to set numerical targets, but the larger the numbers involved the wiser it becomes to have numerical targets in view.

Target setting **3.59** To give an example of target setting, suppose that an employer aims to recruit 1,000 unskilled staff in a travel-to-work locality known to have a 25 per cent. black population of working age. It is reasonable to suppose that somewhere around 250 of those appointed will be black, and that figure could be set as a target. If only 50 black people are appointed some very searching questions should be asked; if 220 or 280 so be it.

3.60 This is an example of target setting related to a particular recruitment exercise. It is large enough to make that a sensible approach. Other methods might be to set a percentage target of 25 per cent. black recruitment generally in this locality, to cover both this exercise and vacancies occurring from time to time. It may make sense to look at the overall results, though little sense to try and draw conclusions from each small-scale recruitment to fill casual vacancies. Another method might be to look at the ethnic breakdown of the existing workforce and at the recruitment potential over a period of years and set a target of reaching a 25 per cent. black workforce in the locality within a determinate number of years.[49]

[49] The last census contained questions relating to ethnic origin and sex and will provide an excellent data base against which the monitoring returns of employers and others can be compared. The Labour Force Surveys published in the Department of Employment's *Gazette* are another useful source of data.

4 DISCRIMINATION IN RELATION TO WORK

4.01 Section 6 of the Sex Discrimination Act and section 4 of the Race Relations Act set out a number of specific heads of potential discrimination in relation to work. The provisions of the two Acts are in identical terms, except in so far as the Race Relations Act includes an additional head of discrimination, namely discrimination in the terms of employment under section 4(2)(*a*). This provision concerns contractual benefits, an area covered by the Equal Pay Act in relation to sex discrimination.

4.02 Complaints under Part II of the Race Relations Act or the Sex Discrimination Act or in respect of the liability of principals or of aiding unlawful acts, are to be heard in the industrial tribunals, (RRA, s.54, SDA, s.63) except in relation to a qualifying body, from the decision of which an appeal may be brought under any enactment. Complaints pertaining to the armed forces in respect of the Race Relations Act are to be heard under the prescribed military procedures under section 75(8).

Employment in Great Britain

Definition of employment

4.03 Where an employee seeks to bring a complaint under Part II of the Sex Discrimination Act or the Race Relations Act which pertain to discrimination in employment, the complainant must be employed at an establishment in Great Britain. "Employment" means employment under a contract of service or of apprenticeship or a contract personally to execute any work or labour and related expressions shall be construed accordingly.[1] The EAT in *Quinnen* v. *Hovells*[2] held that a "contract personally to execute any work or labour" was intended to have a wider connotation than "employment" so as to include persons outside the master and servant relationship *i.e.* the self-employed.[3]

---

[1] RRA, s.78(1), SDA, s.82(1). A J.P. is the holder of an office and not employed, *Knight* v. *A.G.* (1979) I.C.R. 194, EAT.

[2] [1984] I.R.L.R. 227.

[3] This broader connotation does not, however, extend to those who are working under a contract to supply services other than their own labour. Thus in *Mirror Group Newspapers* v. *Gunning* [1986] I.C.R. 145, C.A., a contract between the newspaper company and an independent wholesale distributor fell outside the terms of the comparable section of the SDA, because the contract did not contemplate that the work was necessarily to be performed personally by the contractor.

4.04   For these purposes, employment is to be regarded as being at an establishment in Great Britain unless the employee does his work wholly or mainly outside Great Britain.[4] The exclusion contained in the Sex Discrimination Act, s.10(1) does not apply to employment on a British registered ship, nor to an aircraft or hovercraft registered in Britain and operated by a person who has his principal place of business, or is ordinarily resident in, Great Britain, unless the work is done wholly outside Great Britain. Thus in *Haughton* v. *Olau Line (U.K.) Ltd.*[5] the employee was excluded from the coverage of the Act because the ship on which she worked was registered in Germany and operated mainly outside British territorial waters.[6]

4.05   The Race Relations Act, s.8(1) provides that employment is to be regarded as at an establishment in Great Britain unless the employee does his work wholly or mainly outside Great Britain: section 8(2), however, provides that in the case of employment on a British registered ship or an aircraft or hovercraft registered in the United Kingdom and operated by a person who has his principal place of business or is ordinarily resident in Great Britain, the word "mainly" in section 8(1) shall be omitted. In other words, the employment is deemed to be at an establishment in Great Britain unless the applicant does his work wholly outside Great Britain. In *Deria* v. *The General Council of British Shipping*[7] three British registered Somali seamen were refused work on a British ship requisitioned for service in the South Atlantic at the time of the Falklands war. The vessel unexpectedly completed its voyage in Southampton, rather than Gibraltar. In spite of the fact that the employment would not have been wholly outside Great Britain, the Court of Appeal found against the seamen on the ground that the wording of section 8(2) was apt to cover existing employment, and if it is to be applied to selection for employment, must be read as applying where the applicant "does or is to do" his work wholly outside Great Britain. As the voyage was intended to terminate in Gibraltar, on this construction the employment was excluded from the jurisdiction of the Race Relations Act. This construction was said to have the virtue of enabling the parties to know whether or not any element of unlawful discrimination was taking place at the time of the acts

---

[4] SDA 1975, s.10 and RRA, s.8.
[5] [1986] I.R.L.R. 465, C.A.
[6] It was argued on behalf of the appellant that her case was governed also by the provisions of the Equal Treatment Directive 76/207 which does not specify whether it applies extraterritorially. This argument was ruled out on the basis that the British statute was unambiguous and that there was therefore no place for the application of the Directive. In the light of the dicta of the ECJ in the *Marleasing* case, some doubt must now be cast on this aspect of the decision. See chap. 1 for further discussion of questions of interpretation in the light of Community law.
[7] [1986] I.R.L.R. 108, C.A.

complained of, rather than leaving the matter at large and uncertain until the period of the employment is complete.[8]

4.06   Under the Race Relations Act, s.9, there is an exception for seamen recruited abroad, an exception which is subject to a saving in respect of off-shore oil workers. This exception allowed the continuing recruitment of a substantial part of the crews of British registered shipping abroad, often in the Indian sub-continent. Those seamen recruited overseas have normally earned only a fraction of the wages paid to crewmen recruited in the United Kingdom, but it was feared that if this practice were ended it would have a seriously damaging effect on the economics of British registered shipping. The off-shore oil industry was brought within the scope of the two Acts as regards employment matters in 1987.[9]

Determining who should be offered employment

4.07   It is unlawful under the Sex Discrimination Act, s.6(1)(a) and the Race Relations Act, s.4(1)(a) for an employer to discriminate in the arrangements made for the purpose of determining who should be offered employment. This provision covers recruitment and selection practices, both clearly vital if equal opportunities are to be made available to all classes of potential employees. Such discrimination could be either direct or indirect, as where, say, unjustifiable language or other tests, which have a disproportionate impact on the ability of women or minorities to secure employment are imposed on applicants. The provisions on discriminatory advertising contained in section 38 of the Sex Discrimination Act and section 29 of the Race Relations Act are also relevant in this context.[10]

Advertising

4.08   In this context, section 29(1) of the Race Relations Act provides that:

> "It is unlawful to publish or cause to be published an advertisement which indicates or might be reasonably understood as indicating, an intention by a person to do an act of discrimination, whether the doing of that act would be lawful or, by virtue of Parts 2 or 3, unlawful."[11]

[8] In *Wood* v. *Cunard Line* [1991] 281, C.A.; [1989] I.R.L.R. 431, EAT, a case occurring under comparable provisions of E.P.C.A. 1978, s.141(5), the EAT held that a British seaman working on a British registered ship which only ever plied in the Caribbean was excluded from the coverage of the Act, as his employment was wholly outside Great Britain, notwithstanding that he was given money for the fare home for his leaves which he normally took in the U.K.
[9] The Race Relations (Off-shore Employment) Order, S.I. 19877 No. 920 and The Sex Discrimination and Equal Pay (Off-shore Employment) Order S.I. 1987 No. 930.
[10] It therefore follows that a person may prove discrimination in a case, even though he or she cannot show that he or she would have got the job. There is also the question as to how to assess compensation for the loss of a chance, see chap. 5, *infra*.
[11] See chap. 8 for further discussion of role of the Commissioners.

4.09   Section 38(1) of the Sex Discrimination Act restricts the ambit of the parallel provision on advertising to those acts which indicate an intention of doing an unlawful act only, although section 38(3) further provides that:

> "the use of a job description with a sexual connotation (such as 'waiter', 'salesgirl', 'postman', or 'stewardess') shall be taken to indicate an intention to discriminate, unless the advertisement indicates an intention to the contrary."

4.10   Proceedings in relation to a contravention of those sections[12] can only be brought by the EOC or CRE, as in the case of *London Borough of Lambeth* v. *CRE*.[13] The Race Relations Code of Practice advises employers not to advertise vacancies in such a way that minority candidates are excluded or disproportionately reduced, and that recruitment literature should include a statement that they are equal opportunity employers.[14] Similar advice is also given in the EOC Code.[15]

4.11   The Race Relations Act provides for exceptions to the provisions on discriminatory advertising particularly where:

1. The advertisement indicates that persons of any class defined other than by reference to colour, ethnic or national origins are required for employment outside Great Britain.[16]
2. The advertisement is for a job in which there are genuine occupational qualifications for employing a person of a particular race, colour, ethnic or national origin or sex.

Recruitment practices

4.12   The importance of recruitment practices is testified by the attention given to them in the two Codes of Practice. The Codes enjoin employers not to discriminate directly or indirectly in recruitment, selection or interviewing practice. The CRE Code of Practice advises employers that:

> "to avoid indirect discrimination it is recommended that employers should not confine recruitment unjustifiably to those agencies, job centres, careers offices and schools which, because of their particular source of applicants, provide only or mainly applicants of a particular racial group."[17]

---

[12] SDA, s.72 and RRA, s.63, although the Commission may also proceed by way of a formal investigation and the issuing of a non-discrimination notice under SDA, s.67(1)(*c*) or RRA, s.58(1)(*c*).

[13] [1989] I.R.L.R. 379, EAT, [1990] I.R.L.R 231, C.A.

[14] Code of Practice para. 1.5-1.7.

[15] The Sex Discrimination Code para. 19, which enjoins employers not to present recruitment material in such a way that it reinforces stereotyped roles or the tendency to occupational segregation of the sexes.

[16] RRA, s.29(3). The origin of this provision lies in the concern not to permit racially discriminatory advertisements to appear for jobs abroad.

[17] para. 1(9).

Furthermore the Code states that it is unlawful to use recruitment methods which cannot be shown to be justifiable and which are indirectly discriminatory in that they disproportionately reduce the numbers of applicants from a particular racial group.[18] Thus the practice of "head hunting" for managerial and professional posts, which favours those already in relevant work, may be indirectly discriminatory and difficult to justify objectively unless the vacancy has been openly advertised first.

4.13 The CRE Code recommends that employers should not rely on word of mouth recruitment, where the workforce is predominantly composed of the members of only one racial group, nor should employees be recruited mainly through a trade union where this means that only the members of a particular racial group come forward.[19] The CRE Code also recommends that gate staff should be instructed not to treat applicants from particular racial groups less favourably than others, that staff involved in recruitment should be clearly informed of the selection criteria, given guidance and training on the effects of generalised assumptions about race on selection decisions and made aware of the possible misunderstandings that can occur in interviews between persons of different cultural backgrounds. It recommends that shortlisting and interviewing should not be done by one person alone but at least be checked at a more senior level.[20] The EOC Code contains similar, though less detailed provisions on recruitment, but emphasises that interview questions should relate to the requirements of the job and not include questions about marriage plans or family intentions, as these may be construed as showing bias against women.[21]

Arrangements for selection
4.14 It is unlawful for an employer to discriminate on grounds of sex or race in the arrangements which he makes for the purpose of determining who should be offered employment.[22] It is no defence for an employer to argue that the arrangements were not made with the intention of discriminating, if they operate so as to discriminate in practice. It was held by the EAT in *Brennan* v. *Dewhurst (J.H.) Ltd.*[23] that the argument that the discrimination has to be found in the making of the arrangements rather than in the operation of the arrangements would leave a gap in the plain policy of the Act. In that case, applicants were referred to the shop manager as a first filter, although appointments would have been made by the district manager. The intention of the shop manager not to employ women meant that no women would get through to the final

---

[18] para. 1.10.
[19] para. 1.10(*a*) & (*b*).
[20] para. 1.14.
[21] para. 23(*c*).
[22] RRA, s.(4)(1)(*a*) and SDA, s.6(1)(*a*).
[23] [1983] I.R.L.R. 357.

interview. The Act relates to the arrangements made, not the making of the arrangements, so that when the first selector conducted the interview in such a way as to discriminate against women, this was held to be unlawful under section 6(1)(a).

4.15   In the *Brennan* case it was held that the employer's shop manager who conducted the interview could not be said to be "making arrangements" himself. The style and content of an interview may, none the less, constitute evidence of direct discrimination under section 1(1)(a). Thus in *Saunders v.* Richmond Borough Council[24] a lady golf professional was asked, amongst other questions, "Do you think men respond as well to a woman golf professional as to a man?" She argued that the asking of such questions was in itself discriminatory, in so far as they were questions which may not have been asked of a male candidate. The EAT took the view that the asking of such gender related questions was not in itself discriminatory and may be entirely appropriate where they are related to real aspects of capacity to do the job. Whilst an employer may not assume that all women with small children are unreliable,[25] he may on this reasoning legitimately raise questions about the arrangements which such a woman has made to enable her to attend work regularly. The asking of such questions may constitute evidence of discriminatory attitudes or it may be an entirely appropriate way of testing the suitability of the candidate to perform the duties of the job. The inferences to be drawn from the evidence of questions asked at interview are matters of fact for the tribunal, but tribunals have not been unwilling to draw an inference that discrimination has occurred where a selection panel has been obtrusive or persistent in questioning female candidates about their family responsibilities and child care arrangements.[26]

---

[24] [1978] I.C.R. 75, EAT.

[25] *See Hurley* v. *Mustoe* [1981] I.R.L.R. 208, EAT and *McGuire* v. *Greater Glasgow Health Board*, IT Case No. 2869/89.

[26] *cf. Adams* v. *Strathclyde Regional Council* EAT Case No. 456/88 in which a woman candidate for a teaching post claimed that she was so upset by a question as to how many children she had and of what age that she could not perform properly during the rest of the interview. Her application was dismissed by the industrial tribunal on the ground that the question was designed to put her at ease. The EAT upheld the decision holding that there was nothing inherently adverse in such questions and that this was a question which could equally well have been asked of a man, Caution should be exercised in this respect, however, for as the EAT observed, such questions can give the impression of discrimination to candidates, whether or not it is intended. Some public bodies frame their equal opportunity policies so as to restrict the ambit of such questions. In the IT case of *O'Driscoll* v. *The Post Office* (Case No. 25671/89) the interviewer asked an Irish applicant "Do you have a problem with the drink over here?" meaning, so he said, is the Guiness as good. The applicant, who understood the question as arising from the common stereotype of the Irish as being prone to drink problems, was awarded £600 for injury to feelings because the arrangements made for the interview (*i.e.* the questions asked) gave the impression of racial stereotyping and could have resulted in a poorer subsequent interview

4.16 Where an employer asks the same questions of all candidates, even though the questions may offend the susceptibilities of one candidate more than another, there is no discrimination. In *Simon* v. *Brimham Associates*[27] a Jewish candidate for a job in the Middle East objected to being asked about his religion. The employer explained that the question was asked because if he were of the Jewish faith this might preclude his selection for the post. At this point the candidate withdrew from the interview and took proceedings under the Race Relations Act. The Court of Appeal held that whilst words or acts of discouragement could constitute less favourable treatment, the complainant (surprisingly in the view of the authors) had not established that this question, which would have been asked of any candidate for the post, meant that the candidate had been treated less favourably than the interviewer would have treated some other non-Jewish person. If the candidate in Simon had not been appointed, rather than withdrawing, the action would have fallen under section 6(1)(*c*)-refusal to offer employment.

The terms on which employment is offered

4.17 It is the offer of employment which is caught under either the Sex Discrimination Act, s.6(1)(*b*) or the Race Relations Act, s.4(1)(*b*). Once an offer which is discriminatory on grounds of sex is accepted, the terms of the resulting contract become governed by the Equal Pay Act, whereas under the Race Relations Act the matter is subject to section 4(2)(*a*). The result is that whereas under the Equal Pay Act there is need of an actual male comparator to establish a claim for equal pay, under the Race Relations Act the treatment likely to be afforded to a hypothetical person not of the complainant's racial group etc would found a claim.[28]

4.18 The terms on which employment is offered may include pensions. In *Barclays Bank* v. *Kapur*,[29] employees of East African Asian origin complained that their service in an associated company in Kenya was excluded for pension purposes when they were transferred to the U.K. due to the policy of "Africanisation" in that country. By contrast, the service of expatriate employees who had served in East Africa was included, so that the appplicants were offered employment on disadvantageous terms, Lord Griffiths

---

performance. Likewise a woman candidate for the post of education adviser in *Makiya* v. *Borough of Haringey* Case No. 03023/89, IT, who was asked the question at interview "Given your opinions on equal opportunities and as a woman how would you deal with reactionary male teachers?" was upheld in her claim that a question phrased in that way was inherently discriminatory and revealed the operation of stereotyped assumptions as to the capabilities of men and women.

[27] [1987] I.R.L.R. 307, C.A.

[28] See para. 5.50, on the hypothetical male.

[29] [1991] I.R.L.R. 136, H.L., [1989] I.R.L.R. 387, C.A., [1989] I.R.L.R. 57, EAT.

holding that "a man works not only for his current wage but also for his pension."

4.19 Another important term of employment likely to give rise to discrimination claims is working hours. Although the EAT held in *Clymo* v. *Wandsworth Borough Council*[30] that an employer who stipulated full-time work was not imposing a "requirement" on employees, the question of working hours remains contentious. Many women returning from maternity leave would prefer to work part-time. In the *Clymo* case, for example, a professional librarian was refused "job-share" terms on returning from maternity leave, a facility available to lower grades in the library service of the Borough, but not to the professional grades. The EAT took the view that full-time work was inherent to the way in which the post was specified and not therefore a "requirement", even though in *Home Office* v. *Holmes*,[31] Mr Justice Wait had taken the view that

> "Words like 'requirement' and 'condition' are plain clear words of wide import fully capable of including any obligation of service, whether full-time or part-time."

In Briggs v. *North Eastern Education and Library Board*,[32] the Northern Ireland Court of Appeal held that the fact that the employer requires the employee to carry out the job she is employed to do does not mean that there is not a requirement. It is for the employer to objectively justify the requirement to work full-time in such cases[33] or to refuse to operate flexi-time.

Refusing or deliberately omitting to offer employment

4.20 It is not necessary for race or sex to be the only factor in the decision to refuse employment for the case to fall within either the Race Relations Act, s.4(1)(c) or the Sex Discrimination Act, s.6(1)(c). In *Owen & Briggs* v. *Jones*,[34] the complainant was refused employment on her first interview but seeing the post advertised again she re-applied and was again granted an interview. Though the employer put forward as reasons for her refusal that she had been unemployed for three years and that she had not disclosed

---

[30] [1989] I.R.L.R. 241.
[31] [1984] I.R.L.R. 299, approved by the NICA in *Briggs* v. *North Eastern Education and Library Board* [1990] I.R.L.R. 181, which declined to follow the EAT in *Clymo* v. *Wandsworth Borough Council (supra)*.
[32] In *Briggs* v. *North Eastern Education and Library Board supra* the employers were held to have justified a requirement that a teacher supervise school games for an hour after the finish of normal lessons, rather than at lunchtime. It is for the employer to justify such a requirement in accordance with the circumstances of the case.
[33] For example, in *Todd* v. *Rushcliffe Borough Council* Case No. 11339/90 (EOR Discrimination Case Law Digest No. 8) a housing department employee was found to have been indirectly discriminated against by the requirement to return full-time, whereas in *Gill and Oakes* v. *Wirral Health Authority* Case No. 1615/90 a requirement that midwives returned full-time was held to be justifiable even though it had a disproportionate impact on married women.
[34] [1982] I.R.L.R. 502, C.A.

the fact of her earlier interview, the fact that the job was offered to a white girl with inferior qualifications, to whom the employer expressed racist sentiments, was held by the EAT to constitute a sufficient ground on which the Tribunal could conclude that the refusal to offer employment was contrary to section 4(1)(c).

Promotion, transfer or training opportunities

4.21 It is unlawful for an employer to discriminate in the way in which he affords access to opportunities for promotion, transfer or training under the Sex Discrimination Act, s. 6(2)(a) or the Race Relations Act, s.6(2)(b). Thus promotion systems need to be open equally to all groups, irrespective of their gender, race etc. The EOC Code recommends that promotion and career development patterns are reviewed, especially where employees of one sex are concentrated in sections from which transfers are traditionally restricted without real justification. Where this is the case the EAT in *Francis* v. *British Airways Engine Overhaul Ltd*,[35] which concerned the lack of promotion prospects for a certain all-female grade of aircraft worker, recommended that where there are no promotion opportunities from a particular grade which is predominantly composed of women (or minorities), that an indirect discrimination claim could be formulated as follows: looking at the employees in the job categories from which promotion is possible as one class, in order to be eligible for promotion on the basis of their service and experience, an employee must be a member of that class.

4.22 It is possible that an employer may discriminate directly in allocating opportunities for promotion, or that a requirement or condition may be imposed within the promotion procedure which has an adverse impact on women or members of minorities, *i.e.* which could give rise to the possibility of indirect discrimination. Thus in *Watches of Switzerland* v. *Savell*,[36] the need to comply with the requirements of a promotion system was held to be capable of constituting a requirement or condition for the purpose of establishing indirect discrimination, but in *Perera* v. *The Civil Service Commission and Department of Customs and Excise (No. 2)*,[37] it was held that any such requirement or condition must constitute an absolute bar, if it is to ground a claim that promotion was denied on the basis of indirect discrimination. In all such cases the problem is often that of proof,[38] especially where there is an attempt to rely on statistical evidence on which to found the inference of discrimination. An exception is provided in the Race Relations Act, s. 6, which provides that nothing in section 4 shall render unlawful training which is intended to provide skills which are to be exercised overseas.

[35] [1982] I.R.L.R. 10.
[36] [1983] I.R.L.R. 141, EAT.
[37] [1983] I.C.R. 428, C.A.
[38] See chap. 3.

Special encouragement and training

4.23   Neither the Sex Discrimination Act nor the Race Relations Act permit the use of sex or race as a criterion for appointment to a post except where one of the closely-defined genuine occupational qualifications (GOQS) applies. However, in fact neither the Sex Discrimination Act nor the Race Relations Act requires appointment on merit. It is perfectly legitimate to use the tossing of a coin as a method of selection, which may of course result in the least meritorious person being appointed. So appointment on merit is not mandated, but appointment by reason of sex or race is prohibited.

4.24   So much for the actual point of selection for a post. Prior to that point, certain derogations from the non-discriminatory approach are permitted both in the sex and race fields to deal with underrepresentation. These are conveniently summarised as being intended to overcome chill and bring about skill.

4.25   Until the Sex Discrimination Act 1986, the Sex Discrimination Act and the Race Relations Act were in similar terms. But without any clear explanation for a different approach the law diverged on the question of what discriminatory training is permitted. Probably the general public was rather more tolerant of women-only training than of training restricted to a particular race. Hence the former was freed from ministerial control which a scheme of designated training orders still ensured in the race field, until this too was altered in the Employment Act, 1989.

Overcoming the chill factor

4.26   Even where discrimination at the point of recruitment has been removed, women, or black people as the case may be, may not apply for particular posts if that employer is perceived to have been discriminating in the past either generally or in relation to the particular sort of work ("the chill factor" is a convenient expression). There is only one way of overcoming chill and that is by warmth. Accordingly, both the Sex Discrimination Act, s.48, and the Race Relations Act, s.38, in circumstances of underrepresentation permit the encouraging of women only, or men only, or only persons of a particular racial group to take advantage of opportunities for doing that work. Apparently the Sex Discrimination Act provision is wider because it allows the encouragement to extend to "that work" generally, whilst the Race Relations Act provision restricts the encouragement to "that work at that establishment", and the definition of what constitutes underrepresentation is similarly different.

Definitives of under-representation

4.27   The Sex Discrimination Act definition of underrepresentation is:

"where at any time within the twelve months immediately preceding the doing of the act there were no persons of the sex in question among those doing that work or the number of persons of that sex doing the work was comparatively small."

The Race Relations Act definition is:

"(a) that there are no persons of the racial group in question among those doing that work at that establishment; or
(b) that the proportion of persons of that group among those doing that work at that establishment is small in comparison with the proportion of persons of that group

(i) among all those employed by that employer there; or
(ii) among the population of the area from which that employer normally recruits persons for work in his employment at that establishment."

4.28 Where the conditions of underrepresentation apply, the encouragement can, for example, take the form of specific words of encouragement to the groups concerned to apply for jobs in advertisements (experience shows that there are fewer complaints if the relevant section of the Act is also quoted), or specific advertisements in parts of the press largely restricted to women or ethnic minorities. Section 6 of the Sex Discrimination Act and section 4 of the Race Relation Act would, without these exemptions catch these "arrangements" as discriminatory in themselves. But taking sex or race into account in making a selection decision as to particular people goes beyond mere encouragement. So where a council considered only black and ethnic minority applicants for two gardening apprenticeships (an apprenticeship is treated as employment) the council acted unlawfully: *Hughes and Gissing* v. *Hackney LBC*.[39] It is thought that this is also true of a selection decision as to the composition of a short-list.

If the pitfalls are avoided, use of appropriate encouragement can do much to overcome adverse perceptions.

Discriminatory training for employees

4.29 An employer may, in the conditions of underrepresentation set out above, make provision affording female employees only, or male employees only or only employees of a particular racial group (as the case may be) access to facilities for training which would help to fit them for the work in question. The only difference in the Sex Discrimination Act and the Race Relations Act provisions is that the Race Relations Act refers to employees "at that establishment" whereas the Sex Discrimination Act is not so restricted.

4.30 An employer cannot go so far as to guarantee appointment to particular work post-training if the employee

[39] [1987] EOR 27.

embarks on training, because this would in effect amount not only to lawfully discriminatory training but also unlawful discrimination in appointment to jobs.

4.31 Obviously the special training provision has great potential for career development in cases where there are clear patterns of employment such as women only in secretarial and clerical positions, or blacks only in manual positions. The scope for training to fit persons for supervisory and managerial positions is likely to be considerable, particularly if the training is carried out along with a review of the appointment criteria relating to those higher grade posts. For example, it will often be necessary to ensure that the internal training and previous experience is treated as equivalent to higher academic qualifications if that has been the normal qualification in the past for a supervisory or managerial post.

4.32 There is a real risk that special training schemes will be set up to cater for ethnic minorities and women when the real problem is not that they lack training, but that there was a reluctance to appoint them to supervisory positions because of their race or sex. If the persons on such training schemes look to be already well qualified, the chances are that the organisation concerned has expected ethnic minority or women managers to be better qualified than whites or men, as the case may be, appointed to managerial positions. It is not uncommon when appointments of ethnic minorities or women to managerial positions first take place to appoint only those who are seen as utterly safe appointments so that the rest of the workforce feels reassured.[40]

Discriminatory training generally
4.33 In defined conditions of underrepresentation of particular groups, both the Sex Discrimination Act and the Race Relations Act permit discriminatory training to help fit people for particular work. Apart from certain specified training bodies other organisations once needed designating as training bodies before being permitted to offer such training. The designation requirement however was removed in the field of sex by virtue of the Sex Discrimination Act 1986 and for race by the Employment Act 1989. This relaxation, however, was accompanied by a qualification that it does not legalise anything prohibited by section 6 of the Sex Discrimination Act 1975 or section 4 of the Race Relations Act 1976. Thus it makes clear that any training actually regarded as employment by the Acts *e.g.* apprenticeship, is excluded.

Where it is possible to offer discriminatory training it is also

---

[40] s.8 of the Employment Act 1989 allows for the making of orders to exempt discrimination in favour of lone parents in connection with training. S.I. 1989 No. 2140 & S.I. 1991 No. 2813 so provide.

possible to provide encouragement to take advantage of opportunities to do particular work.

4.34 The conditions of underrepresentation are, in essence, that in the preceding twelve months either no women/men/members of a particular racial group (or comparatively few) were doing that work in Great Britain, or an area of Great Britain.

These "chill and skill" provisions have one thing in common: they are voluntary in nature. There is no power to require their implementation, even in cases where discrimination has been proved. The CRE has recommended that the possibility of ordering such training to take place should be amongst the remedies available to industrial tribunals.

Access to benefits, facilities and services **4.35** The Race Relations Act, s.4(2)(*b*) encompasses discrimination in the provision of benefits, facilities or services, whether contractual or non-contractual, whereas under the Sex Discrimination Act all contractual matters are brought within the purview of the Equal Pay Act. Thus the Sex Discrimination Act, s.6(6) excepts all money payments from the category of benefits in section 6(2)(*a*). Correspondingly the Race Relations Act, s.4(2)(*a*) covers discrimination in the terms of employment, again a topic which falls within the Equal Pay Act.

Benefits, facilities or services also provided to the public **4.36** Those benefits, facilities and services provided by an employer to the public which are also supplied to employees are excluded from these provisions by the Sex Discrimination Act, s.6(7) and the Race Relations Act, s.4(4), unless the benefits, facilities or services differ in some material respect from those supplied to employees, or their supply is regulated by the employee's contract of employment or the benefits, facilities or services relate to training.

Dismissal **4.37** Discriminatory dismissals are unlawful under the Sex Discrimination Act, s.6(2)(*b*) and the Race Relations Act, s.4(2)(*c*). These provisions overlap with those of the Employment Protection (Consolidation) Act 1978 on unfair dismissal, although the differences in qualifying service and in levels of compensation would often suggest an application be made under both statutes. Thus, whilst the level of compensation for unfair dismissal is generally higher because it includes the basic award related to length of service, it does not take into account injury to feelings.

4.38 The EP(C)A 1978 requires a two year qualifying service of not less than 16 hours a week, or 8 hours a week after five years, whilst the SDA and RRA contain no such

limitations. It can be argued that such a service requirement
is indirectly discriminatory against women and indeed the
ECJ so found in respect of broadly similar service
requirements under German social security law in the the
case of *Rinner Kuhn* v. *F.W. Spezial-Gebaudereinigung.*[41] The
decision in Rinner-Kuhn led the EOC to mount a series of
judicial review applications in respect of such limitations; the
first of which to be reported, *R* v. *Secretary of State for
Employment ex p. the E.O.C.*[42], found that such limitations
to women's employment protection rights were justified by
the need to protect and enhance women's employment
opportunities. For further discussion of the concept of
justification see chapter 2.

4.39   Dismissal of a woman on grounds that she marries[43]
or on grounds of her marital status is contrary to the SDA.
In *Coleman* v. *Skyrail Oceanic Ltd*,[44] the employer dismissed
a female employee when she married a man who worked for
a rival travel firm. The two employers colluded and decided
to dismiss the woman in preference to the man because he
was assumed to be the breadwinner, an assumption held by
the majority of the Court of Appeal to be based on sex.

4.40   To fall within the scope of the Acts, a dismissal has to
take place on one of the prohibited grounds. In *Berrisford* v.
Woodard Schools (Midland Division) Ltd,[45] an unmarried
matron of a girls' boarding school run by a Church of
England foundation was dismissed, not, as the Industrial
Tribunal found, by reason of her pregnancy, but because
her pregnancy was a manifestation of extra-marital sex. The
Tribunal found that a male teacher, who had had a woman
living with him who had a child, had been instructed to
regularise the position and that another male teacher who
formed a liaison with the mother of a pupil was given the
choice of leaving the school or terminating the relationship.
On this basis, the EAT upheld the Tribunal decision and
dismissed the argument that because a man cannot become
pregnant there must necessarily be discrimination in any
dismissal connected with pregnancy. Since it was said to be
the example given to pupils which was objectionable, in the
view of the EAT, there was evidence upon which the
Tribunal could conclude that a man so situated would also
have been dismissed if there were comparable visible signs of
extra-marital sexual activity. In such cases it is the drawing
of the framework of comparison which tends to frame the
conclusions.[46]

---

[41] [1989] I.R.L.R. 493.
[42] [1991] I.R.L.R. 493.
[43] *North East Midlands Co-operative Society* v. *Allen* [1977] I.R.L.R. 212.
[44] [1981] I.R.L.R. 398.
[45] [1991] I.R.L.R. 247.
[46] See chap. 2 for a discussion of pregnancy cases and the drawing of the
    framework of comparison.

Pregnancy issues *per se* are considered in chapter 2.

Selections for redundancy

4.41 Where an employer is engaged upon some form of reorganisation in which jobs are re-allocated and some employees may be made redundant, discrimination may occur in the process. If the discrimination occurs in omitting to offer continued employment, the Sex Discrimination Act, s.6(1)(*c*) or the Race Relations Act s.4(1)(*c*) come into effect. In *Timex Corporation* v. *Hodgson*,[47] the employer was engaged in a redundancy exercise and wished to reduce the total of three supervisors to only one. The employers chose to retain the one female supervisor, because they felt that only a woman supervisor would in certain respects be able to look after the women working in the factory, although the two men dismissed had longer service. If the discrimination lay in omitting to offer employment under section 6(1)(*c*), that subsection falls within the ambit of the genuine occupational qualifications set out in section 7, whereas discriminatory dismissals under section 6(2)(*b*) do not. The EAT held that[48]:

> "There are two stages inherent in any selection for redundancy where the job content of the remaining jobs is to be altered: first, the selection of the employees to carry out the revised job and secondly, the dismissal of those not selected to do the revised job. . . In our view the correct analysis is that the employers discriminate against the man by selecting the woman to do the revised job, not in dismissing the man who is not selected for the revised job. The discrimination lies therefore either in." deliberately omitting to offer" the man employment in the revised job. Once the selection for the revised job has been made, the dismissal of those selected necessarily follows. But the dismissal of those not selected is not itself discriminatory: any employee, whether male or female, who has not been selected for the revised job will be dismissed because there is no job for him or her to do."

4.42 Redundancy exercises carried out utilising last-in-first-out (LIFO) may well be indirectly discriminatory, as also may the equally common practice of dismissing part-timers first. In *Clarke and Powell* v. *Eley (IMI Kynoch) Ltd*,[49], part-timers were dismissed before full-timers, who were then selected for dismissal according to a LIFO criterion, in the course of a redundancy exercise. The EAT held that whilst selection of part-timers first was grossly discriminatory in its effects, selection according to a LIFO criterion had a lesser discriminatory effect which might be more easily capable of justification. The use of LIFO criteria were similarly considered to be capable of being contrary to the SDA or RRA in individual cases,

---

[47] [1982] I.C.R. 63, EAT.
[48] *Per* Browne-Wilkinson J. at p. 67.
[49] [1982] I.R.L.R. 482, EAT, [1982] I.R.L.R. 131, IT.

according to the High Court in *R* v. *London Borough of Hammersmith ex.p. NALGO.*[50]

Other detriments   **4.43**   Whether or not a person has suffered a detriment is a question of fact, although it is possible that the detriment could be of such an insubstantial nature as to fall within the *de minimis* rule, as in *Peake* v. *Automotive Products Ltd*[51] (where women were allowed out five minutes before finishing time to facilitate their access to the buses).

4.44   The ECJ held in *Arbeiterwohlfarht der Stadt Berlin* v. *Botel*[52] that the refusal of payment to workers working part-time for attendance at that part of a trade union training course held outside their normal working hours was discriminatory contrary to Article 119. In the British context, such a discriminatory refusal could constitute a detriment contrary to SDA 1975, s.6(2)(*b*), as according to the EAT in *Hairsine* v. *Kingston upon Hull City Council.*[53] British workers only enjoy a right to paid time off under EP(C)A 1978 in respect of the hours during which they would normally be at work. Furthermore, the right to paid time off is qualified by the requirement to have two years service of 16 hours or more per week. These qualifications, essentially similar to those found to be justified by the majority in the Court of Appeal in *R* v. *Secretary of State ex.p. the EOC* because of their potential effect on the employment chances of part-timers, may not necessarily be so regarded in this context.[54]

Sexual   **4.45**   Neither sexual nor racial harassment are terms defined
harassment   in the domestic Statutes. However, the European Commission Recommendation on The Protection of the Dignity of Men and Women at Work[55] provides that conduct of a sexual nature, or other conduct based on sex affecting the dignity of women and men at work is unacceptable if it is:

1. unwanted, unreasonable and offensive to the recipient;
2. used as a basis for employment decisions, such as promotion, or is
3. such as to create an intimidating, hostile or humiliating work environment for the recipient.

4.46   The Commission Recommendation asserts that such conduct may be contrary to the principle of equal treatment

---

[50] [1991] I.R.L.R. 249 See chap. 9 for a discussion of the judicial review aspects of this case.
[51] [1978] 233 Q.B.
[52] Case 360/90, [1992] I.R.L.R. 423.
[53] [1992] I.R.L.R. 211, EAT.
[54] The Court of Appeal was sharply divided on the question of justification but the case was decided on other grounds. See para. 2.63.
[55] [1992] O.J. C27/4.

contained in Directive 76/207, specifically Articles 3 (access to jobs etc), 4 (access to training) & 5 (working conditions, including the conditions governing dismissal). The Recommendation is accompanied by a Code of Practice on measures to combat sexual harassment, which was issued following resolutions of the Council of Ministers[56] and the European Parliament[57] on the protection of the dignity of men and women at work and forms part of the Commission's Third Action Programme on Equal Opportunities for Men and Women.

4.47 In *Grimaldi* v. *Fonds des Maladies Professionelles*,[58] the ECJ held that whilst Article 189(5) provides that recommendations.have no binding force and do not in themselves confer rights on individuals

> "(N)ational courts are bound to take Recommendations into consideration in order to decide disputes submitted to them, in particular where they clarify the interpretation of national provisions adopted in order to implement them or where they are designed to supplement Community measures."

Whilst the Sex Discrimination Act was passed 15 years before the Code was adopted, as Docksey and Fitzpatrick[59] note, the U.K. has agreed that the Sex Discrimination Act represents its obligations under Directive 76/207. It is therefore arguable that the Recommendation and its associated Code of Practice can be prayed in aid as an interpretative device when considering sexual harassment claims brought under the Sex Discrimination Act.

The nature of sexual harassment

4.48 Although British law does not expressly proscribe sexual harassment, the E.C. Code of Conduct defines it as

> "unwanted conduct of a sexual nature, or other conduct based on sex affecting the dignity of men and women at work. This can include unwelcome physical, verbal or non-verbal conduct."

In the Scottish case of *Strathclyde Regional Council* v. *Porcelli*[60] the Lord President of the Court of Session expressed the view that sexual harassment is a "particularly degrading and unacceptable form of treatment which it must be taken to be the intention of Parliament to restrain." Sexual harassment has been considered to be "legal

---

[56] [1990] O.J. C157. The Resolution calls upon the Member States and the institutions and organs of the European Communities to develop positive measures designed to create a climate at work in which women and men respect each others human integrity.

[57] [1991] O.J. C305.

[58] [1990] I.R.L.R. 400.

[59] C.Docksey and B.Fitzpatrick, "The duty of national courts to interpret provisions of national law in accordance with Community law" I.L.J., 20, 2, pp. 113-120.

[60] [1986] I.R.L.R .134 at p. 137.

shorthand for activity which is easily recognised as subjecting her to any other detriment"[61] under the Sex Discrimination Act 1975, s.6(2)(b). What then are the hallmarks of this easily recognisable activity and what remedies does the Act place in the hands of those who feel that they have suffered some form of sexual harassment?

4.49   It was held in the racial harassment case of *De Souza* v. *Automobile Association*[62] that: "before an employee can be said to have been subjected to some "other detriment" that the court or Tribunal must find that by reason of the act or acts complained of a reasonable worker would or might take the view that he had thereby been disadvantaged in the circumstances in which he had thereafter to work."[63]

4.50   The standard of behaviour which might constitute racial or sexual harassment is therefore to be viewed from the point of view of the victim, rather than the alleged perpetrator. What might be acceptable behaviour to one person, may not be to another. Standards will vary as to what constitutes sexual harassment. In *Wileman* v. *Milinec Engineering Ltd.*[64] a director's secretary complained that she had been the victim of sexual harassment by her boss over a period of four and a half years. The complainant sought aggravated damages, and in support of the claim endeavoured to introduce evidence of the director's conduct towards other women, which was not admitted. In discussing the relevance of this evidence Popplewell J. stated that[65]:

> "If this gentleman made sexual remarks to a number of people, it has to be looked at in the context of each person. All the people to whom they are made may regard them as wholly inoffensive; everyone else may regard them as offensive. Each individual then has the right, if the remarks are regarded as offensive, to treat them as an offence under the Sex Discrimination Act 1975."

4.51   Sexual harassment cases have been considered as constituting a species of direct discrimination under section 1(1)(a) *i.e.* as treating the woman less favourably on the grounds of her sex and more specifically in the employment context, as subjecting her to any other detriment under section 6(2)(b). The essential test is therefore whether the woman has been treated less favourably on grounds of her sex than a comparable man would have been treated and that she has thereby suffered a detriment. In order to

[61] *Wileman* v. *Minilec Engineering Ltd* [1988] I.R.L.R. 145.
[62] [1986] I.R.L.R. 103 *per* May L.J. at p. 107.
[63] Note the correspondence between this approach and the E.C. Resolution referred to above with its reference to conduct which creates an intimidating, hostile or humiliating work environment.
[64] [1988] I.R.L.R. 145.
[65] at p. 147.

constitute a detriment under section 6(2)(*b*), treatment need only be such that:

"the putative reasonable employee could justifiably complain about his or her working conditions or environment, whether or not these were so bad as to constitute dismissal or even if the employee is prepared to work on and put up with the situation."[66]

4.52 The expression "subjecting to any other detriment" does not mean anything more than "putting under a disadvantage."[67] An employee could be said to be suffering a detriment if she is disadvantaged in the circumstances in which she has to work. The question is whether the reasonable employee would feel she has been put at a disadvantage in her working life, rather than whether she has been subject to a detriment of some type because she refused to comply with demands which had been made upon her. The EOC Code of Practice provides that:

"all reasonably practical steps should be taken to ensure that a standard of conduct or behaviour is observed which prevents members of either sex from being intimidated, harassed or otherwise subject to unfavourable treatment on the grounds of their sex."[68]

4.53 What if the employer argues that in view of the expressed attitude of the employee towards sexual matters, the conduct complained of cannot be to her detriment? In *Wileman* v. *Minilec Engineering Ltd*[69] the EAT held that there were grounds for the Industrial Tribunal to take into account the fact that the complainant often wore scanty and provocative clothing at work in assessing whether the harassment to which she was subjected constituted a detriment. In the view of the EAT, an Industrial Tribunal is entitled to look at the circumstances in which remarks are made which are said to constitute a detriment. In *Wileman* the extent of any such detriment was also held to be relevant in assessing injury to feelings.

4.54 For a claim to succeed under section 1(1)(*a*) an employee has to have been treated less favourably on grounds of her sex. Such action must be directed towards the employee or intended to affect her in some way. In the

---

[66] *Per* May L.J. in *De Souza* v. *Automobile Association (supra,* p. 87 at p. 107. The American EEOC guide-lines on sexual harassment likewise enjoin sexual harassment not only when compliance with unwelcome requests is made a condition of employment, or the employee has been disciplined or dismissed for refusing to comply with persistent and unwanted sexual overtures, but also where the "conduct has the effect of unreasonably interfering with an individual's work performance or creating an intimidating, hostile or offensive working environment."

[67] *Ministry of Defence* v. *Jeremiah* [1980] I.C.R. 13, C.A.

[68] para. 32(*e*).

[69] [1988] I.R.L.R. 144.

De Souza[70] case, a manager made a racially insulting remark
to a fellow manager in respect of one of the office staff, who
did not herself hear the remark, nor from the evidence did it
appear that she was intended to do so. May L.J. held that
he did not think she could:

> "properly be said to have been treated less favourably by
> whomsoever used the word, unless he intended her to
> overhear the conversation in which it was used, or knew
> or ought reasonably to have anticipated that the person he
> was talking to would pass the insult on or that the
> appellant would hear of it in some other way."[71]

Thus the conduct in question must be directed towards the
complainant or it must be considered to be reasonably likely
to have an effect on the sensibilities of the person in
question. For example, a display of "pin ups" might not be
directed towards any other person, but if it is reasonably
likely that they would be seen by someone who might
consider that they were offensive, such a display could
constitute less favourable treatment of that person.

4.55 In *Strathclyde Regional Council* v. *Porcelli*,[72] two
laboratory male technicians had pursued a course of
harassment towards a female colleague whom they disliked
and whom they hoped would thereby apply for a transfer or
leave. This campaign included sexual innuendoes, suggestive
remarks and intimidating conduct. The question arose as to
whether such treatment was on the grounds of the
respondent's sex. Emslie L.J. held that section 1(1)(*a*) is
concerned with "treatment" and not with the motive or
objective of the person responsible for that treatment. There
need not be a sex related purpose in the mind of a person
who indulges in unwanted and objectionable sexual overtures
to a woman or exposes her to offensive sexual jokes. It is
enough if the treatment occurs because she is a woman. In
that case Grieve L.J. spoke of the weapons used against the
complainer:[73]

> "if any could be identified as what I called 'a sexual
> sword', and it was clear that the wound it inflicted was
> more than a mere scratch, the conclusion must be that the
> sword had been unsheathed and used because the victim
> was a woman."

4.56 The treatment has, however, to occur on the grounds
of the complainant's sex. In *Porcelli*, it was argued on behalf

---

[70] [1977] I.R.L.R. 365, C.A. The de minimis round of the decision in
Peake was held to be the only valid ground for that decision in *Ministry
of Defence* v. *Jeremiah* [1980] I.C.R. 13, C.A. a case in which the rule
that only men had to work in dirty conditions was held to constitute a
detriment.
[71] [1986] I.R.L.R. 134 at p. 137.
[72] [1986] I.R.L.R. 134.
[73] at p. 139.

of the employer that the treatment was not on the grounds of the sex of the complainant, because an equally disliked man would have received perhaps different but no less objectionable treatment. The Court of Session held, however, that where the treatment includes a significant sexual element to which a man would not be vulnerable, it is based upon the sex of the woman. It is no answer to the question posed by section 1(1)(a) that a man would have received different but equally unpleasant treatment. In *Balgobin* v. *London Borough of Tower Hamlets*,[74] the employer had held an investigation into alleged sexual harassment by a cook in a hostel run by the Council. The investigation was inconclusive and the alleged perpetrator and victims of the sexual harassment returned to work together. The victims complained that this action itself constituted a separate head of adverse treatment on ground of their sex, but this argument was rejected by the EAT. The employer would have taken the same action on the completion of an inconclusive disciplinary inquiry into, say, unwelcome homosexual advances by one man towards another. The treatment of, or requiring the employees to work together again was not on grounds of their sex; it was because they were employees, even if the consequence of the treatment was an intolerable situation.

4.57 An important question which arises in racial and sexual harassment cases is whether the employer is liable for the actions of employees, when these are not directly connected with the purposes for which they are employed. In cases where it is doubtful whether the alleged discriminator is acting in the course of his employment and therefore whether the employer is liable, it may be advisable to proceed against both the alleged discriminator personally, as well as the employer. This issue is discussed in chapter 2.

Specific problems of evidence in harassment cases

4.58 One of the problems facing both industrial tribunals, and indeed internal disciplinary hearings, is the extent to which evidence may be admitted of other consensual sexual activity by the victim, as tending to show how far advances or sexual banter were likely to have been acceptable at the time. The EAT in *Wileman* v. *Milinec Engineering* held that "a person may be happy to accept the remarks of A or B in a sexual context, and wholly upset by similar remarks made by C", nor was it considered relevant or of probative value that the complainant subsequently posed for a newspaper in a flimsy costume. The EAT in the earlier case of *Snowball* v. *Gardner Merchant*[75] did, however, admit evidence about the general sexual content of the complainant's conversation as being relevant to whether or not she had suffered detriment. The argument that this was a collateral matter which went

[74] [1987] I.R.L.R. 401.
[75] [1987] I.R.L.R. 397.

only to credit and on which answers in cross examination are final, was rejected. This decision could be subject to the criticism that, if followed, it would have the effect of deterring complainants, who might fear that their entire sexual life could be subject to examination.

4.59   The previous or related conduct of the perpetrator can also be relevant. The IT in *Groundrill* v. *Townhill and Pinefleet Ltd*[76] found that the previous conduct of the perpetrator in respect of two other former women employees was relevant and admissible. Evidence of similar conduct in a new job to which the perpetrator was transferred was admitted as fresh and previously unavailable evidence in a review of the decision in *Larpiniere* v. *Young*,[77] the matter in this case seen as going to credit.

4.60   The EAT in *Bracebridge Engineering* v. *Darby*[78] held that a failure to investigate adequately complaints of sexual harassment could undermine the relationship of mutual trust and confidence between employer and employee. It is clearly important for employers to make it clear that complaints of harassment, whether sexual or racial, fall within the scope of disciplinary proceedings, although it is clearly a sensitive matter for both the victim and the alleged perpetrator as to when the employer should turn from a counselling type of response to formal disciplinary proceedings.[79]

Provisions of the E.C. Code

4.61   The E.C. Code of Practice makes several recommendations to employers to facilitate a climate of opinion at work which inhibits sexual harassment, including:

(a) the issuing of a policy statement which makes clear that such behaviour will not be permitted or condoned and that employees have a right to complain about it,
(b) ensuring that the contents of the policy are communicated to all employees,
(c) promoting the policy in such a way that local management is responsive and supportive to such complaints, and
(d) providing both "awareness" training and more specific training for those responsible for operating the complaints procedure.

4.62   The Code advocates that a clear and precise procedure for dealing with complaints of harassment will have the following features:

---

[76] Case No. 21269/90.
[77] Case No. 191/90.
[78] [1990] I.R.L.R. 3.
[79] See also the IT case of *Mullan* v. *Department of Employment* [1991] in which a small female employee was held upside down by a male colleague who simulated oral sex with her, but whose case was reluctantly and only partially investigated by the DE. Note that under the TURER Act 1993 sections 38 and 39 IT's and the EAT may impose reporting restrictions to protect the identity of individuals involved in cases of sexual misconduct.

(a) A first stage, in which an effort is made to resolve the problem informally.
(b) A "sympathetic friend" or "confidential counsellor" designated as a first port of call for victims of alleged harassment.
(c) A special procedure may be necessary where the normal grievance procedure is not suitable, either because of problems of confidentiality or where, perhaps, the employee's line manager is the alleged perpetrator.
(d) The investigation should be independent and objective, with respect for the rights of both the complainant and the alleged perpetrator to be properly heard and represented by a friend , colleague or trade union representative.
(e) The range of disciplinary penalties should be clearly specified in advance and where consideration is given to transferring one of the parties, wherever practicable, the complainant should be allowed to choose to stay where they are or to opt for a transfer.

Liability of employers for the actions of their employees

4.63 Whilst employers are liable for the actions of employees in respect of discriminatory acts undertaken within the scope of their employment, the employer is afforded a defence under SDA, s.41(3) (or RRA, s.32(3)) if he can "prove that he took such steps as were reasonably practicable to prevent the employee from doing that act, or from doing in his employment acts of that description". In cases of sexual harassment, it is clear that an employer is much more likely to be successful in establishing a defence under section 41(3) if there is a suitable policy in place, which conforms to the main points of the Code. The general issue of the liability of employers for the discriminatory actions of their employees is discussed in chapter 2.

Racial harassment

4.64 The issues which arise in cases of racial harassment are essentially similar to those which occur in relation to sexual harassment, with the proviso that complaints of racial harassment are likely to centre on the creation of a hostile, threatening or demeaning work environment. For example, in *British Leyland Cars Ltd.* v. *Brown*[80], the management feared that a black employee who had been arrested for theft in the plant and granted bail would try to re-enter the premises, perhaps under a false name. The management therefore issued instructions to the security guards to stop every black person and institute a thorough identity check; this instruction resulted in a certain amount of newspaper publicity. A group of black employees sought to establish that they had suffered a detriment under section 4(2)(d), albeit that the CRE also commenced proceedings under s.30 in connection with the issuing of such instructions. On a preliminary point, it was held by the EAT that the

---

[80] [1983] I.R.L.R. 193, EAT.

circulation of the instructions and the setting up of a regime under which black employees would have to undergo special checks was capable of constituting a detriment under section 4(2)(d) of the Race Relations Act, even if no employees had, by the time of the complaint, presented themselves for admission at the gate. The actual detriment suffered was a question of fact for the tribunal, which depended on the knowledge which each employee had of the instructions, his own intentions etc.

4.65   Stereotyped views may result in stereotyped insults and the CRE Code of Practice warns against ignoring, or treating lightly, grievances from members of particular racial groups on the assumption that they are over-sensitive about discrimination. The widespread and unchecked use of racial banter may result in the creation of a hostile, threatening, or more particularly, demeaning work environment leading to complaints of discrimination.[81]. The test as to whether the actions complained of were on racial grounds is answered by analogy with the sex discrimination cases, by considering whether a person not of that racial group would have been vulnerable to the action in question. Whilst the E.C. Code of Practice has no legal status in cases of racial harassment, it can have an indirect impact in so far as it is bound to influence the standard which an employer must reach to be seen as "taking such steps as were reasonably practicable" under section 32(3) to prevent acts of racial discrimination.

Exclusions from SDA

4.66   There are a small number of occupational groups excluded from the provisions of the Sex Discrimination Act, namely ministers of religion, so as to comply with the doctrines of the religion or avoid offending the religious susceptibilities of a significant number of its followers,[82] and prison officers in relation to height requirements.[83]

---

[81] In the IT case (Case No. 08807/88) of *Surinder Chima Singh* v. *The Chief Constable of Nottinghamshire Constabulary* a detective constable of West Indian origins, Glen Williams, eloquently expressed the reality of what such racial banter can entail.

"Sir there are certain ways that as a black person you have to deal with it. The CID tends to be a very close working group.

Now imagine the situation where a black man in a predominantly white office who for quite a while everyone saw as 'Good old Glen, he hasn't got a chip on his shoulder, he's one of the lads, I don't see him as a black man', that sort of attitude. 'He is just Glen.' It wasn't until the point where I started saying, 'I don't want to listen to these remarks anymore, they are offensive. I don't want to hear them', that the atmosphere changed.

The reality is that anybody who refers to a black man as a 'nigger' 'coon' or 'spook', whether it be in jest or not, if that person went up to some ordinary black guy in the street and said that to his face, he would be looking at a fist in the mouth, never mind a grin or a smile or an acceptance.

Regardless of whichever way I might have dealt with those particular comments being made, I guaranteed my survival within the CID. Unfortunately for me it also meant losing my dignity and I reached a point where I could not take that any more."

[82] SDA, s.19.

[83] SDA, s.18.

Exclusions in relation to death and retirement under SDA

4.67 Whilst the Race Relations Act makes no provision for any exclusion of the provisions of the Act in relation to death or retirement, the Sex Discrimination Act originally excluded all such provisions.[84] This blanket exclusion of provisions in relation to death and retirement was held to be contrary to the Equal Treatment Directive Article 5(1) in *Marshall* v. *Southampton and South West Hants Area Health Authority.*[85]

In the *Marshall* case, the policy of the employer was that "normal retirement age will be the age at which social security pensions become payable" *i.e.* age 60 for women and 65 for men. Miss Marshall contended that the application of this policy constituted less favourable treatment under section 1(1)(*a*) of the Sex Discrimination Act, but her case was dismissed in the Industrial Tribunal and in the EAT because it was held to fall within the exception then provided by the Sex Discrimination Act, s.6(4), as a provision made in relation to death or retirement. Miss Marshall had made an alternative claim that her compulsory retirement at the age of 62 was contrary to Article 5(1) of the Equal Treatment Directive.[86] This claim had been upheld in the Industrial Tribunal, but rejected in the EAT on the grounds that the Directive could not be relied on before a United Kingdom court or tribunal. The case was referred to the ECJ which distinguished between the concept of retirement and pension ages and went on to hold that a compulsory retirement age fell within the concept of dismissal under Article 5(1) of the Directive, even if it was also the occasion of the granting of a pension. It was argued that the determination of pension ages for the purpose of social security was a matter which States could reserve to themselves under the EEC Social Security Directive 79/7, but the ECJ distinguished between the determination of pensionable age for the purpose of social security and the imposition of a retirement age within a contract of employment, holding the latter to fall within the Equal Treatment Directive. Whilst in *Burton* v. *British Railways Board (No. 2)*[87] the ECJ had held that the age of access to a voluntary redundancy scheme could be linked to State pension ages without violation of Article 5(1), the situation in *Burton* could be distinguished from that in the *Marshall* case, in that whilst the one had concerned access to voluntary early retirement, the other was concerned with the age of compulsory retirement.

4.68 Since a Directive is only of direct effect against an organ of the state, which a Health Authority was held to be, the rights available to public and private sector employees

---

[84] SDA 1975, s.6(4).
[85] [1986] I.R.L.R. 40, ECJ
[86] Dir. 76/207.
[87] [1982] I.R.L.R. 116. See *Roberts* v. *Cleveland Area Health Authority* (1979) I.R.L.R. 244, C.A.

differed.[88] The result was the decision to enact the Sex
Discrimination Act 1986, which narrowed the exclusion
contained in the Sex Discrimination Act 1975, s.6(4). Whilst
it is lawful to discriminate in provisions made with regard to
death, it is unlawful for a person to discriminate against a
woman in relation to retirement with regard to access to
opportunities for promotion, transfer or training, or by
subjecting her to any detriment, demotion or dismissal.[89]

4.69 It is interesting to note that the words "any other
benefits, facilities or services, or by omitting to afford her
access to them" and "any other detriment" are omitted from
the areas in which discrimination in relation to retirement is
unlawful. One of the purposes of these omissions was to
permit the continued payment of differential pension
benefits, although following the Social Security Act 1975,
ss.53-56, access to pension scheme membership has had to
be equalised since 1978. Differential pension ages under the
State social security system are permitted under the EEC
Social Security Directive 79/7, but following the ECJ case of
Barber v. *Guardian Royal Exchange Assurance*[90], pension
benefits are now seen as "pay" under Article 119[91]. In
holding that differential pension ages did not constitute a
question of access to pensions, as had been held in the
Burton case, but one of pay under Article 119, the ECJ was
reaching a conclusion contrary to the exclusionary provisions
of section 6(1A)(*b*) of the Equal Pay Act, which are in
similar terms to section 6(4) of the 1975 Act. The
amendments made by the Sex Discrimination Act 1986 to
the the Equal Pay Act 1970 and the Sex Discrimination Act
1975, in the light of the *Marshall* case, do not therefore take
account of the post *Barber* status of pensions as pay under
Article 119. Pensions matters are discussed in chapter 7 on
Equal Pay.

4.70 The saving in relation to provisions made in relation
to death is explicable in that a survivor's benefit had been
held to be a form of occupational social security in
Newstead, and under the Occupational Social Security
Directive 86/378 E.C. Article 9(b) there is no obligation to
equalise such benefits until Member States are required by
directive to make such provision in their statutory social
schemes. The Advocate General in Ten Oever concluded
that a widower's pension was pay under Article 119, as it
was paid "in respect of the employment" of the deceased
spouse, a view likely to be sustained by the ECJ.

4.71 An example of the effects of the operation of a

---

[88] See chap. 1.
[89] SDA 1975, s.6(4) as amended by SDA 1986, s.2(1).
[90] [1990] I.R.L.R. 258.
[91] But only benefits accrued by virtue of service after May 1990, according
to the Protocol on Art. 119 appended to the Treaty on European Union
concluded at Maastricht.

common retirement age is given by *Bullock* v. *Alison Ottley School*,[92] in which the school had provided for a common retirement age of 60 for teaching, administrative and domestic staff, but a retirement age of 65 for the gardening and grounds staff, all of whom were men. The EAT held that such a division of the staff into groups was contrary to the "but for" test enunciated by the majority of the House of Lords in *James* v. *Eastleigh Borough Council*,[93] but it is not obvious as to why this should be so as, had the complainant been a man, it is not clear that her situation would have been any different. It is likely, though not decided by the EAT, that the requirement to be a groundsman in order to stay on to age 65 was indirectly discriminatory, as all the grounds and maintenance staff were men and all but two of the teaching, administrative and domestic staff were women. Thus, it can be argued that the *Bullock* case does not rule out differential retirement ages for different groups of staff, though these may, in certain circumstances, be indirectly discriminatory, a view subsequently espoused by the Court of Appeal,[94] which held that the later retirement age for outside staff was objectively justified by the genuine need to recruit and retain this group of staff.

Genuine occupational qualifications

4.72 Both the Race Relations Act and the Sex Discrimination Act provide for a number of "genuine occupational qualifications", under which an otherwise discriminatory act would not be unlawful.

4.73 The Race Relations Act, s.5 provides that where the genuine occupational qualifications apply, section 4(1)(*a*) (selection arrangements) or section 4(1)(*c*) (refusal or omission to offer employment) are excluded, as are the provisions on promotion, transfer and training in section 4(2)(*b*). The exclusions provided for are where, for reasons of authenticity, dramatic performances require a person of a particular racial group,[95] as also for artistic or photographic modelling,[96] employment in an ethnic restaurant,[97] and where the holder of the job will be providing personal services to members of a racial group promoting their welfare, and those services can most effectively be provided by a person of that racial group.[98] In *Tottenham Green Under Fives' Centre* v. *Marshall*,[99] Mr Justice Wood in the the EAT held that where an employer is seeking to rely on the personal services genuine occupational qualification, then:

---

[92] [1991] I.R.L.R. 324. For a discussion of the common basis of comparison aspects of this see chap. 2.
[93] [1990] I.R.L.R. 288, H.L.
[94] [1992] I.R.L.R. 564, C.A.
[95] RRA, s.5(2)(*a*).
[96] RRA, s.5(2)(*b*).
[97] RRA, s.5(2)(*c*).
[98] RRA, s.5(2)(*d*).
[99] [1989] I.R.L.R. 147.

"(a) The particular racial group will need to be clearly and, if necessary, narrowly defined because it will have to be the holder of the post and also that of the recipient of the personal services.

(b) The holder of the post must be directly involved in the provision of the services – to direct others so to do is insufficient as the service must be personal. It does not seem to us that it need necessarily be on a one-to-one basis.

(c) If the post holder provides several personal services to the recipient, then provided that one of those genuinely falls within the subsection, the defence is established.

(d) "Promoting their welfare" is a very wide expression. The facts of each case are likely to vary emormously and different considerations will apply. It would be undesirable to seek to narrow the width of those words.

(e) "Those services can most effectively be provided by a person of that racial group" – the words are not "must be provided" or "can only be provided". The Act assumes that the personal services could be provided by others, but can they be "most effectively provided". Would they be less effective if provided by others?"

4.74 The *Tottenham Green* case concerned the provision of nursery services to Afro-Caribbean children within the context of an explicitly multi-cultural nursery. When an Afro-Caribbean helper left, the Committee decided to advertise for another Afro-Caribbean worker, with a view to maintaining the cultural background link for Afro-Caribbean children, dealing with parents, reading and talking in dialect where necessary and generally looking to the skin care and general health of the Afro-Caribbean children. The Industrial Tribunal found that it was only the dialect requirement which could be most effectively provided by an Afro-Caribbean worker and decided that as that was only a marginal requirement – a desirable extra – found that the requirements of section 5(2)(d) were not satisfied. The case was remitted from the EAT to the same Tribunal after the above guidance was given but the decision remained the same. On a second appeal,[1] Mr Justice Knox held that it is not open to an industrial tribunal to disregard a duty in determining whether a genuine occupational qualification exception applies, unless the matter is *de minimis* or a sham duty invented for the purpose of qualifying for the exception. As neither was the case in this matter, the section 5(2)(d) exception necessarily applied.

4.75 In *London Borough of Lambeth* v. *CRE*,[2] over half of the Borough's tenants were of Asian or Afro-Caribbean origins. When vacancies arose for a head of housing benefit

---

[1] *Tottenham Green Under-Fives Centre* v. *Marshall (No. 2)* [1991] I.R.L.R. 162.
[2] [1989] I.R.L.R. 379, EAT; [1990] I.R.L.R. 231, C.A.

and a group manager within the housing department, it was decided to advertise the posts confining applications to Asian or Afro-Caribbean applicants and relying on section 5(2)(d). The CRE challenged the discriminatory advertisement under section 29, the Borough relying on the personal services exception. The decision of the EAT that these appointments fell outside the terms of section 5(2)(d) was upheld by the Court of Appeal on the ground that these were managerial appointments, whilst the section appears to contemplate either face-to-face or direct personal physical contact between the giver and receiver of the services. The Court of Appeal rejected the argument on behalf of the Borough that the sub-section contemplated a form of positive action in the fields to which it relates. The Court did, however, conclude that as section 3(1) provides that a racial group can be defined by colour, it is open to an industrial tribunal to find that the provider and receiver of the personal services could be of the same colour, even though not of the same ethnic group.

4.76 The above exceptions apply even where the person will be performing such duties for only a part of his working time,[3] although they do not apply in relation to the filling of a vacancy if the employer already has sufficient employees of the racial group in question who are capable of carrying out the duties, and whom it would be reasonable to employ without undue inconvenience to the employer.[4]

4.77 The range of genuine occupational qualifications under the Sex Discrimination Act is much wider, although as with the Race Relations Act provisions, it is only the sections on selection, refusal to offer employment, transfer, training and promotion which are excluded. The qualifications embodied in section 7(2) are as follows:

"Being a man is a genuine occupational qualification for a job only where -

(a) The essential nature of the job calls for a man for reasons of physiology (excluding physical strength or stamina) or, in dramatic performances or other entertainment, for reasons of authenticity, so that the essential nature of the job would be materially different if carried out by a women; or

(b) the job needs to be held by a man to preserve decency or privacy because -

(i) it is likely to involve physical contact with men in circumstances where they might reasonably object to its being carried out by a woman, or

(ii) the holder of the job is likely to do his work in

---

[3] RRA, s.5(3).
[4] RRA, s.5(4)(a), (b), (c).

circumstances where men might reasonably object to the presence of a woman because they are in state of undress or using sanitary facilities; or

(ba) the job is likely to involve the holder of the job in doing his work, or living, in a private home and needs to be held by a man because objection might reasonably be taken to allowing a woman -
  (i) the degree of personal or physical contact with a person living in the home, or
  (ii) the knowledge of intimate details of such a person's life, which is likely, because of the nature or circumstances of the job or of the home, to be allowed to, or available to, the holder of the job, or[5]

(c) the nature or location of the establishment makes it impracticable for the holder of the job to live elsewhere than in premises provided by the employer, and -

  (i) the only such premises for persons holding that kind of job are lived in, or normally lived in, by men and not equipped with separate sleeping accommodation for women and sanitary facilities which could be used by women in privacy from men, and
  (ii) it is not reasonable to expect the employer either to equip those premises with such accommodation and facilities or to provide other accommodation for women; or

(d) the nature of the establishment, or the part of it in which the work is done, requires the job to be held by a man because -

  (i) it is, or is part of, a hospital, prison or other establishment for persons requiring special care, supervision, or attention, and
  (ii) those persons are all men (disregarding any woman whose presence is exceptional), and
  (iii) it is reasonable, having regard to the essential character of the establishment or that part, that the job should not be held by a woman; or

(e) the holder of the job provides individuals with personal services promoting their welfare or education, or similar personal services, and those services can most effectively be provided by a man, or
(f) (repealed by the Employment Act 1989)
(g) the job needs to be held by a man because it is likely to involve the performance of duties outside the United Kingdom in a country whose laws and customs are such that the duties could not, or could not effectively, be performed by a woman, or
(h) the job is one of two to be held by a married couple."

---

[5] s.7(e)(ba) was inserted by the SDA 1986.

4.78   The genuine occupational qualifications are not operative in relation to dismissals or other detriments or in relation to the offer of other benefits, facilities or services. Consequently in *Timex Ltd.* v. *Hodgson*,[6] the supervisory structure was reorganised in the overall context of a redundancy. A male supervisor was selected for redundancy, whilst a woman supervisor of less experience was retained in the context of a reorganisation in which her job was given additional duties of a welfare type for remaining female members of the workforce, which could more effectively be performed by a woman. The EAT held that any discrimination occurred not in the dismissal from the previous job but in the failure to be offered the revised job *i.e.* the discriminatory act was the omission to offer employment rather than the dismissal, which therefore fell within the scope of the genuine occupational qualifications in section 7(2)(*c*). The EAT also held that, provided the Industrial Tribunal was satisfied that the additional duties were genuine, it was not for the Tribunal to instruct the employer how to manage his business.

4.79   The provisions as to decency and privacy in the Sex Discrimination Act, s.7(2)(*b*)(ii) cover not only the state in which the actual duties of the job are performed, but also all matters reasonably incidental to the performance of the job. Thus in *Sisley* v. *Britannia Security Systems Ltd.*,[7] women working twelve hour shifts in a security control centre, who often spent up to five hours resting in a state of undress on the bed provided for that purpose by the employer, fell within the Sex Discrimination Act, s.7(2)(*b*)(ii) even though resting was not strictly part of their job duties. The genuine occupational qualifications relating to decency and privacy, along with the provisions in paragraphs (*a*), (*c*), (*d*), (*f*), or (*g*), are qualified by the Sex Discrimination Act, s.7(4), which provides that they do not apply to

> "the filling of a vacancy when the employer already has male employees-
>
> (a) who are capable of carrying out the duties falling within that paragraph, and
> (b) whom it would be reasonable to employ on those duties, and
> (c) whose numbers are sufficient to meet the employer's likely requirements in respect of those duties without undue inconvenience."[8]

4.80   A man applied for a post as sales assistant in a dress shop in *Etam plc* v. *Rowan*[9] and was refused. His claim that the refusal to employ him was discriminatory was defended

[6] [1981] I.R.L.R. 530, EAT and see para. 4.41.
[7] [1983] I.R.L.R. 404, EAT.
[8] RRA 1976, s.5(4) is in similar term in respect of the genuine occupational qualifications contained in that Act.
[9] [1989] I.R.L.R. 150, EAT.

by the employer on the grounds of decency and privacy, in that a sales assistant may be required to work in the fitting rooms and to measure women who are uncertain of their size. The EAT upheld a finding that the refusal to employ a man was discriminatory, in that it would have been possible to ensure that those aspects of the job could have been executed by one of the 16 existing female staff without great inconvenience.

Special cases

Contract workers   4.81   Under the Sex Discrimination Act, s.6(1) or the Race Relations Act, s.4(1) it is unlawful "for a person, in relation to employment by him at an establishment" to discriminate against a woman or any person on racial grounds. Whilst this section would make the employer of contract workers liable, it leaves untouched the principal for whom the work is being undertaken and who controls many of the terms on which it is done. Consequently, the Sex Discrimination Act, s.9 or the Race Relations Act, s.7 place analogous responsibilities on such principals to those placed upon employers generally, except for the functions of selection, engagement and dismissal which would remain with the person who is in strict law the employer. The section requires the existence of a contract for the supply of labour between the contractor and the principal,[10] although the individuals performing the work may be either employed or, following the expanded definition of employment in the Sex Discrimination Act, s.82(1) or the Race Relations Act, s.78(1), self-employed.

4.82   Although the contractual status of such workers is open to doubt,[11] they nonetheless fall within the scope of the Act, provided they are engaged under a contract to execute personally any work or labour.[12] Persons undertaking training under the ET scheme are not contract workers within the meaning of this section. In *Daley* v. *Allied Suppliers Ltd.*[13], the EAT held that YTS trainees were under a contract of training and not a contract to execute work.

---

[10] See *Rice* v. *Fon-A-Car* [1980] I.C.R. 133, EAT in which it was held that a taxi driver who responded to requests for taxi services passed on through a central agency was not a contract worker because there was no contract between the agency and the customer for the supply of taxi services.

[11] "Where A contracts with B to render services exclusively to C, the contract is not a contract for services (or of services) but a contract sui generis, a different type of contract from either of the familiar two." *Construction Industry Training Board* v. *Labour Force Ltd.* (1970) 3 All E.R. 220, *per* Cook J. at p. 225.

[12] See *Mirror Group Newspapers* v. *Gunning* [1986] I.C.R. 145, C.A. *Tanna* v. *Post Office* (1981) I.C.R. 374, EAT.

[13] (1983) I.C.R. 90, EAT.

Vocational training **4.83** Section 13 of the R.R.A. and Section 14 of the SDA, as amended by the Employment Act 1989, provides that it is unlawful to discriminate on grounds of gender, marital status or race in the terms on which training to help fit a person for employment is offered, or by refusing or deliberately omitting to offer training, terminating training or subjecting a trainee to any other detriment.[14] These provisions are subject to the proviso in sub-section 2 of the respective sections that they do not apply to discrimination rendered unlawful by RRA, s.4(1) or (2) or s.6(1) or (2) of the SDA, or to provisions which would be rendered unlawful by any of those provisions but for the operation of other provisions of the Acts, *i.e.* sections 47 and 48 of RRA and sections 37 and 38 of SDA allowing special encouragement and training in conditions of under-representation. These sections are therefore without prejudice to the operation of discriminatory training undertaken to remedy under representation of women or of minority employees.

Partnerships **4.84** Whereas under the Race Relations Act, s.10 only partnerships of six or more partners are brought within the Act in relation to the appointment of partners, following the enforcement proceedings brought by the European Commission against the United Kingdom,[15] the Sex Discrimination Act 1986, s.2(2) amended the Sex Discrimination Act 1976, s.11 to include all partnerships, no matter what the number of partners involved.

4.85 These sections render it unlawful to discriminate in the arrangements made for determining who should be offered partnerships, the terms on which partnerships are offered, or refusing or deliberately omitting to offer a partnership.[16] In a case where a person is already a partner it is also unlawful to discriminate in the provision of access to benefits, facilities or services or in expelling a person from a partnership, or subjecting him or her to any other detriment.[17]

4.86 The Sex Discrimination Act adds the proviso that sections 11(1)(*b*) and (*d*) do not apply to provisions in relation to death and retirement except in so far as they apply to the terms on which a woman is offered a partnership, or to the expulsion of a woman from a partnership, in order to accommodate the effects of the Marshall case as implemented by the Sex Discrimination Act 1986.

---

[14] The Training and Enterprise Councils (TECS) which are now responsible for providing such training are required to have equal opportunity policies as a condition of their funding.
[15] *Commission of the European Communities* v. *United Kingdom* (Case No. 61/81) [1982] E.C.R. 2601.
[16] RRA, s.10(1)(*a*)-(*c*), SDA, s.11(1)((*a*)-*c*).
[17] RRA, s.10(1)(*d*)(i),-(ii) SDA, s.11(1)(*d*)(i).-(ii)

Trade unions and employers' organisations

4.87　Trade unions and employers' associations are covered by the Race Relations Act, s.11 and the Sex Discrimination Act, s.12 which proscribe discrimination in the terms on which membership is offered, refused, or varied, or in the way in which access is provided to benefits, facilities and services or in subjecting the applicant or member to any other detriment.

4.88　Positive action in regard to training members to assist them to take up office in such organisations or encouraging only members of a particular racial group to take advantage of opportunities for holding such posts in the organisation is permitted under the Race Relations Act, s.38(3) where there are no persons of a particular racial group holding such posts or where the proportion of persons of that racial group holding such office is disproportionately small. A similar provision exists in the Sex Discrimination Act, s.48(2) in relation to positive action in favour of women.

4.89　Under the Sex Discrimination Act, s.49, provision is made for reserving seats for women on any elected bodies of organisations covered by section 12 or to create extra seats for women where, in the opinion of the organisation, it is needed to secure a reasonable minimum of members of that sex serving on the body concerned.

4.90　Under Article 4(b) of the Equal Treatment Directive[18] Member States must take measures to ensure that:

> "any provisions contrary to the principle of equal treatment . . . in rules governing the independent occupations and professions shall be, or may be, declared null and void or may be amended."

The European Court of Justice held that the United Kingdom was in breach of this obligation in enforcement proceedings[19] as regards the rules of trade unions, professional bodies and traded associations. No enforcement machinery exists as yet, however, through which aggrieved members or would-be members may enforce their Community rights.[20]

4.91　Discriminatory terms contained in collective agreements, employers' rule books or the rules of qualifying bodies are rendered void by the Sex Discrimination Act 1986, s.6. This section was also passed following the successful enforcement proceedings brought by the Commission against the United Kingdom government, an

---

[18] Council Dir. 76/207.
[19] Case 165/82, *Commission of the E.C.* v. *U.K.*: [1983] E.C.R. 3431; [1984] 1 C.M.L.R. 136,1984] I.C.R. 192; [1984] I.R.L.R. 29, ECJ.
[20] Note that this right arising under a Directive is only enforceable as against an organ of the state, which is unlikely to be the case for this type of body. See p. 221 for discussion of the legal status of E.C. Directives.

action which succeeded even though collective agreements in the United Kingdom are almost invariably not legally enforceable, following upon Trade Union and Labour Relations Act 1974, s.18. The Government chose to implement the ECJ decision by declaring such terms void rather than amending them, and indeed took this opportunity to repeal section 3 of the Equal Pay Act 1970. That section conferred upon the Central Arbitration Committee the power to amend collective agreements which contained terms which were not inclusive as between men and women. The CAC had, prior to the decision of the Court of Appeal in *R. v. C.A.C. ex p. Hymac*,[21] taken a liberal view of its powers to amend agreements, but the *Hymac* decision had largely nullified those powers. By virtue of the Sex Discrimination Act 1986, s.6(5), any term which has been incorporated into the terms of an individual's contract of employment and which are beneficial to her, although discriminatory, are unaffected by the avoidance of the relevant term of the collective agreement and may be modified in the county court by virtue of the Sex Discrimination Act, s.77(5). Thus the only remedies available to a person who experiences discrimination as the result of a discriminatory term in a collective agreement, which has been incorporated into her contract of employment, is to apply to an industrial tribunal under section 2 of the Equal Pay Act 1970, if the term is unlawful by virtue of that Act, or to a county court under the Sex Discrimination Act, s.77(5), if it is discriminatory by virtue of the Sex Discrimination Act.

However, the Trade Union Reform and Employment Rights Act 1993 amends the SDA 1986 and introduces a new sub-section 6(4A) into that Act. This provides for such actions to be brought in an Industrial Tribunal, although the new provisions are, however, limited to actions by which the offending term may be declared void. The new sub-section provides a right of action in the Industrial Tribunals for individuals who may be affected by unlawfully discriminatory terms of collective agreements, unlawfully discriminatory rules made by employers, trade unions, employers associations, professional organisations or qualifying bodies under SDA 1986, 6(1)–(2). Section 4A(*a*) applies this right to persons who believe that such a rule may have effect in relation to them at some future time and that the rule could lead to an act being done to him or her which would be unlawful if done at the present time. (A person who was actually affected could take direct action in respect of any detriment suffered.) Section 4A(*b*) applies this new right to those seeking employment as respects rules made by or on behalf of an employer or employers association. Section 4A(*c*) applies this right to those seeking membership of, or authorisation from, a qualifying body. It remains true, however, that there is no forum in which

[21] [1979] I.R.L.R. 461.

discriminatory terms of a collective agreement may be amended, a state of affairs lamented by the EOC.

Qualifying bodies 4.92   Under the Race Relations Act, s.12 and the Sex Discrimination Act, s.13, it is unlawful for a body which can confer an authorisation or qualification which is needed for, or facilitates, engagement in a particular profession or trade to discriminate against a person in the terms upon which the authorisation or qualification is conferred, by refusing or deliberately omitting to grant an application or withdrawing or varying the terms upon which the authorisation or qualification is awarded. Thus in *British Judo Association* v. *Petty*,[22] the EAT held that this section was apt to cover the refusal to award a licence to women to referee national men's judo competitions, even though the Judo Association argued that it was not awarding a qualification to facilitate the candidates' entry into the occupation, but simply upholding standards of refereeing. The test is whether the qualification in fact facilitates entry into the profession or occupation, whether it is intended to do so or not.

4.93   The Sex Discrimination Act goes further than the Race Relations Act, and in section 13(2) provides that where a body is required to satisfy itself as to the good character of a potential member before awarding a qualification which facilitates entry into a trade or profession, it shall have regard to any evidence that the applicant has practiced unlawful discrimination in carrying on any trade or profession.

4.93   In the enforcement proceedings taken against the United Kingdom[23] the European Court of Justice held that s.13 did not satisfy Article 4(6) of the Equal Treatment Directive, which requires Member States to legislate to ensure that the internal rules of qualifying bodies can be amended or declared null and void where they are incompatible with the provisions of E.C. law. The Sex Discrimination Act, s.6(2) now renders void non-contractual rules of qualifying bodies which would be unlawful by virtue of the Sex Discrimination Act 1975.

The Trade Union Reform and Employment Rights Act introduces a new section 6(4)(c) into the SDA 1986 which gives a right of action in respect of such rights in the Industrial Tribunals, but note the observations in paragraph 4.91 above.

Employment agencies 4.95   Discrimination by employment and vocational guidance agencies is unlawful under the Race Relations Act, s.14 and the Sex Discrimination Act, s.15. Discriminatory

---

[22] [1981] I.R.L.R. 484, EAT.
[23] n. 113.

activities undertaken by local education authorities under the Employment and Training Act 1973 are rendered unlawful by subsection 2, as these would otherwise be saved by the provisions in the Race Relations Act, s.41, although the amended Sex Discrimination Act, s.51, does not save prior statutory provisions, except in so far as these are concerned with the protection of women.

An employment agency is defined as a person who, for profit or not, provides services for the purposes of finding employment for workers or supplying employers with workers.

Police   4.96   For the purpose of the two Acts, the holding of the office of constable is to be treated as employment by the chief officer of police, or police authority, in relation to actions taken by them respectively under the Race Relations Act, s.16, and the Sex Discrimination Act, s.17(2). The Sex Discrimination Act, s.17(2), provides that men and women shall not be treated differently except as to uniform, equipment or height requirements and in relation to special treatment accorded to women in connection with pregnancy or childbirth, or in relation to pensions paid in respect of special constables or police cadets.

Barristers   4.97   In view of the fact that barristers fell without Part II of the Acts because they work neither under a partnership agreement nor under a contract, whether of service or for services, a gap was exposed in the legislation. The Courts and Legal Services Act 1990 ss. 64 and 65 inserted a new section in each of the Acts[24] as respects barristers in England and Wales and advocates in Scotland, which provide that it is unlawful to discriminate on grounds of race or sex as regards the making of offers of pupillage or a tenancy, the terms on which pupillages or tenancies are offered, or in the giving, witholding or accepting of briefs. But although akin to the work provision, the new sections are inserted in Part III of each Act and therefore the proceedings are brought in the County Courts (or Sheriff courts in Scotland).[25]

[24] RRA 1976, s. 26A & B, SDA 1975, s.35A &B.
[25] By virtue of being placed within Part III of the Acts, legal aid is available in County Courts and there is no statutory limit on compensation, but on the other hand, married barristers do enjoy protection on grounds of their marital status.

5 EQUAL PAY

The legal framework

5.01   The Equal Pay Act was first passed in 1970, but employers were given five years in which to implement equal pay. The Equal Pay Act did not come into force until the end of 1975, by which time the Sex Discrimination Act 1975 had been passed and the Equal Pay Act was re-enacted as Schedule 1 to the Sex Discrimination Act. The two Acts are intended to "provide in effect a single comprehensive code" in the field of employment,[1] although the two Acts have not been consolidated.[2] The distinction between the two Acts is that the Equal Pay Act is concerned with equalising terms and conditions of employment between men and women, whereas the Sex Discrimination Act is concerned to eliminate discrimination in relation to non-pay matters, such as access to training or promotion opportunities, although these clearly could be the subject of implied terms in the contract of employment. However, since Britain acceded to the Treaty of Rome, Article 119, which enshrines the principle of equal pay for work of equal value, it has become an important source of law in this area.[3]

5.02   There are three types of explanation for the persistence of the overall gap of 23 per cent. between the hourly rates of pay earned by full time women workers and those earned by full-time male workers.[4] They are (a) the occupational segregation of men and women, (b) differences in pay for the same or similar work and (c) the under-valuation of female-dominated jobs. Whereas (a) can be attacked by the Sex Discrimination Act, and (b) is subject to the like work and work to which equal value is attributed legs of the Equal Pay Act 1970, (c) is appropriate for review under the equal value amendments to the 1970 Act introduced in 1983. The comparable worth provisions contained in section 1(2)(c) of the 1970 Act are capable of achieving an improvement in the relative position of women workers without needing to wait until women have had time

---

[1] *Shields v. E. Coomes (Holdings) Ltd.* [1978] I.C.R. 1159, *per* Bridge L.J. at p. 1178.

[2] One of the proposals for change contained in the EOC review of the sex discrimination legislation, "Equal Pay for Men and Women," EOC, 1990 was that the two Acts should be consolidated to avoid problems of overlap.

[3] See chap. 1 for a further discussion of the relation between domestic and European law relating to equal pay.

[4] Jill Rubery, "The Economics of Equal Value", EOC, 1992.

to work their way into a wider range of occupations and reach the higher levels of the occupational hierarchy. This would more certainly be the case were those provisions contained in the type of pro-active pay equity system which exists in Ontario, under which employers are required to develop and post a plan to achieve comparable worth between male and female dominated groups in the labour force within a set period. Nonetheless, the British provisions, though cumbersome and slow, have had and are having an effect on the earnings differential between men and women, which having persisted unchanged for 10 years between 1977 and 1987 has now slowly begun to shrink.

Article 119   5.03   Article 119 enshrines the principle of equal pay, which the ECJ in the second *Defrenne*[5] case declared "forms part of the foundations of the Community." Article 119 provides as follows:

> "Each member state shall during the first stage ensure and subsequently maintain the application of the principle that men and women should receive equal pay for equal work."

The principle of equal pay was restated in the Equal Pay Directive 75/117, Article 1 of which provides as follows:

> "The principle of equal pay for men and women outlined in Article 119 of the Treaty, hereinafter called the 'principle of equal pay,' means for the same work or for work to which equal value is attributed, the elimination of all discrimination on grounds of sex with regard to all aspects and conditions of remuneration. In particular, where a job classification system is used for determining pay, it must be on the same criteria for men and women and so drawn up as to exclude any discrimination on grounds of sex."

5.04   The Equal Pay Act, as enacted, failed to provide for equal value claims except where the employer had voluntarily undertaken a job evaluation study. Following upon enforcement proceedings brought by the Commission against the United Kingdom Government,[6] the Equal Pay (Amendment) Regulations 1983 (often referred to as the Equal Value Regulations) were introduced to provide a right to equal value claims. These Regulations were introduced under the European Communities Act 1972 and amend the provisions of the Equal Pay Act 1970.

5.05   The rights arising under Article 119 in respect of direct and overt discrimination were held to be directly

---

[5] *Defrenne* v. *Sabena*, Case 43/75: [1976] ECJ 455 at p. 473. and see chap. 1 generally for a discussion of the relation between Community and national law.
[6] Case 61/81: [1982] E.C.R. 2061 and Case 61/82: [1982] E.C.R. 3431.

effective by the ECJ in *Defrenne (No. 2)*. As the ECJ in *Jenkins* v. *Kingsgate (Clothing Productions) Ltd.*[7] held that Article 1 of the Equal Pay Directive simply restates the principle of equal pay contained in Article 119 and "in no way alters the content or scope of that principle," it follows that Article 1 of the Directive, with its explicit reference to work of equal value, is directly effective. In *Jenkins*, the ECJ also held that the concept of direct effect applies "to all forms of discrimination which may be identified solely with the aid of the criteria of equal work and equal value referred to by the Article in question, without national or Community measures being required to define them with greater precision in order to permit their application."[8] Nonetheless, doubts were expressed by Lord Oliver in *Pickstone* v. *Freemans*[9] that a right which is dependant for its exercise upon the complex national provisions of the Equal Value Regulations could be of direct effect.

5.06   Where the State is the respondent to an action, a complainant might rely on directly effective rights, in so far as Community law obligations have not been fully or correctly implemented. The basis of the decision in *Pickstone* v. *Freemans* was, however, the notion of the indirect or interpretative effect of the Equal Pay Directive, as discussed in Chapter 1. Cases where a question of Community law is at issue may be referred to the ECJ under Article 177 and indeed must be so referred by a national court of last resort. The result has been a wide range of ECJ decisions having application to matters of equal pay, which have considerably extended and modified the scope of the domestic law.[10]

The Equal Pay Act 1970

5.07   The Equal Pay Act operates by implying into the contract under which a woman is employed an equality clause[11] whenever a woman is engaged in like work with a man,[12] work rated as equivalent[13] or work to which equal value is attributed.[14] Section 1 of the Equal Pay Act provides as follows:

"1. If the terms of a contract under which a woman is employed at an establishment in Great Britain do not include (directly or by reference to a collective agreement or otherwise) an equality clause they shall be deemed to include one.

2. An equality clause is a provision which relates to terms

---

[7] [1981] I.R.L.R. 228 at p. 234.
[8] At p. 234.
[9] [1988] I.R.L.R. 357 at p. 364.
[10] The underlying questions of the circumstances and methods by which community law can be given effect in the U.K. are discussed in chapter 1.
[11] Case 61/81: [1982] E.C.R. 2061 and Case 61/82: [1992] E.C.R. 3431.
[12] EqPA 1970, s.1(2)(*a*).
[13] EqPA 1970, s.1(2)(*b*).
[14] EqPA 1970, s.1(2)(*c*).

(whether concerned with pay or not) of a contract under which a woman is employed (the woman's contract), and has the effect that

(a) where the woman is employed on like work with a man in the same employment

(i) if (apart from the equality clause) any term of the woman's contract is or becomes less favourable to the woman than a term of a similar kind in a contract under which that man is employed that term of the woman's contract shall be treated as so modified as not to be less favourable, and

(ii) if (apart from the equality clause) at any time the woman's contract does not include a term corresponding to a term benefiting that man included in the contract under which he is employed, the woman's contract shall be treated as including such a term."

Similar provisions covering women doing work rated as equivalent are contained in subsection 1(2)(*b*) and for work of equal value in subsection 1(2)(*c*).

The scope of the Act

5.08 An equality clause can relate to any term in the contract under which a woman is employed, not merely in relation to pay,[15] except for those terms excluded by section 6(1). Thus the equality clause does not operate in relation to terms which are affected by the laws which regulate the employment of women,[16] although the scope of these laws has been reduced by the Sex Discrimination Act 1986, s.8 and section 6 of the Employment Act 1989.[17] Neither does an equality clause extend to those contractual provisions under which a woman is afforded access to special treatment in connection with pregnancy or childbirth,[18] (a provision present also in Article 2(3) of the Equal Treatment Directive) although in other respects the Act applies to men as to women.[19]

5.09 The Act applies to a woman of any age[20] working at an establishment in Great Britain[21] under a contract of service or of apprenticeship or a contract personally to

---

[15] EqPA 1970, s.1(2).
[16] s.6(1)(*a*).
[17] See chap. 2, n. 171, for details of the protective legislation which has been retained following the Employment Act 1989.
[18] EqPA 1970, s.6(1)(*b*).
[19] EqPA 1970, s.1(13). Thus there is no statutory right to paternity leave, although this has been advocated by the EOC and the TUC.
[20] EqPA 1970, s.11(2).
[21] An employee is to be regarded as being employed in Great Britain unless the employee does her work wholly or mainly outside Great Britain. For an extended definition of employment in Great Britain, both for the purposes of the EqPA and the SDA see the SDA 1976, s.10. and paras. 4.03–4.07.

execute any work or labour.[22] The EAT in *Quinnen* v. *Hovells*[23] held that a "contract personally to execute any work or labour" was intended to have a wider connotation than "employment" so as to include persons outside the master and servant relationship, *i.e.* the self-employed.[24] The Act applies to Crown employments, except for the armed services, as it applies to private employments.[25]

The Equal Pay Act and the Sex Discrimination Act

5.10   The Equal Pay Act and Sex Discrimination Act are complementary to each other and are to be construed as one code. Bridge L. J.in *Shields* v. *E. Coomes (Holdings) Ltd*[26] put the matter as follows:

> "In the sphere of employment the provisions of the Sex Discrimination Act 1975 and the Equal Pay Act 1970 aimed at eliminating discrimination on grounds of sex are closely interlocking and provide in effect a single comprehensive code. The particular provisions designed to preclude overlapping between the two statutes are complex, and it may often be difficult to determine whether a particular matter or complaint falls to be addressed under one statute or the other. But what is abundantly clear is that both Acts should be construed and applied as one harmonious whole and in such a way that the broad principles are not frustrated by a narrow interpretation or restrictive application of particular provisions."

5.11   The Equal Pay Act was passed five years prior to the Sex Discrimination Act but, was re-enacted in 1975 as a schedule to the later Act with considerable consequential amendment. Nonetheless the two Acts operate on somewhat different principles. The Equal Pay Act is restricted to contractual terms and conditions of employment and implies an equality clause into the contracts of all women engaged upon like work, work rated as equivalent or work of equal value. Whilst section 6(6) of the Sex Discrimination Act provides that section 6(2) of the Act does not apply to benefits consisting of the payment of money which are regulated in a woman's contract of employment, the Equal Pay Act is not restricted to payments of money only. Equal Pay Act, s.1(2) provides that:

> "An equality clause is a provision which relates to terms

---

[22] EqPA 1970, s.1(6).

[23] [1984] I.C.R. 525.

[24] This broader connotation does not, however, extend to those who are working under a contract to supply services other than their own labour. Thus in *Mirror Group Newspapers* v. *Gunning* [1986] I.R.L.R. 27, C.A., a contract between the newspaper company and an independent wholesale distributor fell outside the terms of the comparable section of the SDA 1975, because the contract did not contemplate that the work was necessarily to be performed personally by the contractor.

[25] EqPA 1970, s.1(9)(10).

[26] [1987] I.C.R. 1159, C.A. at p. 1178.

(whether concerned with pay or not) of a contract under which a woman is employed."

5.12   SDA, s. 8(5) also excludes from section 6(2) any contractual terms modified or included by virtue of an equality clause. Thus the statutory equality clause applies to contractual terms and conditions of employment other than money where the woman is employed on like work, work rated as equivalent or work of equal value with a male comparator. The Sex Discrimination Act has an advantage for applicants in that it does not call for the existence of an actual comparator and defines discrimination as existing where the discriminator "treats her less favourably than he treats or would treat a man", *i.e.* hypothetical comparisons can be made. The effect is, therefore, that a woman suffering discrimination in respect of the payment of money under her contract of employment may only proceed under the Equal Pay Act (SDA, s.6(6)). She must proceed under the Equal Pay Act in relation to other contractual terms if like work, work rated as equivalent or work of equal value to an actual comparator exists. She may proceed under the Sex Discrimination Act in relation to contractual terms, except those related to the payment of money, if like work or work of equal value does not exist. Thus, a woman experiencing discrimination in fringe benefits is restricted to the Equal Pay Act if she falls within the ambit of comparison laid down by that Act, but otherwise she could proceed under the Sex Discrimination Act alleging that she has been treated less favourably than a man would have been treated.

5.13   The terms on which employment is offered are regulated by Sex Discrimination Act, s.6(1)(*b*) where, had the offer been accepted, the term would have fallen to be modified by an equality clause under the Equal Pay Act (SDA, s.8(3)), providing that the employer would not have been able to mount a successful genuine material difference defence under Equal Pay Act, s.1(3) (SDA, s.8(4)). Therefore, an offer of employment containing discriminatory terms outside the scope of the Equal Pay Act, perhaps because there are no males engaged upon any form of comparable work, does not contravene Sex Discrimination Act, s.6(1)(*b*).

5.14   The defences which may be mounted by the employer are different under the two Acts. Whereas under the Equal Pay Act there is a defence that the inequality is due to a genuine material factor other than sex, the Sex Discrimination Act provides no comparable defence for direct discrimination under section (1)(1)(*a*), whilst providing a defence that any occurrence of indirect discrimination under section (1)(1)(*b*) may be justifiable. The defence of justifiability was held in *Rainey* v. *Greater*

Glasgow Health Board[27] to be equivalent to the genuine material factor defence under the SDA, s.1(1)(*b*).

5.15 Only the Sex Discrimination Act can apply to non-contractual matters, as also to any alleged discrimination on grounds of marital status. Allegations of victimisation under both the Sex Discrimination Act and the Equal Pay Act are to be heard under the Sex Discrimination Act, s.4. Unsurprisingly, the EOC in its document "Legislating for Change", proposed that the two Acts be integrated as one Equal Treatment Act incorporating the hypothetical comparisons presently contained only in the Sex Discrimination Act.

5.16 Article 119 encompasses any "consideration, whether in cash or in kind, which the worker receives, directly or indirectly, in respect of his employment." This broader definition of pay encompasses non-contractual benefits, such as post-retirement travel concessions in *Garland*. The question arises, therefore, as to whether it is more appropriate in such situations to allow the matter to be adjudicated under the Sex Discrimination Act or to interpret the Equal Pay Act so as to conform with the definition of pay in Article 119. Where the question turns on a hypothetical comparison of the sort which is permissible under the Sex Discrimination Act but not under the Equal Pay Act, the issue is far from academic. However, as the ECJ held in *McCarthy's* v. *Smith* it is not possible to rely on purely hypothetical comparisons under Article 119, which therefore has no application in the absence of comparators, whether or not these are contemporaneous. Equally, Article 1 of the Equal Pay Directive 75/117 applies the "principle of equal pay" only to situations where men and women are undertaking the same work, or work to which equal value is attributed. Non-contractual matters outside the scope of concrete comparisons of equal work or equal value are therefore matters of equal treatment under Community law and fall within the Equal Treatment Directive, which, though it only has vertical direct effect, may have a wider indirect interpretative effect, as discussed in chapter 1.

Exclusions in relation to death and retirement

5.17 The Act does not apply to provisions in relation to death or retirement, other than a term which, in relation to retirement, affords access to opportunities for promotion, transfer or training or provides for a woman's dismissal or demotion.[28] Prior to the Sex Discrimination Act 1986 all provisions in relation to death or retirement were excluded by the Act but following the decision of the ECJ in *Marshall* v. *Southampton and South West Hants Health Authority*[29] such a blanket exclusion could not be maintained. The Marshall

---

[27] [1987] I.R.L.R 26, H.L.
[28] EqPA 1970, s.6(1)(*b*) as amended by the SDA 1986.
[29] [1986] I.R.L.R. 140 and see paras. 4.66–4.70.

case was initially brought under the Sex Discrimination Act because the Health Authority's rules as to retirement did not constitute a term of the contracts of their employees, but were a retirement policy or practice handed down to employees. Had the rules as to retirement constituted a term of the employees' contracts, the facts of the case would have fallen to be decided under the Equal Pay Act, rather than the Sex Discrimination Act. The ECJ held that the Authority's practice was contrary to Article 5(1) of the Equal Treatment Directive, as would equally have been the case had the retirement rules constituted a term of the employee's contract. Therefore, the Sex Discrimination Act 1986 modified the exclusionary rules as to death and retirement in the Equal Pay Act, s.6(1)(*b*), as stated above, to reflect the amendments made to section 6(4) of the Sex Discrimination Act 1976.

The scope of the equality clause

5.18   An equality clause can only operate where there is a contractual term relating to the matter in dispute.[30] In *Hayward* v. *Cammell Laird*,[31] the House of Lords held that the natural and ordinary meaning of a term in a contract of employment is a distinct provision or part of a contract, which has sufficient content to make it possible to compare it from the point of view of the benefits which it confers with a similar provision in another contract. In the *Hayward* case, the employers had argued that in considering whether the appellant cook was receiving equal pay with her selected comparators (shipyard painters, laggers and joiners), regard should be had to the whole package of benefits which constituted her remuneration, including sick pay, holiday entitlements and the like. The EAT and the Court of Appeal had decided in favour of the employer's argument in view of the potential for leap-frogging, which they said was a probable consequence if employees were able to compare separately, say, provisions on pay, holidays, entitlement to a car allowance etc., allowing both men and women to reach equality at a new and higher level than either had enjoyed separately. The House of Lords held, however, that it would be wrong to depart from the natural and ordinary meaning of the word "term", because of the difficulty of its application to particular examples, especially when those examples do not arise in actual cases. A further difficulty arises if a broad construction is adopted, equivalent to remuneration as a whole. Section 1(2)(*c*)(ii), which deals with the situation where a woman's contract lacks a particular term (the absent term), would be deprived of any ground on which to operate, in that all contracts of employment necessarily contain a term relating to pay in

---

[30] *Pointon* v. *University of Sussex* [1979] I.R.L.R. 119, C.A. Quaere within whether a contractual term as to pay relates to appointment at the discretion of management according to skill, ability and experience as in *Pointon* or is a term relating to the salary earned, as in *Benveniste* v. *University of Southampton, infra*, p. 182.

[31] [1988] I.R.L.R. 257, H.L.

that broader sense. Thus the statutory equality clause is to be applied to the individual terms of a contract and not to the overall package of employee benefits.[32] A similar view of the need to consider each element of the employee's total remuneration separately was enunciated by the ECJ in the pensions case of *Barber* v. *Guardian Royal Exchange.*[33]

Validity and revision of contracts

5.19 A term of a contract is void by SDA, s.77 or RRA, s.72 where its inclusion renders the contract unlawful by virtue of either the Equal Pay or Sex Discrimination Acts or where it provides for the doing of an act which is thus unlawful. Where a contract includes an unlawful discriminatory term but is otherwise beneficial to a complainant, that term shall be unenforceable against that party. On the application of an aggrieved party to a contract containing such an unenforceable term, a county or sheriff court may make such order as it thinks just for modifying or removing any such term, under subsection 5 of the relevant section of each Act. For example, if a contract included discriminatory sick pay terms, if those terms were simply rendered void there would be no entitlement to sick pay at all.

Non-contractual terms

5.20 Whilst the Equal Pay Act is restricted to contractual terms, Article 4 of the Equal Pay Directive applies the principle of equal pay not only to individual contracts of employment, but also to the provisions of collective agreements, wage scales and wage agreements, notwithstanding that their terms may not be legally enforceable in the U.K. unless incorporated in the individual contract of employment. The European Commission brought enforcement proceedings against the U.K.[34] in respect of the

---

[32] It was argued on behalf of the employer that the broad definition of pay contained in Art. 119 "the ordinary basic or minimum wage or salary and any other consideration in cash or in kind, which the worker receives, in respect of his employment" suggests a broad reading of pay. In respect of s.1(2)(c), however (the equal value provisions under which the *Hayward* case was brought), which was intended to give full effect to the U.K. obligations under the Treaty of Rome following the decision of the ECJ in *Commission of the European Communities* v. *U.K.* [1982] I.R.L.R. 133, Art. 1 of the Equal Pay Directive (held to be simply declaratory of the meaning of Art. 119 and not to add to or change its meaning in any way in *Jenkins* v. *Kingsgate (Clothing Productions) Ltd.* [1981] I.R.L.R. 228, ECJ) provides that "the principle of equal pay calls for the elimination of all discrimination on grounds of sex with regard to all aspects and conditions of remuneration . . .". It is therefore perfectly consistent with Art. 119 to compare one aspect of remuneration with another in the application of the EqPA

[33] [1990] I.R.L.R. 240, ECJ.

[34] Case 165/82, *Re Equal Treatment: E.C. Commission* v. *United Kingdom*: [1983] E.C.R. 3413, [1984] 1 C.M.L.R. 43.

Equal Treatment Directive. The ECJ held that the obligations arising under the Equal Treatment Directive extended to non-legally-binding collective agreements, as such agreements have important *de facto* consequences for the employment relationships covered by them. Consequently, the Sex Discrimination Act 1986, s.6(3) applies section 77 of the SDA 1975 to the terms of unenforceable collective agreements, administrative rules applied in an employer's undertaking or to the rules of trade unions, employer's associations or qualifying bodies, which are capable of incorporation in the employee's contract of employment. In *Ruzius-Wilbrink*[35] the ECJ held that in a case of indirect discrimination the disadvantaged group, men or women, are entitled to have the same system applied to them as other workers, in proportion to their working hours. This dictum was applied to collective agreements in *Kowalska*.[36] However, it is difficult to imagine a county court amending an indirectly discriminatory collective agreement on redundancy which led to differential severance payments. Such payments would in any event only be caught by section 77 if they were incorporated into the contract of employment. The EOC has called for jurisdiction in such matters to be given to industrial tribunals or a similarly constituted body on the application of any interested party or the EOC.[37]

The Trade Union Reform and Employment Rights Act 1993 amends the Sex Discrimination Act 1993 by inserting within it a new subsection 6(4A), under which it will be possible to bring an action in the Industrial Tribunals to declare void a discriminatory provision in a collective agreement. The opportunity was not taken, however, to provide a mechanism whereby such terms could be amended, in view of the fact that Article 4 of the Equal Pay Directive provides that Member States must take the necessary measures to ensure that such provisions may be 'declared null or void *or* may be amended.'[38]

5.21 It may be objected that SDA 1986, s.6 leaves no suitable forum in which collective agreements containing discriminatory terms which are not apt for incorporation may be amended, even though actions could be brought under the Sex Discrimination Act in so far as employers act on the terms of such agreements to the detriment of individuals. The irony of this situation is that it was section 9 of the SDA 1986 which repealed section 3 of the EqPA 1970 *i.e.* it brought to an end the jurisdiction of the Central Arbitration Committee in equal pay matters.

---

[35] Case 102/88, ECJ.
[36] Case 33/89: [1990] I.R.L.R. 447, ECJ.
[37] Equal Pay for Men and women: Strengthening the Acts, 1990, EOC, p. 16
[38] See para 4.90 for further details of these provisions.

The concept of pay

5.22 Whilst the concept of pay has been restricted to contractual terms under the EqPA 1970, Article 119 defines pay in broader terms.

Article 119

"For the purpose of this Article, "pay" means the ordinary basic or minimum wage or salary and any other consideration whether in cash or in kind which the worker receives, directly or indirectly, in respect of his employment from his employer. Equal pay without discrimination based on sex means:
  (a) that pay for the same work at piece rates shall be calculated on the same unit of measurement;
  (b) that pay for the same work at time rates shall be the same for the same job."

Fringe benefits

5.23 The phrase "directly or indirectly in respect of his employment" shows that Article 119 is not limited to contractual terms and conditions of employment. In the first *Defrenne* case, the ECJ held that "pay" extends "to all emoluments, in cash or kind, paid or payable, on condition that they are paid, even indirectly, by the employer to the worker as a result of the latter"s employment."[39] In *Garland* v. *British Rail Engineering*,[40] one of the earlier cases heard with reference to Article 119, "pay" was held to include post-retirement travel facilities granted, as an extension of the terms and conditions enjoyed whilst working, to the wives and dependant children of railwaymen, but not to the dependants of railwaywomen. It is notable that this conclusion was unaffected by the fact that the travel facilities were a concession to which retired staff had no contractual or other legal right.

Sick pay

5.24 The scope of "pay" under Article 119 has been held to include the German equivalent to statutory sick pay in *Rinner-Kuhn* v. *FWW Spezial-Gebaudereinigung*.[41]. Under the relevant German legislation employers were only obliged to pay sick pay to workers employed for ten hours or more a week. Mrs Rinner-Kuhn"s employers, an office cleaning firm, refused to pay her wages during a short period of absence due to illness. The ECJ held that "the continued payment of wages in the event of illness falls within the definition of pay within the meaning of Article 119"[42] and went on to hold that such a legislative

"provision as the one in question results in practice in discrimination between male and female workers and is, in principle, to be regarded as contrary to the objective pursued by Article 119 of the Treaty. It would only be otherwise if the different treatment between the two

---

[39] Case 80/70: [1974] 1 C.M.L.R. 108 at ground 6.
[40] Case 12/81: [1982] 1 C.M.L.R. 696; [1982] E.C.R. 359; ECJ, [1982] 2 C.M.L.R. 174, H.L.
[41] [1989] I.R.L.R. 493, ECJ
[42] At ground 8.

categories of workers is justified by objective factors unrelated to any discrimination on grounds of sex."

5.25 Thus, where an employer draws a distinction between full-time and part-time workers, to the detriment of the latter, such a practice is indirectly discriminatory under Article 119. In effect this decision pre-empts Article 3 of the draft part-time workers directive[43] and entitles all part-timers irrespective of their hours. It is not certain as to whether U.K. statutory sick pay and maternity pay, both qualified by service requirements, could be said to constitute pay under Article 119.[44] Whilst the employer administers those payments, he does not actually bear the costs of them, whereas since 1989 the employer has borne the full costs of statutory redundancy payments, even though their form and extent are governed by statute. It could be argued that as SSP and SMP both spring from the employment relationship and are administered by the employer, they constitute pay under Article 119, even though the cost is borne by the State. Were they to be held to constitute aspects of social security, then it is the terms of the Social Security Directive 79/7 which would govern the situation.

Redundancy and unfair dismissal compensation

5.26 Although contractual redundancy payments were held to constitute pay in *Hammersmith & Queen Charlotte's Special Health Authority* v. *Cato*[45] the EAT in *Secretary of State for Employment* v. *Levy*[46] held that statutory redundancy benefits do not constitute pay. By contrast, the ECJ has taken the view that statutory redundancy payments are a form of pay. In *Barber* v. *Guardian Royal Exchange*,[47] ,the ECJ held that "where the worker is entitled to receive the benefit in question from his employer by reason of the existence of the employment relationship",[48] the fact that a benefit is in the nature of pay cannot be called into question because it also reflects "considerations of social policy," although this aspect of the decision has been subject to criticism.[49] Statutory redundancy pay was held to be a form of pay made in respect of the employee's former employment in order to facilitate his adjustment to the loss of his job and to provide him with a source of income whilst seeking new

---

[43] Proposal for Council Directive on the approximation of the laws of the Member States relating to certain employment relationships with regard to working conditions. [1990] O.J. C224/4. See also the Art. 100A draft Council Directive on the approximation of the laws of the Member States relating to certain employment relationships with regard to distortions of Competition [1990] O.J. C224/6.

[44] See notes by Skyszczak in I.L.J., 19, 2, pp. 114-120, and by Rubenstein in EOR, 28, at pp. 39-41.

[45] [1987] I.R.L.R. 483, EAT.

[46] [1989] I.R.L.R. 469, EAT.

[47] Case 262/88, [1990] I.R.L.R. 240, ECJ.

[48] At ground 18.

[49] Shrubsall *Barber* v. *Guardian Royal Exchange, Industrial Law Journal*, 19, at pp 244-250.

work.[50] In *Barber*, as in *Garland*, it was the employment nexus which was seen as decisive, even if, as the Court had already held in *Defrenne II*,[51] the discrimination arises directly from legislative provisions. The EOC commenced judicial review proceedings in respect of the "decision" of the Secretary of State not to amend domestic law with respect to the discriminatory hours and service requirements for eligibility for redundancy pay and unfair dismissal.[52] In *R. v. Secretary of State for Employment ex. p. EOC*,[53] the High Court concluded not only that redundancy pay, but also potential compensation for unfair dismissal, is a consideration received directly or indirectly in respect of employment and constitutes pay under Article 119, a view upheld in the Court of Appeal. A majority in the Court of Appeal held that the EOC did not have standing to proceed against the Secretary of State, but that it was open to the EOC to support suitable test cases in the Industrial Tribunals. As questions of justifiability are matters of fact on which there is no right of appeal, curious and discrepant results could occur.

Merit pay

5.27   The scope of Article 119 "extends to agreements which seek to regulate wage-earning work collectively, as well as to contracts between individuals" according to the ECJ in *Kowalska* v. *Frei und Hansestadt Hamburg*.[53] In the *Danfoss* case,[54] the ECJ had brought within the scope of the equal pay principle not only substantive pay rates but also the processes by which pay is determined. The case concerned a collectively bargained pay structure, within which there was a system of discretionary pay awards to individuals within each grade. This system resulted in an average difference of 6.85 per cent. between the pay of men and women and was characterised by the ECJ as having a total lack of "transparency" *i.e.* the employees could not readily check the basis on which their pay was calculated.[56] In those circumstances the ECJ argued that the burden was thrown upon the employer to justify the average difference in pay which had been shown. Many pay and merit rating

---

[50] Whilst the Employment Act 1989 equalised the maximum age for redundancy benefit, it did not apply to the facts of the *Barber* case, nor obviously did it provide that a statutory redundancy benefit is a part of pay. The ECJ in *Kowalska* v. *Frei und Hansestadt Hamburg* Case 33/89 [1990] I.R.L.R. 447, ECJ held that severance "payments constitute a form of deferred remuneration to which the worker is entitled by virtue of his employment, but which is paid to him at the time of the termination of the employment relationship."

[51] [1976] E.C.R. 455 at para. 40.

[52] Should the Art. 100A draft directive on part-time work be adopted it will provide that employees working over eight hours per week enjoy social protection and occupational social security rights *pro rata* to their hours.

[53] [1991] I.R.L.R. 493, H.C. at p. 500, [1993] I.R.L.R. C.A.

[54] Case 33/89, [1990] I.R.L.R. 447.

[55] Case 109/88 *Handels-og Kontorfunktionaerernes Forbund i Danmark* v. *Dansk Arbedjsgiverforening (acting for* Danfoss) [1989] I.R.L.R. 532, ECJ.

[56] Thus giving effect in part to the failed directive on the burden of proof in discrimination cases COM (88) 269.

systems in Britain are far from "transparent" in this sense and if they produce differences in pay between men and women could be open to challenge. In the subsequent *Nimz*[57] case, the ECJ held that a system of rules (in this case contained in a collective agreement) governing the passage of employees to a higher salary grade also fell within the concept of "pay" contained in Article 119.

Equality in pensions

5.28 Traditionally men and women have been treated differently in pensions matters; the notion of a male norm has greater force in this area than almost any other. Pension scheme rules have tended to be based on the implicit assumptions that male breadwinners would work until 65, with many women, by virtue of their family commitments, lacking the long-term commitment to a career that would be necessary to qualify for substantial pension benefits. Pensions have often not been offered in industries and occupations in which women predominate, and where they do exist there can often be indirectly discriminatory rules excluding part-timers. Restrictive treatment of transferees and early-leavers is particularly disadvantageous to women, with their commonly more fluid pattern of employment. In the U.K. the lower state pension age for women, first introduced ironically during the course of the Second World War, is commonly reflected in the rules of occupational pension schemes. The greater longevity of women, combined with their generally earlier dates of retirement, has meant that actuarial considerations have led either to higher contributions needing to be made on their behalf or to lower rates of pensions for women in money purchase schemes. The Occupational Social Security Directive 86/378 introduced the principle of equal treatment in pensions matters, but left a number of crucial exceptions for later action, such as differential pension ages and the provision of survivors' benefits. Although the explanatory memorandum attached to the Commission's first draft of the proposal recognised that occupational pension schemes generally fall within the scope of the second paragraph of Article 119, the Occupational Social Security Directive 86/378 adopted an approach to the introduction of the principle of equal treatment in this area which recognised that pension scheme managers and others had made their arrangements on the basis that differentiation in pensions matters was permissible and that time would be needed to adjust. In *Barber* v. *Guardian Royal Exchange*[58] [1990], the ECJ held, however, that pensions are pay for the purposes of Article 119, with

---

[57] [1991] I.R.L.R. 222. In this case the rather special facts of the situation were that the rules of a collective agreement provided that only half the service of part-time workers was to be taken into account in qualifying for movement to the next grade, where a part-timer worked between half and three-quarters time and the part-timers comprises a considerably smaller group of men than women.

[58] Case 262/88: [1990] E.C.R. 1889; [1990] 2 C.M.L.R. 513; [1990] I.R.L.R. 240.

the consequence that for occupational pensions
discriminatory pension ages as between men and women are
unlawful. In placing pensions firmly within the orbit of
Article 119, the *Barber* case gives immediate effect to the
principle of equal pay with regard to pensions. As
Fitzpatrick observes, *Barber* has not only moved the
boundary between Article 119 and the equality directives,
but also between Article 119 and the social security and
occupational social security directives.[59]

5.29   The facts of the *Barber* case were that Mr Barber was
made redundant at age 52. He was only entitled to receive a
lump sum, together with a deferred pension at age 62, when
a woman in similar circumstances would have been entitled
to be treated as "retired" and would have received an
immediate pension. Mr Barber brought proceedings under
both the SDA 1976 and Community law, but his claim was
dismissed by the tribunal. The Court of Appeal referred the
question of whether pensions are "pay" under Community
law to the ECJ, which, to the profound disquiet of the
pension funds, answered "yes."

5.30   The principal question referred to the ECJ was
whether a U.K. contracted-out pension is a part of "pay"
for the purposes of Article 119. The U.K. government had
contended that pensions which are contracted-out of SERPS
are a matter of social security and subject to Article 118,
which is not of direct effect. Indeed, the Occupational Social
Security Directive 36/378, the provisions of which were
implemented by the Social Security Act 1989,[60] speaks of
implementing the principle of equal treatment in this area.
In *Defrenne No. 1*[61] the ECJ held that a pension which is
directly imposed by law without any element of consultation
within the industry or undertaking concerned, and to which
the employer contributes as a matter of legal, rather than
contractual, duty falls outside the scope of Article 119. In
the United Kingdom all occupational pensions have to seek
the approval of the Occupational Pensions Board in order
that they can achieve "contracted out" status. To achieve
this status they must provide benefits at least as good as
those available under SERPS, for which they substitute for a
contracted-out employee. All occupational pension schemes
in the United Kingdom are therefore cast within a statutory
framework, so that the question arose as to whether or not
they constitute pay under Article 119.

5.31   The pension scheme in *Defrenne No. 1* was excluded
from the ambit of Article 119 because it was a special

---

[59] "Equality in Occupational Pensions – The New Frontiers after Barber,
Barry Fitzpatrick", Modern Law Review, 54, 2, pp. 271-280.
[60] With the result that several large employers have made common cause in
suing the Commission for negligent and misleading advice on this matter,
on which they relied to their detriment.
[61] Case 80/70: [1971] E.C.R. 445, ECJ.

scheme for staff of SABENA which was wholly determined by legislation, even though its scope was restricted to civil air crew. In *Liefting* v. *Academish Ziekenhuish bij de Universiteit van Amsterdam*,[62] the ECJ did not rely on that distinction when it held that differential sums which public authorities are required to pay under a legislatively determined occupational pension scheme for civil servants may be contrary to Article 119, if they are included within the computation of gross pay. A similar result was achieved in *Worringham and Humphries* v. *Lloyds Bank*,[63] in which the Bank required male staff to contribute to the pension scheme at a younger age than female staff. In order to ensure equal net pay, a sum was added to the gross pay of male employees, this addition being held to be contrary to Article 119 by the ECJ. In *Newstead* v. *Department of Transport*,[64], the ECJ held that contributions to a contracted-out pension scheme did not fall within Article 119, being matters of social security governed by Article 118. *Newstead* was concerned with the deduction of contributions to a widows' pension scheme which were demanded only of male civil servants and which led to a difference of net, but not of gross, pay, between male and female civil servants. The contributions of unmarried civil servants, such as Mr Newstead, were returned with interest on death or retirement. *Worringham* and *Liefting* were distinguished on the grounds that in those cases the making up of the net pay of male employees to compensate for the employee's contribution to a pension scheme increased their gross pay. The effect of that increase in gross pay, although subsequently deducted into a pension scheme, was to increase pay for the purpose of other salary-related benefits such as redundancy, unemployment benefits and family allowances.

5.32   In the German case of *Bilka Kaufhaus* v. *Weber von Hartz*,[65] however, the ECJ held that an occupational pension scheme which supplemented social security provisions, and which was based on an agreement between an employer and its staff committee, on which the firm's employees were represented, constituted deferred remuneration received by the worker in respect of his employment. In other words, it constituted "pay" within Article 119. The way was open, therefore, for the ECJ in *Barber* to conclude that contracted out occupational pension schemes are a part of "pay" and fall within the directly effective provisions of Article 119, notwithstanding that they are fitted within a statutory framework. The basis of such schemes is:

---

[62] (1984) E.C.R. 3225, ECJ. *Griffin* v. *London Pensions Fund Authority* (unreported at the time of writing) to the effect that the local authority pension scheme is not subject to the effects of the *Barber* decision.

[62] (1984) E.C.R. 3225, ECJ.

[63] [1981] I.R.L.R. 178, ECJ.

[64] [1988] I.R.L.R. 68, ECJ.

[65] Case 170/84: [1986] I.R.L.R. 317, ECJ.

"an agreement between workers and employees or a unilateral decision taken by the employer. They are wholly financed by the employer or by both the employer and the workers without any contribution being made by public authorities in any circumstances. Accordingly, such schemes form part of the consideration offered to workers by their employer."

Such schemes are not of general application "with the result that affiliation to those schemes derives of necessity from the employment relationship with a given employer." The ECJ took the view that this approach was not affected by the interposition of the pension fund trustees between the employer and the worker, even if this means acting in ways contrary[65.1] to the trust deed, according to the Advocate General *Coloroll.*

5.33   As regards the imposition of a discriminatory pension age, the ECJ had held in *Defrenne III*, which concerned the compulsory retirement of an air hostess at age 40, that

"the fact that the fixing of certain conditions of employment – such as a special age limit – may have pecuniary consequences is not sufficient to bring such conditions within the field of application of Article 119, which is based on the close connection which exists between the nature of the services provided and the amount of remuneration."

5.34   The U.K. Government and the respondents in Barber argued that, following *Burton* v. *British Rail*,[66] a differential pension age was a condition of access to a benefit and therefore fell within the scope of the equality directives. Were that to be the case, there could be no question of direct effect as against a private employer such as the Guardian Royal Exchange. In *Burton* British Rail had offered early retirement to all employees within five years of their normal retirement age *i.e.* 60 for men and 55 for women. It was held by the ECJ that this was a question of working conditions under Directive 76/207.[67]. Advocate General Walter van Gerven reconciled the approach of the ECJ in *Bilka* with *Burton* by distinguishing between an age

---

[65.1] Case C200/91 at ground 57.

[66] [1981] 3 C.M.L.R. 100, EAT; [1982] 2 C.M.L.R. 136, E.C.J; [1982] E.C.R. 555, ECJ. See also *Roberts* v. *Tate and Lyle Industries*, Case 151/84, [1986] 1 C.M.L.R. 714 [1986] E.C.R. 703, *Marshall* v. *Southampton and South West Hants Health Authority*, Case 152/84 [1986] E.C.R. 723; [1986] 1 C.M.L.R. 688, ECJ; *Beets-Proper* v. *van Lanschot Bankiers NV*, Case 262/84 [1986] E.C.R. 773, [1987] 1 C.M.L.R. 616, ECJ.

[67] The ECJ reasoned that as the age for early retirement was tied to the state pension age, and that as Art. 2 of of the Equal Treatment Directive makes the 1976 Directive subject to the later Social Security Directive E.C. 79/7, Art. 7 of which reserves to the Member States the determination of pensionable age, that the differential age for early retirement was not discriminatory.

condition or limit which governs the selection of employees for dismissal, as in *Burton*, and a condition which governs the grant of a terminal payment to those employees whose dismissal has already been decided. *Bilka* concerned the conditions for the grant of a pension, as *Rinner-Kuhn* concerned the conditions for the grant of sick pay. The Court, however, in reasoning criticised as "weak" by Honeyball and Shaw,[68] simply held that

"Art. 119 prohibits any discrimination with regard to pay between men and women, whatever the system which gives rise to such inequality. Accordingly, it is contrary to Art. 119 to impose an age condition which differs according to sex in respect of pensions paid under a contracted-out scheme, even if the difference between the pensionable age for men and that for women is based on the one provided for by the national statutory scheme."

5.35   One argument advanced by the employers in *Barber* was that if it were possible in the instant case to weigh the value of a greater lump sum and a deferred pension against the right to an immediate pension, the value of the overall remuneration package would not be greatly affected. The ECJ took the view, however, that equality is mandated in respect of each element of the remuneration package, so that it is not possible to set-off an advantage in one respect against a disadvantage in another, on the basis that "genuine transparency, permitting an effective review, is assured only if the principle of equal pay applies to each of the elements of remuneration granted to men and women." Exactly what would constitute a discrete item in such a review remains unclear and would be open to argument. This aspect of the case is, of course, consonant with the views previously expressed by the Lords on the need for a term by term review of the remuneration package under the Equal Pay Act in *Hayward* v. *Cammel Laird*, even despite what the Lords saw as the hypothetical danger of leap-frogging claims.

The time limitation   5.36   The consequences of the *Barber* decision for pension schemes were mitigated only by the limitation of the ruling to claims in being or arising as from the date of the judgement (May 17, 1990), the ECJ holding as follows,

"The Member States and the parties concerned were reasonably entitled to consider that Article 119 did not apply to pensions under contracted out schemes and that derogations from the principle of equality between men and women were still permitted in that sphere.

In these circumstances, overriding considerations of legal certainty preclude legal situations which have exhausted

[68] S. Honeyball and J. Shaw, "Sex, Law and the Retiring Man", *European Law Review*, 1991, at pp. 47-58.

all their effects in the past from being called into question where that might upset retrospectively the financial balance of many contracted out pension schemes. It is appropriate, however, to provide for an exception in favour of individuals who have taken action in good time in order to safeguard their rights. Finally, it must be pointed out that no restriction on the effects of the aforesaid interpretation can be permitted as regards the acquisition of entitlement to a pension as from the date of this judgement.

It must therefore be held that the direct effect of Article 119 of the Treaty may not be relied upon in order to claim entitlement to a pension with effect from a date prior to that of this judgement, except in the case of workers or those claiming under them who have before that date initiated legal proceedings or raised an equivalent claim under applicable national law."[69]

This aspect of the decision caused great uncertainty because it was not clear whether the provisions on equality in pension schemes applied only to persons

(a) beginning to contribute to a pension after May 17, 1990, or
(b) in receipt of pensions benefits only in respect of periods of service after May 17, 1990, or
(c) beginning to receive pension benefits after May 17, 1990, whether referable to service before of after that date, or
(d) in receipt of any pension payment made after May 1990, whether referable to service before of after that date.

Pensions as pay   5.37   The Advocate General in the *Coloroll*[70] etc., cases opted for interpretation (b) above; he argued that pensions are a form of deferred remuneration which accrues during service and that a distinction can be drawn between the accrual of such rights and the falling due of an occupational pension. The reasoning seems compelling, in view of the Court's stated wish not to upset retrospectively the financial balance of existing schemes. The principle of legal certainty would require that pension rights fall to be determined by the rules applying at the time of the period of service during which those rights were acquired. Yet such limitations are exceptional in view of the declaratory nature of a judgement under Article 177, which clarify and define a rule of Community law as it must be or ought to have been understood from the time of its coming into force. It is not a sufficient justification for the imposition of such a limitation

---

[69] paras. 43-45
[70] Joined cases C109/91 (*Ten Oever* v. *Stichting Bedrijfspensioenfonds voor het Glazenwassers-en Schoonmaakdedrijf*), C110/91 (*Moroni* v. *Firma Collo GmbH*), C152/91 (*Neath* v. *Hugh Steeper Ltd*), C200/91 (*Coloroll Pension Trustees Ltd.* v. *Russel, Mangham and Others*).

that serious economic and financial consequences would flow from the decision. Such a limitation is only appropriate where the parties have acted in good faith, ie on the legitimate expectation that their conduct was in accordance with Community law, as, for example, in *Defrenne No 2*.[71] If pension schemes were required to adjust their calculations in respect of past service to allow employers to pay out pensions to men in full at age 60, the financial balance of those schemes would be upset. Although it could be argued that a pension contribution which will result in a pension payment at some future date cannot have exhausted its legal effects until the pension is paid, the better view would appear to be that if pensions are deferred pay, then a given contribution or period of service entitles the employee to a certain sum by way of pension entitlement, which will fall due on retirement, in accordance with the existing rules of the scheme.[72] This view is reinforced by the statement of the Court in paragraph 43 in *Barber* that pension scheme managers were reasonably entitled to conclude that Article 119 did not apply. Clearly tranfers of pension rights could give rise to problems for the final employer or any other construction.

5.38 The draft Treaty on European Union concluded at Maastricht contains the following protocol signed by all 12 Member States

> "For the purposes of Article 119 of the Treaty establishing the European Community, benefits under occupational social security schemes shall not be considered as remuneration if and in so far as they are attributable to periods of service prior to 17 May 1990, except in the case of workers or those claiming under them who have before that date initiated legal proceedings or introduced an equivalent claim under the applicable national law"

As the Advocate General argues in *Coloroll*, the effect of Article 239 will be to make the protocol an integral part of the Treaty, once ratification has taken place. The protocol, which declares the meaning of Article 119 in this respect, will therefore have the same legal effect as any other Treaty provision, and would vitiate any contrary interpretation.

5.39 Little seems to be left, therefore, of the reservations and exceptions from the principle of equality permitted under the Occupational Social Security Directive 86/378. Once pensions are seen as pay under Article 119 and can be resolved by legal analysis on that basis, the direct effect of the Treaty article displaces any relevant directive to a supplementary or extending effect only. In so far as the

---

[71] [1976] 2 C.M.L.R. 98.
[72] Advocate General's opinion in Coloroll para. 19, but see also David Hudson, "Some reflections on the *Barber* decision", European Law Review, 1992, pp. 163–171.

Directive qualifies rights established under Article 119 it is displaced.[73] The Directive requires that the principle of equal treatment be implemented by January 1st 1993. This was to have been achieved in Britain by the Social Security Act 1989, s.23 and schedule 5.[74] As regards the limitation in time it is notable that Article 5(2) of the Directive provides that:

> "The Directive shall preclude rights and obligations relating to a period of membership of an occupational scheme prior to revision of that scheme from remaining subject to the provisions of the scheme in force during that period."

5.40 In so far as the Directive is wider than occupational pensions as commonly understood, it remains a valid point of reference; Articles 3 and 4 provide that the principle of equal treatment applies to sickness and invalidity benefits as well as to old age and retirement benefits. It also applies to schemes which offer protection in cases of industrial accident, occupational disease and unemployment in respect of any member of the working population and not simply those engaged under a contract of employment. Article 5 requires that there shall be no discrimination in the scope of such schemes or in access to them, the obligation to contribute or the calculation of contributions and benefits. Article 6 applies the provisions of the Directive to direct and indirect discrimination by reference to sex, marital or family status and specifies the requirements of the Directive in greater detail. Article 7 requires that the provisions of legally compulsory collective agreements, staff rules and other arrangements relating to occupational schemes are or may be declared null and void or be amended.

5.41 Yet the qualifications to the principle of equality contained in the Directive are of doubtful validity. Under Article 9 the compulsory application of the principle of equal treatment may be deferred with regard (a) to the discrimination of pensionable age either until the date at which such equality is achieved in statutory schemes or, at the latest, until it is required by a directive, (b) survivor's pensions until such equality is required by directive in

---

[73] Advocate General's opinion in *Coloroll*, etc., para. 32.

[74] The implementation of Sched. 5 has been delayed pending the resolution of the issues raised in the *Coloroll* cases. Para. 7 of the SSA 1989, Sched. 5 applies the principle of equal treatment to what it terms service related benefit schemes, which cover either employed earners. A service related benefit is defined in para. 7(e) in similar terms to the coverage of the Directive. Age related differences are permitted by para. 2(4)(b), differences in survivors' benefits by para. 2(4)(e) actuarial differences in contributions by para. 2(4)(a)(i), *actuarial diffeences in the value of money purchase benefits by para.* 2(4)(b), differences in optional provisions by para. 2(4)(f) and in individual provisions by para. 2(4)(g). The saving with regard to differences in contributions is qualified by the power of the Secretary of State in para. 12 to repeal para. 2(4)(a)(i), which will in any event occur automatically by July 30, 1999. Special treatment for the benefit of women in connection with pregnancy or childbirth is permitted by para. 2(4)(c).

statutory social security schemes or in (c) the calculation of
differential worker contribution rates on actuarial tables at
least until 1999. In contribution defined schemes Article 6(1)
allows different levels of actuarially defined benefit or
differential employer contributions to equalise such benefits.
Differential transfer benefits and terms as to the guarantee of
deferred benefits are also permitted under Article 6(1). All
the above qualifications must be considered highly
questionable.

5.42 The first qualification with regard to pensionable age
was clearly displaced by *Barber*. The qualification as regards
survivor's benefits is questionable, even though, because
they are not paid to the worker, it could be argued that such
payments fall outside the concept or deferred pay. The ECJ
in *Newstead* held that contributions to a windows benefit
scheme which did not affect gross pay fell outside Article
119 because they were in the nature of contributions to a
social security scheme. However, in *Barber* contracted out
pensions were held to constitute pay.[75] In *Garland* the ECJ
jhad already held that a travel benefit paid to the dependants
of a former employee are "pay", whilst in *Razzouk and
Beydoun*[76] differences in the treatment of males and females
with regard to survivors benefits, enshrined in the E.C. staff
regulations, were held to be contrary to the fundamental
right to equal treatment. On this argument the better view
would appear to be that survivors benefits do fall within
Article 119. Likewise, the Advocate General in *Ten Oever*[77]
adopted the view that as entitlement to the benefit arose
from the employment of the deceased spouse, survivor's
benefits should be considered as pay.

5.43 Actuarially determined contributions and benefits may
be seen as constituting direct and overt discrimination
capable of analysis be legal means, contrary to the directly
effective principle of equal pay contained in Article 119, *e.g.*
difdferential transfer values based on the length of time over
which a pension might be expected to be received. The
Advocate General in *Coloroll* concludes that the use of
actuarial tables cannot be justified, because they treat men
and women as a group and do not differentiate between the
multiplicity of factors which determine the longevity of an
individual[78] Thus if this argument prevails differences in

---

[75] *Worringham* holds that where contributions affect gross pay they fall
within Art. 119, whilst the categorisation of pension contributions as
social security matters falling with Art. 118 in Newstead is, it is
submitted, confined to legally determined survivors benefit schemes. The
Advocate General in Barber distinguished between the contributors made
in *Newstead* to a legally required widows pension scheme which was
necessary to achieve contracted out status and therefore akin to the
situation in *Defrenne 1* and the situation in *Barber*.

[76] Chap. 1, n. 50.

[77] Case C109/91 (heard with *Coloroll*.

[78] Paragraphs 34–39. Curtin argues to similar effect in "Occupational
Pension Schemes and Article 119: beyond the fringe?", C.M.L.R. 1987
pp. 215–257. But can direct discrimination be justified at all? It can be

actuarial contributions (and benefits from a money purchase scheme) will fall within Article 119 will be proscribed for service after the date of the judgement in *Coloroll*, including additional voluntary contributions linked to the main scheme. Otherwise, such differences will be regulated by the Directive,[79] which would allow such differences in contributions to persist until July 30, 1999, if they are not eliminated by directive at some earlier date.

5.44   Internal gender based actuarial calaculations of the liabilities of a pension fund are not precluded, only their expression in contributions or benefits.

5.45   Whilst it can be inferred from *Defrenne No. 2*[80] that equality can only be achieved in Community law by upward harmonisation *i.e.* lowering the pension age for men rather than increasing that for women, the Advocate General in *Coloroll* argues that this does not preclude new scheme rules being introduced which would equalise benefits at a lower level in relation to future service.[81]

5.46   Partly as a result of *Barber* the Government has felt moved to sort out the underlying problem, namely, the disparity in the State pension age for men and women. Currently speculation favours uniformity at age 65. Until these matters are resolved, according to the EAT in *Robers v. Birds Eye Walls Ltd*,[82] extra bridging pensions for men to make up for the absence of the state pension between ages 60 and 65 will be contrary to *Barber*, but at the time of writing this decision has been referred to the ECJ by the Court of Appeal.

Operation of the equality clause

5.47   An equality clause will operate in three sets of circumstances, namely where a woman is employed on like work with a man in the same employment, on work which is

inferred from the ECJ decision in *Dekker* [1991] I.R.L.R. 27, that direct discrimination is incapable of justification.

[79] To be implemented by SSA 1989, Sched. 5, para. 2(4)(*a*)(i).

[80] "Since Article 119 appears in the context of the harmonisation of working conditions while the improvement is being maintained the objection that the terms of this Article may be observed in other ways than by raising the lowest salaries may be set aside," ground 15, n. 76. The first para. of Art. 117, with which the social provisions of of the Treaty, as amended by the 1986 Single European Act, commence, provides that "Member States agree upon the need to promote improved working conditions and an improved standard of living, so as to make possible their harmonisation while the improvement is being maintained." The third preamble of the Treaty refers to constant improvement of the living and working conditions of their peoples as the essential objective of its signatories.

[81] Clearly if pensions matters form a term of the contract of employment, (see *Parry* v. *Cleaver* [1970] A.C. 1, *The Halcyon Skies* [1977] Q.B. 14) downward harmonisation may give rise to contractual remedies or alternatively to remedies in trust. The SSA 1989, Sched. 5, para. 3(1) required that equality is to be achieved by a process of levelling-up. Pension fund trustees must act in conformity with Community law, according tothe Advocate General in *Coloroll*.

[82] [1991] I.R.L.R. 19, EAT, [1992] I.R.L.R. 24, C.A.

rated as equivalent with that of a man in the same employment, or where she is employed on work of equal value with a man in the same employment. In each case it is open to the employer to contend that any variation between the terms on which the man and woman are employed is due to a genuine material factor other than a difference of sex, which in the case of women employed on like work or work rated as equivalent must be a difference between her case and his. Following the decision of the House of Lords in *Rainey* v. *Greater Glasgow Health Board*,[83] there is no longer any effective difference between the section 1(3) defence in equal value cases, where the material factor need not be a difference between her case and his, and like work and work rated as equivalent cases, where the statute calls for the genuine material factor to be a difference between her case and his.

The basis of comparison

5.48   The Equal Pay Act provides that where a woman is engaged in either like work, work rated as equivalent (under a job evaluation scheme) or work of equal value, and any term of her contract is less favourable than that of the corresponding clause of her chosen comparator, the equality clause shall operate so as to modify the term in question, unless the difference can be shown to be genuinely due to a material factor which is not the difference in sex. It was argued in *Enderby* v. *Frenchay*[84] that all that the applicant needed to show for the onus to be thrown on to the respondent to establish a genuine material difference defence was a disparity of earnings, if the applicant and the comparator were engaged in like work etc. Thus, the argument runs that if it is established by the applicant that, say, speech therapists and pharmacists are doing work of equal value but their pay is not the same, it is then for the employer to establish a genuine material difference. Conversely, the respondent argued that it is necessary for the applicant not only to establish the difference in pay, but that those differences were attributable to either direct or indirect discrimination, as set out in the 1975 Act. In the case of indirect discrimination, it would be for the applicant to show the existence of a barrier which precluded receipt of the higher pay. Clearly in this respect it is necessary to examine the operation of the 1970 Act in the context of Article 119 and the Equal Pay Directive. Article 119 calls for the application of the principle that men and women should receive equal pay for equal work, but goes on to provide that "Equal pay *without discrimination based on sex* means. . . .". The Equal Pay Directive provides that "the principle of equal pay" entails "the *elimination of all discrimination* on grounds of sex. . ." (emphasis added). The EAT concluded, after reviewing the British and European case law, that it is necessary to establish the existence of such a barrier in equal pay cases which rely upon the

[83] See paras. 5.82–5.98 for a discussion of s.1(3).
[84] [1991] I.R.L.R. 44, EAT [1992] I.R.L.R. 15, C.A. and see also *R.* v. *Secretary of State for Social services ex.p. Clarke* [1988] I.R.L.R. 22.

concept of indirect discrimination. In the Court of Appeal this was seen by Neil L.J. as posing the question of whether the employer has one line of defence or two – may he argue firstly that there is no discrimination because there is no requirement or condition which female employees must satisfy and, secondly, if there is, its imposition is justifiable in the circumstances? Or is it that once it is shown in practice that a predominantly female group is paid less than a male group engaged upon equal work, the employer may only rely on proving that the difference is justifiable? Whilst Neil L.J. accepted that it was arguable that the applicant does not have to establish the existence of such a barrier in equal pay claims based upon indirect discrimination, the question has, at the time of writing, been referred to the ECJ.[85]

The chosen comparator

5.49   The woman may choose as her comparator any male worker in the same employment whom she believes is performing like work, or whose work has been rated as equal under a job evaluation scheme or whom she contends is performing work of equal value.[86] The man chosen need not be representative of a group of male employees, although where this is the case the likelihood is increased that the employer will be able to justify any difference in pay under section 1(3). In *Thomas* v. *N.C.B.*,[87] 1,500 women canteen workers, of whom Mrs Thomas was representative, compared themselves with the only male canteen worker working in the NCB, who for historical reasons bound up with local negotiation at a time of previous labour shortage, was paid on a higher grade. Although anomalous, this was held to be a valid comparison, albeit that the EAT did express some reservations about the possible consequences of this aspect of its decision.

5.50   By contrast with the Sex Discrimination or Race Relations Acts, the Equal Pay Act does not provide for hypothetical comparisons to be made.[88] Under Article 119, however, comparison may be made on the basis of concrete appraisals of the work actually performed by non-contemporaneous employees of different sex within the same establishment or service, although the ECJ recognised in *McCarthys Ltd* v. *Smith*[89] that any disparity between the pay received by a non-contemporaneous male and female

[85] cf *Brooke* v. *London Borough of Haringey* [1992] I.R.L.R. 478, EAT.
[86] See *Ainsworth* v. *Glass Tubes Ltd.* [197] I.R.L.R. 74, EAT.
[87] [1987] I.R.L.R. 451, EAT.
[88] There must be a comparator. In *Meeke* v. *U.U.A.W.* [1976] I.R.L.R. 198, a part-time secretary was found to have been subject to indirect discrimination compared with the rate at which full timers were paid, but as the claim fell within the Equal Pay Act and there were no male comparators, the Tribunal was compelled to dismiss the claim. See also the decision of the ECJ with respect to Art. 119 in *McCarthys* v. *Smith*, n. 74, ground 15.
[89] Case 129/79, *McCarthys Ltd* v.*Smith*: [1980] E.C.R. 1275; [1980] 2 C.M.L.R. 205.

may be explained by the operation of factors unconnected with any discrimination on grounds of sex. *Albion Shipping Agency* v. *Arnold*[90] is a case where economic factors supervened to account for the difference in pay.[91]

The same employment

5.51   A woman may only make comparison with a man who is engaged in the same employment as her chosen comparator, whichever basis of comparison she chooses. Section 1(6) provides that:

> "(M)en shall be treated as in the same employment with a woman if they are men employed by her employer or any associated employer at the same establishment or at establishments in Great Britain which include that one and at which common terms and conditions of employment are observed generally or for employees of the relevant class."

5.52   In *Lawson* v. *Britfish*[92], the EAT held that where employees are working at the same establishment they need not be working under common terms and conditions. Where there are no suitable men working at the establishment where she is employed, a woman may therefore choose to make a comparison with a man employed by her employer or any associated employer at some other establishment at which common terms and conditions are employed. In *Leverton* v. *Clwyd County Council*,[93] the majority of the Court of Appeal held that the existence of common terms and conditions implied that the terms and conditions of the woman and her chosen comparator must be broadly similar. On this view, any gross disparity in the terms and conditions of the woman and the comparators would mean that like was not being compared with like, whilst if the terms and conditions were identical there could be no ground for a claim. Thus in the instant case a nursery nurse who enjoyed school holidays and who worked only school hours, was defeated in her claim with other workers employed by the authority, who were at different grade points on the same set of salary scales, because of the disparity between them in the hours worked. The House of Lords, preferring the dissenting view of May L. J. in the Court of Appeal, held that:

> "The concept of common terms and conditions of employment observed generally at different establishments necessarily contemplates terms and conditions applicable

---

[90] [1981] I.R.L.R. 525, EAT.
[91] In *Wallis* v. *Prudential Portfolio Managers Ltd.* Case No. 35372/91 EOR DCLD 15, 1993, the Liverpool Industrial Tribunal took the view that no precise comparator was necessary in a claim brought under Art. 119 with respect to the occupational pension entitlement of part-timers, observing that in *Barber* and other such cases, no reliance was placed on a person performing equal work.
[92] (1988) I.R.L.R. 53, EAT.
[93] [1988 I.R.L.R. 239.

to a wide range of employees whose individual terms will vary greatly *inter se*. On the construction of the sub-section adopted by the majority below the phrase "observed either generally or for employees of the relevant classes" is given no content. Terms and conditions of employment governed by the same collective agreement seem to me to represent the paradigm, though not necessarily the only example, of the common terms and conditions of employment contemplated by the sub-section."[94]

5.53 It is submitted that this must have been the intention of Parliament, if only because the difference in hours referred to is capable of constituting a genuine material difference under section 1(3), and can therefore find an appropriate place in the scheme of the Equal Pay Act.[95] It could be argued that as neither Article 119 nor the Equal Pay Directive contain an express limitation of the sphere of comparison such as is provided by section 1(6), it is possible under Community law to make a broader comparison. For example, if a certain function has been contracted-out in whole or in part, with the result that employees now work for a new employer under inferior terms and conditions, comparisons may be possible with their former colleagues. Against this view the ECJ in *McCarthys* stated that "comparative studies of entire branches of industry" would concern "indirect and disguised discrimination", and therefore fall outside Article 119, which was confined to comparisons made within the same establishment or service. Two comments need to be made here. First, the ECJ has placed less reliance on the *Defrenne* concept of disguised discrimination in its later case law, save that the law must be clear and the facts ascertainable without need of other legislative instruments. Second, a wide definition of "service" could encompass privatisation situations or other examples where the comparisons to be made are simple, direct and concrete.

Definitions of "associated"

5.54 Two employers are defined as being associated employers in section 1(6)(c) if:

"one is a company of which the other (directly or indirectly) has control or if both are companies of which a third person (directly or indirectly) has control."

Two companies are associated if one has voting control over the other.[96] In *Gardiner* v. *London Borough of Merton*,[97] it was held that the word "company" is not apt to cover all bodies corporate, so that two local authorities would not be

---

[94] [198] I.R.L.R. 29 at p. 31. cf *British Coal Corporation* v. *Smith* EAT/29/91.
[95] The majority of the Court of Appeal and the IT found that the differences did amount to a s.1(3) defence.
[96] *Umar* v. *Pliastar Ltd.* [1981] I.R.L.R. 727.
[97] [1980] I.R.L.R. 472.

considered as being associated employers. Consequently in *Hasley* v. *Fair Employment Agency*,[98] when an employee of the Fair Employment Agency sought equal pay with an official of the Northern Ireland Equal Opportunity Commission, her claim failed on the ground, firstly, that neither body was a company but a public corporation, and secondly, that being the case, it was immaterial that both were under the *de facto* control of the Department of Economic Affairs for purposes of establishment.

The methods of comparison

5.55 Section 1(4) provides that:

"A woman is to be regarded as employed on like work with men if, but only if, her work and theirs is of the same or a broadly similar nature, and the difference (if any) between the things she does and the things they do are not of practical importance in relation to terms and conditions of employment; and accordingly in comparing her work with theirs regard shall be had to the frequency or otherwise with which any such differences occur in practice as well as to the nature and extent of the differences."[99]

Like work

5.56 Thus like work must be the same as, or broadly similar to, the work of the chosen comparator, and whatever differences occur must not be such as would reasonably be thought capable of giving rise to differentials in pay or of putting the two jobs into different categories or grades in an evaluation study.[1] In approaching this question, Tribunals must first ask whether there is like work or work of a broadly similar nature. In considering whether work is of a broadly similar nature, the Tribunals have been enjoined to take a broad approach and not to make too minute an examination, nor to place emphasis upon trivial distinctions which in the real world are not likely to be reflected in the terms and conditions of employment.[2] It follows that where there are differences in responsibility which justify differences in grading, there can be no like work.[3] Greater responsibilities when performing a similar task can lead to the conclusion that like work does not exist, as in *Eaton Ltd.* v. *Nuttal*[4] (a male stock control clerk was responsible for items of greater value than his female colleague).

5.57 The second issue is whether there are any differences of practical importance, and how frequently these differences

[98] [1989] I.R.L.R. 106, NICA.
[99] EqPA 1970, s.1(4).
[1] *British Leyland* v. *Powell* [1978] I.R.L.R. 57, EAT.
[2] *Capper Pass Ltd.* v. *Lawton* [1977] I.C.R. 83, EAT (male assistant chef in directors" dining room found comparable with cook in canteen).
[3] *Capper Pass Ltd.* v. *Allen* [1980] I.C.R. 194, EAT.
[4] [1977] I.C.R. 272, EAT and see *Coley* v. *Hinckley & Bosworth Borough Council* (unreported) 1983, summarised in Towards Equality, EOC, 1989, p. 62. and *Fletcher* v. *Greenbank Terotech Ltd.* EOR, DCLD 12, Summer 1992.

occur. It is not sufficient merely to compare the contractual obligations of the persons concerned but to examine the actual work performed. Thus in *Dance* v. *Dorothy Perkins Ltd.*,[5] the obligation to move heavier material around the warehouse when deliveries were received resulted not only in a difference in the contractual obligations but also in the performance of the duties. By contrast, the contract of the male employee in *Shields* v. *Coomes Holdings Ltd.*[6] had a special responsibility for assisting with security, but the Court of Appeal found that this responsibility was not frequently exercised in practice and neither did the male employee possess any special skills; nor had he undergone any special training in dealing with security matters. The contractual difference was, therefore, held not to be one of practical importance for terms and conditions. A mere preparedness to work shifts or undertake night duty does not constitute such a difference.[7] It is also necessary to show that such additional duties are performed to a significant extent if they are to be of practical importance.[8] Where the work performed is not sufficiently similar to constitute like work, it is not relevant that those differences are of a much smaller order and in no way commensurate with the difference in pay.[9]

Work rated as equivalent

5.58   Where a job evaluation study has been completed it can be relied upon under section 1(2)(*b*) even if it has not been implemented,[10] although the parties must have accepted its validity.[11] The claimant must base her case upon the study as it is,[12] and can only challenge the results under section 1(2)(*b*) if there is a plain error on the face of the record. Methods of job evaluation To fall within section 1(2)(*b*), a job evaluation scheme must satisfy the requirements of section 1(5) in that the scheme must analyse the demands made upon the worker under various headings such as effort, skill, decision.

Methods of job evaluation

5.59   The main distinction in job evaluation methods is between the whole job, or felt fair, methods and the analytical methods. The EAT, in an appendix to the

---

[5] [1978] I.C.R. 760, EAT and see *McCabe* v. *I.C.L. Ltd.* (unreported) IT 292 Case No. 59/79.

[6] [1978] I.R.L.R. 263, C.A. and *Waddington* v. *Leicester Council for Voluntary Service* [1977] I.R.L.R. 32, EAT, *Doncaster Education Authority* v. *Gill EOR DCLD 14.*

[7] *Dugdale* v. *Kraft Foods* [1976] I.R.L.R. 369, *N.C.B.* v. *Sherwin* [1978] I.R.L.R. 122, EAT.

[8] *Electrolux Ltd.* v. *Hutchinson* [1976] I.R.L.R. 410, EAT (the frequency with which additional duties, such as preparedness to transfer to other physically more demanding work or to work at nights, occurred was relevant in considering whether these differences were of practical importance).

[9] *Maidment & Hardacre* v. *Cooper & Co Ltd.* [1978] I.R.L.R. 462, EAT.

[10] *O'Brien* v. *Sim Chem Ltd.* [1980] I.C.R. 573, H.L.

[11] *Arnold* v. *Beecham Group Ltd.* [1982] I.C.R. 744, EAT.

[12] *England* v. *Bromley Borough Council* [1978] I.C.R. 1, EAT.

decision in *Eaton Ltd.* v. *Nuttal*[13] set out a note of the
principal methods of job evaluation:

"Job ranking

This is commonly thought to be the simplest method.
Each job is considered as a whole and is then given a
ranking in relation to all other jobs. A ranking table is
then drawn up and the ranked jobs grouped into grades.
Pay levels can then be fixed for each grade.

Paired comparisons

This is also a simple method. Each job is compared as a
whole with each other job in turn and points (0, 1, or 2)
awarded according to whether its overall importance is
judged to be less than, equal to or more than the other.
Points awarded for each job are then totalled and a
ranking order produced.

Points assessment

This is the most common system in use. It is an analytical
method, which, instead of comparing whole jobs, breaks
each job down into a number of factors – for example
skills, responsibility, physical or mental requirements and
working conditions. Each of these factors may be analysed
further. Points are awarded for each factor according to a
predetermined scale and the total points decide a job's
place in the rank order. Usually the factors are weighted,
so that, for example, more or less weight may be given to
hard physical conditions or to a high degree of skill.

Factor comparison

This is also an analytical method, employing the same
principles as points assessment but using only a limited
number of factors, such as skill, responsibility and
working conditions. A number of key jobs are selected
because their wage rates are generally agreed to be 'fair'.
The proportion of the total wage attributed to each factor
is then decided and a scale produced showing the rate for
each factor for each key job. The other jobs are then
compared with this scale, factor by factor, so that a rate is
finally obtained for each factor for each job. The total pay
for each job is reached by adding together the rates for its
individual factors."

5.60 Job evaluation schemes based only upon the use of
paired comparisons or other felt fair methods in which there
is no analysis of the job under a number of headings, as
required under section 1(5), fall outside the definition. In
Bromley v. *H. J. Quick Ltd.*,[14] the employer had
commissioned consultants to carry out what is often termed
a hybrid job evaluation study. The consultants first used a

---

[13] *Supra* n. 4 and see EOR 24, March/April 1987 for a report of an EOC
   sponsored survey of the practices adopted by independent experts.
[14] [1987] I.R.L.R. 456, EAT; [1988] I.R.L.R. 249, C.A.

panel of management and employees, including women, to perform a paired comparison of a selection of representative jobs, which were then placed in rank order. These comparisons were based upon job descriptions but the tasks were not broken down or analysed in any way. The jobs were then analysed by factors such as skill and the contribution of each of these factors to the total rank order of the jobs was obtained by multiple regression analysis. The factors were assigned weightings on the basis of the regression analysis. The panels then adjusted the rank order of the benchmark jobs to remove any anomalies they perceived and the remaining jobs were slotted in by management on a felt fair basis. Only in the case of an appeal against the grade given were the remaining jobs analysed according to the factor plan. The jobs of the appellants were therefore analysed, but not those of their chosen comparators, who had not appealed against their grading.

5.61 By a majority, the EAT rejected the argument raised on behalf of two appellant female clerical workers that this method of job evaluation fell outside the definition given in section 1(5) and considered that a concentration upon the form and nature of a job evaluation could lead to a failure to identify the real mischief which the Act was designed to meet. The EAT upheld the finding of fact by the Tribunal that the scheme was not discriminatory at any stage and that those responsible for the operation of the scheme had constantly reminded the panels of the dangers of discrimination in their deliberations.[15]

5.62 The Court of Appeal held that the majority of the EAT had erred in the decision that the study fell within section 1(5). It was held that section 1(5) requires that the work of the woman and her comparators has been analysed under the required heading using "analytical" techniques, a usage specifically approved in this context by Dillon L. J. It is not sufficient that the benchmark jobs have been so analysed, if the jobs in question have not.[16] A job evaluation scheme includes not only the determination of points for

---

[15] It was considered that the "blemishes" on the scheme in having slotted in the remaining jobs without full evaluation and in management members having altered a couple of the rank orderings were not sufficiently serious to invalidate the scheme as a whole. In the view of the dissenting member these defects were sufficiently serious to bring the scheme outside s.1(5).

[16] Whilst Woolf L.J. held that the scheme as a whole would have satisfied s.1(5) had the jobs of the appellants been analysed, Dillon L.J. specifically declined to go this far. It is surely a moot point as to whether a scheme which operated in such a way that the factors are weighted so as to provide a rationalisation for the results of the initial felt fair approach, which incorporates existing workplace values, does meet the requirements of s.1(5). See also EOR 23 p. 48 and EOR 24, p. 22 for a further discussion of the necessity for weighting of the factors in analytical job evaluation and the likelihood that in this process, accepted

each job, but the allocation of jobs to pay bands on the basis of those points, according to the EAT in *Springboard Sunderland Trust* v. *Robson*.[17]

Equal value claims

5.63   The equal value claims provided for under section 1(2)(c) arose out of the need to harmonise United Kingdom domestic law with British obligations under the Treaty of Rome. Article 119 provided for equal pay for equal work. This was a narrower concept than the requirement laid down in the I.L.O. Convention 100 of "equal pay for work of equal value." Nonetheless, when the Equal Pay Directive 75/117 was adopted in 1975 as part of the Social Action Programme, Article 1 provided that:

> "The principle of equal pay for men and women outlined in Article 119, hereinafter called the 'the principle of equal pay,' means, for the same work or for work to which equal value is attributed, the elimination of all discrimination on grounds of sex with regard to all aspects and conditions of remuneration."

It was held in the second *Defrenne* case[18] that Article 119 was directly applicable in Member States where there is "direct and overt discrimination which may be identified solely with the aid of criteria based on equal work and equal pay."[19] In *Jenkins* v. *Kingsgate (Clothing Productions) Ltd.*[20] the ECJ held that Article 1 of the Directive restates the principle of equal pay set out in Article 119 of the EEC treaty so as to facilitate its practical application and "in no way alters the content or scope of that principle as defined in the Treaty."[21] Thus, the right to equal pay for work of equal value was viewed by the Commission as integral to the application of Article 119, in spite of the caveat entered at the time of the adoption of the Equal Pay Directive by the United Kingdom Government that "work to which equal value is attributed" applied only where such equal value had in fact been attributed by an existing job evaluation scheme. This argument did not prevail when the Commission brought enforcement proceedings against the United Kingdom Government (and seven other Member States) in 1982.[22] The ECJ held that the United Kingdom was in breach of its obligations under the Treaty in not providing a remedy in its national courts for equal value claims where no system of job classification exists. Subsequently, the United Kingdom Government introduced a discussion document proposing changes in the Equal Pay Act to provide a right for women

---

social mores which incorporate traditional notions of what are more valued and less valued skills, will be built into the results. Some method of factor weighting is inevitable and unavoidable.

[17] [1992] I.R.L.R. 261, EAT.

[18] *Defrenne* v. *Sabena* [1976] C.M.L.R. 98.

[19] At p. 123. See chap. 1 for a discussion of the concept of direct and indirect discrimination in Community law.

[20] [1981] I.C.R. 692, ECJ; [1981] I.R.L.R. 388, C.A.

[21] At p. 614.

[22] *Commission of the European Communities* v. *U.K.* [1982] I.R.L.R. 333.

to bring equal value claims, which eventually resulted in the
Equal Pay (Amendment) Regulations 1983.[23]

**The Equal Pay
(Amendment)
Regulations 1983**

5.64   The Equal Pay (Amendment) Regulations were
introduced under the European Communities Act 1972,
under which an Order can only be accepted or rejected by
Parliament and cannot be amended. The Parliamentary
procedures established under the European Communities
Act allow only minimal time for debate, so that even though
the language (and the substance) of the regulations were
severely criticised, it was not possible to amend them. In
order to implement the regulations, amendments had to be
made to the procedural regulations of the Industrial
Tribunals, changes which again generated fierce controversy.
The procedural regulations are now incorporated within the
Industrial Tribunal (Rules of Procedure) Regulations 1985.[24]
Both the Amending Regulations and the procedures
established for equal value claims are of considerable
complexity and have given rise to some problems of
interpretation in the Tribunals. See Chapter 6 for a more
complete discussion of the procedural issues in equal value
cases.

5.65   The essence of the procedure established under
section 1(2)(c) is that an independent expert is appointed by
the Tribunal to prepare a report on whether or not the
claimant is performing work of equal value to her chosen
comparator. The Tribunal will then decide, on the basis of
the independent expert's report and other evidence, whether
the woman is performing work of equal value to the man.
This is clearly a slow, cumbersome and expensive process
and in consequence a screening test has been provided under
which the Tribunal can first weed out "hopeless cases."

5.66   An employee who wishes to bring an equal value
claim must first pass the screening test designed to sift out
the "hopeless cases." The statutory language in which this
test is laid down was criticised as incomprehensible when the
Order was laid before Parliament[25] and indeed the EAT
sought guidance on its interpretation from the Court of
Appeal in the first reported case under the section.[26]

5.67   Section 2A (1) provides that the Tribunal shall not
determine the question of whether the applicant and her
male comparator are performing work of equal value unless:

"(a) it is satisfied there are no reasonable grounds for
determining that the work is of equal value; or

[23] S.I. 1983 No. 1794.
[24] S.I. 1985 No. 16 and No. 17 (Scotland).
[25] Described as "eleven unfathomable lines. . .virtually incapable of
comprehension" by Mr Barry Jones M.P. (H.C. Deb., 6th ser., Vol.
489).
[26] *Forex Neptune (Overseas) Ltd.* v. *Miller* [1987] I.C.R. 170.

(*b*) it has required a member of the panel of independent experts to prepare a report with respect to that question and has received that report."

Section 2A(1) requires that the Tribunal may not determine whether the work is of equal value unless there are no reasonable grounds for so determining, or it has sought the opinion of an independent expert. The effect of this obscure phraseology is that the Tribunal has the power to stop the case without commissioning an expert report, only if there are no reasonable grounds for thinking that the case could succeed. The converse would appear to be that unless there are no reasonable grounds for considering that the case could succeed, a report must be commissioned. The claimant therefore needs only to establish an arguable case at this juncture for the Tribunal to have to seek the opinion of the independent expert.

5.68   The EOC, in its document "Equal Pay: Strengthening the Acts."[27] advocates that the section 2A(1) procedure should be replaced by an interlocutory procedure. A study reported in the EOC document shows preliminary hearings under section 2A(1) to last from 2 to 10 days, often with much of the evidence which will later be encompassed by the report of the independent expert, being presented.

5.69   The Commission is of the opinion that the "no reasonable grounds" defence should be repealed, pointing out that there is normally a place for a pre-hearing assessment under the Tribunal rules. Under the Employment Act 1989, s.20, regulations may be introduced to permit a pre-hearing review, rather than a pre-hearing assessment, under which tribunals will be empowered to require a party to pay a £150 deposit, if he or she wishes to proceed any further.

5.70   An employee may be frustrated in her desire to pursue an equal value claim by the existence of a job evaluation scheme which she believes does not adequately reflect the value of the job on which she is engaged. She may believe that she is doing work of equal value with a male worker, but the results of the existing job evaluation may say otherwise. She may challenge the validity of an existing job evaluation scheme by bringing an equal value action under section 1(2)(*c*), provided she has an arguable case under section 2A(1) and can satisfy the requirements of section 2A(2).[28]

---

[27] EOC 1990.
[28] Where there is an existing job evaluation scheme s.2A(2) provides that there shall "be no reasonable grounds for determining that the work of a woman is of equal value as mentioned in s.1(2)(*c*) above if: "(a) that work and the work of the man in question have been given different values in a study such as is mentioned in s.1(5) above; and (b) there are no reasonable grounds for determining that the evaluation contained in the study was (within the meaning of subs. 3, below) made on a system

5.71 Under that subsection, a Tribunal may not hear an equal value claim if there is a job evaluation scheme in existence as defined in section 1(5)[29] if there are no reasonable grounds for determining that "the study was made on a system which discriminates on grounds of sex." An evaluation scheme discriminates on grounds of sex under section 2A(3) where:

> "the difference, or coincidence, of values set by that system on different demands under the same or different headings is not justifiable irrespective of the sex of the person on whom those demands are made."

5.72 It should be noted that on the statutory language, an applicant who seeks to challenge the results of an existing job evaluation scheme by securing the report of an independent expert on the value of her work would have to establish only an arguable case that the allotment of different points for the two jobs was made under a system which discriminates on grounds of sex, *i.e.* if she has anything more than a "hopeless case," the Tribunal must proceed to appoint an independent expert and receive his report before deciding whether the woman and her male comparator are performing work of equal value.

5.73 What of a job evaluation which is on its face neutral, but which is thought to have an adverse impact upon the valuation of the jobs done by women, a far more common and realistic case than a scheme corrupted by elements of direct discrimination? The EOC, in its pamphlet Job Evaluation Schemes Free of Sex Bias,[30] argues that a scheme which tends systematically to attribute a lower value to the jobs done by women than to those done by men, must be tainted by indirect discrimination in the choice of factors to be ranked and/or in the weighting of those factors. This is clearly a circular argument for it presumes that the jobs done by men and women in the particular situation are necessarily of equal value and that an unbiased scheme would merely reflect that state of affairs. There is no Olympian height from which one can look down to decide whether or not a given job evaluation incorporates a correct weighting of the skills and attributes possessed or demanded of men and women. All job evaluation is ultimately subjective; it is merely more systematic than non-evaluated pay structures. This accounts for the fact that almost all schemes incorporate an element of negotiation between

---

which discriminates on grounds of sex." Subs.3 provides that: "An evaluation contained in a study such as is mentioned in s.1(5) above is made on a system which discriminates on a grounds of sex where a difference, or coincidence, between values set by that system on different demands under the same or different headings is not justifiable irrespective of the sex of the person on whom those demands are made."

[29] *Supra*, para. 5.59.

[30] 1984 Job Evaluation Schemes Free of Sex Bias, EOC, Manchester and see the comments in n. 16.

management and employees to ensure the acceptability of the results. A job evaluation scheme which produces unacceptable results, results which do not create a framework in which the workforce can assent to the resulting structure of differentials is not achieving the purposes for which it was undertaken.

5.74 All job evaluation will therefore incorporate the values of the surrounding culture to a greater or lesser extent, and it can only be as that culture becomes more sensitive to issues of discrimination and places greater weight upon what are seen as typically female skills or qualities, that there will be an opportunity to upgrade the values attributed to "women's work." Thus, it would not be surprising to find that a study might undervalue skills learnt in the home, such as cooking, sewing or child care, with the result that jobs which incorporate those skills (and such jobs are typically undertaken by women), would receive a lower ranking under a job evaluation scheme when compared with typically male jobs of similar skill levels. This would be even more likely where the study used a rank order or paired comparison method, which relies upon an intuitive sense of the relative values of a series of benchmark jobs, to determine the weighting to be given to the different job factors. Such a study would be simply reproducing and rationalising existing perceptions of the value of different skills. It is just because such schemes reproduce the values of the surrounding culture that there is unlikely to be any discriminatory intent in such a situation, although this does preclude the bringing of an equal value claim.[31]

5.75 These problems were demonstrated in the German case of *Rummler* v. *Dato-Druck GmbH*.[32] In this case, which was brought under the provisions of Article 1(2) of the Equal Pay Directive, a female employee challenged the use of absolute muscular effort as a criteria in the construction of the firm's job evaluation scheme. Article 1(2) stipulates that a job classification scheme "must be based on the same criteria for men and women and so drawn up as to exclude any discrimination on the grounds of sex." The employee contended that the scheme contravened Article 1(2) because it did not measure the heaviness of the work relative to the strength of the person performing the task, *i.e.* women's lower levels of strength should have been taken into account. This argument was rejected on the grounds that it would be discriminatory to rely on criteria which were not impartial between the sexes. The ECJ, however, held that although a job classification scheme may utilise a criterion more commonly found amongst men than women, the Directive

---

[31] See R. v. *Birmingham City Council, ex p. E.O.C.* [1988] I.R.L.R. 430, C.A.

[32] [1987] I.R.L.R. 32, cited by Dillon L.J. in *Bromley* v. *H.J. Quick Ltd. supra*, in rehearsing the need for an objective approach to job evaluation, whilst admitting that a subjective element was inevitable.

requires that job classification schemes be designed so as to take into account the particular characteristics of both men and women and that it is for national courts to assess whether the scheme allows fair account to be taken of all the criteria. Thus, a job evaluation scheme may be held to be discriminatory if it fails to take into account manual dexterity (often seen as characteristic of the work done by women) whilst giving recognition to gross physical effort, which is usually thought to be more characteristic of manual work undertaken by men. For a detailed discussion of the components of a gender neutral comparison system see the Ontario case of *Haldimand Norfolk (No. 6).*[33]

5.76   A study is said to be discriminatory where the values set under that study are not justifiable irrespective of the sex of the person on whom the demands are made. Seemingly, any objection that the values set by the system are not justifiable would suffice; the requirement that the system is not justifiable because it incorporates an element of either direct or indirect discrimination is implicit.

5.77   The requirement that job evaluation schemes be justifiable irrespective of the sex of the person concerned is clearly a matter of fact. The test for justifiability in the Equal Pay Act[34] is that enunciated by the ECJ in *Bilka-Kaufhaus GmbH* v. *Weber von Hartz*[35] that a policy or practice which has a discriminatory effect is only justifiable if "the means chosen for achieving that objective correspond to a real need on the part of the undertaking, are appropriate with a view to achieving the objective in question and are necessary to that end."[36] Thus the objectives enshrined in the job evaluation scheme in question must be objectively necessary to the undertaking and appropriate to that end, if the net effect of the procedures adopted is to create a requirement with which a considerably smaller proportion of women than men can comply if they are to achieve a favourable evaluation. The objective of creating a rational and acceptable pay structure via job evaluation would normally be justifiable according to this test if the scheme produced results which were within the band of outcomes which a reasonable employer might accept.[37] In sum, gross and obvious distortions which clearly undervalued the contribution of women workers to the enterprise might not be justifiable. Where the results fall within that area in which reasonable and informed persons might legitimately disagree, the results are likely to be seen as justifiable.

---

[33] (1991) *Pay Equity Reports* 105.

[34] See chap. 2 for a full discussion of the concept of justifiability in the SDA, s.1(*b*)(ii).

[35] [1986] I.R.L.R. 317.

[36] At p. 320.

[37] Cf. "Pay Equity-Surprising Answers to Hard Questions", *Challenge*, May/June 1987, pp. 45–51, in which Barbara F. Bergman argues as a

5.78   The blocking effect of a job evaluation scheme may lead to hurried attempts to institute one, as in *Dibro Ltd* v. *Hore*[38] where the EAT held that even if the study was commenced after the initiation of proceedings, section 2A(2) still provides that there shall be no reasonable grounds for determining that the work of a man and woman are of equal value. The EAT held that such evidence is admissible even after the independent expert's report has been received, right up to the point of decision on the equal value claim. It follows that if employers do not like the independent expert's report, they could commence their own job evaluation before the tribunal makes its decision. The existence of an analytical job evaluation scheme which was untainted by discrimination would be a complete defence under section 2(A)2. The EOC has recommended that job evaluation schemes should no longer be a bar to equal value claims, but simply be admissible as evidence, on a par with the report of a specially commissioned expert. The evidence may provide a complete defence, but the present law that it automatically does so must be wrong.

Like work and work of equal value

5.79   The other obstacle which has been seen as preventing an equal value claim is the requirement in section 1(2)(c) that an equal value claim can only be brought under that subsection where a woman is employed on work to which neither section 1(2)(a) or (b) applies, in other words, which is neither like work nor work which has been rated equivalent to that of a man in the same employment. Although the Court of Appeal in *Pickstone* v. *Freemans plc*[39] held that the words of section 1(2)(c) are plain, and unambiguously preclude an equal value claim where there is a man engaged upon like work with the applicant, the House of Lords[40] construed this provision as applying only where the woman sought to make comparison with a man who was himself engaged in like work. The House of Lords held that s.1(2)(c) must be read as if it provided "where a

result of studies of the American concept of "comparable worth", that salary structures do routinely undervalue those jobs in which women predominate.

[38] [1990] I.R.L.R. 129 and see *Henderson* v. *Jaguar Cars* EOR, DCLD 11, IT.

[39] [1987] I.R.L.R. 218, C.A. The Court of Appeal took the view that the words of s.1(2)(c) were unambiguous and precluded such a claim, in spite of the fact that the result would be that the U.K. would thereby have failed fully to implement its obligations under the Equal Pay Directive. Consequently the Court of Appeal held that as the Equal Pay Directive had been held in *Jenkins* v. *Kingsgate* (*supra*, see n. 67) to clarify but not in any way to alter or amend the principle of equal pay expressed in Art. 119, and that the inequality in pay between the claimant and her comparator could be identified without recourse to further national measures, as required by the ECJ in *Worringham* v. *Lloyds Bank* (No. 69/80) [1981] I.C.R. 558 ECJ, there was therefore a directly enforceable Community right to pursue an equal value claim in such circumstances, notwithstanding the wording of s.1(2)(c).

[40] [1988] I.R.L.R. 357, H.L.

woman is employed on work which, not being work to
which paragraph *(a)* or *(b)* above applies *as between the
woman and the man with whom she claims equality.*" (Words
in italics implied by the House of Lords). This construction
achieves the result required if the 1983 Regulations[41] are to
give effect to the decision of the ECJ in *Commission of the
European Communities* v. *United Kingdom,*[42] that the United
Kingdom was obliged under the EEC Treaty and the Equal
Pay Directive to provide an unqualified right to claim equal
pay for work of equal value. Lord Templeman stated the
procedure to be followed in cases brought under section
1(2)(*c*) as follows:[43]

> "To prevent exploitation of para. (c) the Tribunal must
> decide in the first instance whether the complainant and
> the man with whom she seeks parity are engaged on 'like
> Work' under para. (a). If para. (a) applies no ACAS
> report is required. If para. (a) does not apply, then the
> Tribunal considers whether para. (b) applies to the
> complainant and the man with whom she seeks parity; if
> so, the Tribunal can only proceed under para. (c) if the
> job evaluation study obtained for the purposes of para. (b)
> is itself discriminatory. If para. (b) applies then, again, no
> ACAS report is necessary. If paras. (a) and (b) do not
> apply, the Tribunal must next consider whether there are
> reasonable grounds for determining that the work of the
> complainant and the work of the man with whom she
> seeks parity is of equal value. If the Tribunal are not so
> satisfied, then no ACAS report is required . . . Para. (c)
> enables a claim to equal pay as against a specific man to
> be made without injustice to an employer. When a woman
> claims equal pay for work of equal value, she specifies the
> man with whom she claims equal value. If the work of the
> woman is work to which para. (a) or (b) applies in
> relation to that man, then the woman cannot proceed
> under para. (c) and cannot obtain a report from an ACAS
> expert. In my opinion there must be applied in para. (c)
> after the word 'applies' the words 'as between the woman
> and the man with whom she claims equality.' This
> construction is consistent with Community law. The
> employers' construction is inconsistent with Community
> law and creates a form of permitted discrimination
> without rhyme or reason."

The equal value   5.80   The requirement under section 1(2)(*c*) is for the
claim   Tribunal to decide:

> "whether the woman is employed on work which . . . is,
> in terms of the demands made on her (for instance under
> such headings as effort, skill and decision) of equal value
> to that of a man employed in the same employment."

---

[41] S.I. 1983 No. 1794.
[42] Case 61/81, (1982) I.C.R. 578.
[43] *Per* Templeman L.J., at p. 362.

To accomplish this comparison the procedure calls for the Tribunal to commission a report from an independent expert, unless, as explained above, there are no reasonable grounds for determining that the work is of equal value. This section has been widely interpreted by commentators as calling for the use of "analytical" methods of job evaluation,[44] a view confirmed by the Court of Appeal in *Bromley* v. *H & J Quick Ltd.*[45] The procedure utilised in bringing an equal value claim is discussed in Chapter 6.

5.81   An employee who is found to be doing work of a higher value than her comparators is not to be frustrated in her attempt to achieve equal pay, following the decision of the ECJ in *Murphy* v. *Bord Telecom Eirann.*[46] It is open to employers to argue that any differences in pay between the applicant and her chosen comparator are due to a genuine material difference other than a difference of sex, under section 1(3)(*b*), prior to the commissioning of a report from an independent expert.[47]

Genuine material differences

5.82   The employer is provided with a defence in equal pay cases under section 1(1)(*a*) or (*b*), or in equal value cases under section 1(1)(*c*), that the variation in pay "is genuinely due to a material factor which is not the difference of sex." The statute further provides that in cases occurring under section 1(1)(*a*) or (*b*), *i.e.* in like work cases or where the work has been rated as equivalent, that the factor must be "a material difference between the woman's case and the man's."

5.83   The difference between the wording in equal value and other equal pay cases is related to the dictum established by Lord Denning in *Clay Cross (Quarry Services) Ltd.* v. *Fletcher*[48] that "a difference between her case and his" referred to a difference in the personal equation of the woman as compared to the man, to what appertained to her in her job and to him in his. That case was concerned with the situation where a man had been taken on to perform the same function as an existing woman employee, but because the man, who was the only suitable applicant, would not come for any less than he was already earning, he was paid more than the woman. The Court of Appeal rejected the appeal to extrinsic forces and stated that:

> "An employer cannot avoid his obligations under the Act by saying: 'I paid him more because he asked for more.'

---

[44] See para. 5.59.
[45] [1988] I.R.L.R. 249.
[46] [1988] I.R.L.R. 267 and see *Wells* v. *F. Smales & Sons Ltd.* (unreported), Case No. 10701/84, IT
[47] See Industrial Tribunals (Rules of Procedure) Regulations (S.I. 1985 No. 16) (I.T.R. 1985) reg. 8(2E) and *Forex Neptune (Overseas) Ltd.* v. *Miller* I.C.R. 170, EAT.
[48] [1979] I.C.R. 1; [1987] I.R.L.R. 361, C.A.

or 'I paid her less because she was willing to come for less.' If any such excuse were permitted, the Act would become a dead letter. Those are the very reasons why there was unequal pay before the statute. They are the very circumstances in which the statute was intended to operate."[49]

5.84 This distinction has, however, been overruled in *Rainey* v. *Greater Glasgow Health Board*[50], in which the House of Lords applied the conclusions reached by the European Court of Justice in *Bilka Kaufhaus* v. *Weber von Hartz*.[51] The *Rainey* case was concerned with the consequences of the decision in 1980 to set up a limb fitting service within the N.H.S. Until that date, all limb fitting work in Scotland had been carried out by private contractors. In order to set up a limb fitting service within a reasonable period, the defendant Health Board took into its employ a number of limb fitters who had formerly been employed within the private sector. Limb fitters in the private sector were earning more than the Whitley Council N.H.S. rates and in order to attract a sufficient number of experienced staff, the Health Board agreed that they could be transferred at their existing rates of pay and be represented in future negotiations by their existing trade union, A.S.T.M.S. All further employees were taken on at the lower Whitley Council rates. The applicant claimed equal pay with the male employees taken on from the private sector and the employer argued that the difference between the two rates of pay was genuinely due to a material factor other than the difference of sex.

5.85 The House of Lords did not follow *Clay Cross*, with its restriction of material factors to those which are rooted in the personal equation between the employees. Lord Keith held:[52]

"The difference must be 'material,' which I would construe as meaning 'significant and relevant,' and it must be between 'her case and his.' Consideration of a person's case must necessarily involve consideration of the circumstances of that case. These may well go beyond what is not very happily described as "the personal equation" . . . . In particular, where there is no question of intentional sex discrimination whether direct or indirect, a difference which is connected with economic factors affecting the efficient carrying on of the employer's business or other activity may be relevant."

5.86 Lord Keith drew support for this view of section 1(3) from the decisions of the European Court in *Jenkins* v.

---

[49] *Per* Denning M.R., at p. 4.
[50] [1987] I.R.L.R. 26, H.L.
[51] [1986] I.R.L.R. 317, ECJ.
[52] At p. 29.

Kingsgate (Clothing Productions) Ltd.[53] and *Bilka Kaufhaus* in interpreting Article 119 of the Treaty of Rome. In *Jenkins*, female part-time and male full-time workers were engaged upon like work. There was a differential in pay between the the two groups and the question was referred to the ECJ as to whether this differential was contrary to the principle of equal pay for equal work enshrined in Article 119. The ECJ held that such a differential between part-time and full-time workers was not contrary to Article 119 "in so far as it is attributable to factors which are objectively justified and are in no way related to any discrimination based on sex."[54] If it is not possible to explain such differences other than by discrimination based upon sex, having regard to the difficulties of women in working full-time, the inequality will be contrary to Article 119. It is for the national courts to decide whether the difference in pay is in reality discrimination based on sex, having regard to the facts of the case, its history and the employer's intentions. When the case was remitted to the EAT,[55] Mr Justice Browne-Wilkinson considered that it was unclear from the judgment of the ECJ whether the employer had to show merely that he intended to achieve some other objectively necessary economic end, or whether he had to show that the practice was reasonably necessary to achieve that end. He interpreted the requirement in section 1(3) as calling for such objective justification, whether or not it was required in respect of Article 119.

5.87 In the subsequent *Bilka* case, the ECJ held that a policy which has the effect of creating a pay differential between men and women undertaking like work (here by giving pensions only to full-time workers) may only be justified where it is undertaken in pursuit of an objective which corresponds to a real need on the part of the undertaking, is appropriate with a view to achieving the objective in question and is necessary to that end. Lord Keith concluded that the true meaning and effect of Article 119 in this context is that same as that attributed to section 1(3) by the EAT in *Jenkins*, and furthermore argued that there was no difference between the need to demonstrate objectively justified grounds of difference for purposes of section 1(3) and the requirement for justification in cases of indirect discrimination under section 1(1)(*b*)(i) of the Sex Discrimination Act 1975.

5.88 In *Rinner Kuhn*, the German Government had argued that the exclusion of part-timers was justified because such workers "are not integrated in and connected with the undertaking in a way comparable to that of other workers."

---

[53] [1981] I.C.R. 592.
[54] [1981] I.C.R. 592 [1981] I.R.L.R. 228, ECJ.
[55] *Jenkins* v. *Kingsgate (Clothing Productions) Ltd. (No. 2)* [1981] I.R.L.R. 388.

These arguments were dismissed as "generalised
statements", not meeting the objective standards of
justification enunciated in *Bilka; i.e.* corresponding to a real
need, necessary and appropriate to achieve that end. A
legislative provision, which in practice gives rise to
discriminatory effects, may only be justified where the
Member State is "in a position to establish that the means
selected correspond to an objective necessary for its social
policy and are appropriate and necessary to the attainment of
that objective", as in the social security case of *Commission
v. Belgium*[56] in which the ECJ concluded that supplements
paid to those with responsibility to support a family fulfilled
a legitimate objective of social policy. In *Kowalska*, the ECJ
held that it is for the national court to judge whether a
provision in a collective agreement which is in practice
discriminatory is objectively justified, and where this is not
the case the injured employees must be treated in the same
way and have the same system applied to them as other
workers, in proportion to their hours. In Britain, maternity
and redundancy benefit and unfair dismissal entitlements are
limited by hours and service restrictions. The Equal
Opportunities Commission brought an action for judicial
review in respect of such service restrictions, but the
Divisional Court in *R. v. Secretary of State for Employment ex
p. the EOC*,[57] held that it was not unreasonable for the
Secretary of State to conclude that amendments to the
legislation might have adverse consequences for women
seeking to work part-time. In the Court of Appeal, although
Lord Justice Hirst held that the Secretary of State had
objectively justified the service thresholds, Lord Justice
Dillon said that there was no evidence that abolishing the
five year threshold for part-time workers would cause any
significant reduction in the availability of part-time
employment, and furthermore "recent history underlined
that according women the equal status which was justly their
due had not led to the dire results foretold by the prophets
of doom." He observed that no other E.C. state had a
comparable threshold for part-time workers.

5.89 In *Bilka* a policy or practice which creates a pay
differential between men and women was held to be contrary
to Article 119 unless it could be objectively justified on
economic grounds, *i.e.* it imports a full blown concept of
indirect discrimination, in which the intentions of the
employer are not relevant, but merely the results of the
practice and whether or not it is objectively justifiable.
Where a pay difference results from indirect discrimination,
the ECJ has consistently held that the burden rests upon the
employer to provide an objective justification for the practice
in question. Thus part-timers were refused a pension in
Bilka, sick pay in *Rinner Kuhn*, and severance pay in

---

[56] [1991] I.R.L.R. 393, ECJ [1993] I.R.L.R. 10.
[57] [1991] I.R.L.R. 493, H.C.,]1993] I.R.L.R. 10, C.A.

Kowalska, whilst in *Danfoss* it was the operation of incremental criteria which required objective justification. What, however, if unequal pay arises from direct discrimination? Must the employer establish objectively justified grounds of difference under section 1(3) to succeed in resisting a claim, or need he show only that the difference between the two cases is "genuinely due to a material ("significant and relevant" as per Lord Keith in Rainey) factor which is not the difference of sex" *i.e.* is the test a subjective one in cases of direct discrimination leading to unequal pay? It would be ironic if that were the case, in that under the Sex Discrimination Act direct discrimination is not capable of justification at all, let alone subjective justification. Yet in *Calder and Cizarkowsky* v. *Rowntree Macintosh*[58] Mr Justice Knox in the EAT concluded that the dictum of Lord Keith in *Rainey* to the effect that there was no difference between the requirement to establish a genuine material difference under the Equal Pay Act and the defence of justification under the SDA, s.1(1)(*b*) implied that only where unequal pay arose from indirect discrimination did the *Bilka* standard apply. Whilst all the ECJ cases on justification do concern indirect discrimination, it is submitted that Lord Keith is better understood as holding that in cases of indirect discrimination occurring under the SDA, no lower standard is to apply than that which obtains in the Article 119 cases *i.e.* an objective one. It appears to be against the policy of the Act to draw the inference that where direct discrimination occurs in equal pay cases subjective justification is possible under the Equal Pay Act, whereas no justification is possible at all under the SDA. Not only are the two Acts to be construed harmoniously, *per* Lord Denning in *Shields* v. *Coomes Holdings*, but such a result would appear to be contrary to the fundamental nature of the principle of equality in Community law. In the pregnancy case of *Dekker*, the ECJ held that where direct discrimination is established contrary to the Equal Treatment Directive, the only question which arises is whether the conduct falls within the exceptions provided for in the Directive, and not whether there are grounds for justification available under national law. Thus by analogy it could even be argued, especially as there are no comparable exceptions contained in the Equal Pay Directive, that once direct discrimination is established in a pay matter, no form of justification which is available under national law, whether objective or no, can be permitted to qualify the right to equal pay.[58.1]

5.90 Under section 1(3) the respondent is required to prove not only that the variation is genuinely due to a material

---

[58] [1992] I.R.L.R. 166, EAT.
[58.1] *Ten Oever* the A.G. in *Coloroll* (joined cases C109/91, C110/91, C152/91 and C200/91 argues the question as to whether the use of sex based actual tables can be justified, although rejecting the argument on factual grounds.

factor, but also that the material factor is not due to the
difference in sex, according to the EAT in *The Financial
Times Ltd* v. *Byrne (No. 2).*[59] Although this involves the
respondent in proving a negative, it is for the employer to
satisfy the tribunal on the balance of probabilities that each
part of the section is established. As Mr Justice Wood makes
clear in the *Financial Times* case, this may result in a trial
within a trial where the applicant alleges that the material
factor put forward is tainted by sex discrimination. Should
the applicant choose to call evidence to establish that the
respondent's alleged material factor is infected with
discrimination, that evidence will need to be tested by the
normal principles as to the burden of proof in discrimination
cases under section 1 of the SDA.[60]

5.91   Whilst the EAT in *Davies* v. *McCartneys*[61] held that
there was no limit to the factors upon which a respondent
may rely under section 1(3) provided they are genuine and
not attributable to sex, it is submitted not only that such
factors must be capable of objective justification, but also
that they cannot encompass the actual constitution of the
jobs in issue. Matters such as the demands of the job are
properly part of the enquiry as to whether there is like work
or work of equal value which it is inappropriate to consider
at the stage of the section 1(3) defence, especially if that
point is taken before equal work or equal value is
established.

5.92   In *Hayward* v. *Cammell Laird*[62] the House of Lords
considered the question as to whether a difference in pension
rights or sick pay might constitute a genuine material
difference between men and women engaged upon work of
equal value, where the men enjoyed a higher hourly rate of
pay. In an interesting *obiter dicta* (the argument, not having
been raised in the Tribunal, was not open to the employers
on appeal) the Lord Chancellor held that for section 1(3) to
operate, the unfavourable term in the woman's contract
would have to be due to the existence of the more favourable
term, *i.e.* in the words of the section it has to be "genuinely
due to a material factor which is not a difference of sex."[63]

---

[59] [1992] I.R.L.R. 163, EAT.
[60] In a number of tribunal cases the material factor defence put forward by
    the employer has been rejected as being tainted by sex discrimination, as
    in *Todd* v. *Lloyds Bank*, EOR DCLD 2, *Smith* v. *British Coal*, EOR,
    D.C.L.D.7 (separate bargaining structures); *Grieg and Grieg* v. *Hazell,
    Watson and Viney* EOR DCLD 6 (employer feebleness in resisting all
    male printing chapel): *Lucas* v. *West Sussex County Council* EOR DCLD
    7 (market forces): *Fleming* v. *Short Bros* EOR DCLD 9 (negotiated bonus
    scheme).
[61] [1989] I.R.L.R. 439, EAT and see also *Maher* v. *Vauxhall Motors* EOR
    DCLD 10 in which the Industrial Tribunal found that the operation of
    the company's grading scheme and the question of equal value were so
    intimately related that it was impossible meaningfully to deal with the
    former before the latter.
[62] [1988] I.R.L.R. 257.
[63] At p. 261.

Goff L. J. observed that it may be possible to argue that the difference was due to the existence of two separate pay structures wholly devoid of sex discrimination, but where discrimination is embedded in a pay structure, then that pay structure will not constitute a material factor which is not a difference of sex.

5.93 Where a wage structure gives rise to a difference in pay between men and women engaged upon work of equal value, the genuine material factor defence in section 1(3) is only available if that difference in pay has been objectively justified, according to the ECJ in *Bilka*. The ECJ in *Kowalska* held that a collective agreement, which in practice results in discrimination as between female and male workers, is contrary to Article 119, but it is for the national court to to establish how far it is justified on objective grounds unrelated to discrimination based on sex. In *Reed Packaging Ltd.* v. *Boozer and Everhurst*,[64] the EAT held, however, that where two despatch clerks were paid on a staff scale and the comparator, also working as a despatch clerk, was paid on a scale for manual workers which was negotiated with a different trade union, the resulting difference in wages was due to a material factor other than sex. The existence of two such pay scales, neither of which were discriminatory in themselves, was held to constitute an "administratively justified reason" in accordance with the decision in *Rainey*. Likewise, in *Enderby* v. *Frenchay Health Authority*, the EAT held that the fact that the pay of the two groups in question was determined by separate collective agreements, neither one of which was tainted by discrimination when considered separately, was a genuine material difference. The Court of Appeal has referred the question as to whether this is capable of constituting a genuine material difference to Luxembourg.

There is, however, a difference between finding that the cause of the difference in pay is not tainted by sex discrimination and concluding that the variation was due to a material factor other than sex, as section 1(3) requires. In *Barber* v. *NCR Manufacturing*[65] clerical workers whose tasks were directly related to the activitites of the shop floor worked a 39 hour week, whilst other clerical staff worked only 35. The two groups were paid the same hourly rate, until in separate pay and hours negotiations the hours of the direct clerical workers were reduced to 38, without loss of gross pay. Basing themselves on the reasoning of the EAT in *Enderby* the majority in the Industrial Tribunal had held

---

[64] [1988] I.R.L.R. 332, EAT. The EAT had reached a similar conclusion in *Waddington* v. *Leicester Council for Voluntary Social Services* [1977] I.R.L.R. 32. Cf the decision in *Grieg and Grieg* v. *Hazell, Watson and Viney*, *supra* in which the employer's attempt to place the burden of differential pay between a male and a female group on the trade unions was rejected as managerial feebleness".

[65] [1993] I.R.L.R. 95, EAT.

that the difference in hourly rate was justified, but Lord
Coulsefield, upholding the appeal, held that although the
difference in hourly rates was thereby explained, it was not
justified by objective factors unrelated to sex *i.e.* there was
no rational ground for the difference in hourly rates. The
reasoning in *Barber* v. *NCR* could pose a considerable threat
to agreements made through the process of collective
bargaining which, whilst acceptable to the parties,
nonetheless result in discrimination as between men and
women which cannot be objectively justified as constituting
necessary and appropriate means of achieving the needs of
the business.

5.94   Yet it must be observed that it is common form that a
scale for manual workers in such circumstances covers
mainly males, whilst that for staff will consist largely of
females. In such circumstances, the existence of two pay
scales may constitute a form of indirect discrimination which
permeates the local labour market in such a way that few
employers or employees would be consciously aware, rather
than being evidence of the existence of an objectively
justified factor unrelated to the sex of the workers. Where
the practice of separate collective bargaining structures has
been tainted by discriminatory attitudes, they may not be
accepted as constituting a genuine material difference
different from sex, as in the IT case of *Smith* v. *British Coal
Corporation.*[66] In that case, the tribunal felt bound to enquire
"whether those pay structures themselves arise because of a
difference in sex."

5.95   An employer may argue that a grading scheme which
results in pay differences between men and women, so long
as it operates irrespective of sex, may constitute a material
difference, even though the scheme is not based upon job
evaluation.[67] Such schemes are likely to be examined
critically, however. The burden of proving that such a
scheme is not tainted by discrimination lies upon the
employer, who will be subject to the normal standard of
proof in civil cases.[68] Likewise, an employer who protects
the pay of an employee on a job transfer or reorganisation,
i.e. the employee's pay is protected by a "red circle," may
argue that such a practice constitutes a genuine material
difference, so long as the "red circle" does not perpetuate
previous discrimination.[69] Likewise, where under Article 119
a comparison is made over time between successive

[66] EOR, DCLD 7, EAT/29/91 (unreported at time of writing).
[67] See the dissenting opinion of May L.J. in *Leverton* v. *Clwyd County
Council* [1968] I.R.L.R. 239 at p. 244.
[68] *National Vulcan Engineering Insurance Group Ltd.* v. *Jade* [1977] I.C.R.
800, [1976] I.R.L.R. 406, EAT.
[69] *Methven & Musolik* v. *Cow Industrial Polymers Ltd.* [1980] I.C.R. 463,
I.R.L.R. 289, C.A. *Charles Early and Marriot (Whitney) Ltd.* v. *Smith*
[1977] I.C.R. 700: *Snoxell* v. *Vauxhall Motors Ltd.* [1977] I.R.L.R. 121,
EAT.

employments, changed circumstances may constitute a genuine material difference.[70]

5.96 Where collective bargaining has been tainted by sex discrimination it cannot found a defence under section 1(3). Lester and Rose[71] argue that discriminatory collective agreements may be evidence that there has been discrimination in the way in which access has been afforded to the benefit of collective bargaining by the employers, contrary to SDA section 6(2)(*a*) or by the trade union concerned contrary to section 12(3)(*a*). It may, however, be difficult to establish exclusion from the full benefit of collective bargaining *on grounds of sex* unless it is possible to trace prior discrimination into the present bargaining structure, on the analogy of the lasting effects of prior discrimination in job grading in *Snoxell* v. *Vauxhall Motors*[72]. The essence of a separate claim under the SDA is that it must concern exclusion or other discrimination in the process of collective bargaining, because section 6(6) excludes from section 6(2) contractual rights to the payment of money, and section 8(5) excludes terms modified or included by virtue of a statutory equality clause implied by the EqPA. As any detriment suffered as a result of collective bargaining in respect of non-contractual matters can be the subject of a direct claim under the SDA, the only remedy for discrimination in the *process* of collective bargaining can be a declaration, unless damages for injury to feelings can be established. Many employers, and especially many trade unions, would be loath to be the subject of such a declaration, but as there is no mechanism for enforcement a declaration can only achieve its objective by moral pressure. Again, as collective bargaining is a process involving both unions and employers, any discrimination by either party which occurs as a result of that process must have been aided by the other side, contrary to section 42, but it is submitted that this argument can only be sustained if the process of collective bargaining has resulted in the parties signing a collective agreement.

5.97 A genuine material factor must be current at the time of the claim. If it is rooted in circumstances which no longer obtain, it will cease to be material as a ground on which unequal pay can be resisted by the employer. In *Benveniste* v. *University of Southampton*,[73] the plaintiff had been appointed in 1981 at a time of great financial stringency in British universities. For this reason, Ms Benveniste was

---

[70] *Albion Shipping Agency Ltd.* v. *Arnold* [1981] I.R.L.R. 525, EAT. But where a "red circle" has persisted over time it may not still constitute a s.1(3) defence. See *Outlook Supplies* v. *Parry* [1978] I.R.L.R. 12, EAT.
[71] A.Lester & D.Rose, "Equal Value Claims and Sex Bias in Collective Bargaining, *Industrial Law Journal*", 20, No. 3, pp. 163-175.
[72] [1973] I.R.L.R. 123, EAT.
[73] [1989] I.R.L.R. 122, C.A; and see *The Post Office* v. *Page*, unreported, EAT No. 554/87.

appointed six points below the point on the salary scale at
which a person of her age would normally have been
appointed. It was argued that this financial stringency was a
genuine material factor within the terms of section 1(3), but
Neil L. J. held that "the material difference between the
appellant's case and the case of the comparators evaporated
when the financial constraints were removed"[74] in 1982. An
analogy with "red circle" cases was rejected and although no
direct criticism of this practice was offered, it must follow
from the reasoning of *Benveniste* that all differences ground
in historical circumstances should be examined critically to
see if those reasons remain material at the present time. A
difference in pay which results from a genuine grading error
is not a material factor defence[75], because such a mistake
cannot constitute objectively justified grounds.

5.98   The question as to whether the genuine material
factor must justify the whole of the difference has proved
toublesome. In *Enderby* v. *Frenchay Health Authority*, the
EAT held that the tribunal had erred in rejecting the
employer's genuine material factor defence of market forces,
because that factor did not account for the whole of the
difference. Mr Justice Wood preferred the view that where
market forces are genuinely material it is the whole of the
difference which is justified. It followed from this decision
that in *Byrne* v. *Financial Times Ltd.*[76] the EAT upheld the
decision of the tribunal not to order further and better
particulars of the degree to which the several genuine
material factors relied on by the employer contributed to the
difference in pay, on the ground that it is often impossible
in practice to attribute a particular percentage or amount to
a particular factor when fixing a wage. Whilst in *Calder and
Cizarkowsky* v. *Rowntree Macintosh Ltd*[77]. the EAT held that
an industrial tribunal is not bound as a matter of law to seek
to apportion a rate of pay between the different factors that
go to make it up, either as a matter of historical fact or
economic justification, the Court of Appeal in *Enderby*
referred the question to the ECJ as to whether a factor
which accounts for only a part of the difference justifies all,
a due proportion, or none of the inequality in pay.

[74] At p. 131. And see *Swift* v. *William Freeman* EOR DCLD 1 on the
   rejection of anachronistic attendance bonus which had been in fact
   assimilated into normal pay, and also *Fleming* v. *Short Bros* EOR DCLD
   9 in which a different and separately negotiated bonus paid only to a
   largely male group was held to have been tainted by discrimination.
[75] *McPherson* v. *Rathgael Centre for Children and Young People* [1991]
   I.R.L.R. 216, NICA See also *Duffy* v. *Barclays Bank* EOR DCLD 10 in
   which a grading scheme, though bona fide, was not properly applied.
[76] [1991] I.R.L.R. 491, EAT.
[77] [1993] I.R.L.R. 212, C.A.; [1992] I.R.L.R. 265, EAT in which a shift
   premium paid to men on rotating shifts was held to be a genuine material
   difference, even though a part of it was attributable to working unsocial
   hours, a factor also present for women workers on a twilight shift.

6 INDUSTRIAL TRIBUNAL PROCEEDINGS AND REMEDIES

6.01 In this chapter we shall cover various matters, concerned with the bringing of tribunal proceedings relating specifically to discrimination, which are not otherwise dealt with; and with remedies in the industrial tribunals. Thus we shall not attempt to deal with matters of a procedural nature which might affect industrial tribunal cases generally, but only those where discrimination cases throw up specific issues. Moreover, one matter in particular which involves interlocutory applications, namely discovery and inspection of documents, is dealt with not here but in the chapter on proof, as is material on the statutory questionnaires.

Assistance with proceedings

6.02 Legal aid is not available for representation at tribunal proceedings, although the cost of being represented at such proceedings can be considerable. This is particularly true in equal value cases, where the procedure is longer and where employers frequently engage their own expert witness. The cost and complexity of such proceedings are apt to deter applicants who cannot call on the backing of their trade union or the EOC. Both the EOC and the CRE have powers to support litigants in tribunal proceedings[1] but have only limited budgets for this purpose. We deal with this function of the Commissions in chapter 8. Neither body supports fully more than a small proportion of the cases where their assistance is sought, although each helps with preliminary steps in many more cases. Both Commissions have published guidance documents to help litigants[2]. Some other organisations such as Women Against Sexual Harassment, unions, and law centres offer some support. Because of the difficulties of bringing discrimination cases, calls for legal aid to be available have been made in many quarters.[3]

---

[1] SDA, s. 75: RRA, s. 66.
[2] "How to prepare a case for an Industrial Tribunal" (EOC); "Race cases in Tribunals A Guide to Bringing Cases" (CRE).
[3] They are summarised in the CRE's second Review of the Act document (CRE, September 1992).

6.03 Frequently employers are insured for the costs of defending discrimination claims. We hope that insurers are insisting on proper employment practices as a condition of granting the insurance. It also sometimes happens that employees find that they are covered to bring discrimination proceedings under legal expenses insurance that they have taken out. Since these policies are sometimes sold as add-on policies to household insurance, their existence may have been forgotten and legal advisers could help by enquiring as to insurance.

6.04 In practice moral support from a friend or colleague is also very helpful, as it can be a lonely experience to take a case. There will almost inevitably be times in a long case when morale flags, particularly when so much of the respondents' evidence in the general type of discrimination case will be directed at pointing out the applicant's failings to explain the less favourable treatment. This sort of evidence can come as a terrible shock, no matter that it is presaged by the respondent's written case. Note that clauses 38 and 39 of the Trade Union Reform and Employment Rights Bill set out restrictions on publicity in cases invloving sexual misconduct, and will lead to new rules for the tribunals and the EAT.

Parties **6.05** The typical case will be the employee or prospective or ex-employee against the employer. However, because there is a special defence available to employers of taking reasonably practicable steps to prevent discrimination from occuring[4] it will often make sense to join as a party the person who is alleged to have done the act of discrimination. If the employer's defence succeeds, that person could still be held liable, whereas failure to join the person actually responsible may mean that discrimination could be proved without anybody being held liable for it. Joining the person alleged to be responsible is possible because the Acts say that such an employee is deemed to aid the doing of the act by the employer even in cases where the employer's defence succeeds, and knowingly aiding another person to do an unlawful act is itself unlawful.[5] This potential personal liability under the Acts may not be widely known. (Indeed, some tribunals still argue against it!). If the Commissions were to focus some publicity upon it, it might serve to make individual employees more interested in ensuring that discrimination does not occur, if only from self-interest.

6.06 Frequently, several Applicants will claim discrimination arising out of substantially the same facts and consolidation of the proceedings will be ordered.[6] In equal

---

[4] RRA, s. 32(3) and SDA, s. 41(3).
[5] RRA, s. 33(1) and (2) and SDA, s. 42(1) and (2).
[6] Industrial Tribunals (Rules of Procedure) Regulations 1985, r. 15.

pay claims in particular there may well be a very large number of originating applications. It will probably be best, if all the applicants can agree, to pick out certain claims as representative and proceed on those, leaving the others adjourned pending the outcome of the "test cases". Or the tribunal may order the selection of representative cases. In *Ashmore* v. *British Coal Corporation,*[7] representative claims (which arose after an interlocutory order was made when some 1500 claims were presented) were heard and failed. An application to have heard one of the cases which had been stayed failed and it was struck out under the Rules of Procedure as an abuse of process as being vexatious.[8] The Court of Appeal upheld the striking-out, even though when originally stayed the Tribunal Chair had noted that the decision on the representative cases would not be binding on any others.

6.07 It also not uncommonly happens, especially when proceedings are protracted and the Applicant remains employed by the Respondent, that the Applicant complains of victimisation and files a new originating application. The Tribunal will normally order consolidation if the first hearing has not progressed too far, or alternatively that the same tribunal should hear the victimisation case later.

Time limits and proceedings

6.08 To hear a case a tribunal needs to have jurisdiction, which it will have if the case falls under the statutory provisions and is in time; or out of time but where it is considered by the tribunal to be just and equitable to hear the case. A preliminary hearing to deal with any time point is quite usual, either if the tribunal of its own motion sees a difficulty, or if a party raises it.

Time limit for presenting an application

6.09 Applications to an Industrial Tribunal in respect of discrimination cases other than equal pay claims must normally be presented to the tribunal within three months beginning when the act complained of was done.[9] The exceptions are:

(i) where the Commissions can bring proceedings in their own name, see chapter 8, below (*e.g.* in respect of an unlawful advertisement), when the period is six months; and

(ii) where there is an appeal from a non-discrimination notice, see chapter 8, below, where the period is not later than six weeks after the notice is served.[10]

[7] [1990] I.R.L.R. 283; [1990] I.C.R. 485 C.A. See also Rules of Procedure, r. 14(3).
[8] Rules of Procedure, r. 12(2)(*e*).
[9] SDA, s.76(1); RRA, s.68(1).
[10] See chap. 8 *post*.

Beware, statutory provisions as to time using the words "beginning when" something happens count that day as the first day of the time period, so effectively in the normal case the period is three months less one day. So if the act was done on June 25 the last day for commencing proceedings is September 24. It is different where the provision says "after" an event, as in the case of the appeal from a non-discrimination notice.

6.10 An application is "presented" when it arrives at the Central Office of Industrial Tribunals and it is not necessary for it to be registered by the office in order to say that proceedings have commenced. Whilst rule 1 requires that an application sets out the names of the parties and the relief sought, these stipulations are discretionary, rather than mandatory, so that where a complaint was made in respect of the rejection of the complainant for a particular post, it was not fatal that the application did not specify whether the complaint was of sex or race discrimination.[11]

6.11 In relation to a dismissal, the relevant date is the date at which the contract is terminated, not that on which notice is given.[12] Whilst an act which occurred more than three months prior to the commencement of proceedings in an industrial tribunal cannot give rise to a cause of action, providing that the proceedings have been commenced within the time limits, acts prior to the time limit can be taken into account as similar fact type of evidence. In *Clarke* v. *Hampshire Electro-Plating Co Ltd*,[13] jowever, the EAT seemed to take the point that, where a black applicant is rejected at one date and a white comparator was appointed at a later date, the cause of action of the black applicant crystallised at the later date so as to set time running. They also held that the coming into existence of a comparator was a ground for exercising discretion, if an applicant reasonably took the view before then either that he had no cause of action or that it was unlikely he would establish a prima facie case without a comparator. This notion of crystallisation of the claim seems to be perceived as useful by tribunals, and the *Clarke* case is, we think, destined to be amongst those regularly referred to in decisions on jurisdiction.

6.12 In the case of a continuing act or an omission, the Race Relations Act, s.68(7) and the Sex Discrimination Act, s.76 provide that:

"(a) where the inclusion of any term in a contract renders the making of the contract an unlawful act, that act shall

---

[11] *Dodd* v. *British Telecom* [1988] I.R.L.R. 16; [1990] I.C.R. 116 EAT.
[12] *Lupetti* v. *Wrens Old House Ltd.* (1984) I.C.R. 348, EAT.
[13] [1991] I.R.L.R. 490.

be treated as extending throughout the duration of the contract, and

(b) any act extending over a period shall be treated as done at the end of that period, and

(c) a deliberate omission shall be treated as done when the person in question decided upon it,

and in the absence of evidence establishing the contrary, a person shall be taken for purposes of this section to have decided upon an omission when he does an act inconsistent with doing the omitted act or, if he has done no such inconsistent act, when the period expires within which he might reasonably have been expected to do the omitted act if it was to be done."

6.13 In *Calder* v. *James Finlay Corporation Ltd.*,[14] the respondent was refused a subsidised mortgage because an unwritten rule of the scheme was that it was only open to men. She left the firm eight months after last being refused an application for a subsidised mortgage, but filed a complaint based on the Sex Discrimination Act within three months of the termination of her employment. The EAT found that the Industrial Tribunal had erred in finding her complaint out of time, in that section 76(6)(*b*) treats a continuing act as having been done at the end of the period in question, here the termination of her employment. As section 6(2)(*a*) of the 1975 Act renders it unlawful to discriminate in the way in which employees are afforded access to benefits, and that way of affording access to the subsidised mortgage scheme was a continuing act, section 76(6)(*b*) treats it as taking place at the end of the employment and therefore it falls within the time limit.

6.14 A similar conclusion was reached in *Barclays Bank plc* v. *Kapur & Others*[15] in which ethnic minority employees complained that their service in an associated company in East Africa was excluded for pension purposes, whilst that of ex-patriate employees who had served in East Africa was included. Whilst the initial exclusion took place in 1970 and 1971, the employees complained under the Race Relations Act, s.4(2)(*b*) that there was discrimination in the way in which they were afforded access to the pension scheme and that by virtue of section 68(7)(*b*) that act, being a continuing act, fell to be treated as done at the end of the period. The Court of Appeal held there was a continuing discriminatory act here, in that the way the applicants were afforded access to benefits (*i.e.* without benefit of their overseas service) was a continuing discrimination and there was not simply an act of discrimination in the year when the relevant decision was first made. Neill L.J. held that the right to a pension formed part of the overall remuneration of the employee, and that if

14 [1989] I.R.L.R. 55, EAT.
15 [1991] I.R.L.R. 136, [1991] I.C.R. 208; [1991] 2 A.C. 355, H.L.

his pension entitlement could be shown to be less favourable than that of other employees, that disadvantage continued throughout his employment. The House of Lords followed this approach.[16]

6.15 By contrast, in *Sougrin* v. *Haringey Health Authority*[17] the Court of Appeal held that there was no continuing act of discrimination where after a regrading exercise a black nurse was paid less than a comparator. It would have been different, however, if there had been a discriminatory policy of paying black nurses less which continued in operation.

Discretionary waiver of time limits

6.16 There is a discretion vested in the tribunals in effect to waive the time limits. The Sex Discrimination Act, s.76(5) and the Race Relations Act, s.68(5) provide that:

> "A court or tribunal may nevertheless consider any complaint, claim or application which is out of time if, in all the circumstances of the case, it considers that it is just and equitable to do so."

The discretion vested in courts and tribunals to entertain applications out of time is wide, so limiting the scope for appeal. For an appellant to succeed he must show that the court or tribunal took a demonstrably wrong approach to the matter, or it took into account facts which it ought not to have done, or the decision was so unreasonable that no properly instructed tribunal could have reached it. The court or tribunal may take into account anything which it judges to be relevant, and though it is not required to hear the entire case before making its decision, it may want to hear enough evidence to gauge the strength or weakness of the complaint.[18]

6.17 Beware, the discretion does not apply to appeals from non-discrimination notices where no power exists to extend the time; nor can it be extended by consent, because after the six week period the notice becomes final and has to be entered on the public register kept by the relevant Commission, and there is no power to take it off again. If, however, the Commission has exceeded its jurisdiction, it might be possible to quash a notice and the register entry by judicial review, for which three months is the usual period for bringing proceedings.

---

[16] In a county court case one of us persuaded the judge that a policy of excluding gypsies from the lounge bar of a public house which was communicated to a plaintiff was a continuing act for as long as the policy existed.

[17] [1991] I.R.L.R. 447; [1991] I.C.R. 791, EAT, upheld by C.A. June 4, 1992:45 at 42, EOR Sept/Oct 1992.

[18] *Hutchinson* v. *Westward Television Ltd.* [1977] I.C.R. 279; [1977] I.R.L.R. 69, EAT. Where a complaint is out of time and the Applicant's representative fails to ask for an extension of time on the basis that it would be just and equitable, a Tribunal Chairman is not obliged to raise the matter: *Dimtsu* v. *Westminster City Council* [1991] I.R.L.R. 450, EAT.

Equal Pay-Claim in time

6.18 Whether there is a time limit for the bringing of a claim under the Equal Pay legislation is currently the subject of conflicting decisions in the EAT. The best advice for an Applicant, if it is feasible to do so, is to present the claim within six months of the termination of the employment to which it relates or face a trip to the Court of Appeal. (There is no problem while an Applicant is still employed because lack of equal pay continues.) Whilst section 2(1) provides that claims may be presented to an Industrial Tribunal in respect of the contravention of an equality clause, and section 2(3) allows such a claim pending in any court which could be more conveniently disposed of in an Industrial Tribunal to be referred to a tribunal, section 2(4) provides that:

> "No claim in respect of the operation of an equality clause relating to a woman's employment shall be referred to an industrial tribunal otherwise than by virtue of subsection (3) above, if she has not been employed in the same employment within six months preceding the date of the reference."

6.19 In *British Railways Board* v. *Paul*, the EAT held that the time limit prescribed by the subsection applied only to a reference to a tribunal by the Secretary of State and not to an original claim. (Damages or arrears of remuneration may not be awarded, however, in respect of any period earlier than two years before the date of the claim.) In *Etherson* v. *Strathclyde Regional Council*, the EAT held that the word "reference" was not to be so narrowly construed and it applied to all claims presented as well as references by the Secretary of State.[19]

6.20 As there are no procedures prescribed for bringing a claim directly based upon EEC law, the EAT in *Stevens & Others* v. *Bexley Health Authority* had taken the view that there was no time limit on bringing a claim.[20] A later EAT in *Livingstone* v. *Hepworth Refractories plc*,[21] however, followed the guidance of the ECJ in *Emmot* v. *Minister for Social Welfare*[22] to adopt procedures no less favourable than those in domestic law, provided they make exercise of Community law rights possible.[22.1] So the procedures including the time limits of the SDA were held applicable. The same would be true of an equal pay claim based directly on EEC law as regards Equal Pay Act procedures.

Conciliation in employment cases

6.21 Copies of complaints under the Race Relations Act and the Sex Discrimination Act are sent to an ACAS

---

[19] *British Railways Board* v. *Paul* [1988] I.R.L.R. 20 EAT; *Etherson* v. *Strathclyde Regional Council* EAT June 11 1992; 45 at 43 EOR 1992.
[20] [1989] I.R.L.R. 240; [1989] I.C.R. 224, EAT.
[21] [1992] I.R.L.R. 63, EAT.
[22] [1991] I.R.L.R. 387, ECJ.
[22.1] See *Cannon* v. *Barnsley Metropolitan Borough Council*, EAT [1992] I.R.L.R. 474; *Rankin* v. *British Corporation* [1993] I.R.L.R. 69, EAT. (See p. 30, n. 83 *ante*.)

conciliation officer under the Race Relations Act, s.54 or the Sex Discrimination Act, s.64. It is the duty of the conciliation officer to facilitate a settlement in individual cases. He neither possesses investigatory powers nor is he under a duty to promote racial or sexual equality. He must act if he is requested to do so by either party, or he may act in the absence of such requests if he considers that there is a reasonable chance of success. Nothing communicated to a conciliation officer in the course of his duties under the Acts is admissible without the consent of the party who made the communication.

6.22 It is generally recognised that conciliation in a discrimination case is often more difficult than in other types of employment cases, because there is principle at stake. Applicants will often perceive themselves as bringing the case to save others from discrimination. Respondents will often refuse to accept the possibility that discrimination has occurred, even though it may have happened unintentionally. Where employers are prepared to make concessions, however, they may agree to action in respect of equal opportunities generally, even though a tribunal could not order widespread change in the event of a finding of discrimination. It is not uncommon for applicants in discrimination cases to have second thoughts about settlements after the event, particularly when they get home and see their children and wonder whether they have made enough noise to ensure they will not have to go through something similar. It is a wise precaution for a representative to ask the applicant to initial any settlement personally.

6.23 It is not uncommon for employers to try and buy silence about the issues in the case by paying over the odds in a settlement but insisting on a confidentiality clause. Sometimes for one reason or another this suits the applicant's purpose as well, but more often than not the applicant will go away feeling unhappy about the position. Such settlements are often less effective for the employers than they hoped because aspects of the settlement leak out in other ways and the settlement begins to look like a cover-up. Thus, in a local authority context, such a settlement will not achieve its purpose if a councillor thereafter starts asking awkward questions.

6.24 A settlement of a Tribunal claim, which is made with the assistance of an ACAS conciliation officer, constitutes an exception to the provisions of the Race Relations Act, s.73(3) and the Sex Discrimination Act, s.77(3) which render void any term in a contract which purports to limit or exclude any provision of the two Acts. It follows that agreements without ACAS assistance, other than actually in front of the tribunal and recorded in the decision, are not binding. The ACAS officer will use a form known as COT 3. A COT 3 agreement drawn up under the Employment

Protection (Consolidation) Act will not be regarded as covering claims under the RRA, SDA or Equal Pay legislation unless expressed to do so. The same rules will be applied to a claim relying on Community law following the *Livingstone* case referred to in the section on time limits above.

Procedure in equal value claims

6.25 Both equal pay claims and claims for equal value under section 1(2)(*c*) operate under the Industrial Tribunal (Rules of Procedure) Regulations 1985.[23] The detailed Rules of Procedure for Industrial Tribunals are contained in Schedule 1 of the regulations.

6.26 A special and more complex procedure is provided in respect of equal value claims. The average time taken to conclude an equal value case is 17 months, long enough to provoke the President of the EAT in *Aldridge* v. *British Telecommunications plc*[24] to observe that the delays are "scandalous and amount to a denial of justice to women seeking a remedy through the judicial process." This procedure has to provide a means whereby a comparison can be made of the value of the applicant's work and that of her selected male comparators. This comparison is undertaken by an independent expert appointed by the Tribunal. The procedures in respect of equal value claims have been incorporated into the 1985 regulations as Schedule 2, the regulations being numbered in such a way that in so far as possible a matter is dealt with in the same numbered section in Schedule 2 as it in the main body of the regulations contained in Schedule 1.

6.27 1. Before proceeding to hear an equal value claim, the Tribunal shall invite the parties to adjourn the proceedings for the purpose of seeking a settlement and shall, if both or all of the parties agree, grant such an adjournment under Regulation 12(2A).

In this respect it should be noted that the under the Sex Discrimination Act 1975, s.64(1), ACAS Conciliation Officers are empowered to act in cases brought under section 2(1) of the Equal Pay Act and copies of the Originating Application will have been forwarded to ACAS from the COIT. Whilst possibilities of conciliation are not therefore exhausted and may nonetheless occur at the commencement of proceedings, the likelihood of reaching a settlement at this stage is thereby reduced.

6.28 2. The Tribunal must consider whether it is satisfied that there are no reasonable grounds for determining that the work is of equal value under section 2A(1). If there are

[23] S.I. 1985 No. 16.
[24] [1990] I.R.L.R. 10, and see *British Coal* v. *Smith*, EAT/29/91.

no such reasonable grounds, the Tribunal must dismiss the application at this stage, before a report is commissioned from an independent expert. The intention behind this provision was that only "hopeless cases" should be excluded at this stage, so that all that is required on behalf of an applicant at this stage is an arguable case.

6.29   3. Under Regulation 8(2E) the Tribunal may, on the application of a party, if it considers it appropriate to do so, hear evidence and permit the parties to address it on the question of whether there is a genuine material difference other than a difference of sex under the Equal Pay Act 1970, s.1(3), before it requires an expert to prepare a report. The EAT in *McGregor* v. *G.M.B.A.T.U.*[25] held that the interpretation and application of the material factor defence should be the same whether it fails to be considered at the first or a subsequent hearing. Should the defence succeed at the preliminary stage, the application may be dismissed without calling for a report from an independent expert. Consideration of a material factor defence at this stage is without prejudice to further consideration of this issue after the Tribunal has received the expert's report,[26] even though this could be characterised as giving two bites at the same cherry and unnecessarily adding to costs.

6.30   A material factor defence cannot be taken as a preliminary point but, save in wholly exceptional circumstances, requires evidence. In *R.* v. *Secretary of State for Social Services ex p. Clarke and others*[27] in response to claims by female speech therapists that their work was of equal value with male clinical psychologists and pharmacists, the employer health authorities sought to establish as a preliminary point that they were bound to pay only those salaries approved by the Secretary of State under the relevant N.H.S. Regulations following upon agreement in the Whitley Councils. The Divisional Court, on an application for judicial review as to whether the Secretary of State's approval of the Whitley Council rates was contrary to Community law in so far as it failed to incorporate the principle of equal pay for work of equal value and was therefore held that section 1(3) requires evidence to be called as to whether the variation is genuinely due to a material factor other than a difference of sex, and that this requires evidence as to the reasons for the variation. Only if the variation in pay were genuinely shown to be due to the Regulations could they constitute the material factor under section 1(3).

6.31   A Tribunal is not bound to embark upon an enquiry under Regulation 8(2E), but if it hears evidence that the

[25] [1987] I.C.R. 505.
[26] Reg. 8(2E).
[27] [1988] I.R.L.R. 22.

employers have a genuine material factor defence prior to the commissioning of a report from an independent expert, the Tribunal must decide the point if there is sufficient evidence and only adjourn the case for preparation of a report from an independent expert where there is insufficient evidence.[28] If the tribunal decides that the employer has made out a defence under section 1(3), the Tribunal must dismiss the claim without commissioning a report.

6.32 If the material factor defence is heard prior to the commissioning of a report from an independent expert, the point must be considered on the presumption that the work is of equal value and it is for the employer to show that the difference is due to a genuine material factor and that this is a factor other than sex.[29] The onus of establishing a defence under section 1(3) lies on the employer whenever it is heard, but in the absence of a finding of equal value at this early stage, clarity about the burden of proof is particularly necessary. The EOC, in their document "Equal Pay: Strengthening the Acts"[30] argues that there should be an obligation to plead particulars of any section 1(3) defence at the initial stage, so that all the issues are identified at an early stage. The EOC takes the view that the section 2A(1) hearing is neither necessary nor desirable, in that it facilitates delaying tactics and is redundant in view of the general power of tribunals[31] to hold pre-hearing assessments and to issue a costs warning, where there are no reasonable prospects of success.

6.33 4. The Tribunal shall, after consideration of the above matters, require an expert to prepare a report with respect to the question according to the provisions Regulation 7A(2) and (3).

6.34 5. Such a requirement shall be made in writing and shall specify the name and address of the parties, the address where the applicant is or was employed, the question at issue and the name of the person with reference to whose work the question arises. A copy of the requirement shall be sent to each of the parties.

6.35 6. Regulation 7A(3) provides that the requirement shall stipulate that the expert shall:

---

[28] *Reed Packaging Ltd.* v. *Boozer* [1988] I.R.L.R. 333, EAT.

[29] *Financial Times* v. *Byrne (No.2)* [1991] I.R.L.R. 163, EAT. *In Byrne* v. *Financial Times* [1991] I.R.L.R. 417, the EAT had refused an application for further and better particulars of the employer's defence under s.1(3) which would have required the employer to have allocated a specific sum to any particular pleaded. This was dismissed as being impossible to quantify accurately.

[30] Equal Pay Strengthening the Acts, EOC, 1990.

[31] Industrial Tribunal (Rules of Procedure) Regulations 1985 (S.I. 1985 No. 16) Sched 1, r. 6.

(a) take account of all such information supplied and all such representations made to him as have a bearing on the question;
(b) before drawing up his report, produce and send to the parties a written summary of the said information and representations and invite the representations of the parties upon the material contained therein;
(c) make his report to the Tribunal in a document which shall reproduce the summary and contain a brief account of any representations received from the parties upon it, any conclusions he may have reached upon the question and the reasons for that conclusion or, as the case may be, for his failure to reach such a conclusion;
(d) take no account of the difference of sex and at all times act fairly.

6.36   7. The Tribunal shall adjourn the hearing under Regulation 4 when it requires an independent expert to prepare a report. The parties may complain to the Tribunal under Regulation 5 not less than 42 days after the expert has been required to prepare the report, that there is likely to be undue delay in the preparation of the report. The Tribunal may, on consideration of any explanation or information as to the progress of the report, revoke the requirement upon the expert and commission a fresh report. Although the powers provided under regulation 5 have not hitherto been exercised, where an applicant fails to furnish the necessary information, a tribunal may consider dismissing the claim for want of prosecution.

A copy of the report shall be sent to the parties upon its receipt by the Tribunal and a date fixed for the resumed hearing, such date to be not less than 14 days after the Report has been sent to the parties (Reg. 6).

6.37   8. Under Regulation 7A(7), the report shall be admitted in evidence at the resumed hearing, unless it is excluded under the powers contained in Regulation 7A(8). Under that regulation the Tribunal may, if it thinks fit, determine not to admit the report where, on the application of one or more of the parties or otherwise, it forms the view:

(a) that the expert has not complied with the stipulations set out in Regulation 7A(3) (above), or
(b) that the conclusion contained in the report is one which, taking due account of the information supplied and representations made to the expert, could not reasonably have been reached, or
(c) that for some other material reason (other than disagreement with the conclusion that the applicant's work is or is not of equal value or with the reasoning leading to that conclusion) the report is unsatisfactory.

6.38 Regulation 7A(9) provides that the tribunal shall take account of the representations of the parties and may, subject to Regulation 8(2A) and (2B), permit any party to give evidence, call witnesses and question witnesses upon the question of admitting the expert's report, as provided for in Regulation 7A(8). Where a party wishes to contest the factual basis of the independent expert's report, this is best done before the report is admitted under Regulation 7A(8). A party who objects to the admission of the report may make representations under Regulation 7A(9), give evidence and call witnesses upon any matter relevant to the criteria set out in regulation 7A(8)(*a*), (*b*) and (*c*) above. This is subject to the proviso in Regulation 8(2A) that the independent expert may be called and cross-examined on his report. It is, however, only possible for a Tribunal to refuse to admit the report if the conclusion is one which could not reasonably have been reached in the light of the information supplied and the representations made or the report is in some other way unsatisfactory, *i.e.* it can only be rejected where the expert has gone badly wrong and mere disagreement with his conclusions or his reasoning is not sufficient.[32] In *Aldridge* v. *BT* the EAT held that the tribunal was entitled to take the expert's oral testimony into account in deciding to admit the report. They went on to hold that in view of the inevitable delay which would ensue if a fresh report were required, tribunals should hear all the necessary evidence at the admission stage, which could include evidence from the experts commissioned by the parties. After hearing the experts for the parties the tribunal should give such weight as it sees fit to the independent expert's report and to those of the experts for the parties, along with any other evidence. It is for the tribunal to reach the factual conclusions on equal value, particularly in the light of the requirement laid down in Article 2 of the Equal Pay Directive of a right "to pursue their claims by judicial process after possible recourse to other competent authorities."

6.39 This rule must be understood in the context of Regulation 8(2C) which provides that the parties may not give evidence upon any matters of fact upon which a conclusion in the report of the expert is based, except as provided by Regulations 7A(9) or 8(2D). The purpose of this provision is to prevent continual attack upon the factual basis of the report. Regulation 8(2D) (discussed below) provides that evidence may be admitted and witnesses questioned where the matter is relevant to a genuine material factor defence under section 1(3), or the expert failed to reach a conclusion due to the failure of the parties to supply the necessary information.

---

[32] *e.g.* the independent expert's report was not admitted in *Allsop* v. *Derbyshire Police Authority*, EOR Case Law Digest, 4, because the expert refused to answer questions under cross examination as to the basis of the reports commissioned by the parties.

6.40 In *Tennant Textile Colours Ltd.* v. *Todd*,[33] the report of the expert had been admitted, after which the employer sought an adjournment, to procure a report from their own expert witness. The Tribunal allowed the adjournment but ruled that the findings of fact in the report of the independent expert would be binding on both parties "in circumstances where the report had already been admitted in evidence." The employers appealed by way of a case stated to the Northern Ireland Court of Appeal, which held that whilst Regulation 8(2C) provides that new evidence may not be admitted at this stage, parties may make submissions about the findings of fact and may refer back to facts adduced at some prior stage in the hearing, as when considering whether the report should have been admitted under Regulation 7(A9), or whether there was a section 1(3) defence under Regulation 8(2D). Although the primary fact finding role of the Tribunal is thus placed within the remit of the expert, it remains the function of the Tribunal to decide whether equal value has been established. Lord Lowry in the NICA also held that:

> "Reports obtained in the circumstances created by the present Act and Rules must obviously carry considerable weight, as was clearly intended, but there is no provision or principle that the party challenging an independent expert's report has to 'persuade the Tribunal that the independent expert's report should be rejected' or that the Tribunal 'could only reject the independent expert's report if the evidence were such as to show that it was so plainly wrong that it could not be accepted,' as stated in paragraph 23 of the Tribunal's decision. The burden of proving a claim under the Act of 1970 is on the applicant. The burden does not in point of law become heavier if the independent expert's report is against the applicant. Nor, if that report is in favour of the applicant, is the burden of proof transferred to the employer."

6.41 Whilst it is clearly right that there is no change in the burden of proof, an applicant may be driven towards commissioning a report from her own expert witness to overcome this problem, with all the attendant burdens of cost and complexity.

It is now commonplace for one or both of the parties to commission a report from their own expert. The EAT ruled in *Lloyds Bank* v. *Fox*[34] that whilst a party that had appointed its own expert could require the other side to

---

[33] [1989] I.R.L.R. 3, N.I.C.A.
[34] [1987] I.R.L.R. 103, EAT in which each side had commissioned an independent report. The Bank appointed a new expert, after the Tribunal had criticised the report of the expert originally appointed. The Bank sought an order to require the complainant to be interviewed by the new expert, but Wood J. held that the Tribunal only had powers to order written interrogations and not to require that a party consent to be interviewed.

furnish further and better particulars or discovery of documents under Rule 4(1)(*b*), tribunals have no power to require that the other party consent to be interviewed by the opposing expert in the course of preparing his report.

6.42   9. The Tribunal may require the expert to explain any matter in his Report or give further consideration to the question under regulation 7A(10), and the expert shall make his reply in writing, setting down any conclusions which may result from further consideration and his reasons for that conclusion. Copies of the expert's reply shall be sent to the parties, which shall be given such weight as the Tribunal thinks fit.

6.43   10. In those instances where an expert's Report is not admitted, regulation 7(13) requires that it shall be treated as if it has not been received and no further account shall be taken of it. The result will be the appointment of a new expert. In *Davies* v. *Francis Shaw*[13] the expert's report was not admitted on the grounds that he had failed to take account of the representations of the parties and had failed to give any reasons for his conclusions. The applicant in that case tried to persuade the Industrial Tribunal to accept her expert's report, but did not succeed in this submission.

Procedure at the hearing

6.44   1. Proceedings on equal value claims are to be conducted in an informal manner, as applies to other Industrial Tribunal proceedings and likewise the Tribunal is not bound by any rule of law as to the admissibility of evidence in courts of law (Reg. 8(1)).

2. On the application of a party the Tribunal may compel the attendance of the expert under Regulation 8(2A), who may be cross examined on his report and any other matters pertaining to the question on which the expert was required to report.

3. A party may, on giving reasonable notice of his intention to do so, call his own expert witness on the question on which the expert was asked to report under regulation 8(2B); any other party may cross examine such a witness. A party which is unhappy about the conclusions of an expert's report, although unable to ensure that the report is not admitted under Regulation 7(8) above, may present an alternative opinion about the conclusions to be drawn from the facts of the case in this way, even though Regulation 8(2C) precludes the giving of evidence or calling or questioning of witnesses upon any matter of fact upon which the expert's report is based.

4. Notwithstanding regulation 8(2C), under Regulation 8(2D)(b) a party may give evidence, call or question witnesses upon matters of fact upon which the conclusions of the expert's report is based, where the expert reached no conclusions on the question of equal

value because of a refusal by a person to furnish information or documents to the expert.

5. The matter may be disposed of or dismissed in the absence of either party subject to the consideration of any written representations made under Regulation 7(3).

6. Costs may be awarded in respect of frivolous, vexatious or otherwise unreasonable actions.

7. The costs of the independent expert are born by the Secretary of State. The main burden falling on parties to equal value cases is the expense of the initial preparation and the emerging trend to commission an expert, whose report can be contrasted with that of the independent expert. Once one party has commissioned its own expert, it becomes a practical necessity for the other side to match this expertise. Further substantial costs may be incurred in questioning any material factor defence put forward by the employer, as was the case, for example, in *Lloyds Bank* v. *Fox*. The result is that without financial support from a trade union or the EOC a complainant needs a high level of commitment effectively to pursue an equal value claim.

Reform of the Equal Value Provisions

6.45 Proposals have been made for simplifying and speeding-up this procedure, in particular by the EOC.[35] These proposals include ways of speeding up the initial steps of the proceedings by the introduction of a preliminary review to clarify and record each party's case, at which the respondents would be under an obligation to set out the nature of any genuine material factor defence on which they propose to rely. Correspondingly it is proposed that the "no reasonable grounds" requirement would be removed and that the genuine material factor defence should only be available after equal value has been established.

Another proposal to speed up and standardise the procedure is the appointment of a "chief independent expert", and a cadre of other full-time independent experts. A Chief Independent Expert might be able to ensure greater uniformity of procedures and impose a more brisk timetable on the production of reports.

6.46 The President of the EAT questioned the place of the independent expert in *Aldridge* v. *British Telecommunications* and advocated that his role become that of an assessor to the Tribunal itself, emphasising that it is for the Tribunal to make the decision as to equal value. Justice has previously mooted that equal value claims should be referred to arbitration before the Central Arbitration Council (CAC), but attractive as this might be from the point of view of

[35] Case No. 27668/85A, I.T. Manchester, July 15, 1988.
[36] Equal Pay: Strengthening the Acts, Equal Opportunities Commission, 1990.

trade unions and, perhaps, employers, Community law calls for a judicial remedy to be available.[37] In Ireland an Equality Officer hears such cases, with appeal to the Labour Court. The argument against that approach is that once such an officer is required to produce a reasoned report and safeguards are built in to the system to ensure that the process is operated in a fair and objective manner, it may be no quicker than a reformed industrial tribunal procedure.

6.47 Many of the benefits of referring equal value cases to the CAC may be derived from other recommendations of the EOC, *e.g.* that not only should the terms of the award in any successful case be extended to all other employees engaged on the same or broadly similar work to the applicant also but, that where the discrimination was rooted in the terms of a collective agreement, the tribunal should have the power to require that the offending term be modified or abandoned within a stipulated period, rather than deeming the term void, as now.[38]

6.48 Whilst Article 4 of the Equal Pay Directive provides that collective agreements, wage scales, wage agreements or individual contracts of employment which are contrary to the principle of equal pay may be declared null and void or may be amended, in *Nimz* v. *Freie und Hansestadt Hamburg* the ECJ ruled that:

> "where there is indirect discrimination in a provision in a collective agreement, the national court is required to disapply that provision, without requesting or awaiting its prior removal by collective negotiation or any other procedure, and to apply to members of the group which is disadvantaged by that discrimination the same arrangements which are applied to other employees, arrangements which, failing the correct application of article 119 of the EEC Treaty in national law, remain the only valid system of reference."

6.49 This decision suggests that it is not sufficient simply to render void any discriminatory provisions in a collective agreement, without providing an alternative remedy for those affected. The EAT recently held in *McKechnie* v. *UBM Building Supplies (Southern) Ltd.*[39] that industrial tribunals may rely on directly enforceable Community rights, so that tribunals may be able to rely on *Nimz* in applying the same arrangements to those disadvantaged by

---

[37] Council Directive 75/117 on the application of equal pay for men and women calls in Art. 2 for claimants to be able to pursue their claims "by judicial process".
[38] The Sex Discrimination Act 1975, s.77(5) provides that such a term may be modified by application to a county court. County courts seem singularly ill-equipped to undertake such work and to the best of the writers' knowledge no such applications have ever been made.
[39] [1991] I.R.L.R. 222.

the discrimination as are applied to other employees. In Britain this means that those disadvantaged by an indirectly discriminatory provision in a collective agreement can look to the application of an equality clause where the term in question has been incorporated into their contracts of employment.[40] or at least to a declaration that they are to enjoy comparable rights with their comparator group, as was done in *Secretary of State for Scotland and Greater Glasgow Health Board* v. *Wright and Hannah*.[41]

Hearings   6.50   In proceedings under the RRA and SDA, the applicant presents his or her case first because the burden of proof lies on the applicant. Sometimes the cases will be linked with unfair dismissal claims under the EPCA. If the unfair dismissal case stood alone in a case where the dismissal is admitted the respondent goes first, but where it is joined with a discrimination claim then it is usual for the applicant to start unless the parties agree otherwise, which they sometimes do.

6.51   Except in Scotland, the applicant is usually allowed an opening speech. If the case is fairly simple, sometimes tribunals in England and Wales do not allow opening speeches. It is quite usual in England and Wales to deal with liability alone in the main hearing and leave the question of compensation, if it arises, to agreement or a further hearing. Tribunals do differ in approach, however, and it is well worth asking the tribunal during opening which approach they will take. In Scotland the question of compensation is dealt with in the main hearing. Whenever compensation is dealt with, it is as well to deal with injury to feelings when the applicant first gives evidence, because such evidence seems very contrived when the only issue is the amount of compensation and much more natural at the end of a description of what has happened.

6.52   In England and Wales, but not in Scotland, witnesses other than the parties themselves are permitted to sit in the tribunal room and hear the rest of the case. It is possible to apply to the tribunal for them to be excluded. It is actually very difficult to cross-examine effectively each of a number of people on an interviewing panel when they are all present in the tribunal. However imaginative the questions, there is bound to be some repetition and witnesses can square their evidence if they hear what each other says. Sometimes, though, if the respondents are spinning a ludicrous line it helps the applicant for them to be seen to be consistently

---

[40] *e.g.* in *Alexander and others* v. *Standard Telephones and Cables Ltd. No. 2* [1991] the terms of a redundancy procedure which could well have been discriminatory (had the issue been in point), in that it relied upon service as a criteria for selection, was held not to be capable of incorporation into the individual workers contracts of employment.

[41] [1991] I.R.L.R. 187.

ludicrous! It has happened that a respondent has had so many witnesses in the tribunal that the atmosphere has become intimidating for the applicant and a tribunal may see that as a reason for excluding witnesses.

6.53 The course of a trial is no different in a discrimination case from other tribunal cases. The strict rules of evidence do not apply, so hearsay is admissible, but otherwise normal conventions are followed. Thus examination-in-chief, cross-examination and re-examination of witnesses are as usual and representatives of parties are expected to put their case to the opposing witnesses. The state of mind of the witnesses on the respondent's side who made the relevant decision about the applicant is crucial in a direct discrimination case and therefore cross-examination of those witnesses is extremely important. As a Manchester Industrial Tribunal in the case of *Freeman* v. *Salford Health Authority* said, "So much of an applicant's case depends upon in-depth cross-examination of the respondents" witnesses."[42] The importance for the tribunal of hearing what the respondent has to say about his or her reasons for the decisions in question has been recognised in the rule that unless the circumstances are exceptional the tribunal should not dismiss the case at the end of the evidence for the applicant.[43] Indeed, quite often the applicant's own oral evidence does not carry the matter very far at all on the issue of liability if, for example, he or she is complaining about a decision not to short-list after a written application from outside.

6.54 The most difficult problem for representatives in making speeches when unfamiliar with the particular tribunal is to judge how far the tribunal understands the nature of discrimination, and how much to take for granted on this topic. It is better to be safe than sorry and err on the side of full explanation since the tribunal is likely to indicate what it is already aware of, but in the nature of things cannot indicate much about what it does not know. Most of the jurisdiction of the tribunals concerns unfair dismissal, and these days Wages Act claims, and they may not have much familiarity with discrimination cases. The notion of reasonableness serves them well in the unfair dismissal jurisdiction, but in the discrimination area it is often doing things in ways which have traditionally been regarded as reasonable, such as appointing people who "fit in", that is the cause of the problem.[44] If the applicant has had an opening speech, then at the end the respondent has the first closing speech followed by the applicant. In Scotland, of

---

[42] The Tribunal was arguing for Legal Aid to extend to discrimination cases:cited in the CRE's consultative document for Second Review of the RRA, 1991.
[43] *Oxford* v. *D.H.S.S.* [1977] I.R.L.R. 225; [1977] I.C.R. 884.
[44] See *Baker* v. *Cornwall County Council* [1990] I.R.L.R. 194; [1990] I.C.R. 452, CA.

course, there are no opening speeches so at the end the Applicant's speech is first.

Remedies 6.55 Industrial Tribunals have three remedies at hand on a well-founded complaint of discrimination: a declaratory order; an order for compensation; and a recommendation. The limits pertaining to each are set out below. But there is an overall qualification, however, that the tribunal shall make such of those orders "as it considers just and equitable".[45] It has been held that these words refer to the issue whether or not to make an order not to the contents of the order: *Hurley* v. *Mustoe (No. 2)*.[46] Thus a declaration has to deal with the legal rights, compensation be based on usual principles of assessment in tort, and a recommendation made according to what is practicable -not in any of those cases according to what is just and equitable.

6.56 In certain circumstances the Commissions have the power to bring proceedings in their own names in the Industrial Tribunals before commencing proceeding in the county court to obtain injunctions for persistent discrimination, or to restrain the doing of further acts concerning unlawful advertisements or pressure or instructions to discriminate. If such a case is well founded and it is just and equitable, the tribunal may make either a declaratory order, or a recommendation, or both.

Declaratory Order 1. **A Declaratory Order** The duty is to make where just and equitable "an order declaring the rights of the complainant and the respondent in relation to the act to which the complaint relates".[47] This calls for no comment, save that it would seem to be a rare situation in a well-founded complaint where a tribunal not making an order of compensation, or a recommendation, did not find it appropriate to make a declaratory order.

Compensation 2. **An Order for Compensation** The tribunal's duty, where it is considered just and equitable, is to make "an order requiring the respondent to pay to the complainant compensation of an amount corresponding to any damages he could have been ordered by a county court or by a sheriff court to pay to the complainant if the complaint had fallen to be dealt with" [there].[48]

6.57 But there is a limit imposed which does not apply in the sheriff or county courts, namely, that for the time being imposed by the Secretary of State, which is currently

---

[45] SDA 1975, s.65; RRA 1976, s.56.
[46] *Hurley* v. *Mustoe* [1983] I.C.R. 422, EAT.
[47] SDA 1975, s.65(1)(*a*); RRA 1976, s.51(1)(*a*).
[48] SDA 1975, s.65(1)(*b*); RRA 1976, s.56(1)(*b*).

£11,000. Where there is an award under both the Sex Discrimination Act, and the Race Relations Act the total is not to exceed the limit, and where a monetary order is made because a recommendation has not been complied with, it should not take the total sum awarded beyond those limits.[49] We predict that the future will see many efforts made to get round the limit on compensation: for example, by arguing that it applies to each act of discrimination within the time limit; and if that line fails, by filing several originating applications in future cases, each alleging separate incidents between the same parties. A limit designed for the unfair dismissal jurisdiction where in the nature of things an applicant can allege only one act has been applied to a jurisdiction where the applicant may be complaining of many acts and the ramifications have yet to be worked out. However, it should be noted that if an unfair dismissal was based on grounds of race or sex and a reinstatement order was made and not complied with where practicable to do so, a "higher additional award" may be made.[50]

The exception for indirect discrimination

6.58 In an indirect discrimination case the Race Relations Act 1976, s.57(3) and Sex Discrimination Act 1975, s.66(3) provide that[51] "no award of damages shall be made if the respondent proves that the requirement or condition was not applied with the intention of treating the claimant unfavourably on racial grounds [on the ground of his sex or marital status as the case may be]".

Types of damages

Compensation for financial loss

6.59 Although the usual tort principles apply (subject to the upper limit applicable in this jurisdiction), the subject of financial loss merits specific attention here. Particularly in the area of discrimination in relation to applicants for jobs, or promotion, the situation may not be straightforward. The simple case is where it is clear that the applicant would have got the post but for the discrimination; yet it may be the case that there was discrimination in relation to the appointment and it is unclear whether or not the applicant would have got the job but for the discrimination; and finally, it may be the case that discrimination is proved, but it is clear that the applicant definitely would not have got the post even if there had been no discrimination. The fact that it is possible for there to be discrimination in the "arrangements made"[52] for determining who should get a post as well as in the final selection makes the two latter possibilities all the more likely to occur.

6.60 Is compensation for actual loss payable if they do? If it is unclear whether the applicant would have got the job

---

[49] *Infra* p. 119.
[50] EPCA 1978, s.71.
[51] An equivalent provision is embodied in SDA 1975, s.66(3). See *Orphanos* v. *Queen Mary College* [1985] I.R.L.R. 349; [1985] A.C. 761, H.L.
[52] See *ante* p. 127.

but for the discrimination, what the applicant has lost is the chance of getting the post. There has been a tendency for tribunals simply to award a sum for injury to feelings in these circumstances, and indeed it may be that advocates have not thought to ask for more. But it is well-established[53] that a sum can be awarded for loss of a chance, to be assessed according to the circumstances. So generally there can be awarded a proportion of the compensation for pecuniary loss which would have been awarded had it been clear that the applicant would have got the job but for the discrimination.

6.61   Obviously compensation based upon loss of a chance cannot be awarded in the situation where it is clear that the applicant would not have got the post even if there had been no discrimination. Even here, however, limiting the compensation to damages for injury to feelings may not always be appropriate. There is also the head of compensation based upon expenditure rendered futile by the unlawful acts. If the effect of the discrimination is such that the applicant was never really considered seriously at all for the post, as (s)he was entitled to be, it is arguable that the applicant should be entitled to compensation in respect of expenditure incurred in putting him or herself forward (for example postage, costs of interview attendance if these were not otherwise met) because (s)he would not have incurred that expenditure had (s)he known that (s)he would not be seriously considered at all. Everyone of course takes the chance in applying that someone else better may apply.

6.62   Subject to the statutory limit for compensation, damages for financial or other loss can relate to loss which has been incurred at the time of the hearing, and any prospective future loss. Obviously where the result of the discrimination is that a person is without a job and that situation continues, an estimate of the likely time which will elapse before a job is found has to be made, based upon the state of the job-market.

6.63   It is very often the case that an Industrial Tribunal will hear the case on the issue of liability without hearing evidence on the issue of compensation, and in the event of finding the case proved, express the hope that the parties will reach a settlement on the issue of compensation and not need to reinstate the case for a hearing on this issue. (In Scotland, however, evidence relating to compensation should normally be led along with the other evidence.) If a tribunal which has not heard any evidence or submissions on the subject of compensation were to find on liability and purport to make an award of compensation, the way for the dissatisfied party to deal with that situation is to ask the tribunal for a review of its decision.

[53] See *Chaplin* v. *Hicks* [1911] 2 K.B. 786.

Even if the issue of compensation is to be adjourned by the tribunal, it is as well for the applicant to give evidence at the original hearing as to the effect of the alleged discrimination on his or her feelings, because it will probably be more convincing as part of the whole picture than later when the amount of compensation is the sole issue.

Damages for injury to feelings

6.64 The Sex Discrimination Act and the Race Relations Act both make it clear that compensation may include damages for injury to feelings. Save for a run of Scottish cases concerning sexual harassment, the level of damages awarded by courts and tribunals under this head tended to be very low. For example, an Industrial Tribunal is reported by the CRE in their 1985 Review of the Act to have awarded £30 to a young man who lost a YTS placement as a result of discrimination and was said by the tribunal to be "shattered". This was perhaps a particularly low award, but the typical award did not rise above a few hundred pounds. However two decisions of the Court of Appeal in 1988 gave the green light for considerably higher awards under this head, as well as making clear that an award may include aggravated damages.

Principles for compensation for injury to feelings

6.65 *Alexander* v. *The Home Office*[54] sets out the basic principles for the assessment of compensation for injury to feelings. In the county court Mr Alexander had been awarded compensation of £50 when he proved racial discrimination by the prison service in not permitting him to work in the prison kitchens. His induction report, which was considered by those dealing with allocation of work, said that "he shows the anti-authoritarian arrogance that seems to be common in most coloured inmates". So he was not treated as an individual, but by reference to a damaging racial stereotype. In making the award the county court took into account that he had been vindicated by the court in his assertion of his rights. His appeal to the Court of Appeal as to the level of compensation was allowed and an award of £500 substituted. It is clear from the Court's reasoning that £500 now represents a figure at the lower end of the scale of damages for injury to feelings. May L.J. said:[54]

> "As with any other awards of damages the objective of an award for unlawful racial discrimination is restitution. Where the discrimination has caused actual pecuniary loss, such as the refusal of a job, then the damages referable to this can be readily calculated. For the injury to feelings, however, for the humiliation, for the insult, it is impossible to say what is restitution and the answer must depend on the experience and good sense of the judge and his assessors. Awards should not be minimal, because this would tend to trivialise or diminish respect

[54] [1988] I.R.L.R. 190, [1988] I.C.R. 685, C.A.

for the public policy to which the Act gives effect. On the other hand, just because it is impossible to assess the monetary value of injured feelings, awards should be restrained. To award sums which are generally felt to be excessive does almost as much harm to the policy and the results which it seeks as do nominal awards. Further, injury to feelings, which is likely to be of a relatively short duration, is less serious than physical injury to the body or the mind which may persist for months, in many cases for life.

Nevertheless damages for this relatively new tort of unlawful racial discrimination are at large, that is to say that they are not limited to the pecuniary loss that can be specifically proved. . . . [C]ompensatory damages may and in some instances should, include an element of aggravated damages where, for example, the defendant may have behaved in a high-handed, malicious, insulting or aggressive manner in committing the act of discrimination".[55]

6.66   It was held that the judge was wrong to take into account that Mr Alexander had been vindicated in court in mitigation of the damages to which he was entitled. The Court of Appeal thought it appropriate to take into account, in aggravation of damages, that an unjustified, prejudiced and damaging appraisal of Mr Alexander had been disseminated within the prison system.

6.67   The subsequent case of *Noone* v. *North West Thames Regional Health Authority*[56] concerned a Sri Lankan microbiologist who was not appointed to a consultancy post on grounds which the Court of Appeal held to be racial. She had superior qualifications, greater experience and more publications than the successful candidate. The Industrial Tribunal found her interview "little more than a sham". They had awarded £5000 compensation for injury to feelings. The EAT in fact allowed an appeal against liability but indicated that £1000 would have been an appropriate figure. When the Court of Appeal restored the industrial tribunal's finding of racial discrimination it substituted an award of £3000. The Court took into account the fact that section 56 of the Race Relations Act 1976 imposes an upper limit on compensation awarded by industrial tribunals (which is fixed by the Secretary of State), and that such a figure should make allowance, not only for a sum for injury to feelings, but also any actual loss, and any sum payable for failure to comply with a recommendation. The limit at the relevant time was £7,500. The Court were of the view that the appellant's injury to feelings was severe and that the award should be at the top end of the bracket, but that

---

[55] At p. 193 in the I.R.L.R. version.
[56] [1988] I.R.L.R. 195, C.A.

£5,000 was too high. Since the upper limit is now £11,000, on this reasoning the top of the range should be well over £4,000. This reasoning seems to give the Government of the day power, by raising or lowering the limit for compensation, to determine the appropriate range of awards for injury to feelings. It is ironic that after the Industrial Tribunal decision the CRE had made representations to the Secretary of State to lift the upper limit bearing in mind the award of £5,000 for injury to feelings by the tribunal. Had this been done, the award might have stood in the Court of Appeal.

6.68   In the case of *Sharifi* v. *Strathclyde Regional Council*[57] a tribunal award of £750 compensation for race discrimination in respect of intangible loss, covering loss of opportunity, disadvantage in the job market and injury to his feelings was set aside by the EAT and an award of £1,500 substituted. Dr Sharifi applied for a post as a Divisional Scientist in the respondent's Water Department and had not been short-listed, whilst many white applicants without equivalent or indeed any appropriate qualifications were selected. The Appeal Tribunal said that an award of £500 for injured feelings is at or near the minimum appropriate level of award. They added, however, that there was no need to make separate assessments in respect of the various elements of the award.

6.69   Indications, therefore, are that the tribunals have welcomed the liberating influence of *Alexander*. Scottish tribunals had in any event gone their own way, as indicated earlier, largely it would seem under the influence of the Chairman Doris Littlejohn (who is now the Scottish President of Industrial Tribunals), and awarded substantial sums in sexual harassment cases. It may, however, be that bad cases of both racial and sexual harassment would in any event call for particularly large sums to be awarded under the heading of aggravated damages.

Can exemplary damages be awarded?

6.70   After dicta in the Court of Appeal in *Alexander* v. *Home Office* and the decision of that Court in *Bradford Council* v. *Arora*[58] it seemed that exemplary damages could be sought in an appropriate discrimination case.[59] However, the Court of Appeal in a public nuisance case *AB* v. *South West Water Services Ltd.*[60] held that the question whether it was right to apply the principles in *Rookes* v. *Barnard*[61] to a

---

[57] [1992] I.R.L.R. 259. And see the *Deane* case fn 62 below. See also *Murray* v. *Powertech (Scotland) Ltd.* [1992] I.R.L.R. 257 where the EAT suggest that claims for injury to feelings in a discrimination case are "almost inevitable".
[58] *City of Bradford* v. *Arora* [1991] I.R.L.R. 165, [1991] I.C.R. 226, C.A.
[59] Case No. 36145/86 (Birmingham) was an example: cited in *Arora*.
[60] [1993] 1 All E.R. 609.
[61] [1964] A.C. 1129, H.L.

tort created since that case was not argued in *Arora* and it was not appropriate to do so. The Employment Appeal Tribunal in *Deane* v. *Ealing LBC*[62] followed this decision in a race discrimination appeal and ruled that a claim for exemplary damages must therefore fail.

6.71 Unless this point gets before the House of Lords and is reconsidered, therefore, we shall see no more awards for exemplary damages in discrimination cases in Britain. Nevertheless it is probably worth pleading a claim in appropriate cases, because one of the Commissions may well feel it worthwhile to pursue a test case on this issue.

Community Law and the compensation limit

6.72 A new dimension was provided by the decision of Southampton Industrial Tribunal in June 1988 in the case of *Marshall* v. *SW Hants Health Authority*.[63] The tribunal ruled in a sex discrimination case that the statutory ceiling on awards for compensation breached Article 6 of the 1976 EEC Equal Treatment Directive.[64] The Directive obliges Member States to adopt "within the framework of their legal systems, all the measures necessary to ensure that the Directive is fully effective". In the 1984 case, *Von Colson & Kamann* v. *Land Nordrhein-Westfahlen*,[65] the European Court had held that this obliged Member States to provide remedies which were effective deterrents to recalcitrant employers and if states opted for compensation it had therefore to be adequate. The tribunal ruled that the limit (it has since been increased to £10,000) did not provide an adequate remedy for unlawful discrimination and was not a deterrent to any save a very small employer. The Tribunal in fact awarded £19,405 compensation to the applicant. (She had been forced to retire early because of her sex.) Obviously, this case had the potential to bring about the ending of the compensation limits under the Sex Discrimination Act 1975.

6.73 The *Marshall* case was appealed to the EAT on the basis that the award of £19,405 wrongly included a substantial sum for interest. The EAT allowed the appeal. (However, provision has since been made for the payment of interest on Tribunal awards).[66] No appeal was brought against exceeding the statutory limit on compensation, though Wood J. observed that it was a point which the Authority could well have taken. Nevertheless, the ratio of the case on the interest point was in part that where a State has provided access to the courts the remedies are for the State, subject only to the principle of *de minimis*, and Article 6 has no direct effect. On further appeal to the Court of

---

[62] [1993] I.R.L.R. 209.
[63] See *Marshall* v. *SW Hants Health Authority* (No. 2) [1990] I.R.L.R. 481; [1991] I.C.R. 136.
[64] EEC Council Directive No. 76/207.
[65] Case No. 14/83 [1984] E.C.R. 1981.
[66] The Industrial Tribunals (Interest) Order 1990 S.I. 1990 No. 479.

Appeal, the employers were allowed to rely on the limit on compensation. That Court held that a complainant cannot rely on Article 6 of the Equal Treatment Directive to override the statutory limit on compensation because the Von Colson Court had held that the provisions as to compensation in the Article were not sufficently precise or unconditional to have direct effect. However, Dillon L.J. dissenting was of the view that since the employers here were the representatives of the State they could not rely on the State's own failure to implement Article 6. The Court of Appeal clearly thought the statutory limit probably was too low.

6.74 On further appeal the house of Lords referred certain questions to the European Court of Justice. Advocate General Van Gerven's Opinion delivered on January 26, 1993 concludes in esssence that if national legislation does not embody an adequate system of sanctions there can be reliance on Article 6 of the directive in any event as against a public body of that member state. But the fact that there is an upper limit on compensation is not by itself enough to mean national legislation falls foul of the Directive. It all depends whether the compensation would be adequate in relation to the damage sustained having regard to the most important components of compensation including loss of income, injury to feelings ("moral damage") and interest. And certainly there should not be less effective sanctions for Community Law than for corresponding national law. In the instant case it was the interest element which took the award well over the limit. At the time of writing the ECJ has yet to rule but the writing on the wall is plain.

6.75 Under the Fair Employment (Northern Ireland) Act 1989 the limit on compensation is £30,000. The first award for injury to feelings made under this Act in the case of *Duffy* v.*Eastern Health & Social Services Board*[67] was for £25,000 including both aggravated and exemplary damages. We take the view that there is no good reason why religious and political discrimination should attract higher compensation than racial or sex discrimination, and the higher level is the more likely to bring about a significant reduction in unlawful discrimination.

Recommendations **6.76** Both the Sex Discrimination Act and Race Relations Act give an Industrial Tribunal the power on a well-founded complaint to make a recommendation if it considers it to be just and equitable. The scope of such recommendations is limited, however, by the terms of the provisions and by case-law thereon. The power is to make:

"a recommendation that the respondent take within a

---

[67] [1992] I.R.L.R. 251, F.E.T.

specified period action appearing to the tribunal to be practicable for the purpose of obviating or reducing the adverse effect on the complainant of any act of discrimination to which the complaint relates."[68]

6.77 The most obvious limitation on the recommendation power is that it is limited to the adverse effect "on the complainant". In the nature of things, discrimination rarely happens on a one-off basis. If a person has been treated in a particular way because of perceptions of, or beliefs about, the group to which that person belongs rather than the individual's merits, then obviously the same thing is likely to happen to other persons from that group. Tribunals are not empowered, however, on a complaint brought by an individual to make even a recommendation with statutory effect to deal with that possibility.

6.78 This may be seen as a major flaw in the legislation. It is farcical that a tribunal might listen for days to similar fact evidence and evidence relating to measures which could have been taken to avoid discrimination, yet be powerless even to make a recommendation themselves. It seems to be the case that the legislators contemplated the Commissions following up individual cases to deal with the wider implications, either by promotional work (employers are often amenable to an approach after having been caught out) or by use of the formal investigation power which the Commissions possess. (We are not aware of the formal investigation power being used in this way.) This can be asserted with some confidence, because the power to issue non-discrimination notices in formal investigations lists the unlawful acts to which it applies and then says "and so applies whether or not proceedings have been brought in respect of the act".

6.79 The statutory effect of a recommendation is that:

"If without reasonable justification the respondent to a complaint fails to comply with a recommendation made by an industrial tribunal . . . then if it thinks it just and equitable to do so . . . the tribunal may . . . [subject to the statutory limit on compensation which is currectly £11,000] increase the amount of compensation required to be paid to the complainant in respect of the complaint . . . or if [an order for compensation had not been made but could have been] the tribunal may make such an order."[69]

6.80 Recommendations for an apology are sometimes made, but if the respondent has denied the discrimination and had it proved against him, unless there has been some

---

[68] SDA 1975, s.65(1)(c), RRA 1976, s.56(1)(c).
[69] SDA, s.65(4), RRA, s.56(4).

change in attitude during the hearing, the absence of an apology up to that point would also need to be reflected in the compensation awarded.

Power to make a recommendation

6.81 Case-law has imposed limitations on the power to make a recommendation. First, it cannot be used to give the applicant priority in respect of future similar jobs over other applicants, so the Court of Appeal in *Noone* v. *N. W. Thames Regional Health Authority (No 2)*[70] held, because other possible contenders for such a post might be better qualified for that post. However, the *Noone* post was a highly specialised consultancy post. It is open to question whether, when an employer has many similar vacancies of a less specialised kind, it is not being unduly sensitive not to allow a recommendation that the next such vacancy should be offered to the applicant. This is particularly the case where the applicant is demonstrably better than the person who got the post to which the complaint relates. The *Noone* case does make clear that a recommendation that a person be notified of the vacancy which next occurs is lawful. Second, questions of monetary compensation are to be dealt with under the power to award compensation and not under the power to make a recommendation. A tribunal may not, therefore, make a recommendation that an employer should increase a person's wages.[71]

Reasoned decisions

6.82 A tribunal is required to furnish a reasoned decision in race relations, sex discrimination and equal pay cases under Regulation (9) (5) of the Industrial Tribunal (Rules of Procedure) Regulations 1985. In equal value cases, a copy of the report supplied by the independent expert is appended to the decision.

6.83 In *Meek* v. *City of Birmingham District Council*, Bingham L.J. set out the approach to be adopted by tribunals when reasons are required:

> "It has on a number of occasions been made plain that the decision of an Industrial Tribunal is not required to be an elaborate formalistic product of refined legal draftsmanship, but it must contain an outline of the story which has given rise to the complaint and a summary of the Tribunal's basic factual conclusions and a statement of the reasons which have led them to the conclusions which they do on those basic facts. The parties are entitled to be told why they have won or lost. There should be sufficient account of the facts and of the reasoning to enable the EAT or, on further appeal, this court to see whether a question of law arises."[72]

---

[70] [1988] I.R.L.R. 530 C.A.
[71] See *Irvine* v. *Prestcold Ltd.* [1981] I.R.L.R. 281, C.A.
[72] [1987] I.R.L.R. 250, C.A.

6.84 In *Hampson* v. *DES*[73] Balcombe L.J. relied upon the decision in *Meek* arguing that, in the absence of authority on the meaning of "full reasons," no less standard is required than was formerly the case when only "reasons" were prescribed. He was critical of the findings of justifiability by the Tribunal in *Hampson* because the standards used to test the Department's justification of the requirements placed upon the applicant were not identified, nor was it clear what precise findings of fact had been relied upon in coming to the conclusion that the requirement was justifiable.

Costs **6.85** Costs are not normally awarded in the Industrial Tribunals. An Industrial Tribunal has the power to award costs under Regulation 11 of the Industrial Tribunal (Rules of Procedure) Regulations 1985 if, in the view of the tribunal, the proceedings were brought or conducted frivolously, vexatiously or otherwise unreasonably. The restriction as to frivolous or vexatious action does not apply in respect of a party who applies for an adjournment.

6.86 Cost awards are uncommon and lie within the discretion of the Tribunal, both as to whether they are awarded and as to their sum. In making such an award, the Tribunal may take into account the means of the party in question. The costs of the EOC or CRE in assisting applicants constitute a first charge upon any costs or expenses recovered by the assisted person.[74]

6.87 A costs warning may be issued against either party at a pre-hearing assessment under Regulation 6 of the Industrial Tribunal (Rules of Procedure) Regulations 1985[75] if the Tribunal is of the opinion that there is no reasonable prospect of success. The introduction of the pre-hearing assessment has not resulted in a costs award being made in a substantial number of cases, and in a fair number of the cases in which a costs warning was given the applicant was ultimately successful at the full hearing.

6.88 Nonetheless, the Employment Act 1989 introduced a provision under which regulations provide for a pre-hearing review. At that review the tribunal is empowered to require a deposit of up to £150 from a party as a condition of proceeding further if there is no reasonable prospect of success, or the proceedings are judged to be being brought frivolously, vexatiously or otherwise unreasonably. It will be interesting to see whether the Commissions will ever pay deposits as part of their assistance. The review will take place without the benefit of any evidence being heard and must entail the prospect that a deposit will be required in a

---

[73] [1989] I.R.L.R. 69 (the case subsequently went to H.L.).
[74] SDA, s.75 (3)(*a*), RRA, s.66(5)(*a*).
[75] S.I. 1985 No. 16.

certain proportion of cases which will ultimately be successful. Discrimination cases are not normally thrown out without hearing the Respondent's side and giving the Applicant the chance to cross-examine, and knowing this should make tribunals wary of taking deposits on the strength of the papers alone.

Appeals to the EAT

6.89 Appeal may be made to the EAT on a point of law only, within 42 days beginning with the notification of the written decision. Appeals in discrimination and equal pay cases are governed by the normal Employment Appeals Tribunal Rules 1980 and are the subject of a Practice Direction dated February 17, 1981. The Practice Direction contains the observation that it is not necessarily a good excuse for delay in appealing that legal aid has been applied for or support is being sought from the EOC or CRE. In such circumstances, the appellant should inform the registrar, and the other party, of his intentions within the normal time limit for appeal and seek the latter's agreement for an extension to the normal time limit. Employee appellants have had a very poor success rate in discrimination cases in front of the EAT in recent years, such that it has become a matter of comment by the editor of the Industrial Relations Law Reports.[79]

[79] See [1992] I.R.L.R. 333.

7 DISCRIMINATION OUTSIDE EMPLOYMENT

Education

Part lll of each of the Sex Discrimination Act 1975 and the Race Relations Act 1976 deals with discrimination in other fields than employment. Each opens with the subject of Education.

7.01 In the context of education, it is perhaps worth repeating the general point that, if less favourable treatment occurs on the prohibited grounds, *direct* discrimination occurs even though the person acting on those grounds was paternalistic or well-intentioned. Much discrimination as a result of sterotyping falls into this category. A teacher stops a girl doing science-based subjects, because of a belief that girls in general are better at arts subjects, despite the fact that the particular girl has the right aptitude for science-based subjects. A teacher stops an Afro-Caribbean boy doing academic subjects, because of a belief that Afro-Caribbeans are good at sport but not academic subjects, despite the fact that the particular boy is academically bright. In both cases, the teacher is doing as much harm as one who malevolently sets out to do down girls and blacks, and this is the way that the law looks at it.

7.02 In *Debell, Sevket and Teh* v. *London Borough of Bromley*,[1], there was sex discrimination where a headmistress departed from a written policy for the allocation of pupils by age to different classes and made decisions on the basis of sex. She tried to even up the number of each sex in each class for socialisation and curriculum opportunity reasons. The complainant girls were kept in a class of predominantly third year pupils with a female teacher, instead of being moved to a class of predominantly fourth year pupils as had happened to some younger boys. The headmistress also claimed that a class with a female teacher was best for the girls concerned.

7.03 The law of *indirect* discrimination says in effect that a practice which has a discriminatory result will be unlawful unless justifiable.[2] In the context of education, one will be

[1] See EOC Sex Discrimination Paper No. 7.
[2] See chap. 2 *supra*.

looking for an educational justification for the practice. Educational thinking on various subjects, however, tends to develop and change as understanding increases. This means that not only do practices have to be examined to assess whether they have discriminatory impact, but also that the justification should be re-examined from time to time to see whether it still holds good. A good example is the CRE's Formal Investigation of Calderdale Local Education Authority. The LEA operated an English Language testing system. Before admission to main-stream schooling, children either had to be exempt or pass the test. Those who did not were predominantly of Asian origin and were placed either into special language centres or special language classes within schools. The effect was that they were separated from other children and there were other disadvantages including a narrower curriculum. No doubt when the system was set up it had been thought the best was of teaching English as a second language, but in the meantime, educational research and thinking had reached the conclusion that teaching English as a second language was actually best done in the ordinary classroom with special help on tap. The LEA conceded in the light of this development that their procedures were not justifiable, and the CRE concluded that they amounted to indirect discrimination. The Secretary of State accepted these findings.

The provisions dealing with education

7.04   Section 17 of the Race Relations Act 1976 and section 22 of the Sex Discrimination Act 1975 are phrased in similar terms and make unlawful the following types of discrimination by certain bodies in charge of educational establishments: Discrimination

"(*a*) in the terms on which it offers to admit him or her to the establishment as a pupil; or

(*b*) refusing or deliberately omitting to accept an application for his or her admission to the establishment as a pupil; or

(*c*) where he or she is a pupil of the establishment -

(i) in the way if affords him or her access to any benefits, facilities or services, or by refusing or deliberately omitting to afford him or her access to them;

(ii) by excluding him or her from the establishment or subjecting him/her to any other detriment."

7.05   The establishments to which this applies with the responsible body are set out in the relevant section together with orders made from time to time under section 24(1) of the Sex Discrimination Act 1975. As the educational system changes, so the sections and orders alter. Reference should be made to the current provisions.

7.06   It should be noted that under section 17 of the Race Relations Act and section 22 of the Sex Discrimination Act, unlawful discrimination occurs only in respect of a particular establishment. Under these provisions it is not possible to compare the treatment of say girls or black pupils in one school with that of boys or white pupils, as the case may be, in another school. But section 18 of the Race Relations Act and section 23[3] of the Sex Discrimination Act impose a wider duty on local education authorities.[4]

7.07 Possibly the worst case of direct discrimination under both Acts to come to light was in the admission process of St George's Hospital Medical School. A computer programme used to sift UCCA admission application forms and grade them for a decision to be made as to whether the applicant would be interviewed had a built-in bias against women and "non-caucasians", which deliberately mimicked the decision-making of the academics who read the forms before the computer took over the task. The real question for everybody in education is how typical this bias in decision-making is of other educational institutions, (although of course the manifestation of the bias in a computer programme may be very rare).[5]

7.08 An indirect racial discrimination case which went to the House of Lords was *Mandla* v. *Dowell-Lee*[6] in which it was held to be indirectly discriminatory to require agreement to the wearing of a school uniform cap because turban-wearing orthodox Sikh boys could not comply consistently with their cultural norms and could not therefore enter the school, and the requirement was not justifiable.

7.09 More complex was the CRE's investigation into access to the Watford Grammar Schools (in fact all-ability schools) where the selection process seemed to involve a need for a minimum number of reasons to be specified by parents in choosing the schools. This had an indirectly discriminatory impact on those Asian children whose parents' first language was not English and who encountered difficulty in expressing themselves in writing. The Commission found indirect racial discrimination (but the passage in the report dealing with justifiability is barely more than an assertion by the Commission, and would hardly have satisfied an appeal court if a tribunal had been so skimpy with its reasons on justifiability: see Balcombe LJ in *Hampson* v. *DES*).[7]

The single-sex exemption

7.10 Where the single-sex exemption under the Sex Discrimination Act 1975 applies, a single-sex establishment

---

[3] See *Infra.*
[4] See *R. V. Secretary of State for Education and Science ex P. Keating* [1985] L.G.R. 469.
[5] See Medical School Admissions: A CRE formal investigation.
[6] [1983] 2 A.C. 548.
[7] See [1989] I.R.L.R. 69.

Sex Discrimination Act 1975, s.26

is exempt from the Sex Discrimination Act duty not to discriminate in admissions. There are transitional arrangements for establishments becoming co-educational in section 27 and Schedule 2.

A single-sex establishment is defined by section 26 of the Sex Discrimination Act 1975 as an establishment which admits pupils of one sex only, or where the admission of pupils of the opposite sex is exceptional, or comparatively few in number and confined to particular courses of instruction or teaching classes. A school which is not a single-sex school may nevertheless discriminate in its admission of boarders and in relation to boarding facilities if it takes both boarders and non-boarders, but the boarders are wholly or mostly of one sex only. Section 27 of the Sex Discrimination Act enables schools to gain sanction for transitional arrangements in becoming co-educational, by application for a "transitional exemption order" under Schedule 2 of the Act.

7.11 It should be noted that, unlike the Race Relations Act 1976, the Sex Discrimination Act 1975 has no provision equating segregation with less favourable treatment.[8] In this way, the Act does not prohibit the continuation of separate facilities for boys and girls within a co-educational school, provided that the facilities afforded to each sex can justifiably be regarded as providing equal opportunities. Any facility or course provided must be available to both sexes. By contrast, segregation of black pupils from white pupils on racial grounds amounts in law to less favourable treatment of both groups.

7.12 Since the cultural practices of particular racial groups may be such as to require single-sex education for their children, lack of sufficient places provided by a local authority to meet this need might be indirectly racially discriminatory in that it would have the effect of denying them access to schools of their choice. This would, however, fall to be dealt with not under section 17 of the Race Relations Act 1976 which relates to *particular establishments*, but under section 18 which sets out a wider duty of local education authorities (education authorities in Scotland).

Duties on Education Authorities

7.13 Section 18 of the Race Relations Act 1976 and section 23 of the Sex Discrimination Act 1975 are in similar terms and impose a duty on those education authorities in carrying out their functions under the Education Acts not to do any act which constitutes discrimination (excepting functions already covered by sections 17 RRA Dection and 22 SDA). An example usually referred to in this context is the award of discretionary educational grants, but the provision can

---

[8] See RRA 1976, s.1(2), and see the Cleveland case on the meaning of segregation, *infra* n. 11.

also cover wider educational functions. For example, a local education authority could fall foul of the Sex Discrimination Act provisions by treating girls less favourably in, say, the provision of places for advanced physics, even though the underlying reason for this is that the extra facilities exist for boys in exempt single-sex schools. This is a necessary implication from the fact that the single-sex establishment exception does not apply in relation to section 23.

7.14 In *R* v. *Secretary of State for Education and Science, ex p. Keating*,[9] it was held that a local education authority was obliged to have regard to the Sex Discrimination Act 1975 in carrying out its duty under section 8 of the Education Act 1944 to provide secondary schools in its area "sufficient in number, character, and equipment". Thus, if the policy of the authority was to provide single-sex education for both boys and girls, the treatment of one sex less favourably than the other was contrary to section 23 of the 1975 Act. The local education authority's publication of a proposal to close the only boys' comprehensive school in its area would therefore, being an act done pursuant to section 8 of the Act of 1944, constitute discrimination on the grounds of sex.

7.15 The *Keating* case was an example of the use of judicial review procedures to obtain relief. In that case it was the parents who took proceedings. In *R* v. *Birmingham City Council*,[10] (a case which went to the House of Lords) it was the EOC who took judicial review proceedings. This method of proceeding is an ideal way of avoiding the cumbersome procedure of a formal investigation where the facts are not in dispute, and what is in issue is the lawfulness of what has occurred. The decision was similar to that in the *Keating* case, though here the council was discriminating unlawfully in providing more grammar school places for boys than for girls.

7.16 The parental choice provisions were held by the Court of Appeal to override the Race Relations Act insofar as there was a conflict in the case of *R* v. *Cleveland County Council ex p. CRE*. A local education authority had taken the view that a parental choice of school had been expressly made on racial grounds, yet felt obliged to comply with it because of the wording of the Education legislation. The Court upheld the view of the authority against a contrary finding by the CRE in a formal investigation that the Race Relations Act provision in section 18 prevailed. It held that discrimination in carrying out duties in relation to parental choice was protected by section 41 which protects acts done in pursuance of any enactment. The case was unfortunate inasmuch as it had been the intention of the Commission to

[9] [1985] 84 L.G.R. 469.
[10] [1989] I.R.L.R. 173.

concentrate on the law as it applied to the perception of the situation by the local authority and not to name or involve the family, but they were named by the press and dragged into the matter.[11]

7.17   Section 19 of the Race Relations Act 1976 and section 25 of the Sex Discrimination Act 1975 further impose a general duty in the public sectors of education to secure that facilities for education and any ancillary benefits or services are provided without discrimination. These provisions are really concerned with *planning* in education to ensure freedom from discrimination. As the Equal Opportunities Commission point out, as far as the Sex Discrimination Act 1975 is concerned, the purpose of the planning is not to ensure that there is a balance between the sexes, but that pupils and applicants for admission have access to education provision irrespective of sex. With appropriate modification, the same could be said of race. In the course of planning, questions may have to be asked why existing imbalances exist, and whether the cause is discrimination.

Enforcement   **7.18**   The Secretary of State has the exclusive power to enforce this general duty using Education Act powers.[12] Those same powers also apply to breaches of the other provisions, creating liability for discrimination in addition to an individual's right to enforce them in the County Court. In this sector of education there are also two modifications to the normal enforcement procedure. First, an individual has to give notice to the Secretary of State before commencing legal proceedings and this has an effect on the time limit for their commencement.[13] Second, neither the EOC nor the CRE can issue a non-discrimination notice in a formal investigation, but instead give notice of findings of discrimination to the Secretary of State, who can use his Education Act powers if appropriate.

LEAs and the promotion of good race relations   **7.19**   The education provisions in the Sex Discrimination Act and the Race Relations Act are concerned with the elimination of discrimination. But LEAs, being local authorities, are also subject to the wider duty under section 71 of the Race Relations Act 1976,[14] requiring them in addition:

> "to make appropriate arrangements with a view to securing that their various functions are carried out with due regard to the need –
>
> (a) to eliminate unlawful racial discrimination; and

---

[11] Times Law Report, August 25, 1992. The parent was held not to have acted on racial grounds.
[12] RRA 1975, s.19 and SDA 1975, s.25.
[13] See at the end of this chap.
[14] See also chap. 9.

(b) to promote equality of opportunity, and good
relations, between persons of different racial groups."

Clearly (a) above covers much the same ground as section 19
of the Race Relations Act 1976, but (b) goes beyond,
particularly insofar as it relates to the promotion of good
race relations. This adds a whole new dimension to the
educational function of LEAs. However, the opting out
arrangements for schools obviously mean that the influence
of LEAs will diminish in the future.

Goods, facilities and services

7.20   Both the 1975 and 1976 Acts contain similar sections
prohibiting discrimination in the provision of goods,
facilities and services to the public or a section of the public.
It is generally unlawful for any person concerned with the
provision (for payment or not) of goods, facilities or services
to the public, or a section of the public, to discriminate
either by refusing or deliberately omitting to provide them,
or to provide them of like quality, in the like manner, and
on the like terms as he normally provides them (section 20,
RRA, section 29, SDA).

7.21   However, certain differences have arisen between the
SDA and RRA. First, the reference to "the public or a
section of a public" has meant that the activities of private
clubs vis-a-vis membership matters are outside of the
prohibition. Under the Race Relations Act 1976, this has led
to a separate provision dealing with such associations (see
s.25), but not, despite, it seems, a need, under the Sex
Discrimination Act 1975.[15] Second, a restrictive
interpretation of the application of the provision to the
functions of public authorities by the House of Lords in R
v. Entry Clearance Officer, Bombay ex p. Amin[16] has led to a
new section 19A in the Race Relations Act 1976 to ban racial
discrimination in the exercise of planning functions, but
there is no similar ban on sex discrimination.

7.22   Use of the word "normally" in sections 20 RRA and
section 29 SDA indicates that they do not extend to cover
provision on a one-off occasion.[17] They do, of course, cover
even a one-off case of discrimination where the provision is
sufficiently frequent for the word "normally" to be
appropriate.

---

[15] See EOC "Legislating for Change."
[16] [1983] 2 A.C. 818.
[17] On the similar provision on the RRA 1968 see Dockers Labour Club and
Institute Ltd. v. Race Relations Board [1976] A.C. 285, at p. 297 per Lord
Diplock, and on the 1976 Act Hector v. Smethwick Labour Club Institute
(1988) (unreported).

Public or section thereof

7.23 The words "to the public or a section of the public" limit the application of the sections. The leading cases on the meaning of those words all arose in the context of the Race Relations Act 1968. The House of Lords held that a Conservative Club was not offering the facility of membership to a section of the public,[18] and similarly nor was a working men's club, in refusing to admit a member of another club, offering facilities or services to a section of the public, even though the clubs were all affiliated in a union.[19] The consideration which weighed with their Lordships was whether there was genuine selection on personal grounds in electing candidates for membership. Even the fact that there were more than a million members of the union normally entitled to avail themselves of affiliated membership rights did not make them a section of the public. By contrast, the House held that children in the care of a local authority were a section of the public to whom foster-parents provided services or facilities.[20] The cases remain authoritative on the meaning of the words "to the public or a section of the public". Nevertheless, the sequel to these cases was that the Race Relations Act 1976 legislated specifically to bring private clubs within that Act, whilst foster-parents were themselves taken outside the Act.[21]

7.24 The latter was achieved by section 23(2) of the Race Relations Act 1976 which says that:

"section 20(1) does not apply to anything done by a person as a participant in arrangements under which he (for reward or not) takes into his home, and treats as if they were members of his family, children, elderly persons, or persons requiring a special degree of care and attention".

Since the reference is to the person who "takes into his home," the exception would cover the foster-parent who discriminates on racial grounds, but not discrimination by local authorities or private agencies in providing their services to children or others in need of such provision, except insofar as they were satisfying racial preferences expressed by the homeowners. (However, if the authorities or agencies were by written circular to invite the expression of racial preferences, it would seem that they would fall foul of the ban on discriminatory advertisements since "advertisement" is defined very widely. There is no exception relating to section 23(2), and the ban applies whether the act of discrimination would be lawful or not, and where the advertisement might reasonably be understood as indicating an intention to discriminate).

[18] *Charter* v. *Race Relations Board* [1973] A.C. 885.
[19] *Dockers Labour Club and Institute Ltd.* v. *Race Relations Board. supra*, p. 129.
[20] *Applin* v. *Race Relations Board* [1975] A.C. 259.
[21] See RRA 1976, ss.23(2), 25.

The meaning of "goods, facilities and services"

7.25   There is no attempt to provide a close definition of "goods, facilities and services" in the legislation. Instead, the phrase is exemplified. The Acts do, however, state that references:

> "to affording by any person of access to benefits, facilities or services are not limited to benefits, facilites or services provided by that person himself, but include any means by which it is in that person's power to facilitate access to benefits, facilities or services provided by any other person."[22]

This is a general provision, but its main application is likely to be in relation to section 29 of the Sex Discrimination Act 1975 and section 20 of the Race Relations Act 1976.

7.26   The examples given of the provision of facilities and services by the legislation are not intended to be exhaustive:[23]

> "(a) access to and use of any place which members of the public are permitted to enter;
> (b) accommodation in a hotel, boarding house or other similar establishment;
> (c) facilities by way of banking or insurance or for grants, loans, credits or finance;
> (d) facilities for education;
> (e) facilities for entertainment, recreation or refreshment;
> (f) facilities for transport or travel;
> (g) the services of any profession or trade, or any local or other public authority."

A few points need to be made here. There is an exception relating to insurance under the Sex Discrimination Act 1975;[24] "education" is defined as including any form of training or instruction, "profession" as including any vocation of occupation, and "trade" as including any business.[25]

What is being provided

7.27   What if the goods, facilities or services are of such a nature that they cater in practice for members of one sex only, or one particular race only – would the provider have to modify the service accordingly? The example of a sari shop raises the same problem under both pieces of legislation. There is no doubt that a white man is entitled to buy a sari on the same terms as an Asian woman, but does the shop also have to sell clothes that specifically cater for persons of other ethnic origins or for men? The Sex Discrimination Act 1975, s.29(3) attempts to solve a similar problem "for the avoidance of doubt" in the context of sex

[22] RRA 1976, s.40(1) and SDA 1975, s.50(1).
[23] *R. v. Entry Clearance Officer, Bombay ex p. Amin* [1983] 2 A.C. 818 *per* Lord Fraser, at p. 834 and Lord Scarman at p. 842.
[24] See SDA 1975, s.45.
[25] SDA 1975, s.82(1); RRA 1976, s.78(1).

discrimination. Where the provision of a skill is normally for one sex only, and it is commonly exercised in a different manner for different sexes, it can either be provided in the like manner to a person of the other sex, or if it is considered reasonably impracticable to do so, it can be refused. Presumably since the provision is only for the avoidance of doubt, it follows that a sari shop need not also stock clothes which cater for persons of non-Asian ethnic origin or men.

7.28 There is a distinction, it seems, between what is there to be provided and the circumstances of the provision itself. The legislation is aimed at discrimination relating to the latter, not the former. In some circumstances drawing the line may not be altogether easy, and may become most acute in the context of indirect discrimination when what constitutes goods, facilities or services will need to be distinguished from conditions or requirements applied to persons seeking those goods, facilities or services. Thus, in the case of building societies who made loans only on houses with front gardens, the CRE took the view that the facility or service was that of making loans upon mortgage in respect of houses, and a requirement or condition was applied to persons that they could only make use of the facility or service if they came forward with houses with front gardens. Since disproportionately few Asians could comply with this in the circumstances prevailing in Rochdale, this amounted to unlawful indirect discrimination, with the building societies admitting that they could not justify the practice.[26]

Facilities, services and the public sector

7.29 Among the examples of the application of section 20 of the Race Relations Act and section 29 of the Sex Discrimination Act is reference to the services "of any local or other public authority". It is, however, misleading to suppose that when applied to the public sector the provision is comprehensive. Judicial interpretation has meant that this is not the case. The leading case on this point is the House of Lords decision *R* v. *Entry Clearance Officer, Bombay ex p Amin*.[27] Mrs Amin was a British Overseas Citizen. Pursuant to legislation introduced in 1968, her right to entry to the United Kingdom depended on a special voucher scheme. Vouchers were only available to heads of household and generally a woman was assumed not to be the head of a household. For this reason, Mrs Amin was refused a voucher. The House of Lords were clear that this amounted to sex discrimination, but a majority held that it was outside section 29 of the 1975 Act because the supply of vouchers was the provision of neither a facility nor a service.

[26] CRE Formal Investigation Report: Mortgage Allocation in Rochdale (1985).
[27] [1983] 2 A.C. 818 approving *R.* v. *Immigration Appeal Tribunal ex p. Kassam* [1980] 2 All E.R. 330.

7.30 Two reasons were relied upon. First, section 29 was held to apply "to the direct provision of facilities or services and not to the mere grant of permission to use facilities".[28] If this is right, it is difficult to see why issuing somebody a ticket to enter a swimming bath should not equally be regarded as the mere grant of permission to use a facility, yet nobody could really doubt that it was intended that the Acts cover discrimination by refusing somebody such a ticket. Second, the section was held to apply only to acts which "are at least similar to acts that could be done by private persons". There was said to be a "necessity" for construing the Act in that way, although the House entirely failed to explain this assertion. Had the House of Lords not said otherwise, one could have been forgiven for thinking that the necessity was to construe the "goods, facilities and services" as widely as possible so as to provide a remedy in the county courts for as much racial and sex discrimination as possible. Privatisation may undermine their reasoning.

7.31 Prior to the *Amin* case in *CRE* v. *Riley*,[29] a county court judge held that the granting of planning permission fell within section 20 of the 1976 Act, and issued an injunction to restrain the bringing of pressure on a planning authority to commit racial discrimination. In the light of *Amin*, the CRE found itself unable to embark on an accusatory investigation relating to an allegation of discrimination in the making of a planning decision by a local authority. In consequence, a provision in the Housing and Planning Act 1986 brought planning functions specifically within the 1976 Act in a new section, section 19A.

To be fair to their Lordships in *Amin*, the case did not stand alone. Two earlier Court of Appeal cases were approved in *Amin*. In the first, *R* v. *Immigration Appeal Tribunal, ex p Kassam*,[30] it was held that the Home Secretary when exercising powers under the Immigration Act 1971 to control entry to the United Kingdom was not providing a "facility". In the second case, *Savjani* v. *I.R.C.*[31] it was held, distinguishing *Kassam*, that insofar as it operated the tax relief system the Inland Revenue was providing a "service" within section 20 of the 1976 Act. The case concerned a requirement that a taxpayer born in the Indian subcontinent should produce a full birth certificate to substantiate a first-time claim for tax relief for a child born in the United Kingdom. Such a birth certificate cost £2.50. For other taxpayers claiming the same relief, a short birth certificate costing nothing sufficed. In *Amin*, Lord Fraser referred to this decision as follows: "In *Savanji* Templeman L.J. took the view that the Inland Revenue performed two separate

---

[28] *Ibid. per* Lord Fraser at p. 834.
[29] CRE Annual Report 1982 p. 18.
[30] [1980] 2 ALL E.R. 330.
[31] [1981] Q.B. 458.

functions – first a duty of collecting revenue and secondly a service of providing taxpayers with information." He went on, "In the present case the entry clearance officer in Bombay was in my opinion not providing a service for would-be immigrants; rather he was performing his duty of controlling them".[32]

7.32   The notion of a "duty of controlling" contrasted with the provision of a facility or service is particularly important when it comes to sorting out the functions of, say, the prison service into those not covered by the law enforcement provision of the Acts and those which are. Southampton County Court held in *Alexander* v. *Home Office (Prison Department)*[33] that allocation of work to prisoners in the prison (including highly desirable kitchen work) was within section 20. Presumably, access to education facilities for prisoners would also be within the provision. Matters such as allocation of security classifications, however, may be seen as an exercise of the duty of controlling prisoners.

7.33   The CRE, in criticising the *Amin* decision, make the point that the lack of a financial remedy under the 1976 Act:

"occurs precisely where the individual is most vulnerable. In the private sector, if there is discrimination at one source the individual generally has both the opportunity of going elsewhere to another provider of services and also has his or her remedy under the Act. The individual appears to have neither when facing an immigration officer, prison officer or police officer prepared to discriminate improperly."[34]

7.34   *Some* of their activities will of course be inside section 20 of the Race Relations Act 1976 and section 29 of the Sex Discrimination Act 1975, but they will tend to be those ancillary to the main functions of the officials concerned.

7.35   Public authorities are of course amenable to judicial review. Even where there is no duty under the legislation not to discriminate, a public body will generally be acting wholly unreasonably if it does so and open itself up to judicial review.

7.36   When section 95 of the Criminal Justice Act 1991 was passed, it adopted the position that all those engaged in the administration of criminal justice were under a duty not to discriminate against any person "on the ground of race or sex or any other improper ground" and imposed on the

---

[32] *Amin* Case, *supra*, p. 835.
[33] CRE Annual Report 1987. The case went on to the Court of Appeal on question of damages. Liability was not an issue there.
[34] CRE Review of the RRA 1976 (1985) at p. 8.

Secretary of State a duty to publish information to facilitate "the performance by such persons of their duty".

7.37 The case of *James* v. *Eastleigh Borough Council*[35] highlighted a new problem. Concessions have often been offered to people of state pension age. In this case, a 61 year old man complained that concessionary entry to a swimming pool was not available to him in circumstances where it would be available to a woman because the state pension ages are different. The House of Lords held that this amounted to direct sex discrimination. (A similar problem can occur in the race field if a service provider makes use of the voting register as a basis for eligibility for a facility because this register is based on nationality which itself is a prohibited ground under the 1976 Act).

Section 20 of the RRA 1976, section 29 of the SDA 1975 and the private sector

7.38 The application of section 20 of the Race Relations Act and section 29 of the Sex Discrimination Act in the private sector is subject to few problems. Thus, retailers who refuse a woman hire-purchase facilities unless her husband enters into a guarantee when they would not have done the same for a man in similar circumstances, commit sex discrimination.[36] Similarly, refusal to serve women at the bar in a wine club where they were served only at tables when men could be served at the bar fell foul of section 29.[37]

7.39 The absence of a provision under the Sex Discrimination Act 1975 dealing with discrimination by associations, equivalent to section 25 of the Race Relations Act 1976, was rejected as a reason for construing section 29 of the Sex Discrimination Act differently from section 20 of the Race Relations act 1976 by the Court of Appeal in *Jones* v. *Royal Liver Friendly Society*.[38] The Society offered its policies to anyone prepared to apply and pay the premium and was therefore providing facilities to the public or a section thereof. Accordingly, it amounted to unlawful discrimination to refuse to allow female members to participate in the elections for the governing body of the friendly society. The point to be gleaned from this case is that the activities of clubs and associations are not *per se* outside of section 20 of the Race Relations Act 1976 and section 29 of the Sex Discrimination Act 1975, but only if they provide their facilities or services in such a way that they cannot be said to be provided to the public or a section thereof.

Exceptions

7.40 The Sex Discrimination Act has a special exception in section 45 permitting differential treatment in insurance where it:

---

[35] [1990] I.R.L.R. 288.
[36] *Quinn* v. *Williams Furniture Ltd.* [1981] I.C.R. 328, C.A.
[37] *Gill* v. *El Vino Co. Ltd.* [1983] Q.B. 425.
[38] *The Times*, December 2, 1982 C.A.

1. "was effected by reference to actuarial or other data from a source on which it was reasonable to rely and
2. was reasonable having regard to the data and any other relevant factors."

7.41 There is no equivalent provision in the Race Relations Act 1976, and indeed racial discrimination relating to the granting of insurance policies is not uncommon. The EOC refer to the "near-universality of the present practice" of differential treatment on the grounds of sex in insurance, and to the only test case on the scope of section 45, *Pinder* v. *Friends Provident*,[39] in which the County Court found it reasonable for a company to justify its practice of charging women 50 per cent. more than men for Permanent Health Insurance, which it had done since 1953, largely by reference to social security statistics at the time. The court took the view that once the case for differential treatment was made out it was largely a matter of commercial judgment how large it should be. Leaving county court judges to make judgments under the rubric of words like "reasonable" in the context of how far sex discrimination should be permitted is apt to produce such a result.

7.42 Both section 20 of the Race Relations Act and section 29 of the Sex Discrimination Act have a small premises exception, but since this is an exception which also applies to the sections dealing with discrimination in the disposal or management of premises it is dealt with below under that heading.

Territorial extent   **7.43** Section 20 of the Race Relations Act and section 29 of the Sex Discrimination Act only apply to the provision of goods, facilities and services outside Great Britain in limited circumstances. They apply in relation to facilities for travel outside Great Britain where the refusal or omission occurs in Great Britain, and apply generally in relation to any ship registered at a port of registry in Great Britain, or in relation to any aircraft or hovercraft registered in the United Kingdom and operated by a person with a principal place of business or ordinary residence in Great Britain. The Sex Discrimination Act, but not the Race Relations Act, also applies in relation to any ship, aircraft or hovercraft which is the Queen's in right of the Government of the United Kingdom. Neither Act applies to various financial facilities for a purpose to be carried out, or in connection with risks wholly or mainly arising outside Great Britain. There is a general caveat, however, that nothing done within another country or its territorial waters to comply with that country's laws is rendered unlawful by these provisions.

Political parties   **7.44** Section 33 of the Sex Discrimination Act 1975 contains an exception for political parties to the effect that

[39] *The Times*, December 16, 1985.

section 29 is not to be construed as affecting any special provision for persons of one sex only in the constitution, organisation or administration of the political party and nothing in section 29 renders unlawful an act done to give effect to such special provision. The Secretary of State can amend this section by Order. This is perhaps rather odd, in that it could permit a Secretary of State to render unlawful the arrangements of an opposing political party. Special women's groups are of course permitted under this provision. Political parties are those having as a main object promotion of parliamentary candidates for the Parliament of the United Kingdom, or having formal links with such a party.

7.45 There is no similar exemption in the Race Relations Act 1976, which raises the question of the lawfulness of special black groups within parties. Political parties will, *vis-à-vis* their members either be within section 20 as providing facilities or services to a section of the public, or, if more exclusive, but having 25 or more members, within section 25 of the Act. Giving special extra facilities for meetings etc. to black members will therefore constitute unlawful discrimination unless a general exemption can be prayed in aid. If, as is likely, the purpose of the black group is to meet the special needs of that racial group in regard to their education, training or welfare, or any ancillary benefits, then section 35 can be relied upon to legitimize the group.

Premises and housing

7.46 The law under the Sex Discrimination Act and the Race Relations Act is identical in the provisions relating to the creation of liability in the disposal or management of premises[40] and in relation to consent for assignment or sub-letting,[41] and the principal exception for small dwellings.[42] The law applies only to premises in Great Britain. The term "premises" includes land of any description. There is a difference between the two Acts inasmuch as the CRE can issue codes in the field of housing and has done so, whereas EOC cannot.

7.47 It is unlawful for a person, having the power to dispose of premises, to discriminate in the terms on which he offers them, or by refusing an application for them or in the treatment of a person in relation to any list of persons in need of premises of that description. The term "dispose" includes granting a right to occupy premises, so the

---

[40] SDA 1976, s.30 and RRA 1976, s.21.
[41] SDA 1975, s.31 and RRA 1976, s.24.
[42] SDA 1975, s.32 and RRA 1976, s.22.

provision covers discrimination against both the prospective purchaser and the prospective tenant. Except insofar as they may knowingly aid an unlawful act, persons such as estate agents, accommodation bureaux and building societies who may be involved in a housing transaction will not *normally* be covered by this provision, lacking as they do the power to dispose of the property. Their facilities or services will, however, be covered by section 29 of the Sex Discrimination Act 1975 and section 20 of the Race Relations Act 1976. There is a "private transaction" exception: there is no liability where a person, who owns an estate or interest in property which he wholly occupies, discriminates unless he uses the services of an estate agent or advertises in any way.

7.48   The reference to a list of persons is apt to cover those on a local authority housing list. Perhaps the most notable finding of racial discrimination under this head was by the CRE in its Formal Investigation of the London Borough of Hackney. There may be an overlap between section 20 and 21 of the Race Relations Act 1976 in that one example given of facilities or services under section 20 is "the services of . . . any local . . . authority". The finding in the Hackney investigation was, in summary, that the Council had practised:

> "unlawful direct discrimination against black applicants and tenants who had been allocated housing from the waiting list, or who had been homeless or decant cases, in that whites had received better-quality allocations of properties than blacks."

7.49   This finding was expressed in legal terms as amounting to the following contraventions:

> "of section 20(1)(b) read together with section 1(1)(a) of the Act by refusing or deliberately omitting to provide them with housing accommodation (provision of such accommodation being a service of the local authority) of the like quality to that afforded to white persons in similar need of housing accommodation and/or in contravention of section 21(1)(c) read together with 1(1)(a) of the Act in its treatment of them in relation to lists of persons in need of council accommodation."

7.50   This formal investigation is referred to above under the heading of "proof of discrimination" and is significant for the reason set out in the preface to the Report. "It is worth noting that an important precedent was set in issuing this non-discrimination notice against Hackney Council, in that it is the first time such a notice has been issued solely on the basis of statistical evidence."

7.51   It is also unlawful for a person who manages premises to discriminate against a person occupying them in the way he affords access to any benefits or facilities, or by refusing or deliberately omitting to afford access to them; or by evicting or subjecting the person to any other detriment. The term "manages" is clearly far wider than the notion of having power to dispose, and therefore is capable of covering actions by housekeepers and estate agents, for instance, who may manage property by collecting rents and/or arranging particular facilities or benefits for occupants. If it seems inherently unlikely that a landlord would, for example, take a black person as a tenant and then proceed to harass that person on racial grounds so as to fall foul of this provision, it should be borne in mind that personalities do change in estate agents' offices and so forth, and so do the personalities of the principals for whom they act, or persons in neighbouring properties, who may bring pressure to bear on them to discriminate. Being given a tenancy is therefore no guarantee of freedom of discrimination. It is also conceivable that sexual harassment of a woman tenant could occur and put the person concerned in breach of this provision.

7.52   Both the Sex Discrimination Act 1975, s.35(3) and the Race Relations Act 1976, s.23(1) deal with the problem of overlap between various parts of the legislation, so that the sections dealing with discrimination in the provision of goods, facilities and services and of accommodation do not render unlawful discrimination in the provision of accommodation for the purposes of residential employment or education where it is permitted elsewhere in the legislation.

7.53   Section 24 of the Race Relations Act 1976 and section 31 of the Sex Discrimination Act 1975 deal with the situation where the tenant of a property requires the consent or licence of a landlord in order to assign the tenancy or sublet part of the accommodation. They render unlawful discrimination by a landlord by refusing the consent.

The small premises exception

7.54   Section 22 of the Race Relations Act and section 32 of the Sex Discrimination Act permit discrimination by a person in letting accommodation (and an equivalent provision applies to discrimination in granting consent to assign or sublet) if that person, or a near relative (as defined) resides and continues to reside on the premises, and shares a significant part of the accommodation with other persons living on the premises, and the premises are small. Where there is residential accommodation for one or more households (under separate letting or similar agreements), in addition to that of the landlord or his near relative, the premises are small if there is not normally residential accommodation for two such households, and only members of his household live within the accommodation occupied by the landlord or his near relative. In other cases, the premises are small if there is not normally residential accommodation on the premises for more than six persons in addition to the landlord or his near relative and any members of that household

Planning: The Race Relations Act 1976

7.55 For reasons which are set out under the heading concerned with the provision of goods, facilities and services, discrimination by a planning authority in carrying out its planning functions was thought, in the light of the *Amin* case, to be outside the scope of the Race Relations Act 1976. In the context of racial discrimination this was a significant loophole in the Act, because although judicial review was available to deal with discrimination by a planning authority itself, there was no remedy for the racist pressure to discriminate that was put upon authorities in respect of some developments.

7.56 It seems that sex discrimination in carrying out a planning function is also outside the Sex Discrimination Act, but is not thought to be a problem in that area. In any event, the position has been altered by legislation only in the context of the Race Relations Act 1976, to which a new section, section 19A, has been added by the Housing and Planning Act 1986, which makes it unlawful for a planning authority to discriminate. A planning authority is defined in England and Wales as a county, district or London borough council, a joint planning board, a special planning board or a National Public Committee, and in Scotland as a planning authority or regional planning authority, and includes an urban development corporation and a body having functions under Schedule 32 of the Local Government, Planning and Land Act 1980. Planning functions are defined in the legislation.

7.57 Inasmuch as this is an example of a decision to which a right of appeal attaches being subject to the discrimination legislation, the provision is an interesting development. If one of the arguments against extension of the legislation to other areas is that there are statutory rights of appeal, or complaints bodies in existence, an explanation is needed as to why the same argument was not applied to planning authorities.

RRA 1976, s. 25

Discrimination by Associations other than trade unions or similar organisations

7.58 Section 25 of the Race Relations Act covers discrimination by any association of persons whether incorporated or not, and whether a profit-making organisation or not, where it has twenty-five or more members and admission to membership is regulated by its constitution and is so conducted that the membership do not constitute a section of the public.[43] But organisations to which section 11 applies (organisation of workers, employees etc.) are exempted.

---

[43] See *supra*, para. 7.23.

7.59   It is made unlawful for such an association to discriminate against a non-member in the terms on which it is prepared to admit him to membership, or by refusing or deliberately, omitting to accept his application for membership. In practice, one major problem with clubs is that they will normally require applicants for membership to be sponsored by existing members. This will often be a problem for black potential applicants trying to get into an all-white club, and represented a challenge for the courts to use the indirect discrimination law to break down barriers in relation to a matter which goes to the heart of the membership system. Birmingham County Court, hearing an appeal from a non-discrimination notice, showed that it was willing to conclude that the traditional rule needed modifying in a case where the membership of a club was all white in the middle of multi-racial Handsworth.

7.60   In relation to members or associates (persons having some or all membership rights without actually being members) it is made unlawful to discriminate by depriving the person of those rights or varying them, in the way access to benefits, facilities or services are afforded, or by refusing or deliberately omitting to afford access to them; or by subjecting the person to any other detriment.

7.61   Section 26 provides for an exception to section 25 for certain associations providing the discrimination is not on the ground of colour. Those are associations where the main object is to enable the benefit of membership to be enjoyed by a particular racial group defined otherwise than by reference to colour. So, for example, a Polish cultural society, an Irish dance group or a Welsh choral society can discriminate *vis-a-vis* membership applications and in its relation with members or associates, but not on the ground of colour.

Barristers and advocates

7.62   Section 64 of the Courts and Legal Services Act 1990 deals with discrimination by, or in relation to, barristers, and s65 does the same for advocates in Scotland. They do so by inserting provisions in Part III of the SDA and RRA, and thus proceedings lie in the county courts (designated in the case of a race claim) or sheriff courts. Otherwise the provisions are akin to those dealing with employment, and so we have decided to deal with them in chapter 4.

Exceptions under the Sex Discrimination Act 1975

Voluntary bodies

7.63   Section 34 of the Sex Discrimination Act 1975 contains a wide exception relating to voluntary bodies, *i.e.* a body carrying on its activities other than for profit and not set up under any enactment. It is not unlawful for such a body to restrict either its membership or the benefits, facilities or services it provides to its members to one sex (disregarding any minor exception), even though membership of the body is open to the public, or to a section of the public. In addition, where any such body has as its main object to confer benefits on one sex (disregarding any exceptional or relatively insignificant provision to persons of the other sex), it is not unlawful to have a provision to that effect or to do anything to give effect to such a provision.

Sex Discrimination Act 1975, s. 35, special cases

7.64　It is lawful to provide facilities or services to one sex only at, or as part of, an establishment for persons requiring speical care, supervision or attention *e.g.* a hospital or reception centre provided by the Supplementary Benefits Commission.

7.65　Likewise, it is lawful to provide facilities or services restricted to one sex at a place occupied or used (permanently or for the time being) for the purposes of an organised religion if the restriction is to comply with the directives of that religion or to avoid offending the religious susceptibilities of a significant member of its followers. An exception for religious susceptibilities, even where not stemming from religious doctrine, seems to be an open invitation to members of a religion to masquerade their prejudices as "religious susceptibilities." No doubt they would answer to God rather than the law in such matters.

7.66　It is also lawful to provide facilities or services restricted to one sex where they are provided for, or likely to be used by, two or more persons at the same time, and the facilities or services are such, or the persons are such, that users of one sex are likely to suffer serious embarrassment at the presence of a member of the other sex. The same applies where the facilities or services are such that a user is likely to be "in a state of undress" and a user might reasonably object to the presence of a member of the opposite sex. A single-sex facility or exercise can also be provided, if it is such that physical contact between the user and any other person is likely and that other person might reasonably object if that user were of the opposite sex.

Charities

7.67　Section 43 of the Sex Discrimination Act 1975 provides a general exception for provisions in charitable instruments conferring benefits on persons of one sex only (disregarding exceptional or insignificant benefits to the other sex),[44] but Sections 78 and 79 provide a means to alter to charitable instruments or endowments of an education character.

Sports activities

7.68　Section 44 of the Sex Discrimination Act 1975 provides that nothing

---

[44] See *Hugh-Jones* v. *St John's College, Cambridge* [1979] I.C.R. 848. Special arrangements were made in the Employment Act 1989.

"shall, in relation to any sport, game or other activity of a competitive nature where the physical strength, stamina or physique of the average woman puts her at a disadvantage to the average man, render unlawful any act related to the participation of a person as a competitor in events involving that activity which are confined to competitors of one sex."[45]

Communal accommodation

7.68 Section 46 of the Sex Discrimination Act 1975 permits sex discrimination in admission to communal accommodation and associated benefits, but the section nevertheless demands "fair and equitable" treatment of men and women.

Special Race Relations Act provisions

7.69 Parts V and VI of the Race Relations Act contain certain provisions which have no exact counterpart in the Sex Discrimination Act.

Charities

7.70 Discriminatory provisions in charitable instruments are rendered lawful by section 34 of the 1976 Act. The exception is where there is provision for conferring benefits on persons of class defined by reference to colour. In this case, the offending reference is effectively disregarded, leaving either a wider class, or persons generally, as the case may be, as persons who may benefit.

7.71 Although the 1976 Act does not deal with the point, both the Charity Commissioners and the Board of Inland Revenue have indicated that they regard working towards the elimination of racial discrimination, and promoting equal opportunity and good relations between persons of different racial groups as being charitable objects. Case-law to the contrary should therefore be regarded as outmoded, on the basis that the law of charity develops with the social climate.[46] This means that the way is open for a civil rights movement to take advantage of charitable status in fund-raising activities.

RRA 1976, s.35:

Special needs in relation to education, welfare and training

7.72 The Race Relations Act 1976, s.35 renders lawful any act done in affording persons of a particular racial group access to facilities or services to meet the special needs of persons of that group in relation to their education, training or welfare, or any ancillary benefits.

7.73 It is probable that "special" in this context means that the need does not have to be exclusive to the racial group to

---

[45] See *Bennett* v. *Football Association Ltd.* Court of Appeal July 28, 1988 unreported. *GLC* v. *Farrar* [1980] I.C.R. 266, *British Judo Association* v. *Petty* [1981] I.C.R. 660, [1981] I.R.L.R. 484.
[46] See *Re Strakosch* [1949] Ch. 529 and the annual report of the Charity Commission 1983 para. 20.

be benefited; it could also be a need that is experienced by all, but experienced to a much greater degree by members of a particular racial group.

7.74 Typically, special language training facilities have been regarded as covered by this provision. In addition, matters such as special housing need, or special need for counselling on starting businesses have been addressed under this rubric. The needs must relate to education, training or welfare, or any ancillary benefits, however. Accordingly, whilst advice for new Afro-Caribbean businesses may be covered, for example, as by and large there is a specially felt need for such education or training in that community, the provision of actual business funds would be outside the provision. Likewise, whilst training courses may be laid on, and financial support provided to those on the courses, under the rubric of "ancillary benefits", the financial support should not go beyond what is truly ancillary.

7.75 Section 35 ought to be perceived as providing exemption for essentially temporary schemes in the sense that once the need is met, the statutory protection will fall away. Of course this may take years to achieve.

RRA 1976, s.36 **7.76** Such schemes are protected where it appears to the person concerned that the persons in question do not intend to remain in Great Britain after their period of education or training here.

RRA 1976, s.39 **7.77** This provision renders lawful discrimination on the basis of nationality, place of birth, or length of residence in selecting persons to represent a country, place or area in any sport or game, or in the rules of a competition relating to eligibility to compete in a sport or game.

Sports and competitions

Procedure and remedies in the County Court

7.78 Generally, proceedings relating to discrimination in non-employment matters have to be brought in the county courts in England and Wales, and the sheriff court in Scotland.[47] Appeals lie to the Court of Appeal in England and Wales and to the Court of Session in Scotland. In the case of proceedings relating to racial discrimination, only designated county courts have jurisdiction. The reason for this is that arrangements exist for the county court judges to sit with the help of Assessors.[48]

---

[47] RRA, s. 57 and SDA, s. 67.
[48] RRA, s. 67.

7.79 As in the case of employment discrimination, individuals may apply to the EOC or CRE as the case may be, to ask for assistance with litigation. Cases are, however, brought in the names of the individuals concerned and whether or not a Commission assists is discretionary. Legal aid may be available.

7.80 As in the case of alleged employment discrimination the questionnaire procedure is available prior to the commencement of proceedings; but thereafter it is available only with leave of the court.[49] Moreover, it is necessary to apply for an order as to the admissibility of the questionnaire and the answers.[50]

7.81 The time limit for commencing proceedings is different in a non-employment case, although the discretionary power of the court to consider a claim out of time is the same as that possessed by an industrial tribunal. The limitation period is six months beginning with the date of the act complained of.[51] The exception is the case of those education complaints where the Secretary of State for Education has general responsibilities and has to be informed before a claim is commenced. In those cases, the period is eight months. Within that period the proceedings cannot be commenced until either the Secretary of State has said he does not require further time to consider the matter, or two months have elapsed. The period is, however, modified under the Race Relations Act 1976 in all those cases where an individual has applied to the CRE for assistance with the proceedings within the time limit. In effect, two further months are automatically added, and if the CRE has served notice extending the time by which it has to respond to the application, one further month is added. Thus, in an education case under the Race Relations Act 1976 where notification has to be given to the Secretary of State, and where an application for assistance is made to the CRE who extend the time for responding, the limitation period is eleven months (and even then is subject to the county court's discretion).[52] For more detail and interpretation of the time provisions, see chapter 6 on the tribunal position.

7.82 The principles which apply to the questions of discovery and proof in the county court are the same as those applying to the Industrial Tribunal jurisdiction and are dealt with there.[53] Discovery by lists is the usual way in the county court. The strict rules of evidence apply in the county court, whereas they do not in the industrial

[49] RRA, s. 65(4).
[50] County Court Rules, Ord. 49, r.17(6).
[51] RRA, s. 68, SDA, s.76.
[52] See generally RRA, s.68.
[53] See chap. 3.

tribunals. Where the two jurisdictions differ is in the field of remedies available. Whereas in the Industrial Tribunal there is a limit on compensation and injunctive relief is not available, in the county court or sheriff court the position is different. The two statutes say that cases "may be made the subject of civil proceedings in like manner as any other claim in tort, or in Scotland for reparation of breach of statutory duty" and add "all such remedies shall be obtainable in such proceedings as . . . would be obtainable in the High Court or the Court of Session, as the case may be."[54] It is reasonably clear that this means that the normal limit on damages in the county court does not apply. Full injunctive relief is also available.

7.83 As to heads of damages, the same rules apply as in the Industrial Tribunal to awards of damages in indirect discrimination cases, and as to damages for injury to feelings.

7.84 Judicial statistics reveal that non-employment discrimination litigation initiated by individuals is sparse, which raises the question whether those courts can build up much expertise.[55]

7.85 Sometimes formal consequences flow from a finding of discrimination in the county courts. For example, these are matters to be taken into account by the Director General of Fair Trading under the Estate Agents Act and the Consumer Credit Act. Also, licensing magistrates are specifically enjoined to take into account findings of sex discrimination. Presumably they may, without being required to do so, take into account findings of racial discrimination.

7.86 Much of the county court litigation where racial discrimination is proved does concern discrimination on licensed premises. (Proof is generally fairly easy, since the defences available for failure to serve are few, and resort is often had to evidence of "testing" the public house using comparable black and white testers to back up the original complainant. The testing is arranged either by local community relations councils or by the CRE exercising its powers to assist individuals.)

---

[54] RRA, s. 57 and SDA, s. 66.
[55] See the Annual Judicial Statistics.

8 THE COMMISSIONS

8.01 The Equal Opportunities Commission (EOC) and the Commission for Racial Equality (CRE) have largely equivalent duties and functions in their respective fields of operations. The CRE's are somewhat wider. When it came into being, it replaced both the Race Relations Board and the Community Relations Commission. The latter body's functions have been generally subsumed in the CRE's duty to "promote good relations between persons of different racial groups generally."[1] No equivalent duty exists for the EOC.

General duties

General duties in common

8.02 The general duties in common are:

1. to work towards the elimination of discrimination;
2. to promote equality of opportunity;
3. and to keep under review the working of the constituent legislation and, when required, by the Secretary of State or otherwise think it necessary, draw up and submit proposals for amending that legislation.[2]

The first two general duties are amplified by a list of more specific duties and powers which enable the tasks to be carried out, on which more below. Under the power to Review the legislation, the EOC produced documents in 1988, "Legislating for Change" and "Equal Treatment for Men and Women: Strengthening the Act" and in 1990 a set of proposals called "Equal Pay for Men and Women: Strengthening the Acts". In mid-1985, in a document entitled "Review of the Race Relations Act 1976: Proposals for Change",[3] and in 1992 in a further document entitled "Second Review of the Race Relations Act 1976" the CRE has sent proposed changes to the Secretary of State.

Status and manner of operation of the Commissions

8.03 The two Commissions are independent of Government (though funded out of Departmental Votes: the EOC now comes under the Department of Employment and the CRE the Home Office). Thus, in the exercise of its law

---

[1] RRA 1976, s.43(1)(*b*).
[2] SDA 1975, s.53, RRA 1976, s.43.
[3] See Jeanne Gregory "Sex, Race and The Law, Legislating for Equality" (EOC, 1987) ch.8.

enforcement functions, the CRE has on more than one occasion been involved in litigation against the Home Office.[4] In addition, both Commissions now use judicial review as a method of resolving legal issues involving public bodies, failing other methods; and this will inevitably lead to more confrontations between the Commissions and the Government which sponsors them.[5]

8.04   It is doubtful how far real independence from Government can in fact be maintained when Government holds the purse strings, appoints the Commissioners, approves Additional Commissioners for formal investigations, approves the decision-making arrangements internally, frequently sends in review teams, provides observers to sit in on chief executive appointments, and receives the papers for Commission meetings.

8.05   The Commissions each consist of up to 15 Commissioners. Much of their work is delegated to committees under arrangements approved from time to time by the Secretary of State.[6] The Commissions are served by staff who, although paid at civil service rates, are by statute specifically not civil servants. As from the summer of 1987, the Commissions came under the jurisdiction of the Parliamentary Commissioner (Ombudsman).[7]

Publications, and the Codes Funding of research and educational activities

8.06   Each Commission is obliged to produce an Annual Report and Accounts.[8] The Report is to the Secretary of State who lays the same before Parliament. Each Commission also publishes much material each year under various other powers. Both Commissions have the power to undertake or assist (financially or otherwise) the undertaking by other persons of any necessary or expedient research and educational activities.[9]

8.07   Each Commission may issue codes of practice in the employment field,[10] following consultation. A draft code needs the approval of the Secretary of State and to be laid before Parliament. A tribunal must take it into account if it appears relevant to a question in the proceedings. One of the purposes of such codes is to inform the reader as to what

---

[4] *Home Office* v. *CRE* [1982] Q.B. 385; *Alexander* v. *Home Office* [1988] I.R.L.R. 190.
[5] See chap. 9 on Judicial Review.
[6] For the law relating to the functioning of the Commissions see SDA 1975, Sched. 3. Evelyn Ellis in *Sex Discrimination Law* (1989), p. 238 suggests abolishing the EOC Commissioners altogether leaving just the chair.
[7] See Parliamentary and Health Services Commissioners Act 1987.
[8] SDA 1975, ss.53, 56, Sched. 3, RRA 1976, ss.43, 46, Sched. 1.
[9] SDA 1975, s.54, RRA 1976, s.45.
[10] RRA 1976, Sched. 4 inserting s.56A in SDA 1975, and RRA 1976, s.47. See Codes in a Cold Climate Administrative Rule-Making by the CRE by C. McCrudden 1988 M.L.R. 409.

steps are reasonably practicable to avoid the occurrence of discrimination. Taking such steps gives the employer a defence in employment cases. The CRE was recently given power to produce codes in the field of housing and has done so.[11]

8.08 When the Commissions conduct formal investigations, they are obliged to produce reports which are either published or made available for inspection.[12] Non-discrimination notices issued in the course of investigations are to be made available for inspection.[13] Each Commission has a general power to make charges for educational or other facilities, or services made available by them.[14]

CRE's power to fund organisations

8.09 The CRE has a power for which there is no EOC equivalent: to give financial or other assistance to any organisation appearing to the Commission to be concerned with the promotion of equality of opportunity, and good relations between persons of different racial groups.[15] The giving of such financial assistance is subject to the Home Secretary's approval, which in practice takes the form of financial limits above which items need to be referred specifically to the Home Office for approval and below which they do not. This function of the CRE is by statute given specifically to a committee of at least three, and not more than five, Commissioners of whom one is a deputy chairman of the Commission. Under current arrangements it is the Public Affairs Committee which exercises this function.

8.10 The power is used, for example, to fund many racial equality officer posts throughout the country, and the funding is subject to arrangements for the approval by the Committee of annual work plans of racial equality councils. In practice, funding of such posts attracts considerably more funding to racial equality councils from local authorities. It is often mistakenly assumed that racial equality councils are emanations of the CRE. They are not. The councils are autonomous bodies with their own constitutions, which employ the racial equality officers, albeit in some cases entirely with CRE funded monies. At the time of writing, several million pounds are spent on RECs. Examples of the use of the CRE's funding power are set out in the Annual Reports. In practice, it is the financial commitment to RECs which means that only a small proportion of the CRE's budget is spent on law enforcement. If the RECs were to be

---

[11] s. 47, RRA was amended by s. 137(2) and (5) of the Housing Act 1988 and s. 180 of the Local Government and Housing Act 1989.
[12] SDA 1975, s.60; RRA 1976, s.51.
[13] SDA 1975, s.70; RRA 1976, s.61.
[14] SDA 1975, s.54(2); RRA 1976, s.45(2).
[15] RRA 1976 s.44, Sched. 1, para. 13.

brought fully into law enforcement at a local level, a better balance might be achieved in the CRE's expenditure.

EOC's duty to review health and safety legislation

8.11 The EOC has one duty for which there is no CRE parallel. It is obliged to keep under review discriminatory provisions in the health and safety legislation and submit proposals for amending it to the Secretary of State, who also has power to call for a report.[16] The Employment Act 1989 made a number of legislative changes in this area.

Law enforcement by the Commissions

8.12 Each Commission has a major law enforcement function. Essentially this function is exercised in one of three ways:

1. Assisting individuals to bring discrimination cases, in the case of EOC including equal pay and equal value cases.
2. Bringing proceedings in the name of the Commission. The power here is, surprisingly, given that the Commissions are both law enforcement agencies, limited in the statutes to a small range of matters, see below. However, the Commissions will often have *Locus standi* to bring judicial review proceedings and, given the burgeoning of such proceedings generally in recent years, it is not surprising to find both Commissions participating in this growth area.[17]
3. Carrying out formal investigations. These are under case-law[18] of two types, which can conveniently be called general investigations, and accusatory investigations. Whether it is right to call a general investigation part of the law enforcement function must be in some doubt since probably in this type of investigation no remedy is available, save the power to make recommendations. The power to conduct general investigations is perhaps closer to the power to conduct research. There are two important advantages to the Commissions of doing general investigations as opposed to research: powers to compel provision of information can be sought from the Secretary of State and the research convention of anonymity of subjects need not be followed in the reports.

The power to assist individuals to bring cases

8.13 This power is, in most respects, similar for both organisations. The CRE has imposed upon it a time limit of two months (which it can extend by notice to three months), within which it has to respond to a request for assistance.[19] The EOC has no such obligation.[20] The CRE often finds it

---

[16] SDA 1975, s.55.
[17] See chap. 9.
[18] See in particular *R. v. CRE ex p. Hillingdon* LBC [1982] A.C. 779 and *CRE v. Prestige Group plc* [1984] I.C.R. 473.
[19] RRA 1976, s.66(3), (4).
[20] See SDA 1975, s.75.

difficult to give a final decision whether or not to provide actual representation in court or tribunal as the case may be, even within the extended period of three months, because enquiries will not be complete. It therefore adopts the practice of deciding to provide continued advice and assistance until those enquiries are complete and it can make a fully informed decision. This is generally the result of delays by respondents in returning answers to the statutory questionnaire.[21]

8.14 The Commissions *must* consider applications in respect of proceedings or prospective proceedings under the relevant legislation. In practice this is done by Legal Committees. They have a *discretion* whether to grant assistance and as to the form it will take. The decision in practice will be taken on the basis of a report and assessment of the application prepared by staff in the light of enquiries made. The criteria upon which the Commissions can grant assistance are set out in the statutes and are similar in both cases:

> "the Commission shall consider the application and may grant it if they think fit to do so on the ground that -
>
> (*a*) the case raises a question of principle, or
> (*b*) it is unreasonable, having regard to the complexity of the case of the applicant's position in relation to the respondent or another person involved or any other matter, to expect the applicant to deal with the case unaided, or
> (*c*) by reason of any other special consideration."[22]

Factors to be taken into account by the Commissions

8.15 Both Commissions now give applicants for assistance a written explanation of the factors which the Commissions take into account and their priorities in making decisions on applications. The EOC takes the following matters into consideration:

> "i) whether the case is likely to clarify important points of law or principle
> ii) whether the case is likely to affect large numbers of people
> iii) whether the case is likely to bring about change
> iv) whether the case has a strong liklihood of success
> v) whether the case has a likely potential for Commission follow-up work

The Commissioners also consider whether the case falls within one of the Commission's current priorities."[23]

---

[21] See RRA 1976, s.65.
[22] SDA 1975, s.75(1); RRA 1976, s.66 (1)(1).
[23] EOC's document sent to applicants for assistance 1992.

8.16 The CRE's criteria are similar. The CRE were criticised in *Racial Justice at Work* for not taking a strategic stance in relation to assisting individuals, other than in relation to cases testing important points of law. There may come a point, however, at which complainants cease to bring their complaints to an agency if it is perceived as selecting cases on the basis of its own strategic concerns with little regard to individual injustice. The statutory criterion pertaining to whether it is unreasonable to expect the applicant to proceed unaided means that the Commissions could not anyway lose sight of that factor without falling foul of the law. It also not infrequently happens that cases selected for support for one reason turn out later to be significant for quite different reasons, and, given this serendipity factor, strategic omniscience at the outset is not possible. Nevertheless clearly a strategy is important in bringing about wider change.

8.17 Whilst both Commissions will discuss informally with the applicant a refusal of assistance, it is not their practice to give written reasons.

8.18 It is important for both applicants for assistance and respondents to proceedings to realise that a refusal of assistance by the Commission may, having regard to the statutory criteria, say nothing in itself as to the merits of the applicant's case against the respondent. Cases for which the Commissions have refused assistance have succeeded in tribunals. Indeed if, for example, the Commissions are to carry out a policy of encouraging, say, unions to support discrimination cases, refusals of assistance for cases with merit *vis-à-vis* respondents are inevitable. For county court cases (non-employment) legal aid may be available, but this is not the case for the conduct of Industrial Tribunal proceedings (employment).

8.19 The forms of assistance which the Commission may grant may include:

"(*a*) giving advice;
(*b*) procuring or attempting to procure the settlement of any matter in dispute;
(*c*) arranging for the giving of advice or assistance by a solicitor or counsel;
(*d*) arranging for representation by any person including all such assistance as is usually given by a solicitor or counsel in the steps preliminary or incidental to any proceedings, or in arriving at or giving effect to a compromise to avoid or bring to an end any proceedings."[24]

---

[24] SDA 1975, s.75(2); RRA 1976, s.66(2).

8.20   The Commissions seem to differ on the question whether the power to assist covers assistance with enforcement in the county court of awards made by Industrial Tribunals. The CRE takes the view that it does; the EOC seemingly not. It appears to be the sort of "assistance as is usually given by a solicitor . . . incidental to any proceedings." The CRE's view is to be preferred, unless applicants are to be left ultimately to their own devices at the mercy of unscrupulous respondents who ignore tribunal awards.

Legal Aid   **8.21**   Expenses incurred by a Commission under the power to assist constitute a first charge on any costs or expenses recovered, but subject to any charge under legal aid legislation[25]. Whether the individual himself can recover costs which the Commission can then recover depends on the rules of the particular tribunal or court. For the EAT it was held in *Walsall MBC* v. *Sidhu*[26] that if assistance is given by the Commission on the terms that the individual would not personally incur any costs, then the Commission, not being a party, could not through that individual recover any costs. However, the position is probably different if the Commission retains a discretion to ask the individual to pay the costs which it exercises upon costs being awarded to the individual.

Proceedings in the name of the Commission   **8.22**   The power to bring proceedings under the Act in the name of a Commission for law enforcement purposes is very limited in scope. Where it applies, the Commission has exclusive jurisdiction. The following are the areas covered: discriminatory advertisements; instructions to discriminate; pressure to discriminate; persistent discrimination and preliminary proceedings in Industrial Tribunals relating thereto.

Discriminatory advertisements   **8.23**   Proceedings in respect of an unlawful advertisement can be brought only by a Commission.[27] Of course an unlawful advertisement may itself be some *evidence* that an act unlawful under the provisions of the Act under which an *individual* can bring proceedings has been committed. If, for example, it is alleged that a discriminatory appointment to a job has been made, it will be material evidence that it followed an advertisement for the job indicating an intention to do an act of discrimination of just that sort.

Definition of advertisement   **8.24**   An advertisement is very widely defined as including:

"every form of advertisement or notice, whether to the public or not, and whether in a newspaper or other

---

[25] SDA 1975, s.75(4); RRA 1976, s.66(6).
[26] [1980] I.C.R. 519.
[27] SDA 1975, s.72; RRA 1976, s.63.

publication, by television or radio, by display of notices, signs, labels, showcards or goods, by distribution of samples, circulars, catalogues, price lists or other material, by exhibition of pictures, models or films, or in any other way."[28]

It is unlawful to publish or cause to be published an advertisement which indicates, or might reasonably be understood as indicating, an intention to do an act of discrimination.[29] At this point the two pieces of legislation take a different line.

8.25 The Sex Discrimination ban applies only to advertisements indicating an intention to do any act unlawful under Parts II or III of that Act. It does not apply to an advertisement if the intended act would not in fact be unlawful. There is also a clarifying provision to the effect that the "use of a job description with a sexual connotation (such as 'waiter', 'salesgirl', 'postman' or 'stewardess') indicates an intention to discriminate unless the contrary is indicated." The Race Relations Act ban is wider, applying to advertisements indicating an intention to discriminate, whether or not the discrimination would be unlawful by virtue of Parts II or III of that Act. Because of this approach it becomes necessary to spell out a list of exceptions in detail. The ban does not apply if the intended act would be lawful by virtue of any of the Race Relations Act 1976, ss. 5, 6, 7(3) and (4), 10(3), 26, 34(2),(b), 35 to 39 and 41. Two other specific examples relate to the services of an employment agency if the intended act concerns employment which the employer could by virtue of section 5, 6 or 7(3) or (4) lawfully refuse to offer to persons against whom the advertisement indicates an intention to discriminate; and to advertisements relating to employment outside Great Britain requiring persons by reference to their nationality. Since there is no reference to section 4(3), for example, in this list, it follows that although it is lawful to discriminate on racial grounds in relation to employment for the purposes of a private household, it is nevertheless unlawful to advertise such a discriminatory intention.

8.26 The two pieces of legislation are similar in providing a time limit of six months for proceedings, and a defence to a publisher if he proves that he reasonably relies on a statement made by the person who caused it to be published that the advertisement would be lawful under the exempting provisions. It is a criminal offence knowingly or recklessly to make such a statement which is false or misleading.

8.27 In practice, proceedings in relation to unlawful advertisements have been rare. Signs put up by landlords

---

[28] SDA 1975, s.82; RRA 1976, s.78.
[29] SDA 1975, s.38; RRA 1976, s.29(1).

such as "no blacks" have now largely disappeared. There has been litigation in relation to "no travellers" signs in public houses. The Court of Appeal in *CRE* v. *Dutton*[30] held that such a sign is potentially discriminatory and needs to be justified. The case is authority for the hitherto unresolved point that the advertisement provisions cover indirect discrimination.

8.28 Many of the problems for the Commission relate to keeping "positive action" advertisements within the bounds of what is permitted by law. Since the various exceptions are vaguely worded, this is not an easy task, and the Commissions have normally preferred to act by way of guidance and conciliation. As a result, cases are relatively few. For an example see *Lambeth LBC* v. *CRE*.[31]

Instructions and pressure to discriminate

8.29 It is convenient to deal together with these two instances where the Commissions can bring proceedings, since it is common for both to be alleged in the same proceedings. The provisions in the two pieces of legislation are approximately the same.[32] The Sex Discrimination Act is clearer on what actually constitutes pressure, and it took litigation to clarify the same point in relation to the Race Relations Act. These particular breaches of the law do not entail the same problems of proof as beset discrimination proceedings generally. There is normally available the direct evidence of the person given instructions or subjected to pressure. Both Commissions have brought proceedings under these heads, and are usually successful because this type of case does not depend on inference.

8.30 It is unlawful for a person who has authority over another person, or in accordance with whose wishes that other person is accustomed to act, to instruct him to do any act unlawful under Parts II or III of the two pieces of legislation, or procure or attempt to procure the doing him by of such an act. It matters not that no unlawful act occurs in consequence. (If it does, of course, an individual may be able to bring proceedings himself, and it is not unusual in such a case for the Commission's proceedings to be joined with those of the individual. It is convenient in those cases for the Commission to provide representation to the individual under its power to assist, and facilitate the conduct of the proceedings.) In *CRE* v. *Imperial Society of Teachers of Dancing*,[33] it was said that for a person to be accustomed to act in accordance with the instructions of someone:

"requires that there should be some relationship (between

---

[30] [1989] I.R.L.R. 8 C.A.
[31] [1990] I.R.L.R. 231, [1990] I.C.R. 768 C.A.
[32] 1989 EOC 23.
[33] SDA 1975, ss.39, 40; RRA 1976, ss.30, 31.

them). It does not seem to us to be possible to construe the section as meaning that it is sufficient to show that the other person is accustomed to act in accordance with the wishes of persons in the same position as the person giving the instructions."[34]

This seems to be an extremely literal interpretation.

8.31 It is unlawful to induce or attempt to induce a person to do any act which contravenes Part II or III of either legislation. The Sex Discrimination Act 1975, s. 40 spells out the fact that either a carrot or a stick, as it were, suffices:

"(1) It is unlawful to induce, or attempt to induce, a person to do any act which contravenes Part II or III by–

(*a*) providing or offering to provide him with any benefit, or
(*b*) subjecting or threatening to subject him to any detriment."

8.32 In the case of the Race Relations Act there is no similar provision, but the same is true. In *CRE* v. *Imperial Society of Teachers of Dancing*,[35] it was held that a request to someone to act in contravention of the Act can amount to an attempt to induce a contravention.

8.33 Whether a question such as "Is he black?" in answer to, say, a job centre trying to place that person with the employer amounts to instructions or pressure to discriminate will depend on whether in all the circumstances it is clear that the employer is instructing or requesting the job centre not to send the person because of his colour. It does not necessarily follow that that is so, though it may very well be. A person's colour may, for example, being an obvious feature, be a handy way of identifying him when he arrives. So a mere request for information needs to be distinguished from discriminatory instructions or pressure; and some cases have turned on this point.[36]

Persistent discrimination Preliminary proceedings relating thereto

8.34 A Commission has power to bring special proceedings within five years of a non-discrimination notice or a court or tribunal finding of unlawful discrimination if it appears to the Commission that, unless restrained, that person is likely to commit an unlawful act or apply a discrimintory practice.[37] The proceedings would be in a designated county court or sheriff court for a restraining order. The court may grant the order in the terms applied for, or in more limited

---

[34] at p.477 *per* Neill J.
[35] See n. 33.
[36] See *CRE* v. *Powell and City of Birmingham* 1986 unreported EAT (37).
[37] SDA 1975, s.71; RRA 1976, s.62.

terms. In so doing, the Commission cannot allege discrimination within the jurisdiction of an Industrial Tribunal unless a finding by an Industrial Tribunal on that matter has become final.

8.35 With a view to making an application for a restraining order to the county court, a Commission may present to an Industrial Tribunal a complaint that the respondent has done an act within the jurisdiction of an Industrial Tribunal. The Tribunal can make a finding to that effect and if it thinks it just and equitable to do so in a case concerning the employment provision of the Act it can make an order declaring the rights of a person discriminated against, and/or a recommendation as though the complaint had in fact been presented by the person discriminated against.[38]

Formal investigations[39]

8.36 One may be forgiven for thinking, as both Commissions once did, that a provision with the side-note "power to conduct formal investigation" which reads:

> "the Commission may if they think fit, and shall if required by the Secretary, conduct a formal investigation for any purpose connected with the carrying out of those duties",[40]

sets out a very wide power; and that the following provisions which have the side-notes "terms of reference" and "power to obtain information" apply where there is the power to conduct an investigation.[41] However, the House of Lords in *Re Prestige Group plc*[42] construed those following provisions as actually limiting the power to conduct investigations. Neither Commission can now conduct an investigation into a *named respondent's* activities unless it has a suspicion that an unlawful act may have been committed. This is almost certainly not what Parliament intended,[43] and the powers of the two Commissions are more limited than those of the Fair Employment Agency and its successor the Fair Employment Commission in Northern Ireland, who have been able to investigate a named respondent without suspecting an unlawful act.[44] The CRE had to abandon a number of invalid investigations in the light of the *Prestige* decision.

---

[38] SDA 1975, s.73; RRA 1976, s.64.
[39] G. Appleby and E. Ellis "Formal investigations: The CRE and EOC as Law Enforcement Agencies." (1984) Public Law 236, and Chap. 11 C. McCrudden "The Commission for Racial Equality: Formal Investigations in the Shadow of Judicial Review" in *Regulation and Public Law* (McCrudden ed and others), and passim in *Racial Justice at Work* PSI 1991.
[40] SDA 1975, s.57; RRA 1976, s.48.
[41] SDA 1975, ss. 58, 59 as amended by RRA 1976, Sched. 4; RRA 1976, ss. 49, 50.
[42] [1984] I.C.R. 473.
[43] See CRE's "Review of the Race Relations Act 1976: Proposals for Change" (1985), Appendix C setting out parts of the Parliamentary debates. No doubt in a post *Pepper* v. *Hart* era a different court result would have been reached.
[44] See now Fair Employment (N.I.) Act 1989.

Types of investigations

8.37 The investigations which can be conducted by the Commission now fall into just two categories: *accusatory*, where an unlawful act is suspected to have been committed by a named respondent, or *general* which does not name a respondent as such, but looks at an area of activity. In the category of general investigations, for example, the CRE has investigated the provision of equal opportunities at a particular new shopping centre in Leicester, where there were many businesses situated; the provision of equal opportunities in entry to training contracts in the chartered accountancy profession; and the provision of equal opportunities in certain parts of the hotel trade in named towns. Since the CRE's general duties include the promotion of good race relations, general investigations are also possible under this rubric.[45]

8.38 The CRE has conducted many more formal investigations than has the EOC. However, in recent years the CRE has been sharper in the non-employment areas than in the field of employment, and the majority of the EOC's work concerns employment. Yet it would seem that there is plenty of scope for investigations concerning non-promotion by employers as this is an area where the vast majority of Tribunal cases brought by individuals fails.

Accusatory investigations

8.39 The level of suspicion required for a named person accusatory investigation is, however, low. In relation to the CRE, the House of Lords has pronounced twice on the level required:

> "To entitle the Commission to embark upon the full investigation it is enough that there should be material before the Commission sufficient to raise in the minds of reasonable men, possessed of the experience of covert racial discrimination that has been acquired by the Commission, a suspicion that there may have been acts by the person named of racial discrimination of the kind that it is proposed to investigate."[46]

8.40 In the *Prestige* case the Lords affirmed and quoted the foregoing passage and added (their emphasis):

> " . . . and had at any rate *some* grounds for so suspecting albeit that the grounds upon which any such suspicion was based might, at that stage, be no more than tenuous because they had not yet been tested."[47]

8.41 The question arises whether purely statistical material showing a huge disparity between say the actual black, or

---

[45] *Home Office* v. *CRE* [1982] Q.B. 385.
[46] *R.* v. *CRE ex p. Hillingdon* LBC [1982] A.C. 779, *per* Lord Diplock at p.791.
[47] [1984] I.C.R. 473 *per* Lord Diplock at p.481.

female, employment rate, and what might have been expected to be the case without discrimination, gives rise to the necessary suspicion. If those figures cry out for an explanation, the Commission relying on its experience may take the view that the figures alone are sufficiently suspicious to warrant investigation. Certainly it is the practice of the CRE to rely on statistical material in appropriate cases, and it has not yet been challenged in court. In the light of *West Midlands Passenger Transport Executive* v. *Singh*,[48] such a challenge would seem doomed to failure. In an accusatory investigation, the terms of reference must not go beyond the belief held by the Commissioners as to the unlawful acts which may have been committed.[49] Investigating without a suspicion is not allowed. However, a Commission may in an appropriate case draw the inference that if one discriminatory act appears to have occurred, there may well have been others of a similar kind.[50] The important point is that if that is the Commission's belief it should say so, because the right to make representations:

> "cannot be exercised effectively unless that person is informed with reasonable specificity what are the kinds of acts to which the proposed investigation is to be directed and confined. The Commission cannot 'throw the book at him'."[51]

8.42   The obligation on the Commission to set out its belief in the terms of reference and the supporting grounds for its belief is best seen as a duty to produce a document more akin to the pleadings in a civil case than the bundle of statements which might be received by the defence in a trial on indictment. There is no requirement on a Commission to set out all the *evidence* which is to hand, but, on the other hand, it would necessarily have to set out the general effect of that evidence in reaching its belief.

Conduct of investigations

8.43   A Commission may delegate the functions in a formal investigation to one or more Commissioners, who may include additional Commissioners appointed with the approval of the Secretary of State specially for the purpose of the formal investigation.[52] Certain functions in the conduct of investigations, such as the hearing of representations by respondents, would be very difficult to organise without exercising the power to delegate. The power to appoint additional Commissioners is a useful way of bringing special expertise and familiarity with the subject-matter to bear on a particular investigation, and the choice of an appropriate person can lend considerable weight to the findings of the Commissioners. Inevitably the

---

[48] [1988] I.R.L.R. 186.
[49] *Hillingdon* case, *supra*.
[50] *Prestige* case, *supra*.
[51] *Hillingdon* case, *supra*.
[52] SDA 1975, s.57(2), (3); RRA 1976, s.48(2), (3).

Commissioners will rely on Commission staff to collect evidence upon the basis of which the Commissioners make their decisions.[53]

Terms of reference and representations

8.44 Terms of reference have to be drawn up by the Commission or, if the Secretary of State has ordered the investigation, by him after consulting the Commission. For a general investigation, general notice of the terms of reference suffices. But in the case of a named-person accusatory investigation, a special procedure applies. The legislation says:

"Where the terms of reference of the investigation confine it to activities of persons named in them and the Commission in the course of it propose to investigate any act made unlawful by this Act which they believe that a person so named may have done, the Commission shall–

(a) inform that person of their belief and of their proposal to investigate the act in question; and
(b) offer him an opportunity of naming oral or written representations with regard to it (or both oral and written representations if he thinks fit);

and a person so named who avails himself of an opportunity under this subsection of making oral representations may be represented–

(i) by counsel or a solicitor; or
(ii) by some other person of his choice, not being a person to whom the Commission object on the ground that he is unsuitable."[54]

8.45 This procedure provides an opportunity to raise various matters. Particularly relevant arguments are likely to be: that the grounds of the Commission's belief when properly explained do not warrant an investigation; or that the unlawful acts did take place, but have ceased and adequate steps to ensure no repetition have been taken; or that the terms of reference are too wide. There is no entitlement to call witnesses or adduce evidence during the course of representations, or to cross-examine the witnesses on whose statements the Commission relies[55]. However, if, for example, a legal representative wished to ask a local authority housing manager to talk about the housing management system, the Commission may well in its discretion permit that course of action. It is an occasion for the Commissioners to hear argument as to whether such an investigation is appropriate. There is power in the Commission to vary the terms of reference.[56]

[53] R. v. Commission for Racial Equality, ex p. Cotterell and Rothon [1980] 1 W.R.R. 1580.
[54] SDA 1975, s.58(3A) inserted by RRA 1976, Sched. 4; RRA 1976, s. 49(4).
[55] R. v. CRE ex p. Cotterell and Rothon [1980] 1 W.L.R. 1580; [1980] I.R.L.R. 279.
[56] SDA 1975, s.58(4); RRA 1976, s.49(5).

Powers to compel production of information

8.46 Whether or not the Commission has any power to compel the production of information in the course of an investigation differs according to whether it is a general or an accusatory investigation.[57] In the former case, the Commission only has the power to serve the requisite notice requiring information where it is authorised by the Secretary of State. In the case of an accusatory investigation, the power to serve a notice is an automatic adjunct of that type of investigation.

8.47 The notice must be in prescribed form and served in the prescribed manner and:

"(a) may require any person to furnish such written information as may be described in the notice, and may specify the time at which, and the manner and form in which, the information is to be furnished;
(b) may require any person to attend at such time and place as is specified in the notice and give oral information about, and produce all documents in his possession or control relating to, any matter specified in the notice."

8.48 A notice:

"shall not require a person –

(a) to give information, or produce any documents, which he could not be compelled to give in evidence, or produce, in civil proceedings before the High Court of the Court of Session; or
(b) to attend at any place unless the necessary expenses of his journey to and from that place are paid or tendered to him."

8.49 If a person fails to comply with a notice served on him or the Commission have reasonable cause to believe that he intends not to comply with it, the Commission may apply to a county court, or, in Scotland, a sheriff court, for an order requiring him to comply with it or with such directions for the like purpose as may be contained in the order. The penalty for failure to comply is the same as that for neglecting a witness summons, or diligence in Scotland.

8.50 A person commits an offence if he:

1. wilfully alters, suppresses, conceals or destroys a document which he has been required by a notice order to produce; or
2. in complying with such a notice or order, knowingly or recklessly makes any statement which is false in a material particular.

---

[57] See generally, SDA 1975, s.59; RRA 1976, s.50.

8.51 In practice, in a large general investigation the Commission may prefer not to delay the investigation while it asks the Secretary of State for authorisation for service of a notice requiring information. It may instead, in its report of the investigation, simply praise the cooperation of those who did provide information, and condemn the lack of cooperation of those who did not and list them. The Commission could, it seems, make a finding that a person failed to cooperate. Persons may well prefer to cooperate rather than risk such adverse publicity. Whether the Commission adopts this course of action is likely to depend on how far the purpose of the investigation will be frustrated by lack of cooperation.[58] That may be something which one person from whom information is sought is not in a position to judge. It is also possible that in combination with other known facts, failure to cooperate with a general investigation could lead to the Commission to suspect that unlawful acts may have taken place so as to justify an accusatory investigation.

Recommendations

8.52 It is the duty of the Commissions to make recommendations which appear necessary or expedient in the light of any of their findings in a formal investigation.[59] These recommendations may be directed at any person with a view to promoting equality of opportunity and may relate to changes in policies or procedures or as to any other matters; or at the Secretary of State relating to changes in the law or otherwise. They may be made during an investigation.

Reports of investigations

8.53 The Commissions are obliged to prepare a report of their findings in a formal investigation. If it is a formal investigation required by the Secretary of State, it is his obligation to publish it. (Neither Commission has been required to carry out such an investigation.) In other investigations, the Commission concerned has the choice whether to publish the report or just make it available for inspection and copying. Although the statutes refer to a requirement to prepare a report of "findings,"[60] it would be nonsensical if the Commissions did not in their report make reference to those recommendations of general significance which merit publication and without which the findings would be pointless. There is nothing in the statutes to prohibit the inclusion of such recommendations, or indeed other material such as a non-discrimination notice, in a report. There are, however, certain specific prohibitions on disclosure of information by the Commissions.[61] In preparing

[58] The authors of *Racial Justice at Work* PSI 1991 took the view that the CRE had perhaps avoided going to the Secretary of State too often, p.102: "the concept of an allowable drop-out rate has . . . grown and grown".

[59] SDA 1975, s.60; RRA 1976, s.51.

[60] See n. 59.

[61] SDA 1975, s.61; R.A.A. 1976, s.52.

any report for publication or inspection a Commission has to:

> "exclude, so far as is consistent with their duties and the object of the report, any matter which relates to the private affairs of any individual or the business interests of any person where the publication of that matter might in the opinion of the Commission prejudicially affect that individual or persons."

8.54 It is standard practice for the Commissions to allow persons referred to in the report the opportunity to comment on a draft or draft of the relevant part before publication. It is a step which natural justice would probably in any event require. At the end of the day, however, it is the Commission's report, and respondents have no entitlement to insist on any particular form of words, although they may be able to prevent publication if it would be defamatory, or where no reasonable Commission could have made the findings in question, or formed the particular view on whether an individual or person is being unnecessarily prejudiced by the report.

Disclosure of information

8.55 There are restrictions on disclosure of information given by an informant to the Commission in connection with a formal investigation which apply to Commissioners, Additional Commissioners and staff, past and present alike. Disclosure outside the Commission is a criminal offence except on the order of a court, or with the informant's consent, or in the form of a summary or other general statement published by the Commission which does not identify the informant or any other person to whom it relates, in the formal report of the investigation, or so far as necessary for the proper performance of the functions of the Commission, or for the purpose of certain legal proceedings. (The informant's position is also protected against certain forms of retaliation by employers and the like by the somewhat imperfect and incomplete victimisation provisions of the Act.)

Non-discrimination notice

8.56 If in the course of a formal investigation a Commission becomes satisfied that an unlawful act or practice has taken place, it has the power (except in certain education matters where the Secretary of State has a responsibility) to issue a non-discrimination notice in respect of the person concerned.[62] However before so doing, the statutory procedure again requires that the Commission gives the person notice, specifying the grounds, and provides an opportunity to make oral or written representations at not less than 28 days" notice. There is no entitlement to cross-examine witnesses at these representations.[63] In

---

[62] SDA 1975, s.67; RRA 1976, s.58.
[63] See n. 55.

principle there seems to be no reason why the Commission should not send the draft report of its investigation as the grounds for the proposed notice if it is specific about which points it is relying on. This would conveniently shorten the procedure.

8.57 The non-discrimination notice must be in the prescribed form or as near as possible.[64] It will require the person not to commit any such unlawful acts. Although it cannot require any particular changes in practice, it can, where changes in practice or arrangements are necessary, require that the person inform the Commission of changes and notify other persons of them within specified periods. The Commission has a monitoring function, and to this end the notice can require that information be provided to the Commission for up to five years to enable them to check that the notice has been complied with. It would seem to be good practice for the notice to set out the areas where changes in practice are necessary.

Appeals against non-discrimination notices

8.58 When the non-discrimination notice is served, it should be accompanied by a statement of the facts upon which it is based either fully or by reference to the grounds upon which the "minded letter" was based if those have not changed. An appeal against any requirement in a notice may be made within six weeks to an Industrial Tribunal in an employment matter, or to a designated county court or sheriff court in other matters. The time limit is strict and there is no discretion to extend it. A requirement found to be "unreasonable because it is based on an incorrect finding of fact or for any other reason" may be quashed. There is power to substitute another requirement.

8.59 On such an appeal, the findings of fact upon which the notice was based may be reopened. The procedure is for the person served with the notice to respond to the Commission's statement of the facts upon which it relies by a notice stating which of the findings are disputed. The burden is on the person appealing to demonstrate that the true facts are different from those relied upon by the Commission.[65] A recent example of an appeal against a non-discrimination notice was *Handsworth Horticultural Institute* v. *CRE* where an appeal to the County Court failed in relation to admission requirements in a private club.[66]

---

[64] Sex Discrimination (Formal Investigations) Reg. 1975 (S.I. 1975 No. 1993, as amended by S.I. 1977 No. 843); Race Relations (Formal Investigations) Regulations 1977 (S.I. 1977 No. 841).

[65] For appeals see SDA 1975, s.68; RRA 1976, s.59. For procedure see: *CRE* v. *Amari Plastics Ltd.* [1982] I.C.R. 304, C.A.; affirming [1981] I.C.R. 776, EAT.

[66] For the CRE an investigating Commissioner, an investigating Officer and the former Legal Director gave evidence. The Commission attached particular importance to the case as a test case on private clubs.

8.60 If there is no real dispute on the relevant facts the High Court can entertain judicial review proceedings in relation to a non-discrimination notice. It is possible that the High Court will reconsider whether it is sensible to add in this way to an already cumbersome procedure. In *R. v. CRE ex parte Westminster City Council*,[67] the judicial review failed, there was a subsequent appeal to the Court of Appeal which failed, and the appeal in the Industrial Tribunal was therefore pursued. Nothing seems to have been gained by the High Court exercising jurisdiction, since the Tribunal has powers to quash a requirement in a notice at least as wide as the High Court ("*Wednesbury* unreasonableness" appears, if anything, to be less exacting than the "unreasonableness" test in the statutes); and the Industrial Tribunal has the merit of being the specialised tribunal envisaged by the statute.

8.61 The obligation on the Commission to produce a report of an investigation is not without difficulty of application where there is an appeal against a non-discrimination notice. The statutes say that the report is to be of the findings of the Commission. The Commission would be entitled to publish a report even though the findings are under challenge on appeal. However, it may take the view that it would be unfair to do so in view of the fact that the appeal is the first opportunity that the person concerned will have had to challenge the evidence by cross-examination. Either course is apparently lawful.[68] The disadvantage of delaying the report until after the appeal is decided is that the whole matter will be stale.

Enforcing a non-discrimination notice

8.62 There are several methods of enforcing a non-discrimination notice which has become final. A county court order may be obtained in respect of breach of a requirement. A further formal investigation may be carried out to determine whether the requirements of a notice are being carried out. A county court injunction may be sought if, within five years of the notice becoming final, it appears likely that the person will commit further unlawful acts.[69] Finally, if a local authority is involved, much the same effect as enforcing a non-discrimination notice in the race field could be achieved with judicial review relying on the section 71 duty under the Race Relations Act.

Opportunities for delay

8.63 It will be observed that in relation to an employment investigation it is possible for there to be a whole variety of proceedings in different *fora*; the Industrial Tribunal for appeal against a non-discrimination notice; the High Court for judicial review; a (designated in a race case) county court

[67] [1984] I.C.R. 827 C.A. affirming [1984] I.C.R. 770.
[68] *CRE* v. *Amari Plastics, supra*.
[69] See SDA 1975, ss.67(7), 69, 71; RRA 1976, ss.58(7), 60, 62.

for enforcement of a non-discrimination notice. A resourceful respondent to an investigation, exploiting these and other opportunities in a cumbersome system, therefore has enormous scope for delaying tactics. A note of caution, however: both Commissions have in the past demonstrated a tenacity in sticking with some investigations, for many years if need be, to the bitter end.

9 PUBLIC BODIES

Introduction 9.01 Whether an organisation is a public body and, sometimes, what sort of public body is increasingly of importance in equality law.

First, public bodies are amenable to judicial review proceedings in England and Wales. (In Scotland however the Court of Session's supervisory jurisdiction does not depend on the nature of the body whose decision it is sought to review.) This offers the Commissions and an aggrieved person a useful way of getting a determination where the facts are reasonably clear and point to a possible breach of discrimination law and (i) the law itself needs clarification, and/or (ii) a discriminatory decision needs to be quashed, and/or (iii) a discriminatory system needs to be ended. This is dealt with below.

Secondly, in instances where Community law is relied upon which is not directly applicable but should have been implemented by the state, then whether the respondent body is a manifestation of the state will determine the issue of whether the tribunal or court can apply the Community law. This is dealt with in Chapter 1 above.

Thirdly, local authorities and some housing bodies are subject to a special duty under section 71 of the Race Relations Act 1976. There is no equivalent provision in the Sex Discrimination Act. This distinction between the two statutes turned out to be important when legislation dealing with contract compliance by public bodies was passed. This is dealt with below.

Fourthly, there are statutory rules which apply to the contracting processes of many public bodies which either prohibit them from concerning themselves with the question whether prospective contractors are providing equal opportunities, or limit the extent to which they can do so. This is dealt with below.

Judicial Review

9.02 Both the SDA and RRA allow for proceedings to be brought for certiorari, mandamus and prohibition relying on unlawfulness by virtue of provisions of those Acts.[1] This

[1] s. 62, SDA and s. 53, RRA.

means that judicial review under R.S.C., Ord. 53 may be an alternative way of proceeding to either Industrial Tribunal proceedings in employment matters or County Court proceedings in non-employment matters, provided the body accused of unlawfulness is a public body amenable to such review. (In Scotland, judicial review proceedings may be brought without regard to whether it is a public body.) Where the body concerned is alleged to have adopted a discriminatory policy, judicial review would seem to be appropriate. Where a number of individual discriminatory acts are alleged, however, proceedings under the enforcement provisions in the Tribunals or County Courts are preferable. See the *Hammersmith* case referred to below.[2]

9.03 In addition judicial review provides an alternative way of proceeding for the Commissions instead of formal investigations where there is no real dispute as to the facts. (Evidence on judicial review is by way of affidavit.) In *R.* v. *Birmingham City Council, ex p. Equal Opportunities Commission*, judicial review was used to establish that the provision by the Council of more Grammar school places for boys than girls was unlawfully discriminatory and a declaration was granted.[3]

9.04 Some areas of activity of public bodies are outside the enforcement provisions of the Acts. For example, the House of Lords case of *Amin* v. *Entry Clearance Officer Bombay*[4] is to the effect that the control functions of government do not fall within the provisions making discrimination unlawful in the provision to the public of facilities or services. This puts many of the activities of the police, customs and immigration authorities outside of the scope of the Acts. Nevertheless, it is not to be supposed that they are entitled to act on racial grounds or grounds of sex unless there is specific statutory or ministerial authorisation to do so (obviously, if the concept of citizenship is to mean anything, some discrimination on grounds of nationality is bound to be lawful). Thus even where the equality statutes do not specifically apply, decisions may be challenged relying on the proposition that the public body acts wholly unreasonably (in the *Wednesbury* sense) in taking into account irrelevant considerations. Since allegations of discriminatory treatment by officials at ports of entry are not infrequent, it is inevitable that the CRE will be drawn into challenges in this area.

Locus standi **9.05** Even where the public body is apparently protected by some statutory provision, will judicial review provide the way of testing the validity of the provision against European

[2] *R* v. *London Borough of Hammersmith and Fulham, ex p. NALGO* [1991] I.R.L.R. 249.
[3] [1989] I.R.L.R. 173; [1989] A.C. 115, H.L.
[4] See Chap. 7 for a discussion of this case.

Community law? There is a substantial amount of
Community law on sex discrimination. Thus both the British
and the Northern Ireland EOCs began judicial review
proceedings against the government to challenge the
lawfulness under EC law of the minimum hours requirement
for statutory protection rights on the basis that most
part-time workers are women.[5] The CRE has also challenged
government action (by way of a national security certificate
issued under the Race Relations Act), relying on the
Community law relating to the freedom of movement of
Community nationals.[6] The case of *R* v. *Secretary of State for
Social Security, ex p. EOC*[7] is an example of judicial review
brought by an agency to test the validity of statute law
against community law in which reference was made to the
European Court of Justice under Article 177 of the EEC
Treaty. In that case the statutory framework underpinning
the different number of years of contribution for state
retirement pensions for men and women was challenged.
Although the challenges have failed (treatment of the
substantive issues is to be found earlier in this book), we are
concerned here solely with the use which can be made of
judicial review. Unfortunately, the Court of Appeal in *R* v.
Secretary of State for Employment, exp. EOC[8] held, in the
case concerning the validity of the minimum hours
requirement for statutory employment protection, that there
was no justiciable decision and that EOC in such a case had
no *locus standi* to bring the judicial review proceedings. The
issue should be dealt with in private law proceedings by the
individual against the employer. There is a cogent dissent by
Dillon L.J. which we think makes a great deal more sense.

9.06   The applicant needs leave of the court to pursue the
review, and this will only be granted where the court
considers that he or she has a sufficient interest in the
matter. The Commissions, because of their statutory
function to work towards the elimination of unlawful
discrimination, will often, at least where the validity of U.K.
law is not the issue, have a sufficient interest to maintain
proceedings.[8] They may also be able to support proceedings
brought by an individual where they are brought to clarify
procedures under which the individual is pursuing a claim
under the Act concerned. Thus, in *R* v. *Army Board of the
Defence Council, ex p. Anderson*, a soldier was subjected to
racial harassment in the Army. His complaints had not been
properly dealt with under the Army procedures (a serving
soldier's complaint against his employers is not subject to
the Industrial Tribunal jurisdiction in race matters). He was
aided in judicial review proceedings by the CRE, who were
supporting him in pursuing his case before the Army

---

[5] See *R* v. *Secretary of State for Employment, ex p. EOC* [1991] I.R.L.R.
   493.
[6] An unreported case.
[7] [1992] I.R.L.R. 376.
[8] [1993] I.R.L.R. 10 C.A.

authorities. The outcome was a clarification of the procedures to be followed by the Army to ensure proper standards of fairness and the Army Board's decision was quashed.[9]

9.07 In a case against the Ministry of Defence, two military nurses were supported by the EOC who themselves also brought proceedings. The Government conceded that a policy of dismissing military nurses who became pregnant breached the Equal Treatment Directive, and also that Service personnel could bring proceedings in the Industrial Tribunals as the Directive had displaced the exemption under the SDA. (EOC's standing was not disputed).

9.08 In education matters, parents of children affected by decisions or policies will generally have sufficient interest to maintain judicial review proceedings. *R* v. *Secretary of State for Education and Science, ex p. Keating,*[10] was such a case where it was held that a Local Education Authority was obliged to have regard to the SDA in providing secondary schools. Thus if the policy of the Authority was to provide single sex education, the treatment of one sex less favourably than the other was contrary to section 23 of the SDA, and the parents were able to challenge a proposal to close the only boys' comprehensive school.

9.09 In *R* v. *London Borough of Hammersmith and Fulham, ex p. NALGO*, the court was content to assume in accordance with counsel's submissions

> "that if a public authority proposes to embark upon an employment or redeployment policy which is in breach of the Sex Discrimination Act or the Race Relations Act, or is otherwise unlawful, the public law remedies should be available to the unions and employees affected."

In fact, however, certiorari was refused on the basis that unlawfulness had not been made out in the council's policy of redeployment and redundancy.

> "The most that can be said on the available evidence is that the implementation of the policy might offend the law in individual cases, depending on how the implementation is carried out. . .I have referred to the wealth of conflicting evidence which the parties have brought to bear upon these issues. In my judgement their opposing contentions can only properly be tested on a case-by-case basis in pursuance of the applicants'' private law remedies. The numerous factual issues involved are eminently suitable for consideration by an Industrial

---

[9] [1991] I.R.L.R. 425; see also *R* v. *Department of Health, ex p. Gandhi* [1991] I.R.L.R. 431. These two cases were heard consecutively by the High Court.
[10] [1985] L.G.R. 469.

Tribunal, and are wholly unsuitable for resolution by the single drastic remedy of certiorari."[11]

9.10 We set out below a general statutory duty on local authorities in race matters under section 71, RRA. At the present time, this has only been relied on by local authorities as a shield in judicial review proceedings[12] except in a case brought by the CRE against Tower Hamlets L.B.C. which was eventually settled. However, no doubt it will be relied on in future to take local authorities to task and it is a good question how widely the court will construe the "sufficient interest" criterion in respect of local inhabitants.

Legal aid is available for judicial review proceedings.

9.11 The time limits for judicial review are short and an application has to be made promptly and in any event within three months from the date when grounds for the application first arose, unless the court considers that there is good reason for extending the period.[13]

9.12 The Commissions are themselves both amenable to judicial review, and at one time the CRE tended to be on the receiving end rather than taking the initiative.[14] Various points concerning formal investigations were established in judicial review proceedings. The EOC carried out far fewer formal investigations and therefore never invited the same attention.

Local authorities and section 71 of the Race Relations Act 1976

9.13 The 1976 Act contains a general duty imposed upon local authorities for which there is no equivalent in the Sex Discrimination legislation, though the EOC evidently think such a duty would be desirable. Section 71 reads:

"Without prejudice to their obligation to comply with any other provision of this Act, it shall be the duty of every local authority to make appropriate arrangements with a view to securing that their various functions are carried out with due regard to the need –

(a) to eliminate unlawful racial discrimination; and
(b) to promote equality of opportunity, and good relations, between persons of different racial groups."

The Housing Act 1988 extended the duties to the Housing Corporation and to housing action trusts and equivalent provision has been made in Scotland.

---

[11] [1991] I.R.L.R. 249.
[12] See later in this chap. where the cases are dealt with.
[13] R.S.C., Ord. 53, r. 4.
[14] As Legal Director, CRE one of the authors can recall five sets of judicial review proceedings against CRE when or shortly after he took up the job in 1982.

9.14   The scope of this provision was considered by the House of Lords in *Wheeler* v. *Leicester City Council*.[15] Although the way in which the Council tried to carry out its duty under the section was held to be invalid, the case is important in the main for establishing that section 71 is justiciable and not just a pious aspiration. However since the litigation took the form of a challenge to a council's action, the reasoning of their Lordships is couched in terms of what a council is *empowered* to do under the provisions, rather than in terms of what it is *required* to do. The section is phrased in terms of a *duty*. As, in principle, section 71 is justiciable, it seems that a party with appropriate *locus standi* could bring proceedings to enforce the duty against a local authority (although, given the vague terms of the duty, establishing a failure to carry it out may well prove difficult in practice).

9.15   In *Wheeler*, the Council had licensed a rugby club to use its recreation ground. Three members of the club were invited to join the English rugby team to tour South Africa. The Council supported the Commonwealth Gleneagles Agreement to withhold support for and discourage sporting links with South Africa. It asked the club to endorse these views, condemn the tour, and put pressure on its members not to take part in the tour. The club agreed with the Council in condemning apartheid in South Africa, but said it could only advise its members of the arguments for not going on the tour since to do so was not unlawful, nor was it contrary to the club rules or those of the Rugby Football Union. After the members went on the tour, the Council resolved to ban the club from using the recreation ground for twelve months. The club members applied for an order of certiorari to quash the council decision, and the Council's attempt to rely on section 71 of the 1976 Act succeeded at first instance and in the Court of Appeal, but failed in the House of Lords.

9.16   The club argued that section 71 should be given a narrow construction. It was suggested that the section was only concerned with the actions of the council as regards its own internal behaviour and was what was described as "inward looking". It was said that it had no relevance to the general exercise by the council of its statutory functions as, for example, in relation to the control of open spaces or in determining who should be entitled to use a recreation ground and on what terms. The House of Lords, as had the courts below, rejected this argument. *Per* Lord Roskill:

> "I think that the whole purpose of this section is to see that in relation to matters other than specifically dealt with, for example, [in Parts II and III of the 1976 Act] local authorities must in relation to 'their various functions' make 'appropriate arrangements' to ensure that

[15] [1985] 2 All E.R. 1105, H.L.

those functions are carried out 'with due regard to the need' mentioned in the section. It follows that I do not doubt that the Council were fully entitled in exercising their statutory discretion under, for example, the Open Spaces Act 1906 and the various Public Health Acts . . . to pay regard to what they thought was in the best interests of race relations."[16]

And later he goes on:

"I do not doubt for one moment the great importance which the Council attach to the presence in their midst of a 25 per cent. population of persons who are either Asian or of Afro-Caribbean origin."[17]

9.17   Ultimately, however, the House of Lords held that the decision of the council was invalid. In Lord Templeman's words, with which three other members of the House expressed agreement: "The club could not be punished because the club had done nothing wrong." He goes on:

"Of course this does not mean that the Council is bound to allow its property to be used by a racist organisation or by any organisation which, by its actions or its words, infringes the letter or the spirit of the 1976 Act."[18]

Lord Roskill, who gave the only other reasoned speech with which three members of the House agreed was perhaps less forthright in his reasoning, but his approach may best be summed up in his words:

"Persuasion, even powerful persuasion, is always a permissible way of seeking to obtain an objective. But in a field where other views can equally legitimately be held, persuasion, however powerful, must not be allowed to cross that line where it moves into the field of illegitimate pressure coupled with the threat of sanctions."[19]

He adds:

"If the club had adopted a different and hostile attitude different considerations might well have arisen. But the club did not adopt any such attitude . . . In my view . . . this is a case in which the court should interfere because of the unfair manner in which the Council set about obtaining its objective."[20]

9.18   There appears to be some wavering in the reasoning. If the true ratio is that the club had done nothing wrong, suppose a club were to say it approved of the system of apartheid as suitable for the special conditions of South

[16] At p. 1110.
[17] At p. 1111.
[18] At p. 1113.
[19] At p. 1111.
[20] At p. 1112.

Africa? Quite possibly such a view could be advanced in circumstances where it would not amount to incitement to racial hatred for the purposes of the Public Order Act. Could a Council take action to punish a club in these circumstances? The statements in the speeches that a council would not be bound to allow its property to be used by a racist organisation, and that different considerations might well have arisen had the club been hostile, seem to indicate that a Council would be justified in taking action here.

9.19   It should be borne in mind that the case concerned the termination of a facility once granted. It is possible that a council, which at the outset sets out a policy of granting facilities only where it is satisfied on certain points, may be on stronger ground than a council taking away a facility on a basis which was not apparent when it was granted. A court may grant more leeway to a council which has carefully weighed up a policy and set it out at some length, provided that in accordance with ordinary administrative law principles the council is prepared to consider the facts of the particular case before it in deciding whether to apply the policy. To take the example of contract compliance before the provisions of the Local Government Act 1988, it is improbable that a court would have struck down as wholly unreasonable conditions for entry on to an approved list for tendering which required compliance with the Code of Practice under the 1976 legislation as well as the legislation itself. Strictly speaking, it is not unlawful to fail to comply with the Code, although the failure could have certain consequences in litigation under the Act (see chapter 3). If this is correct, then it follows that ancillary conditions, such as requirements to provide monitoring information, there to ensure compliance with the Code, would necessarily have had to be upheld. In the light of the *Wheeler* decision, however, a condition which prohibited trading links with South Africa was obviously legally more doubtful, since that fell into the areas where opinions could legitimately differ as to what constituted the right approach.

9.20   *R* v. *Lewisham London Borough Council, ex p. Shell U.K. Ltd.*[21] was another decision predating the Local Government Act 1988. The applicant was a United Kingdom company which was part of a multinational group of companies which had subsidiaries operating in South Africa. The Council – 18 per cent. black population – decided, pursuant to section 71, to promote good race relations within the borough by adopting a policy of boycotting the applicant's products subject to alternative products being available on reasonable terms. The Council also sought to persuade other local authorities to follow suit and so maximise pressure on the parent companies of the group to withdraw their interests from South Africa.

[21] 1 All E.R. 938.

9.21 It was held that the purpose of the council's decision was not simply to satisfy public opinion or promote good race relations in the borough, but to exert pressure on the company and the group to sever all trading links with South Africa. Since that purpose had exerted a very substantial influence on the Council's decision and was inextricably mixed up with any wish to improve race relations in the borough, and since the group's policy towards South Africa was not unlawful, it followed that the Council's decision had been influenced by an extraneous and impermissible purpose which vitiated the decision as a whole. A declaration was granted.

Contract compliance

The U.S. experience[22] **9.22** The term "contract compliance", of U.S. provenance, is now commonly used to describe those procedures used by governmental agencies (whether central or local) to ensure that companies to which they give contracts to supply goods or services are pursuing equal opportunities policies as employers. Many black people and women in the U.S.A. point to the operation of contract compliance being an effective instrument of policy for bringing about improvements towards equality. Amongst the most vociferous supporters of contract compliance in the U.S.A. can be found the National Association of Manufacturers, which is the U.S. equivalent of the CBI. Because contract compliance is fairly new in Britain, a brief survey of the position in the U.S.A. may serve the purpose of indicating possible trends here in this developing area.

Presidential executive orders **9.23** During the Second World War, Presidential Executive Orders were used to bar discrimination on the grounds of race, creed, colour or national origin by defence contractors. The rationale was that "the prosecution of the war demands that we utilise fully all available manpower, and that discrimination by war industries is detrimental to the prosecution of the war". The Fair Employment Practice Committee reported that the Orders had had a positive effect, noting that the percentage of black workers employed in the war industries had risen from 3 per cent. in March 1942 to 8 per cent. by the end of the war. However, they also pointed out that the Orders had been repeatedly and consistently breached, and that sometimes had not been applied: "the wartime gains of Negro, Mexico-American and Jewish workers are being lost through an unchecked revival of discriminatory practices."

---

[22] The material collected under this heading owes much to work done by Brian O'Neill when on student placement with the CRE.

9.24 In 1953, an Executive Order extended the ban on discrimination to all government procurement contractors and suppliers, not just those involved in the defence industry. The rationale was stated to be that persons of different races or religions were entitled to fair and equitable treatment. A Government Contract Committee was set up with powers to receive violation complaints, and to further and encourage equal opportunity programmes. By 1954 it had established precontractual discussions, field checks, investigations and conciliation services, and a central reporting system. In 1961 President Kennedy signed his first Executive Order, in which he expanded the justification for the Orders to include efficiency as well as entitlement:

"It is in the general interest and welfare of the United States to promote its economy, security, and national defence through the most effective and efficient utilisation of all available manpower."

A new obligation was placed on contractors

"The contractor will take affirmative action to ensure that applicants are employed, and that employees are treated during employment, without regard to their race, creed, colour, or national origin. . ."

Power was given to the President's Committee on Equal Employment Opportunity to recommend specific sanctions, including termination for non-compliance.

9.25 When in 1964 Title VII of the Civil Rights Act was passed outlawing employment discrimination, attempts to make this the exclusive remedy for employment discrimination failed. The President's power to deal with discrimination by federal contractors remained intact. The current Executive Order is No. 11246 signed by President Johnson. Supervision of contracting agencies was transferred to the Department of Labor and led later to the creation of the Office of Federal Contract Compliance (OFCC). The scope of the contractual provision was expanded to cover not only the performance of work under the contract in hand, but also the contractor's other operations. In 1967, discrimination on the grounds of sex was added to the list of prohibited discrimination. Current requirements are for the setting of goals and timetables by companies subject to the programme for the employment of qualified members of minority groups where they are under-utilised.

9.26 Research on the operation of contract compliance is worthy of note. A study by Leonard of the operations of the Order between 1974 and 1980 found that "the employment goals that firms agree to are not vacuous; neither are they adhered to as strictly as quotas". He says that the higher the goal is set, the better the company performs, but that on average firms achieve only about 10 per cent. of their goals.[23] In 1981, OFCC commissioned research to assess the impact of affirmative action, which reviewed 77,000 companies employing 20 million employees during the period 1974 to 1980. The study was published in 1983. In the period under survey, federal contractors employed 20 per cent. more racial minorities and 15 per cent. more women, whilst the comparable increases for the non-contractors were 13 per cent. and 2 per cent.[24] A 1984 survey by Organisation Resources Counselors, Inc., a firm of management consultants, of chief executives of companies showed 95 per cent. indicating that they would use numbers as a management tool to measure progress, whether or not the government required them to.[25]

Local government and contract compliance

9.27   A number of local authorities set up contract compliance units following the lead given by the Greater London Council in April 1983 (when the G.L.C. was abolished its unit passed to the Inner London Education Authority until that too was abolished).[26] The legal position is that, prior to the Local Government Act 1988, there was no statute law which specifically dealt with the subject of contract compliance. It was therefore neither required nor forbidden, but in principle permissible. In the case of eliminating racial discrimination and promoting equal opportunities and good relations between different racial groups, section 71 of the Race Relations Act 1976, imposing a duty on local authorities, provided a statutory framework within which contract compliance, though not specifically referred to, found a general authority. There is no equivalent provision in the Sex Discrimination legislation, and this was to prove an important distinction under the Local Government Act 1988.

Towards consistency and fairness in contract compliance

9.28   Before the 1988 Act, there were developments aimed at consistency and fairness in the operation of contract compliance.[27] First, the Association of Metropolitan Authorities proposed a model questionnaire. The point of a model questionnaire is that, if widely used, the burden upon companies in providing information is much reduced, since the answers given to one local authority will suffice for others also. Secondly, the CRE produced a set of Principles of Practice relating to contract compliance with the aims of

---

[23] Jonathan S Leonard, *The Impact of Affirmative Action on Minority and Female Employment* (1983).

[24] OFCCP, U.S. Department of Labor *A Review of the Effects of Executive Order 11246 and Federal Contract Compliance Programs on Employment Opportunities of Minorities and Women* 1983.

[25] Organisation Resources Counselors Inc *Managing Diversity: the challenge of EEO to 1990.* 1984.

[26] See I.L.E.A. Contract Compliance EO Unit, 1985-1986 *Contracting for Equality: first annual report of the G.L.C.*", 1986.

[27] See Institute of Personnel Management, *Contract Compliance -The UK Experience* 1987.

maximising the effectiveness of such schemes; minimising any burden schemes may impose; ensuring consistency between schemes; and ensuring fairness in the application of schemes. The Principles did not have the status of a Code under section 47 of the 1976 Act.[28] The views of the CRE following consultation may well have carried weight with a court in the event, say, of judicial review of a council's actions.[29]

The Local Government Act 1988

9.29 Contract compliance concerning race relations and sex equality matters carried out by the public authorities listed in Schedule 2 to the Local Government Act 1988 (see below) is banned by that Act, save for local authorities where it is permitted in certain circumstances which relate to section 71 of the 1976 Act. However, any body not listed in Schedule 2 can carry out contract compliance on the general principle of our law that what is not forbidden is permitted. For such bodies, the CRE's document *Principles of Practice for Contract Compliance* may still be useful. Lawyers acting for such bodies, however, will need to ensure that their own governing constitution or statute does permit such action.

9.30 The Local Government Act 1988 requires the scheduled public authorities to exercise their public supply or works contract functions without reference to the non-commercial matters specified in section 17(5).

Public supply or works contracts are contracts for the supply of goods and materials, the supply of services or the execution of works.

Contractual functions covered by s.17

9.31 The contractual functions covered by section 17 are:

1. the inclusion or exclusion of anybody from a list of approved contractors or lists of persons from whom tenders are invited;
2. the acceptance or non-acceptance of tenders;
3. the selection of the successful contractor;
4. the approval, non-approval, selection and nomination of sub-contractors for proposed or existing contracts; and
5. the termination of a contract.

9.32 Two of the matters listed under section 17(5) as "non-commercial matters" are of particular concern here:

"(a) the terms and conditions of employment by contractors of their workers or the composition of, the arrangements for the promotion, transfer or training of or the other opportunities afforded to, their workforces. . ."

---

[28] See now CRE, *Local Authority Contracts and Racial Equality-Implications of the Local Government Act 1988* CRE 1989.

[29] See *R. v. London Borough of Lewisham, ex p. Shell U.K. Ltd.* [1988] 1 All E.R. 938.

These are known as "workforce matters", and

"(e) the country or territory of origin of supplier to, or
the location in any country or territory of the
businesses activities or interests of, contractors."

The heading (e) obviously knocks on the head any contract
compliance aimed at stopping links with South Africa.

9.33   As drafted, it was arguable that the definition of
"workforce matters" at section 17(5)(*a*) did not include the
policy and practice relating to recruitment and dismissal of
members of the workforce. The only way in which they
would fall within that provision is if they are caught by the
words "composition . . . of their workforce". This clearly
comprises the make-up of the existing workforce.
Recruitment and dismissal policy and practice will inevitably
affect the future composition of the workforce, but it is at
least odd that the definition of workforce matters did not
include those matters explicitly if it was intended to cover
them. This is particularly true in the light of section 18(6),
which makes it clear that the phrase "composition of the
workforce" also includes a reference to "matters which
occurred in the past as well as matters which subsist when
the function in question falls to be exercised". However, a
judicial review case brought by an organisation representing
potential contractors has ruled out this line of argument.[30] A
scheduled public authority cannot therefore have regard to
equal opportunity as concerns recruitment and dismissal in
relation to sex or disability in exercising its contractual
functions.

Race relations   **9.34**   The one area where local authorities, but not the
matters   other scheduled public authorities, are allowed under the
Act to take account of non-commercial matters during the
contractual process is in the field of race relations. This is in
view of the fact that section 71 of the Race Relations Act
1976 places a duty on local authorities to ensure that their
various functions are carried out with due regard to the need
to eliminate unlawful racial discrimination and to promote
equality of opportunity, and good relations, between persons
of different racial groups.

9.35   Section 18 of the Act therefore allows local authorities
to ask approved written questions and include terms in a
draft contract which relate to the workforce matters in
section 17(5)(a) if it is reasonably necessary to do so to
secure compliance with section 71.

It should be noted that the provision relating to approved
questions is quite separate from the provision entitling the

[30] *R* v. *London Borough of Islington, ex p. Building Employers' Confederation*
[1989] I.R.L.R. 382.

inclusion in a draft contract or draft tender of terms or provisions relating to workforce matters. In both cases the local authority has to consider whether its actions are reasonably necessary to secure compliance with section 71. The implication seems to be that it may not in some cases be reasonably necessary to ask all the approved questions. On the other hand, the further implication is that, as regards the *terms or provisions in a draft contract or tender*, it may be reasonably necessary, depending on the circumstances, to stipulate terms or provisions which go beyond the matters referred to in the approved questions. It also follows that it is section 71, and not the Local Government Act or any approved questions under it, which the courts must look to in considering a local authority's view as to what is "reasonably necessary" in the particular circumstances. Terms or provisions might therefore cover such matters as compliance with particular recommendations in the Commission for Racial Equality's Code of Practice pursuant to section 47 of that Act. (The current Code came into operation in April 1984.)

Questions specified under section 18(5), LGA 1988

9.36   The following questions and description of evidence are specified under section 18(5) of the Local Government Act 1988 as approved:

"1. Is it your policy as an employer to comply with your statutory obligations under the Race Relations Act 1976 and, accordingly, your practice not to treat one group of people less favourably than others because of their colour, race, nationality or ethnic origin in relation to decisions to recruit, train or promote employees?
2. In the last three years, has any finding of unlawful racial discrimination been made against your organisation by any court or industrial tribunal?
3. In the last three years, has your organisation been the subject of formal investigation by the Commission for Racial Equality on grounds of alleged unlawful discrimination? If the answer to question 2 is in the affirmative or, in relation to question 3, the Commission made a finding adverse to your organisation,
4. What steps did you take in consequence of that finding?
5. Is your policy on race relations set out –

(a) in instructions to those concerned with recruitment, training and promotion,
(b) in documents available to employees, recognised trade unions or other representative groups or employees,
(c) in recruitment advertisements or other literature,

6. Do you observe as far as possible the Commission for Racial Equality's Code of Practice for Employment, as approved by Parliament in 1983, which gives practical guidance to employers and others on the elimination of racial discrimination and the promotion of equality of

opportunity in employment, including the steps that can be taken to encourage members of the ethnic minorities to apply for jobs or take up training opportunities? Description of evidence –

In relation to question 5: examples of the instructions, documents, recruitment advertisements or other literature."

The major omission from the list of approved questions and description of evidence is a question relating to the actual results of ethnic monitoring (*i.e.* a numerical question). The CRE's suggested questionnaire would have provided such a question. There is a case for the CRE to carry out a general investigation into the working of the approved questions, and if necessary to make recommendations for change to the Secretary of State.

9.37   Section 20 of the Act requires the authorities to notify forthwith any person in relation to whom certain contractual decisions are taken. Those decisions are:

1. to exclude him from an approved list;
2. not to invite him to tender when he had asked to be invited;
3. not to accept the submission of his tender;
4. not to enter into a contract with him when he has submitted a tender;
5. not to approve, or to select or nominate, persons to be sub-contractors for a proposed or subsisting contract; and
6. to terminate a contract.

Section 20 also provides that where the person so requests in writing within 15 days of the date of notification, the authority must provide him, within 15 days of the date of the request, with written reasons for the decision.

9.38   Prior to any decision being taken on the basis of responses to approved questions, or responses to draft terms or provisions, the legislation envisages their consideration in the light of what is reasonably necessary to secure compliance with section 71. This is briefly adverted to in section 18. In practice, this may be a considerable over-simplification of the problem which may face the local authority at that stage. Prior to the Local Government Act 1988, the general approach of local authorities to contract compliance was to proceed by way of advisory and counselling methods, rather than immediate use of sanctions. Answers to approved questions which are inadequate may now lead to a decision not to include on an approved list, whereas previously they could have led to a further approach to the company and satisfaction all round. This could prove to be an unintended consequence of the legislation. There seems to be nothing to prevent the local authority sending a letter saying that they are intending to make a decision against the company on specified grounds, however, unless they are persuaded otherwise. This is not asking unapproved questions, and would be a reasonable administrative step to take which mitigates the otherwise potentially harsh consequences of the Act. If a potential contractor provides further information in consequence of such a letter, that is his decision. However, the whole procedure should not be designed by the local authority to procure further information other than from the questions approved by the Secretary of State, because the courts will probably strike down use of the procedure in that way. It is a different matter, however, for the local authority to say in effect "Well, we have your response to our approved questions. This is the interpretation we place upon it. As a result, the following consequences will ensue, unless you persuade us otherwise."

9.39 Some further points arise in respect of terms or provisions relating to equal opportunities for persons of different racial groups in draft contracts or draft tenders. First, it is essential that negative responses to those terms or provisions are considered fully on the question whether it is reasonably necessary to include them in the contract or tender to secure compliance with section 71. Secondly, where they do become incorporated into a contract, what is the position if they are broken? The Local Government Act does not regulate the contractual effects of breach except in the important respect that a scheduled public authority cannot terminate a subsisting contract by reference to a non-commercial matter. (Section 18(3) expressly applied this position to a local authority acting under the section 18 exemption to section 17 in respect of section 71 of the 1976 Act.) There are, however, two other possibilities. One is a claim in damages, but in practice proof of loss will be virtually impossible. The second is to provide that payment under the contract, or at least some part of the payment, should only fall due upon all the equal opportunity terms of the contract having been met, as well as all other essential terms. The assistance of a skilled contract lawyer would be essential to draft such a term to avoid falling foul of the law relating to penalty clauses.

No charge may be made by a public authority as a condition of inclusion on an approved list.

9.40 The various provisions referred to above do not create any criminal liability but, for the purpose of proceedings for judicial review, those having an interest in a matter are clarified by section 17 and include any body representing contractors (see the *Islington* case). Failure to comply with the section 17(1) duty is actionable by any person who in consequence suffers loss and damage, but a tenderer is limited to damages in respect of expenditure reasonably incurred in submitting the tender.

Effect of section 71, Race Relations Act 1976

9.41   The effect of the Local Government Act 1988 is to make the race relations and sex discrimination position markedly different in this area. The supposed justification for this distinction lay in section 71 of the Race Relations Act 1976, for which there is no equivalent in the Sex Discrimination Act 1975. Contract compliance by all scheduled public authorities in respect of matters covered by the 1975 Act is therefore prohibited. The CRE had called for the section 71 type of duty to extend to all public authorities (*Review of the Act* 1985), and the EOC have now called for a similar provision in relation to sex (*Strengthening the Acts*, 1988). If there were provisions extending a section 71-type duty in respect of both race and sex to all public authorities presumably the contract compliance provisions would have to be widened accordingly. As the CRE pointed out in comments on the Local Government Bill, it is odd that an urban development corporation, for example, is prohibited from carrying out contract compliance in relation to race relations matters when it is likely to take over local authority functions in just those inner-city areas where the ethnic minority concentration is higher, and urban renewal most urgently needed.

Schedule 2, Local Government Act 1988: Public authorities

9.42   The scheduled public authorities are as follows:

"A local authority.

An urban development corporation established by an order under section 135 of the Local Government, Planning and Land Act 1980.

A development corporation established for the purposes of a new town.

The Commission for the New Towns.
A police authority constituted under section 2 of the Police Act 1964 or as mentioned in section 3(1) of that Act, or established by section 24 or 25 of the Local Government Act 1985.

A fire authority constituted by a combination scheme and a metropolitan county fire and civil defence authority.

The London Fire and Civil Defence Authority.

A metropolitan county passenger transport authority.

An authority established by an order under section 10(1) of the Local Government Act 1985 (waste disposal).

A joint education committee established by an order under paragraph 3 of part ll of Schedule 1 to the Education Act 1944.

A water development board in Scotland.

The Scottish Special Housing Association.

The Broards Authority.

The Lake District Special Planning Board.

The Peak Park Joint Planning Board.

A Passenger Transport Executive, that is to say, any body constituted as such an Executive for a passenger transport area for the purposes of Part II of the Transport Act 1988.

A probation and after-care committee, that is to say, any body constituted as such a committee for a probation and after-care area by paragraph 2(1) of Schedule 3 to the Powers of Criminal Courts Act 1973.

A joint committee discharging under section 101 of the Local Government Act 1972 functions of local authorities (within the meaning of that section)."

Central government and contract compliance

9.43 From 1969, there was a clause in all government contracts requiring contractors to conform to the employment provisions of the Race Relations Act as follows:

"Racial discrimination -

(1) The Contractor shall not unlawfully discriminate within the meaning and scope of the provisions of the Race Relations Act 1968 or any statutory modifications or re-enactment thereof relating to discimination in employment.
(2) The Contractor shall take all reasonable steps to secure the observance of all the provisions of clause (1) hereof by all servants, employees or agents of the contractor and all subcontractors employed in the execution of the Contract."

9.44 No attempt has been made to monitor compliance with this clause, notwithstanding the fact that The White Paper on Racial Discrimination preceding the 1976 Act recognised this as unsatisfactory. This differs from the approach to religious discrimination in Northern Ireland, where the government has introduced compulsory monitoring of the religious composition of workforces and tied this in with contract compliance relating to government contracts.[31] Now that the government has set out a scheme of contract compliance for local authorities in Great Britain, it remains to be seen whether they will follow a similar scheme for their own supply and works contracts. It would ill behove central government to pray in aid of the absence of a section 71 duty on themselves, particularly given the developments in Northern Ireland.

Privatisation

9.45 The increasing tendency to privatise entities that were previously part of the public service creates new needs to ensure that equal opportunities are being provided, and contract compliance would seem to be the best way of doing

[31] Fair Employment (N.I.) Act 1989.

this. For example, it is all very well the prison service claiming exemplary equal opportunity policies, but what system other than contract compliance will ensure that they are followed in a privatised prison? And if it is right to have contract compliance here, it is difficult to see why the same should not apply wherever the State buys in service provision.

9.46   Indeed, privatisation presents problems for public bodies other than central government. One of the authors has experience of a case concerning a privatised company where the relevant managers had no idea what policies concerning equal opportunities had existed previously under local authority control, and had been too busy making people redundant to develop their own policies. It seems probable that the effect of much privatisation will be a weakening of existing equal opportunity initiatives. No doubt the policy of the present government is to loosen bureaucracy, but was it also to make the position of women and ethnic minorities more difficult, or was this an unintended consequence? Both EOC and CRE could well mount general investigations to ascertain exactly what happens when privatisation does occur.

10 MATERNITY RIGHTS

10.01 Women enjoy a series of rights intended to protect their position during pregnancy and maternity. These rights have the character of employment protection rather than anti-discrimination provisions. The treatment of pregnancy-related dismissals under the Sex Discrimination Act and Equal Treatment Directive has been discussed in chapter 2. Here we are concerned with the suite of specific statutory protections given to women who are pregnant or who have recently given birth. These rights, which are regulated principally but not solely by the Employment Protection (Consolidation) Act 1978 (EP(C)A 1978) are in the process of being amended by the Trade Union Reform and Employment Rights Act 1993 (TURERA 1993).

Background to the legislation

10.02 The maternity provisions of the TURERA 1993 owe their origins to the Directive on the Introduction of Measures to Encourage Improvements in the Safety and Health at Work of Pregnant Workers and Workers who have Recently Given Birth or are Breastfeeding 92/85/[1] (the Pregnancy Directive) which was adopted by the Council of Ministers on October 19, 1992. The Pregnancy Directive was introduced under Article 118A on the basis of majority voting, as the tenth daughter Directive under the framework Health and Safety Directive 89/391. It is notable that these provisions have been introduced as primary legislation, rather than as delegated legislation under the European Communities Act 1972, thus allowing for Parliamentary debate over the form of the implementation and consequential amendment of other statutes. The implementation date of the maternity provisions of TURERA is likely to be October 1994, two years after the adoption of the Directive.

The first social action programme

10.03 As far back as 1974, the first Social Action Programme called for "action for the purpose of achieving equality between men and women as regards access to employment, vocational training and advancement and to ensure that the family responsibilities of all concerned may be reconciled with their job aspirations." The aim behind the 1983 draft directive on Parental Leave and Leave for Family Reasons, which sprang from the 1974 Programme, was that of enabling working parents to reconcile work with their family responsibilities. It provided for a period of up to

---

[1] [1992] O.J. L348/1.

three months leave to be taken by one of the parents to enable them "to stay at home to take sole or principal charge of his or her child" during the first two years of the child's life. Even though research in Sweden showed that only a modest take-up of such rights was likely, the directive was opposed by the U.K. and in the end was not adopted. On family leave, it would have provided for a limited period of family leave to have been taken by workers for pressing family reasons the illness of a spouse or a child, the death of a near relative etc on terms to be assimilated to paid holiday.

The Social   **10.04**   The Community Charter of Fundamental Social
Charter   Rights of Workers, which was signed by 11 heads of state in 1990, provided that measures should be adopted to enable men and women to reconcile their occupational and family obligations. This led in turn to proposals in the associated Social Action Programme for a Directive on the protection of pregnant women at work, a Recommendation on child care and a Recommendation concerning a code of good conduct on the protection of pregnancy and maternity. In brief, it provides for specific health and safety protection of pregnant and breast feeding women, including protection against dismissal, unqualified by service requirements, together with the right to 14 weeks, maternity leave. The associated Recommendation on a code of good conduct on pregnancy and maternity is not available at the time of writing. The Directive is to be implemented by October 1994, two years after its adoption.

10.05   The Commission has proposed a Council Recommendation on Child Care[2] (not yet adopted at the time of writing), in which it is noted that in all Member States the demand for good quality affordable child care considerably exceeds the existing supply. The draft Recommendation goes on to propose that Member States develop measures to enable women and men to reconcile their occupational obligations with their family obligations arising from the care and upbringing of children. Such measures would include steps to make available affordable, safe and effective child-care, as well as taking steps to ensure that the workplace is organised in such a way as to make it responsive to the needs of workers with children. On the latter point, the Recommendation advocates that both sides of industry, through the process of collective bargaining, should encourage such initiatives. The Recommendation goes on to advise that men should be encouraged to participate more fully in the care and upbringing of children, in order to achieve a more equal sharing of parental responsibilities. The Government is now in the process of introducing 50,000 "out of school" child care places via the agency of the TECs for those parents, "especially mothers", with school age children, who wish to

[2] [1991] O.J. C242/3.

take advantage of training opportunities. The programme will cost 45 million pounds over the next three years.[3]

The Pregnancy Directive

10.06 The provisions of the Pregnancy Directive[4] as regards maternity leave and protection against dismissal associated with pregnancy have been implemented in the Trade Union Reform and Employment Rights Act 1993, but this is unlikely to come into force before October 1994. The result is that a position which was already complicated has been rendered yet more complex. The reason for this is that in some respects the British position is more generous than the Directive, and in others less. Most importantly, the rights to protection against unfair dismissal by reason of pregnancy and the right to return to work are qualified under British law by the need to have worked for the same employer for a minimum of two years. Whilst the period of paid maternity leave is not especially generous by comparison with other Community countries, the right to return to work can be exercised up to 29 weeks after the date at which a woman had given birth. This period of unpaid maternity leave is more generous than is usual in the Community. However, Article 1(3) of the Directive provides that it may not have the effect of reducing the level of protection afforded to pregnant and breastfeeding mothers, as compared with the situation which exists in each Member State on the date on which the Directive is adopted. As the new rights provided for by the Directive are not subject to any qualifying period of service, the TURERA will create a situation where, for example, although the new right to 14 weeks maternity leave is unqualified, the right to return at the end of 29 weeks after the birth of the child can be exercised only by those who have the necessary two years' service. Similarly, any worker dismissed during or at the end of the 14 weeks' maternity leave period will have an automatic right to a statement of the reasons for her dismissal, although after that period the right to a statement of reasons would be exercisable only on request by those who have two years' service.

General maternity rights

10.07 In broad terms women enjoy the following maternity rights:
1. Not to be dismissed unfairly by reason of pregnancy or maternity.
2. To receive statutory maternity pay
3. To return to work 29 weeks after the date of childbirth.
4. To take time off with pay for ante-natal care.

Following the implementation of the Pregnancy Directive women will also enjoy the following further rights:

---

[3] Employment News, no. 214, January, 1993.
[4] For an account of the legislative history of the Directive see the notes by Evelyn Ellis, *Industrial Law Journal*, 22,1,63–67 and by Daniele Muffat-Jeandet, *Industrial Law Journal* 20,2,76.

1. To enjoy a 14 week period of maternity leave
2. To be protected from certain types of health risks specifically related to maternity.

In the following sections we attempt to set out the law as it is prior to the implementation of the Directive by the 1992 TURERA, and section by section to contrast that with the new position.

The right not to be dismissed unfairly

The existing law

10.08 EP(C)A 1978, s.60 presently provides that it is automatically unfair to dismiss a woman because she is pregnant or for a reason connected with her pregnancy.[5] However, to enjoy this right, a woman must have been employed for two years or more if she works 16 hours or more, or for 5 years if she works between 8 and 16 hours a week.[6] For an employee to bring herself within s.60, it is necessary for the employer to know or believe she is pregnant.[7] If a women is dismissed for some other reason, but the employer subsequently learns she is pregnant, that does not bring her within section 60.

10.09 In *Brown* v. *Stockton-on-Tees Borough Council*,[8] the House of Lords held that selection of a woman for redundancy because she is pregnant and will require maternity leave, constituted a "reason connected with pregnancy" within the meaning of section 60. Such words are to be given their ordinary or natural meaning in a redundancy situation. Their Lordships concluded that it would be an abuse of language to say that the reason for her dismissal was not directly and intimately connected with her pregnancy, and went on to state that:

"S.60 must be seen as a part of social legislation passed for the specific protection of women and to put them on an equal footing with men. I have no doubt that it is often a considerable inconvenience to an employer to have to make the necessary arrangements to keep a woman's job open for her whilst she is absent from work in order to have a baby, but this is a price that has to be paid as part of social and legal recognition of the equal status of women in the workplace . . . It cannot surely have been the intended that an employer should be entitled to take advantage of a redundancy situation to weed out his pregnant employees."

---

[5] For example in *George* v. *Beecham Group Ltd* [1977] I.R.L.R. 43 a woman who was on a final written warning for poor attendance was dismissed because of absence associated with a miscarriage. The tribunal found that she was dismissed for a reason connected with pregnancy which was automatically unfair under section 60.

[6] EP(C)A 1978, s.64 and Sched. 13.

[7] *Del Monte Foods* v. *Mundon* [1980] I.C.R. 694, [1980] I.R.L.R. 224, EAT.

[8] [1988] I.R.L.R. 263.

10.10 Such a dismissal will be *automatically* unfair under section 60, but this is not the case if the dismissal occurs because the woman has become incapable of doing her job due to pregnancy[9] or because her employer would contravene a statutory duty or restriction by virtue of her continued employment,[10] unless the employer has failed to offer her any suitable alternative vacancy.[11] Where no such vacancy exists, the dismissal can nonetheless be tested under the normal rules applying under section 57(3). The exception as regards capability applies only to pregnancy as a reason for her incapability and not to other reasons connected with her pregnancy, but in *Grimsby Carpet Co Ltd.* v. *Bedford*,[12] the EAT held that the statutory wording nonetheless covers pregnancy-related incapability. Where a woman ceases to be capable of heavy lifting, for example, that might bring the subsection into action even though such lifting constitutes only a part of the job.[13] The second qualification applies mainly to health and safety related situations, such as, for example, where there is a risk of exposure to ionising radiations.[14]

10.11 Where the employer offers an alternative vacancy, to be suitable, it must take effect immediately on the ending of the contract, (or on the Monday if the contract ends on a Friday, Saturday or Sunday), be such that the work is suitable in relation to the employee and appropriate for her to do in the circumstances and be on terms not substantially less favourable than those obtained in the original contract.[15] It will therefore be automatically unfair for the employer not to offer a suitable vacancy which he knows is available, although there is no obligation to create such a post if it is not available. Whilst the employee will be seeking to establish that there was a suitable alternative vacancy, where the employer alleges that a suitable vacancy was offered it is for him to establish that fact. In the event that a woman does not fulfil the conditions necessary to bring her within section 60, she would still be able to bring an action under section 57, though that will, of course, be subject to the test of reasonableness in section 57(3). An employee may also claim that her dismissal was an act of unlawful sex discrimination, and that issue is discussed in chapter 2.

10.12 A woman who is dismissed during her pregnancy, but before the 11th week prior to the Expected Week of Confinement (EWC), will not qualify for the right to return to work, unless she was dismissed for one of the reasons

---

[9] s.60(1)(*a*).
[10] s.60(1)(*b*).
[11] s.60(2).
[12] [1987] I.R.L.R. 438, [1987] I.C.R. 975.
[13] *Brear* v. *Wright Hudson Ltd* [1977] I.R.L.R. 287, IT.
[14] See chap. 2, n. 170 for a list of remaining health and safety restrictions on the employment of women which survive the 1989 Employment Act.
[15] s.60(3).

specified in section 60(1)(*a*) or (*b*) and has not been
re-engaged.[16] In the event that a woman is dismissed for any
other reason, even though the dismissal may be unfair, the
right to return is lost. The right to return is conditional in
these circumstances upon the woman informing the
employer before the dismissal takes effect, or as soon as
reasonably practicable thereafter, that she intends to return.
If she is dismissed after the eleventh week prior to the
EWC, her right to return up to 29 weeks after confinement
is unaffected and applies whether or not her contract
subsists in the interval. A woman dismissed in the course of
exercising her right to return will be treated as having been
dismissed on the notified day of return.[17] Where a woman is
dismissed in order to avoid liability to pay State Maternity
Pay, the right to SMP is preserved.[18]

Onus of establishing reason for dismissal

10.13   Whilst in unfair dismissal cases the onus of
establishing the reason for dismissal lies upon the employer,
it would be rare indeed for the employer to admit that
pregnancy or maternity was indeed the reason! The
employer will inevitably assert some other reason for the
dismissal, such as misconduct or redundancy and in those
circumstances it is for the applicant to show that pregnancy
or maternity formed a part of the decision, according to the
EAT in *Clayton* v. *Vigers*.[19] In that case, the employer
asserted that the reason for the applicant's dismissal soon
after the birth of her child was the inability of the employer
to find a temporary replacement as a dental nurse in his
practice. The EAT approved the approach of the Court of
Appeal in *Maund* v. *Penwith District Council*, in which an
employee alleged that he had been selected for redundancy
by virtue of this trade union activities. Purchas L.J. held
that in such circumstances "the onus which rests upon the
employee is to show that there is an issue which warrants
investigation, against which an alternative, or competing,
reason may be established. I emphasise that the onus resting
on the employee is not to prove, on a balance of
probabilities, that his contending reason is the principal
reason, but he must prove, on the balance of probabilities,
that the issue exists."[20]

10.14   A maternity leave replacement, who is informed of
her position in writing and who is dismissed to make way
for the return of the person who has been absent on account
of pregnancy or childbirth is deemed to have been dismissed
for some other substantial reason under EP(C)A 1978,
s.57(1)(*b*), but without prejudice to the application of the
reasonableness test contained in s.57(3).[21]

---

[16] s.33(4).
[17] *Infra* n. 16.
[18] SMP Gen. Regs. reg. 3.
[19] [1990] I.R.L.R. 177.
[20] [1984] I.R.L.R. 24 at p. 28.
[21] EP(C)A, s.61(1).

The law as
amended by the
Pregnancy
Directive

10.15   Article 10(1) of the Pregnancy Directive prohibits
the dismissal of pregnant women and women who have
recently given birth, save in exceptional circumstances not
connected with pregnancy which are permitted under
national law, ie in the U.K. context, a non-pregnancy
related fair dismissal. This right is subject to the
requirement that the employer must have been informed of
their condition, as required under national law or practice.
This protection lasts from the beginning of their pregnancy
until the end of the 14 week period of maternity leave
required by the Directive.

10.16   These provisions are being implemented by
TURERA 1993, which provides for an amended section 60
of EP(C)A 1978. The amended section 60(a) provides that
an employee shall be treated as unfairly dismissed if she is
dismissed because she is pregnant or for a reason connected
with her pregnancy. An example of a reason connected with
pregnancy would be a miscarriage or pregnancy-related
illness. Note that these sections are unlikely to come into
effect before October 1994.

10.17   Section 60(b) provides that it shall be unfair if a
woman's 14 week period of maternity leave (as provided for
in Article 8 of the Directive and EP(C)A 1978s 33(1) as
amended by TURERA is ended by dismissal, and the reason
is that she has given birth or for any reason connected with
having given birth. Section 60(c) provides that it is unfair to
dismiss a woman after the end of her maternity leave period
as defined above because she took, or availed herself of the
benefits of, maternity leave. The amended section 60(d)
provides that an employee who gives a medical certificate to
her employee before the end of the 14 week period, stating
that she will be incapable of work after her period of
maternity leave and who is dismissed during the ensuing
four week period, is deemed to be dismissal for a reason
connected with childbirth i.e. in these circumstances there is
an extra 4 weeks protection against unfair dismissal. It is
also unfair by virtue of section 60(f) to dismiss a woman
during or at the end of her 14 week maternity leave by
reason of redundancy if she has not been offered suitable
alternative employment in accordance with the amended
section 38 of EP(C)A 1978, where such employment is
available. In section 60 a reference to a period of maternity
leave is a reference to the period of 14 weeks' maternity
leave introduced by the amended sections 33-38 of EP(C)A,
in accordance with the Directive, rather than to the period
during which she may be absent from work prior to
exercising her right to return under the amended section 39
at the end of 29 weeks after the birth.

10.18   Section 60(e) also renders unfair a dismissal resulting
from a requirement or recommendation that the woman be

suspended from work on medical grounds, in accordance with the amended section 45(1) of EP(C)A.

10.19 The effect of implementing the Directive will be to remove the qualification on the right not to be unfairly dismissed, previously provided by section 60(1)(*a*) in cases where the woman is no longer capable of doing the job, or in section 60(1)(*b*) where her continued employment would be in contravention of a statutory duty or restriction.[22] Most importantly, the new right not to be unfairly dismissed by reason of pregnancy or maternity is not subject to the usual two year qualification period for protection from unfair dismissal. TURERA amends EP(C)A 1978, section 64, which provides for the normal two year qualifying period, by inserting a new section 64(3) and (4), which creates an exception to that requirement where the employee is dismissed for one of the reasons stipulated in section 60 *i.e.* by reason of pregnancy, childbirth or by virtue of the exercise of her rights to maternity leave, except in cases of redundancy governed by section 60(*f*). TURERA also amends EP(C)A section 59, to add pregnancy and childbirth, as defined in the amended section 60(*a*) to (*e*), to the list of reasons which render the selection of an employee for redundancy automatically unfair. This sub-clause gives statutory effect to the decision of the House of Lords in *Brown* v. *Stockton on Tees Borough Council*[23] that the selection of an employee for redundancy because she would require maternity leave was a reason connected with pregnancy.

10.20 Under the amended section 60(*f*) it will be unfair to dismiss a woman who is enjoying her right to 14 weeks' maternity leave by reason of redundancy unless the amended section 38 is complied with. This provides that where redundancy occurs during the period of maternity leave, if it is not practicable for an employer to continue to employ the woman in question under her existing contract of employment, she shall be entitled to be offered a suitable alternative vacancy under a new contract of employment, where such a vacancy exists. The new contract shall be such that the work to be done is suitable to her and appropriate in the circumstances, and the terms and conditions under which it is offered are not to be substantially less favourable than those enjoyed under the previous contract. An employee who does not have two years' service will not, however, be eligible for a redundancy payment.

10.21 It would seem clear that in the terms of the amended s.60, the applicant would have been dismissed for a reason

---

[22] These qualifications fall with the implementation of the Directive and would, in any event following *Dekker*, arguably be contrary to Art. 5 of the Equal Treatment Directive.
[23] [1988] I.R.L.R. 263.

connected with her pregnancy in *Webb* v. *EMO (Air Cargo) Ltd.*[24] In that case, a woman who was engaged as a maternity leave replacement discovered herself to be pregnant and was dismissed because she could not do the job for which she had been engaged. Her lack of service would have been no bar to a successful claim for unfair dismissal under the amended legislation. Nor could an employer argue that in such circumstances the dismissal was reasonable within the terms of EP(C)A, section 57(3), because dismissals which fall within section 60 are automatically unfair and not subject to the test of reasonableness contained in section 57(3).

10.22 Article 2 provides that the rights which arise under the Directive only apply where the employer has been informed of the woman's condition in accord with national law or practice. In Britain, the amended EP(C)A, s.36 provides that if she wishes to take advantage of the right to maternity leave, a woman must inform her employer that she is pregnant and of the expected date of childbirth at least 21 days before the expected date of commencement of maternity leave. Unless a pregnant woman has informed her employer of her condition, it is difficult to see how she could in any event be dismissed on grounds of her pregnancy.

10.23 Thus the Directive, as implemented in TURERA 1993, creates a right not to be unfairly dismissed by reason of pregnancy unqualified by service or capacity to do the job. Even though the Directive speaks of "prohibiting" dismissal during pregnancy, EP(C)A as amended will not prevent such dismissals taking place; it merely makes available the normal remedies for unfair dismissal. Indeed, Article 10(3) calls upon Member States to take the necessary measures to protect workers from the consequences of such unlawful dismissal. The impact of these changes may be quite considerable, in view of the fact that it is obviously the case that potential mothers tend to have shorter service than the majority of employees. Indeed, according to the 1989 Labour Force Survey, 40 per cent. of working women have been continuously employed by the same employer for less than two years, with the figure for mothers of pre-school age children being as much as 56 per cent.

10.24 In the *Dekker* case, the ECJ could be said to have judicially anticipated the Directive, by holding that "(a)s employment can only be refused because of pregnancy to a woman, such a refusal is direct discrimination on grounds of sex." The ECJ went on to hold that such direct discrimination is incapable of justification, even where the proferred justification owes its origin to a national law.

10.25 Article 10(2) of the Pregnancy Directive requires the

[24] [1990] I.C.R. 442.

employer to provide written reasons for the dismissal of any
worker within the scope of the Directive. This requirement
is implemented by TURERA 1993 as a right for any
pregnant worker or woman whose maternity leave period is
ended by dismissal to be provided with written particulars of
the reasons for her dismissal under an amended EP(C)A,
s.53(2A), without the need to make any request for such
reasons and irrespective of her length of service. Beyond that
date the normal rules apply as to the provision of a written
statement of reasons for dismissal.

The right to maternity leave and maternity pay

10.26 Prior to the Pregnancy Directive, women did not
explicitly enjoy a right to a period of maternity leave. Whilst
women have had a right, provided they fulfilled the
necessary conditions, to receive statutory maternity pay
(SMP) for up to 18 weeks if they were absent from work
due to pregnancy or childbirth, and to return to work up to
29 weeks after childbirth, again provided they fulfilled the
necessary but different conditions, they did not explicitly
enjoy a right to a legally designated period of maternity
leave.

10.27 Following the implementation of the Pregnancy
Directive, women will enjoy a statutory right to an explicit
14 week period of maternity leave, and any references to
maternity leave in this chapter refer to that new right. It
must be expected that there will be a period of confusion as
the everyday vocabulary of employers and workers adjusts to
this change and begins to limit references to maternity leave
to the new Community induced right.

The existing right to statutory maternity pay

10.28 The present regime of maternity payments dates
from 1987. Prior to 1978, all pregnant women were eligible
for 18 weeks' maternity allowance, but in 1978 working
women who satisfied the eligibility conditions became
entitled to a period of 6 weeks maternity pay paid by their
employer at nine tenths of their previous normal earnings.
The employer was responsible for the higher rate payment,
but could offset from it the lower National Insurance rates
of allowance and recover the entire cost from the Maternity
Pay Fund. This situation was rationalised in 1987 to make
the employer responsible for the entire payment of statutory
maternity pay, although as with statutory sick pay, the
employer could set the cost of such payments against his
liability to make National Insurance contributions. The
result is that statutory maternity pay is now administered by
the employer, but not paid for by him, with the pattern of a
higher rate of payment for the first six weeks and a lower
rate for the subsequent 12 weeks being preserved. The
standard 18 weeks of state maternity allowance is still
available to women not satisfying the conditions of eligibility
for SMP.

Social Security
Act conditions

10.29 A woman is eligible for statutory maternity pay if she satisfies the conditions laid down in the Social Security Act 1986, (SSA 1986) s.46, in that

(*a*) she has been continuously employed as an employed earner for National Insurance purposes for a period of 26 weeks ending at the end of the fifteenth week prior to the expected week of confinement (EWC) but has ceased to work for him wholly or partly because of pregnancy or confinement.[25] It is worth observing that though a woman need only work until the end of the fifteenth week before confinement to be eligible for SMP she must stay on until the eleventh week to be able to enjoy the right to return, a confusing distinction which may lead to women disqualifying themselves from the latter right.

(*b*) her normal weekly earnings for the eight weeks prior to the qualifying week are not less than the current lower earnings limit for National Insurance contributions (£54 for 1992/93),[26] and

(*c*) her pregnancy has continued up to, or she has been confined before reaching, the beginning of the eleventh week prior before the EWC.[27] and

(*d*) she gives her employer notice (in writing if requested) that she is going to be absent from work wholly or partly because of pregnancy or confinement at least 21 days before her absence from work is due to begin, or as soon as is reasonably practicable.[28] A pregnant woman is also required to furnish evidence to her employer of her expected week of confinement on form Mat B1 signed by a midwife or medical practitioner.[29]

10.30 The calculation of continuity of employment for the purposes of SMP is broadly similar to the calculation of continuity for the purposes of the EP(C)A, although there are detailed differences, *i.e.* if a woman does not work due to a trade dispute she must prove that she had no interest in it, as opposed to having taken part in it, if that week is to count as a week of continuous employment.[30] Likewise, a woman who is dismissed during a stoppage of work must show she had no interest in the dispute if she is to preserve her continuity of employment, even if she is subsequently re-employed.[31]

10.31 A woman who leaves her employment before the qualifying week will normally lose her entitlement to

[25] s.46(2)(*a*).
[26] s.46(2)(*b*).
[27] s.46(2)(*c*).
[28] s.46 (4) &(5).
[29] SMP Gen Regs, reg. 22 and SMP (Medical Evidence) Regs 1987 S.I. 1987 No. 235.
[30] SMP Gen Regs, reg. 13(1).
[31] SMP Gen Regs, reg. 13(2)&(3).

SMP, unless her employment is terminated by the employer for the purpose of avoiding liability to pay SMP.[32] Similarly, a woman who has been in employment for at least eight weeks and is dismissed for a reason falling within EP(C)A, s.60(1)(a) or (b) and who is not offered a new contract under section 60(3), or who declines to accept it and who would, but for her dismissal, have been employed for at least 26 weeks by the qualifying week, will not lose her entitlement to SMP.[33] Neither is this so if she was confined before the qualifying week but would have had 26 weeks' service before the expected qualifying week.

10.32 An eligible employee is entitled to SMP for 18 weeks, to begin not earlier than 11 weeks prior to the EWC, except in cases of premature birth.[34] The mother-to-be has a discretion as to when to leave work, but if she continues after the sixth week before the EWC, she will lose the right to SMP for any week during any part of which she is employed.[35] Any weeks lost will be lost at the lower rate. For an employee who has served for two years prior to the EWC and whose normal working hours are not less than 16, or who has been employed for 5 years or more at not less than 8 hours per week,[36] the first six weeks of SMP are paid at the higher rate of nine tenths of her normal weekly earnings[37]. The remainder of the 18 week period is payable at the lower rate, which is £47.95 per week for 1993/94. Women not eligible for the higher rate, but who are otherwise qualified will be entitled to receive 18 weeks SMP at the lower rate, normally payable weekly or monthly. It is inadvisable to pay SMP as a lump sum, because a woman may become disentitled to it during the course of the 18 week period. For example, SMP is not payable during any week in which the employee worked for the liable employer, or, after her confinement, for any other employer.[38] In the latter case, the liability to pay SMP ceases for the remainder of the period.[39] There is no liability to pay SMP to a woman during any week in which she is outside the E.C. and if a woman should be held in custody she loses the right to SMP as from that week.

---

[32] SMP Gen Regs, reg. 3(1).
[33] SMP Gen Regs, reg. 4(1).
[34] SSA, s.47(1).
[35] SSA, s.47(4).
[36] SSA, s.48(5) but if a woman has been employed for two years for not less than 16 hours per week, she will be deemed to have worked for 16 hours per week if she has worked for not less than 8 hours per week in any period prior to the EWC. A period of continuous employment of not less than 16 hours per week is deemed not to be broken by a period of up to 26 weeks where her employment was for not less than 8 hours. SMP Gen Regs, reg. 16(2) & (3).
[37] SSA, s.48(2).
[38] SSA, s.47(4)–(6).
[39] SMP Gen Regs, reg. 8(2).

10.33 Employers are entitled to recoup payments of SMP from their liability to make National Insurance contributions under the SMP (Compensation of Employers) Regulations.[40] Employers are, of course, obliged to keep records relating to SMP showing the date when it was first paid, the weeks for which it was paid and the amount of such payments, together with details of weeks for which no payment was paid and the reasons for such non-payment.[41]

The new right to 14 weeks' maternity leave

10.34 The Pregnancy Directive, Article 8(1) requires Member States to take measures to provide that pregnant women shall enjoy an uninterrupted period of at least 14 weeks of maternity leave, regardless of their length of service or the hours which they work. This requirement will be implemented by the amended sections 33–38 of EP(C)A 1978. It is important to note that, although there are no service or hours restrictions placed upon the new right to maternity leave, this is not the case, for the right to return to work later than the end of the maternity leave period of 14 weeks.

10.35 The requirements of the Directive will be implemented in the amended Part III of EP(C)A. Section 34 as amended will provide that an employee's maternity leave period will commence with the date which she notifies to her employer as the date at which she intends to commence her period of absence from work,[42] in accordance with section 36, or if earlier, the first day on which she is absent from work wholly or partly because of pregnancy or childbirth, where that day occurs after the beginning of the eleventh week prior to the expected date of confinement,[43] or with the day on which childbirth occurs, if that is earlier.[44]

10.36 The amended section 35(1) provides that the period of maternity leave will run for a period of fourteen weeks from the date of commencement of the maternity leave period. Should a woman be dismissed before the end of that period, her maternity leave will end with the date of her dismissal under section 35(3). Subject to section 35(3), any period in which a pregnant woman is unable to resume her employment at the end of the maternity leave due to a statutory requirement other than a requirement specified in an order made under the amended section 45(3) (suspension on medical grounds on full pay[45]) shall be added to the

[40] S.I. 1987 No. 91.
[41] SMP Gen Regs, Reg. 26.
[42] 34(1)(*a*).
[43] 34(1)(*b*).
[44] 34(2).
[45] See paras. 10.80–10.82 for a discussion of the new provisions made with regard to medical suspension of pregnant workers following a risk

period of maternity leave, according to section 35(2), and
during that period her employment rights continue to accrue
under section 33(1) (see below).

10.37   The right to maternity leave is subject to the
requirement in the amended section 36 that the employee
shall have informed her employer in writing that she is
pregnant and of the expected date of confinement at least 21
days prior to the commencement of the period of maternity
leave, or as soon as is reasonably practicable. If requested,
the employee shall produce a certificate from a midwife or
medical practitioner stating the expected date of childbirth.
The provisions of section 36 reflect the requirement in
Article 2 that in order to benefit from the provisions of the
Directive a woman must have informed her employer of her
condition, in accordance with national legislation or practice.

10.38   During an employee's period of maternity leave,
Article 11(2)(a) of the Directive requires that any rights
connected with the employment contract be "ensured"
during the 14 week period of maternity leave provided for
under Article 8(1), except those with regard to pay. Article
11(2)(b) provides for the maintenance of a payment to and/or
entitlement to an allowance at least equivalent to the sick
pay which such a worker would receive, *i.e.* in the case of a
firm which does not pay contractual sick pay, only SMP. It
follows, however, that where such a firm does pay full pay,
or enhanced statutory sick pay, for a certain period to
employees of the relevant category who are off sick,
maternity pay can be no less generous. Thus there will be a
need to review maternity payment schemes, at least in order
to bring them into line with sick pay.

10.39   In this context it should be noted that, following the
decision of the House of Lords in *Webb*, any detrimental
action against a woman on grounds of her being pregnant is
necessarily discriminatory. It follows that if the terms on
which maternity leave is taken are less favourable than those
which are usual for other forms of legitimate absence, this
could amount to direct discrimination on grounds of
pregnancy. If, therefore, contractual sick pay provisions are
more generous than contractual maternity pay provisions, it
could be argued that the difference is attributable to a
condition which is specific to women ie the capacity to be
pregnant. The Advocate General in the *Dekker* and *Hertz*
cases drew a distinction between dismissal because of
pregnancy or maternity, and matters which concern the
granting of payments for maternity pay, for which the
Member States are free to set conditions.[46] Yet this

assessment of the workplace. It is difficult to know what grounds for
suspension could fall within this sub-section which will not be covered by
the new risk assessment procedures under amended s.45(3).
[46] Cases 177 &179/88 [1990] I.R.L.R. 27 at para. 27.

distinction appears unconvincing if it is used to justify worse terms for maternity leave than apply to sickness or other forms of consensual absence. Rubenstein argues that such a distinction must be drawn to avoid the opposite embarrassing situation where an employer would be obliged to pay full contractual remuneration to workers who are absent on maternity leave, when workers who are absent sick may not be eligible for any contractual sick pay at all.[47] However, Article 11(2) of the Pregnancy Directive appears to resolve this difficulty during the maternity leave period, in that it provides that whereas the non-pay rights of employees absent on maternity leave must be ensured, it is only necessary to ensure that such employees are entitled to the maintenance of a payment or maternity allowance equivalent to that which such a worker would receive if she were away sick.

10.40 What about the period, however, between the end of the maternity leave period and the end of the 29 week period in which qualifying women will retain the right to return? An employee who is absent on account of pregnancy or childbirth whose contract subsists may should be entitled to receive an allowance equivalent to SSP or contractual sick pay until that entitlement runs out, on the argument that if she is not paid because she is absent, she should receive a payment equivalent to those who are absent in other comparable circumstances, *i.e.* the long term sick. Such an argument could only apply, however, to those whose contracts subsist,[48] for otherwise no comparison can be made with the treatment of other employees. Employees who are simply absent in the expectation that they may exercise their statutory right to return in due course, as in *McKnight* v. *Addlestones (Jewellers) Ltd*,[49] would not enjoy the right to any allowance during that period.

10.41 The amended section 33(1) provides that an employee who is absent on maternity leave, as defined in section 34 and 35, shall be entitled to the benefit of the terms and conditions which would have been applicable to her had she not been absent, except, as provided by the amended section 33(2), with regard to pay. It follows that rights to other service related benefits, such as holidays, continue to accrue. Whether rights to, say, holiday pay, will fall within the "pay" exception contained in the amended section 33(2) is unclear. Recent European case law points to a wide definition of "pay", which would include all fringe benefits to which a financial value could be attached. Pensions benefits and contributions are to be maintained as provided by the Social Security Act 1989, sched. 5, para. 5 as regards "unfair maternity provisions" (discussed below).

[47] EOR 42 at p. 26.
[48] See *Institute for the Motor Industry* v. *Harvey* [1992] I.R.L.R. 343.
[49] [1984] I.R.L.R. 453.

If a woman continues to be absent after the end of her 14 weeks' period of maternity leave, but is intending to exercise a contractual right to return or her statutory right to return up to 29 weeks after the birth of the baby, she does not enjoy the protection of the amended section 33(1) as regards the accumulation of her rights, but such absence does not break her continuity of employment.[50]

10.42 Nonetheless, the amended section 33(3) provides that an employee who has both the statutory right to maternity leave and a corresponding contractual right, may take advantage of whichever right is, in any particular respect, the more favourable.[51] Thus, the statutory provisions are a floor and employees may enjoy superior contractual terms with respect to maternity leave, reflecting the terms of Article 1(3) which precludes the reduction of already established rights. It is, of course, not possible to diminish the statutory right to maternity leave by endeavouring to agree what would be adverse contractual terms from the point of view of the employee.

10.43 Under Article 11(2) of the Pregnancy Directive, an employee who is enjoying maternity leave is entitled to the maintenance of payment and/or an adequate allowance, the latter being defined as being at least equivalent to that which the worker would have received as a payment in the event of sickness. The 1990 draft Directive had proposed that the minimum payment be not less than 80 per cent. of the beneficiary's salary over the 14 week period of maternity leave, but this was modified in the course of negotiation in the Council to allow for a minimum allowance at least equivalent to national sick pay. As the Directive allows that entitlement to be subject to national eligibility conditions, workers earning less than the National Insurance threshold may not benefit from the Directive in this respect. This could affect many part-time a low paid women, who would thereby continue to be excluded from the receipt of an allowance. Legislation may need to be introduced by the end of 1994 to ensure that the terms of SMP are at least equivalent to SSP.

10.44 Article 12 of the Directive requires that workers shall be able to pursue claims arising from the Directive by judical process, but there are no specific remedies provided for under TURERA should a woman be denied her right to accumulation of benefit.

Paternity and family leave **10.45** The proposal for an E.C. directive on parental and family leave was opposed by the U.K. and is unlikely to be

---

[50] See p.16 *infra*.
[51] See *infra* the discussion of the right to return for a discussion of such composite rights.

given legislative effect in the foreseeable future. There are permitted derogations from the Equal Treatment Directive in respect of arrangements for the protection of women, particularly as regards pregnancy and childbirth, a situation mirrored in the Sex Discrimination and Equal Pay Acts in respect of special treatment with regard to pregnancy and childbirth. No action relying on these enactments is likely therefore to be successful in establishing a right to paternity leave, nor to any form of extended family leave on account of the illness of any child of the family in respect of either parent. Some employers, particularly in the public sector, and to a less extent in finance and retailing, do provide such facilities, but the practice is by no means widespread. Where such benefits cannot be brought within the exceptions with regard to the protection of women, as in *Hoffman* v. *Barmer Ersatzkasse*[52] (six months maternity leave was held to fall within the pregnancy and childbirth exception), it would be potentially discriminatory to distinguish between the treatment accorded to mothers and fathers. However, in the *Commission* v. *Italy*[53], the reception of an adopted child into the family was equated with the birth of a natural child, so that the refusal of paternity leave to the adoptive father was held to fall outside the maternity exception.

The right to take time off for ante-natal care

The present position

10.46 EP(C)A, s.31A, provides that an employer may not unreasonably refuse paid time off for ante-natal care.[54] Once an employer has accepted that it is reasonable to allow a woman time off for ante-natal care, he may not refuse to pay her, although an employer may be able to argue that it was reasonable for him to refuse time off during working hours where it was reasonably possible for the employee to have made arrangements for ante-natal care outside working hours.[55] On second and subsequent appointments, the employer may request that the woman furnishes a certificate showing that she is pregnant from a midwife, health visitor or medical practitioner and an appointment card.[56] An employee may make a complaint to an industrial tribunal that she was unreasonably refused such time off, if the complaint is presented within three months of the date of the appointment.[57] If the complaint is successful, the tribunal may make a declaration and award compensation of an amount equal to the pay which would have been due.[58] Such time off is to be paid at an appropriate hourly rate, that rate being the amount of one week's pay divided by the normal working hours for the week in question on the day when the time off is taken, or where the number of hours varies from week to week, an average struck over the

[52] Case 184/83 [1984] E.C.R. 3407; [1985] I.C.R. 731.
[53] Case 163/82 [1983] E.C.R. 3273; [1984] 1 C.M.L.R. 44.
[54] s.31A(1) &(4).
[55] *Gregory* v. *Tudsbury Ltd* [1982] I.R.L.R. 267, IT.
[56] s.31A(2) & (3).
[57] s.31A(6) & (7).
[58] s.31A(8).

previous twelve weeks or such shorter period as the
employee has worked.[59]

**The position
under the
Directive**

10.47 Article 5(5) of the Directive requires Member States
to take measures to provide that pregnant workers shall
benefit from a period of leave without loss of pay when
attending medical examination before birth, in cases where
such examinations can take place during during working
hours only. This requirement seems to add nothing to the
prior position in the U.K. and no amendments to EPCA,
s.31A are made by TURERA.

**The right to
return to work**

10.48 At the time when the Pregnancy Directive was
adopted, of all the Community countries, Britain enjoyed the
longest period during which a woman might exercise a right
to return to work, though the extent of paid time off was
not, by comparison, generous. This period, amounting in all
to up to 40 weeks, during which a woman might exercise
her right to return is, however, balanced by the need to have
served the liable employer for the longest period in the
Community two years before that right is enjoyed. Thus, the
introduction through the Pregnancy Directive of a right to
return with no prior service requirements marks a
substantial shift in the UK position, notwithstanding that
this new right must be exercised after a much shorter 14
week period of maternity leave. The result will be a two
tiered system of rights to return, which may be confusing to
both employers and employees, with disparate service and
notice provisions. The right to return at the end of 29 weeks
will be in some respects amended by TURERA, but the
broad structure and, in particular, the notice requirements
will remain unchanged.

**The present right
to return at the
end of 29 weeks**

10.49 The right to return after 29 weeks is complex and set
about with inflexible qualifying conditions, making this
valuable right somewhat of a trap for the unwary. The
return to work provisions have been criticised as being

> "of inordinate complexity exceeding the worst excesses of
> a taxing statute; we find that especially regrettable bearing
> in mind that they are regulating the everyday rights of
> ordinary employers and employees. We feel no confidence
> that, even with the detailed assistance of skilled advocates,
> we have now correctly understood them: it is difficult to
> see how an ordinary employer or employee is expected to
> do so."[60]

10.50 Any consideration of these provisions can only lend
substance to the above contentions. Unfortunately, the

---

[59] s.31A (5).

[60] *Per* Browne-Wilkinson J. (as he then was) in the EAT, in remarks
subsequently endorsed by the Court of Appeal in *Lavery* v. *Plessey
Telecommunications Ltd.* [1982] I.R.L.R. 180 at p. 182.

amendments made following the Pregnancy Directive will do little to redeem this position. Indeed, by imposing another layer of rights, with only minimal amendments made to the existing law, the new position may be thought to be still more complex.

10.51   The right to return to work under EP(C)A 1978, s.45 is

> "a right to return to work with her original employer, or where appropriate, his successor, at any time before the end of the period of 29 weeks beginning with the week in which the date of confinement falls, in the job in which she was employed under the original contract of employment and on terms and conditions not less favourable than those which would have been applicable to her if she had not been so absent."

(i) When is the right exercisable?   The right to return to work can be exercised at any time up to 29 weeks after the week in which the date of confinement falls. Thus, if a baby is born earlier than the EWC it is important to bear in mind that the period of 29 weeks runs from the actual date of confinement. Thus in *F.W.Woolworths plc* v. *Smith*[61] the mother concerned lost the benefit of her statutory right to return in part because, though she gave notice of her intention to return more than 21 days before the expiry of 29 weeks from the date of the EWC, it was less than 21 days from the expiry of 29 weeks from the date of her actual confinement, which had occurred 9 days earlier than expected.

(ii) To what "job" is she entitled to return?   Under section 45(1) a woman is entitled to return to "the job" in which she was employed under the original contract of employment. "Job" is defined in section 153(1) as meaning "the nature of the work which she is employed to do in accordance with her contract of employment and the capacity and place in which she is so employed."

The emphasis in the definition of "job" is on the terms used in the employee's contract of employment rather than the tasks which are actually performed. It follows that where the contract draws the job definition in broad terms, the employer can have considerable flexibility in the allocation of actual tasks to the employee on her return. In many cases, the employee only has the job title specified in the statement of terms issued under EP(C)A section 1(3)(*f*). For example, in *Edgell* v. *Lloyds Register of Shipping*,[62] the complainant was described as a "book-keeper grade 13". Even though

---

[61] [1990] I.C.R. 45, EAT.
[62] [1977] I.R.L.R. 463.

the employee was given a job with less responsibility on her return, as she was still within the parameters of a "book-keeper grade 13", she had no grounds on which to object.

(iii) On what terms is she entitled to return? A woman is entitled to return on "terms not less favourable than those which would have been applicable to her had she not been absent."[63] It follows that a woman who returns is entitled to the benefit of any general pay increases made in her absence, but conversely, if conditions have deteriorated, she must accept these.

Terms for return   10.52   Her period of absence will not break her continuity of service as regards seniority, pension rights and other similar rights, according to section 45(2). This requirement was, however, made subject to the requirements of the Social Security Act 1989 Continuity of Service, Sched. 5, para. 5 as regards "unfair maternity provisions." In this respect, the 1989 Social Security Act implements the provisions of the Occupational Social Security Directive 86/378. Full Implementation of schedule 5 has been postponed pending their solution of the issues in the *coloroll* cases. Under Schedule 5, para. 5, an employer is required to treat a woman who is paid whilst absent from work on account of pregnancy or childbirth as she would have been treated if she had worked normally and been paid accordingly, but such a woman shall only be required to pay contributions related to the amount of contractual remuneration or SMP actually paid. Note that such a requirement will only be operative whilst the woman is in receipt of maternity pay, which in the case of SMP is for only 18 of her maximum of 40 weeks' potential absence before and after childbirth.

10.53   Not only does any period of pregnancy-related absence not break the continuity of service of any woman who is qualified for the statutory right of return, but if she returns after such a period in exercise of her section 45 rights, her period of absence counts towards her total of continuous employment.[64] It follows that a woman who returns otherwise than in the exercise of section 45 rights does not enjoy this statutory protection of the accumulation of her continuous employment. However, a woman dismissed in the course of exercising those rights will be held to have been unfairly dismissed under section 56, and her employment will be deemed continuous up to that date.

---

[63] In *McFadden* v. *Greater Glasgow Passenger Transport Executive* [1977] I.R.L.R. 327 on her return a woman was offered work on the same grade but as a supernumerary. The tribunal held that these were less favourable terms by virtue of the fact that she no longer had her own desk, had lost status and was more vulnerable to redundancy.
[64] EP(C)A 1978, Sched. 13, para. 10.

Where a woman's contract subsists during her absence her continuity of employment would, of course, accumulate in any event.[65] Where the contract does not subsist and she does not satisfy the statutory conditions for the right to return under section 45 her continuity would be be broken, unless her case falls within the provisions of Schedule 13, para. 9(1)(*d*), which relates to absence from work on account of sickness and injury. To obtain the benefit of this provision, it is necessary for an absence of not more than 26 weeks to be preceded and followed by periods of qualifying employment.

Right to return part-time?

10.54   Though there is no statutory right to return on different terms under the maternity provisions of EP(C)A, many women do want to return part-time. An unwarranted insistence on full-time work may be held to be contrary to section 1(1)(*b*) of the Sex Discrimination Act as constituting an act of indirect discrimination. In *The Home Office* v. *Holmes*[66], the EAT held that full-time work could constitute a requirement with which a smaller proportion of women could comply than men. In *Holmes*, such a requirement as regards a clerical officer in the Civil service was held not to be justifiable on its facts, although in *Greater Glasgow Health Board* v. *Carey*[67] it was held to be justifiable to require a health visitor to return full-time, in order to ensure continuity of care throughout the week. Thus there can be no legal certainty that a woman who finds that she only wants to work part-time with a new baby will be able to insist on doing so, though no doubt many employers are prepared to be flexible, at least in times of labour shortage.

What service requirements qualify this right?

10.55   An employee who is absent from work wholly or partly because of pregnancy or confinement enjoys the right to return whether or not her contract of employment subsists during her period of absence, but she must have been continuously employed (whether or not she is at work) for two years or more by the beginning of the eleventh week prior to the EWC.[68] Such employment must normally be for 16 hours or more per week, or if she has been employed for more than five years, between eight and sixteen hours per week.[69] It is obvious that many young women do not satisfy these criteria and are not able to benefit from the right to return under section 45.

---

[65] In the *Institute of the Motor Industry* v. *Harvey* [1992] I.C.R. 470; [1992] I.R.L.R. 343, EAT the EAT has held that a woman's contract of employment is likely to continue when she goes on maternity leave, unless it is terminated by agreement, resignation or dismissal.

[66] [1984] I.R.L.R. 299; [1984] I.C.R. 678.

[67] [1987] I.R.L.R. 484.

[68] EP(C)A, s.33(3).

[69] EP(C)A 1978, Sched. 13, paras. (4)-(6). Where there is a period of not more than 26 weeks within a period of continuous employment of more than 16 hours per week in which the employee's contract normally involves work for between eight and sixteen house per week, that period shall not break the employee's period of continuous employment and shall count in computing the total period.

What notice requirements must be complied with?

10.56 The notice requirements which qualify the right to return under section 45 are precise, demanding and absolute. They constitute a considerable hazard for the potential returner, in that the courts have generally taken a strict view of the need to comply with them.

(i) The woman must inform her employer in writing at least 21 days before her absence begins, or if that is not reasonably practicable, as soon as is reasonably practicable that:
- (a) she will be absent from work wholly or mainly because of pregnancy or confinement,
- (b) that she intends to return to work with her employer, and
- (c) of the EWC, or if the confinement has occurred, the date of confinement.[70]

Even though women may find it difficult to make up their mind about their intentions to return to work, bearing in mind the unknown nature of the responsibilities of motherhood for those having their first child, the question of whether it was reasonably practicable to give notice of their intention to return to work by the due date has been approached by the courts on lines similar to those adopted with regard to unfair dismissal. Thus, in *Nu-Swift International* v. *Mallinson*[71], the employee told her employers she was pregnant. In response to the employer's questions about whether she intended to return to work, she said that she thought she did not, because she had fears about her baby's health. She changed her mind, but did not give notice of her intention to return until the day upon which she left. The EAT held by analogy with the situation with regard to unfair dismissal applications[72] that if the employee was put on notice as to her rights and as to the time limit, then it was "reasonably practicable" for her to comply with the time limit. The EAT went on to hold that the provision was not intended to cover those who change their minds or are not sure either way. It would, therefore, be prudent for any woman who is otherwise qualified for maternity leave to give the requisite notice, unless she is quite certain that she does not want to return.

An employee who is dismissed, by reason of her incapacity to do her job or by reason of a statutory restriction, to whom any suitable alternative vacancy has not been offered, *i.e.* unfairly by virtue of section 60(1)(*a*) or (*b*), and who, but for the dismissal, would have been employed until the 11th week prior to the EWC, shall retain the right to return to work, provided she gives the requisite notice under section 33 before or as soon as is reasonably practicable after the dismissal.[73]

---

[70] EP(C)A, s.33(3)(*d*).
[71] [1979] I.C.R. 229, [1979] I.R.L.R. 29, EAT.
[72] *Dedman* v. *British Building and Engineering Appliances Ltd.* [1974] I.C.R. 53.
[73] EP(C)A, s.33(4).

(ii) An employer may request written confirmation of the employee's continued intention to return to work not earlier than the forty ninth day after the EWC or the actual date of confinement. If such a request is made, the employee must give written confirmation within two weeks of receiving it, or as soon as is reasonably practicable thereafter, on pain of losing the right to return.[74] The request for confirmation must be accompanied by a statement of the effects of not complying with the request.[75] These sections were added by the Employment Act 1980 in response to employer concerns about the effects of section 33(3) in leading employees to indicate that they intend to return, even though they were by no means serious in those intentions.

(iii) An employee must give at least 21 days' notice in writing of the date on which she intends to return -the notified day of return.[76] Originally the requirement was for only 7 days" notice and did not need to be in writing, but this was extended to 21 days by the Employment Act 1980, in response to employer concerns. The requirements under this section were interpreted strictly by the Court of Appeal in *Lavery* v. *Plessey Communications Ltd*,[77] in which a woman whose baby had arrived a couple of weeks later than expected rang her employer only five days before the date at which she and they had originally expected her to come back. The employers took the view that they need not give her job back as she had given only five days' notice of her intended return. Her claim for unfair dismissal under section 56, arising from the claim that she was not permitted to exercise her right to return to work in accordance with section 47, was rejected because she had not complied with the notice requirements then obtaining under section 47. This was in spite of the fact that because the baby was late she would still have had time to comply in full with the notice requirements.

Postponement of notified date of return   10.57   Both the employer and the employee have the right to delay the right to return. The employer may postpone the right to return for up to four weeks after the notified day of return, provided that he specifies the reasons for the postponement and states that she will be able to return on the postponed date.[78] The employer may postpone the return for any reason, and although he must state that reason, it need not necessarily be in writing.

---

[74] EP(C)A, s.33(3A).
[75] s.33(3B).
[76] EP(C)A, s.47(1).
[77] [1982] I.R.L.R. 180, EAT; [1983] I.R.L.R. 202, C.A. And see also the decision of the EAT in Scotland in *Kolfor Plant Ltd.* v. *Wright* [1982] I.R.L.R. 311.
[78] EP(C)A, s.47(2) &(8).

How long can the woman delay her return?

10.58 The employee may delay her return by up to four weeks after the notified date of return, notwithstanding that that date falls after the end of the period of 29 weeks from the week in which the date of confinement falls.[79] She may also delay the notified date of return by up to four weeks, provided that she returns not later than four weeks after the expiry of the 29 week period as defined above.[80] The employee may only postpone her return if she provides a medical certificate stating that she is incapable of work on the notified date of return or on the expiry of the 29 week period, as the case may be, on grounds of disease or bodily or mental disablement.[81] Only one such exercise of her right to postponement is permissible in connection with any one return to work.[82] If the woman concerned is still not well at the end of her four week period and unable to return to work she will lose her right to return. In *Kelly* v. *Liverpool Maritime Terminals Ltd*,[83] a woman found that her pregnancy had exacerbated a previous back injury. She sent in a medical certificate covering the first four weeks beyond the notified date of return, but because she was still unwell, in due course she sent in two further medical certificates. The employer wrote informing her that her rights under section 45 had lapsed and that she would not be able to return to work. An industrial tribunal rejected her claim to have been unfairly dismissed under section 56, a decision which was upheld both by the EAT and the Court of Appeal, on the ground that her second medical certificate could not be understood as constituting a return to work coupled with an immediate request for sick leave. The moral would appear to be that a woman who finds herself in such a situation would be well advised to do her best to return to work, even if she subsequently needs to go off sick. It follows that the child's illness or difficulties in arranging suitable child care cannot be valid reasons for seeking an extension of the right to return. If an employee has notified a day of return, but there is an interruption of work, whether or not this is due to industrial action, which renders it unreasonable for the employee to expect to return to work on the due date, she may return to work when work resumes, or as soon as possible thereafter.[84]

10.59 Where an employee has not notified an expected date of return, but an interruption of work renders it unreasonable to expect the employee to return to work within 29 weeks of the week containing the date of confinement, she may return within 28 days of the end of the period of interruption.[85]

---

[79] EP(C)A, s.47(3)(*a*) &(8).
[80] EP(C)A, s.47(3)(*b*) and (7).
[81] EP(C)A, s.47(3).
[82] EP(C)A, s.47(4).
[83] [1988] I.R.L.R. 310, C.A.
[84] EP(C)A, s.47(5) & (8).
[85] EP(C)A, s.47(6) & (7).

What are the consequences of not permitting a qualified woman to return?

10.60 The remedies available to an employee who is not permitted to return to work are those provided under sections 47, 56 and 86 and Schedule 2 of EP(C)A.[86] Under s.56, an employee who is entitled to return to work and who has exercised her right of return in accordance with section 47, but who is not permitted to return to work, shall be treated for the purpose of the maternity provisions as having been continuously employed until the notified day of return, and as if she had been dismissed with effect from that day, for the reason that she was not permitted to return to work.[87] Thus where, for example, an employer refuses to take back a returnee because the work has been reorganised, the employer's reason for dismissal might be of the business reorganisation type under section 57(1)(*b*). The reasonableness of that decision will fall to be judged under section 57(3) as modified by Sched. 2 para. 2(1). That modified test calls for the reasonableness of the employer's actions in dismissing the employee to be assessed as "if she had not been absent from work." Section 86 provides similarly with regard to redundancy under Part VI. A woman who resigns in protest at the terms on which she is to be allowed to return is not dismissed in the course of returning, and will therefore not be able to bring a claim under section 56, although, provided her contract has persisted through her period of absence, she is not precluded from bringing a case under section 55 if she can legitimately complain that she has been constructively dismissed.[87]

10.61 The provisions of section 56 are subject to section 56A, which excludes section 56 in cases where the employer, together with any associated employer, does not employ more than five people and it is not reasonably practicable to permit her to return to work.[89] It also excludes section 56 in cases where it is not reasonably practicable to permit her to return to work for a reason other than redundancy and the employee unreasonably refuses an offer of suitable alternative employment on terms which are not substantially less favourable.[90]

10.62 Where a woman is made redundant in circumstances covered by section 45(3) (no offer of an existing suitable alternative vacancy) Sched.2, para. 2(2) provides that the dismissal, which by virtue of section 56 is treated as having taken place, shall be treated as automatically unfair. Where it is not practicable to allow the employee to return by virtue of a genuine redundancy situation, section 45(3) prescribes

---

[86] EP(C)A, s.46.

[87] EP(C)A, s.56.

[88] *Institute of the Motor Industry* v. *Harvey* [1992] I.R.L.R. 343, EAT. The EAT held that her contract had persisted through her absence, but in view of a dispute as to terms the applicant did not notify her date of return and therefore failed to exercise her statutory right.

[89] EP(C)A, s.56A(1).

[90] EP(C)A, s.56A(2) &(3).

that the employee must not unreasonably refuse an offer of any suitable available vacancy. Such a vacancy must be suitable and appropriate in the circumstances, and on terms not substantially less favourable than she enjoyed under the old contract. Any failure to make such an offer of an existing vacancy will be treated as automatically unfair by virtue of Sched. 2, para. 3. Thus in *Community Task Force* v. *Rimmer*,[91] the employer did not make an offer of an available vacancy because the consequence of doing so would have been that the organisation would have ceased to be eligible for certain monies from the Manpower Services Commission, as the employee would not have satisfied the eligibility rules as to prior unemployment. Nonetheless, the dismissal was held to be unfair because the test set down in section 45(3) is not qualified by considerations of what is economic or reasonable. Where no such vacancy is available, the employee will be redundant in the normal way and eligible for a redundancy payment. The date on which the employee will be deemed to have been made redundant is the day on which she would have been made redundant if that day is earlier than the notified date of return.[92] Such an employee may, of course, complain that her selection for redundancy was unfair in the normal way.

What is the relation between statutory and contractual rights to return?

10.63 Employees may have maternity provisions in their contracts of employment which are more generous than those available under statute, and the question therefore arises as to the relation between these rights. Section 48(1) provides that where an employee is in such a position she "may not exercise the two rights separately but may in returning to work take advantage of whichever right is, in any particular respect, the more favourable." Such a right has been termed a "composite" right, being composed of the best elements of the statutory and contractual regimes. Such a provision appears on first acquaintance to be highly favourable to the employee, enabling her to rely upon whichever is the best in any particular respect of the two sets of provisions. The provision enables an employer who is concerned about such matters to improve upon the statutory scheme, perhaps by agreement with the representatives of the employees, whilst rendering it impossible to derogate from the statutory standards.

10.64 Yet there are problems with the extent to which an employee can elect to take advantage of the more favourable provisions of a contractual scheme. Thus, in *Bovey* v. *Board of Governors of the Hospital for Sick Children*[93] a physiotherapist wished to return to work part-time after the birth of her child. She had a statutory right to return to her previous job full-time, and a contractual right to return

[91] [1986] I.R.L.R. 203, EAT.
[92] EP(C)A, Sched. 2, para. 5.
[93] [1978] I.C.R. 934, [1978] I.R.L.R. 241, EAT.

part-time to a job at a lower grade. She wished to return part-time to her previous job and sought to combine the most favourable aspects of her composite right to return in order to do this. The industrial tribunal and the EAT held that she had to choose between what were seen as "essentially indivisible" rights to return full-time or part-time. Thus the EAT held that:

> "There must be a limit to the extent to which the right in question, to return to work, can be sub-divided, so as to identify the particular respects in which it is more favourable."

10.65   Yet this interpretation seems unduly limiting, for the phrase "in any particular respect" seems to suggest that the hours to be worked and the grade at which the person works are distinguishable and therefore capable of being treated separately. The view adopted by the EAT appears more like a straight choice between the contractual and statutory rights of the worker, than the exercise of a "composite" right.

10.66   A yet more significant limitation upon the exercise of contractual rights to return to work is provided by section 48(2) which provides that:

> "The provisions of sections 45,46, 47, 56 and 86 and paragraphs 1 to 4 and 6 of Schedule 2 shall apply, subject to any modifications necessary to give effect to any more favourable contractual terms, to the exercise of the composite right described in subsection (1) as they apply to the exercise of the right conferred solely by this Part."

10.67   Thus in the absence of explicit contractual notice terms which are more favourable to the employee, the notice provisions contained in section 33 and on which the exercise of section 45 rights depend, will condition the exercise of any contractual right, as they condition the exercise of the statutory rights. In *Lavery* v. *Plessey Communications Ltd*,[94] the EAT had held that failure to give the requisite seven days notice had vitiated the applicant's statutory right to return. Before the Court of Appeal the argument was based primarily upon the existence of a separate contractual right to return. As her contract had not been explicitly terminated, it was argued that it must have subsisted throughout her absence and up until the moment when the employer refused to allow her to return to work. On this basis it was argued that, if her right to bring an action under section 56 was defeated by the failure to give the requisite notice required under section 33, she was entitled to bring an action under section 55, based upon the employer's repudiation of her contract at the date of her attempted return to work. This argument was not accepted, as section

---

[94] [1982] I.R.L.R. 180, EAT; [1983] I.R.L.R. 202, C.A. and see above for the facts.

48 provides that the two rights may not be exercised
separately and that it is the "composite" right which must
be exercised. In those circumstances failure to give the
necessary notice was fatal.

10.68 A second line of argument was developed before the
Court of Appeal to the effect that if the employee was
dismissed during the subsistence of her contract, Sched. 2,
paras. 6(1) and (4) assist her to bring an action under section
55. Paragraph 6(1) embraces any dismissal which occurs
during the subsistence of the contract of employment after
the eleventh week prior to the EWC, except (as prescribed
in paragraph 6(2)) those dismissals which occur in the course
of an attempted exercise of the right to return in accordance
with her contract to which section 48 applies. Paragraph 6(2)
provides that such employees shall be deemed not to have
been dismissed for the purposes of paragraph 6(1), with the
effect that the provisions of paragraph 6(4) do not apply to
them. Paragraph 6(4) provides that any dismissal falling
within paragraph 6(1) shall not affect the employee's right to
return to work. Sub-paragraph 6(4)(a) further provides that
the existence of that right to return is not to be taken into
account in the assessment of any compensation for unfair
dismissal, whilst sub-paragraph 6(4)(b) stipulates that if an
employee has been dismissed after the eleventh week of her
period of absence due to maternity, that dismissal shall not
affect her right to return provided she repays any
compensation she has received for unfair dismissal or
redundancy. Such compensation could only have occurred in
the context of an application for unfair dismissal under
section 55 because the applicant could not have been
dismissed in the course of exercising her right to return
under section 48, with the possibility of a potential section
56 application. Therefore, although paragraph 6(2) does state
that no dismissal shall be deemed to have taken place when
the dismissal occurs in the context of an attempted return to
work, this deeming provision is said to be only for the
purposes of paragraph 1, the purpose of which is to regulate
the application of paragraph 6(4). The Court of Appeal
construed paragraph 6(2) as deeming that no dismissal could
occur in the context of a return to work, thereby precluding
the possibility of an application under the ordinary law of
unfair dismissal via section 55,[95] a conclusion arguably
opposite to that intended by the legislation.

10.69 A third argument put forward on behalf of the
applicant was to the effect that if there was a composite right
and that composite right contained less rigorous notice
provisions, such provisions would take precedence over their
statutory equivalents, as they would, in that respect, be

---

[95] It was in this context that Browne-Wilkinson J. criticised the maternity
provisions as being of "inordinate complexity"!

more favourable. However, no such clear contractual provisions could be deduced from the evidence, and in that event the exercise of a composite right, for which section 56 is the channel through which any infringement of the right to return is to be processed, depended upon the admittedly defective compliance with the section 33 notice provisions.[96]

10.70 The decision in *Lavery* was followed by the Court of Appeal in *Dowuona* v. *John Lewis Partnership Ltd*,[97] in which an agreement was made between the applicant and the employer to extend the period by which a return must be made by the one weeks holiday to which the employee was entitled. In the event, the baby was premature and neither the baby nor the mother were well. At the end of the due time, a sick note was sent in first for one month and then covering subsequent months. The employers refused to take the applicant back. The Court of Appeal held that it was unrealistic to view the extra week as a return to work followed by a week's holiday, from which the woman failed to return on time due to sickness. The Court took the view that this was an exercise of a composite right under section 48 and that the failure to return on time precluded a claim under section 56. The Court also held that as the dismissal occurred in the context of an attempted return to work in the exercise of a composite right, that Sched. 2, para. 2 precluded a section 55 claim.

10.71 The decision in *Lavery* was distinguished in *Lucas* v.*Norton of London Ltd.*[95] in which an entirely informal arrangement was struck that the applicant would cease work on account of her pregnancy. The employer paid SMP, but thought little more about the matter until the applicant sought to return to work, at which time she was told that her job was no longer available. She was paid two weeks' pay in lieu of notice, which was construed as an acknowledgement by the employer that her contract had subsisted. Even though qualified to do so, she had not sought to exercise her statutory right and indeed had not taken any of the preliminary steps of giving notice of her intention to return at least three weeks before leaving. She was not therefore disbarred by her failure to give notice of intention to return as she was not attempting to exercise a statutory right, but relying solely on the persistence of her contract, varied so as to allow her not to fulfil the obligation to work during the period of absence. Thus, in the view of the EAT, she was not caught up in section 48 and the complex position emerging from the *Lavery* case and was free to pursue her claim for unfair dismissal in the ordinary way, arguably even relying upon pregnancy as the reason for

---

[96] See also the judgement of Lord McDonald in *Kolfor Plant Ltd* v. *Wright* [1982] I.R.L.R. 311.
[97] [1987] I.R.L.R. 310.
[98] [1984] I.R.L.R. 86.

her dismissal under section 60.[99] Whilst it could be argued that this case puts the woman who has not even attempted to protect her rights in a better position than one who has, the outcome does depend on the continued existence of a contract which contains a right to return, without which no contractual dismissal could be said to have occurred. This conclusion is reinforced by the decision of the Northern Ireland Court of Appeal in *McKnight* v. *Addlestones (Jewellers) Ltd*,[1] in that where an employee failed to comply with the requirements necessary for the effective exercise of the statutory right and did not have a contractual right to return, when she left she simply left to have her baby. Any persistence of her contract of employment was said to be purely for the purposes of seeing whether she could effectively exercise her statutory right to return, which, not having given the requisite notice of her intention to be absent, in the event she could not do.

10.72 A third variation in the way these complex provisions can be construed is offered by the EAT in the *Institute of the Motor Industry* v. *Harvey*,[2] in which a senior female executive whose contract was found to have subsisted during her maternity leave became embroiled in a dispute with her employers over the precise terms of her return and the date at which it was to take place. As a result, no section 47 notice of her intended day of return was ever given. She claimed to have been constructively dismissed under section 55 during the course of her maternity leave as a result of the collapse of the relationship of mutual trust and confidence. The EAT held that as her contract had subsisted during her absence and that as there had been no attempt to exercise her statutory right to return, she was not caught by section 48 and could therefore bring an action under section 55. She was not alleged to have been dismissed in the context of exercising either a statutory or a contractual right to return, but simply as a result of the collapse of the relationship between the parties in the course of the negotiations concerning her possible return. Much depends on the facts of the case in such situations, but there is clearly a possibility of the separate exercise of contractual and statutory rights where there has been no attempted exercise of the section 45 right.

10.73 All in all, the criticism of the maternity legislation made by Browne-Wilkinson J. (as he then was) in *Lavery*

---

[99] It would be possible on the facts of the case to take the view that was being attempted was an ineffective exercise of her statutory rights and that therefore the case falls within s.48. Balcombe L.J. in *Dowuona* did not discuss the decision in *Lucas*, as it was not relied upon, although he did state that his silence was not to be taken as an indication that he considered the case rightly decided.
[1] [1984] I.R.L.R. 453.
[2] [1992] I.R.L.R. 343.

that it is of "inordinate complexity" in the context of ordinary every-day employment law seems more than justified.

The right to return at the end of the 14 week maternity leave period

10.74   Article 8 of the Directive provides for a period of 14 weeks' maternity leave, during which time Article 11(2)(a) stipulates that the rights connected with the worker's employment contract must be ensured. This is translated into British law by the amended section 33 of EP(C)A, which provides that a woman absent during her 14 week maternity leave period shall be entitled to the benefit of the terms and conditions which would have been applicable to her had she not been absent. It follows from this provision that a woman so entitled will be entitled to return to work at the end of that period on the same terms and conditions which she formerly enjoyed, and will therefore enjoy a right to unfair dismissal. Indeed the amended section 60(*b*) provides that if her maternity leave period ends with her dismissal for a reason connected with her having given birth, that dismissal shall be automatically unfair. Furthermore, the amended section 60(*c*) provides that if a woman is dismissed after the end of her maternity leave period because she took, or availed herself of the benefits, of maternity leave, then her dismissal shall be unfair. The amended section 60(*b*) also provides that it shall be unfair to dismiss a woman at the end of her maternity leave period by reason of redundancy, if she has not been offered any suitable alternative vacancy, in accordance with the procedure laid down in the amended section 38.

10.75   The new right to return at the end of the 14 week maternity leave period is subject only to the qualification that the woman shall have given notice in writing, twenty-one days before the date of the commencement of her maternity leave, that she is pregnant, and of the expected, or actual, week of childbirth.[3] Thus the new right will be valuable to those who lack two years' service and who wish to return to work, but it is a somewhat draconian option. At the end of the 14 week period of maternity leave, mothers will still be entitled to a further four weeks of SMP (or maternity allowance), which must be sacrificed if a return to work is to be made in due time, unless the new right is modified by a co-existing contractual right which may be exercised concurrently. Once the 14 week period (potentially modified by any contractual rights) has elapsed only those women who satisfy the conditions of the amended sections 39-43 (formerly ss. 45-47) as to service and notice requirements will have a statutory right to return to work.

10.76   The amended section 33(3) provides that, where a woman has both the right conferred by the amended section

---

[3] Amended s.36. The employer is entitled to request a statement of the EWC by a registered medical practitioner or midwife.

33 and a corresponding contractual right, she may take advantage of whichever right is, in any particular respect, the more favourable. It is notable that when compared with the previous section 48 wording for the exercise of "composite" rights, the new formulation omits the words "may not exercise the rights separately", and nor is the new right qualified by the limitations which have been held (by virtue of EP(C)A 1978 Sched. 2, para. 2) to exclude an ordinary unfair dismissal claim under section 55 in *Lavery* v. *Plessey Communications Ltd*. Thus a section 60 based action would be possible in the event of a failure to allow a woman to return from the 14 week maternity leave for one of the specified reasons, even where her leave had been extended by the exercise of contractual rights. Clearly the terms and conditions maintained by the amended section 33 will remain in force during any extended contractual period of maternity leave, so that a refusal to allow a woman to return would constitute a dismissal. Where the woman is not allowed to return for a reason which is unconnected with pregnancy, such as, for example, a business reorganisation, her dismissal will fall to be considered under the ordinary law of unfair dismissal at the end of the contractually extended period of maternity leave.[4] The new wording would not appear to change the effect of *Bovey* v.*Board of Governors of the Hospital for Sick Children*, in that both depend on the phrase "in any particular respect". Much will depend on contractual wording as to the exact effect of combining statutory and contractual rights, or of exercising them separately.

The right to return 29 weeks after childbirth as amended by the Directive

10.77   To enjoy a right to return 29 weeks after childbirth, a woman must first enjoy the right to maternity leave prescribed in section 33.[5] The amended right to return after 29 weeks will be contained in the amended sections 39-44 of EP(C)A, which are introduced by Schedule 2 of the TURERA 1993. The amended section 39(1) makes clear that the right to return at 29 weeks after childbirth supplements the right to 14 weeks' maternity leave provided for in the amended section 33, but is only available to those employees who satisfy the prescribed condition. These provisions are essentially similar to the previous legislation as to length of service and notice. These are that the employee must have been employed for two years at the beginning of the eleventh week prior to the EWC[6] and satisfied the conditions

[4] A note of caution should be sounded here about the possibilities of combining the wide terms as to eligibility for the new statutory right, with a contractual scheme which is possibly superior in the matter of benefits. It could be argued that where, for example, a woman must have two years service to have a contractual right to 30 weeks paid maternity leave, she would not be able to combine the superior length of her contractual leave with the new statutory terms as to eligibility, because until she has her two years service, she does not have the contractual right.

[5] Amended s.39.

[6] EP(C)A amended s.39(1)(*b*).

as to notice prescribed in the amended section 40. One significant difference is that the request for written confirmation of the intention to return to work must not now be made earlier than 21 days before the expiry of the maternity period.[7]

10.78 The amended section 39(2)(a) explicitly provides not only that the woman shall be entitled to return on terms which are not less favourable as to remumeration than those which would have been applicable to her if she had not been absent from work at any time since the commencement of her maternity leave period, but section 39(2)(*b*) also provides that her seniority, pension and similar rights shall be as they would have been if the period of employment prior to the end of her maternity leave (not prior to her absence *sic* as under the previous section 45(2)) was continuous with her renewed employment, subject to the provisions of the 1989 Social Security Act as to unfair maternity provisions, (as to which, see para. 10.52 above); and otherwise on terms and conditions not less favourable than those which would have been applicable had she not been absent from work after the end of her maternity leave period. Thus in any period of post maternity leave absence, benefits do not accumulate though continuity is not broken and the employee has a right to return on terms and conditions as to remuneration which are not less favourable than which would have applied if she had not been so absent, as regards seniority and pensions as at the end of the maternity leave period and otherwise (*i.e.* as regards job duties etc) on terms as if she had not been absent.

10.79 The amended section 41 provides that in the event that redundancy prevents her return to work, the employee shall have the right to be offered a suitable alternative vacancy on terms and conditions not substantially less favourable than those previously enjoyed. The amended section 42 provides for the extension of the period of maternity in the same manner as does the previous section 47. The provisions of Schedule 2 are similarly imported into the right to return at the end of 29 weeks, as are the requirements on the exercise of "composite" rights in the amended section 44 (the old section 48). Therefore *Lavery* v. *Plessey* and *Duowana* v. *John Lewis* are still good law in respect of the 29 weeks right, in so far as the developing line of case law on the exercise of contractual rights prior to or separate from the exercise of the statutory right, has not modified their effect.[8]

Health and Safety Protection for Pregnant and Breastfeeding Workers.

10.80 The principal thrust of the Pregnancy Directive is towards health and safety protection for pregnant and breastfeeding workers, it having been introduced under

[7] Amended s.40(2).
[8] See para. 10.71.

Article 118A of the Treaty of Rome, as amended by the
Single European Act. The Directive is the tenth daughter
directive consequent upon the Framework Health and Safety
Directive 89/391. The Directive provides that guidelines are
to be issued by the Commission with the advice of the EC
Advisory Committee on Health and Safety at Work in
consultation with the Member States, which cover the
assessment of chemical, physical and biological agents
considered hazardous to the safety and health of pregnant
and breastfeeding workers. The guidelines may also cover
movements and postures, mental and physical fatigue and
other types of mental stress connected with the work done
by such workers.

10.81   Articles 3-6 of the Directive introduce a regime
under which employers are bound to make a risk assessment
of any situation where pregnant or breastfeeding workers are
likely to be exposed to the non-exhaustive list of hazardous
substances set out in Annex 1 to the Directive. Where the
assessment reveals a risk to the health and safety of such
workers, the employer shall take steps to ensure that the
exposure of the worker to such risks is avoided, by
temporarily adjusting the working conditions or working
hours of the worker concerned.[9] If such adjustments are not
feasible, the employer shall move the worker to another job.
If that is not feasible, the employee shall be granted leave in
accordance with national legislation.[10] The Trade Union
Reform and Employment Rights Act 1993 enacts a provision
whereby employees suspended from work on medical
grounds in accordance with any enactment or code of
practice enacted under the Health and Safety at Work Act,
will have the right to be offered suitable alternative work,
where this is available, before being suspended on medical
grounds.[11] Any employee suspended on such medical
grounds will have the right to remuneration equivalent to
normal pay, for the period of suspension.[12] Exposure to
certain substances is prohibited for pregnant[13] or
breastfeeding[14] workers.

10.82   Under Article 7, Member states are obliged to
introduce a procedure under which pregnant or
breastfeeding workers may not be obliged to perform night
work on production of a medical certificate stating that this
is necessary for the safety and health of the worker
concerned. Where a transfer to day-time work is not
feasible, there shall be a right to an extension of maternity
leave or other leave from work.

[9] Art. 3 of 92/85.
[106] Art. 3(3).
[11] Amended EP(C)A, ss.45-46, enacted in TURERA Sched. 3.
[12] Amended EP(C)A, s.47.
[13] Dir. 92/85/Annexe 2(a).
[14] Dir. 92/85/Annexe 2(b).

Conclusions **10.83** The law protecting maternity is complex and fragmentary. The rights arising from the Pregnancy Directive, though in some ways more limited than existing statutory rights, are not subject to the same constraints as to their exercise. Nonetheless, because there will be two layers of statutory rights with regard to maternity leave and the right to return as from October 1994, the position remains fraught with the possibility for misunderstandings between employers and their employees. These potential difficulties look as if they will be aggravated by the possibility of contractual rights being capable of separate exercise in relation to the 14 week period of maternity leave, but only being capable of being exercised as a "composite" right to return after 29 weeks.

10.84 Yet the new laws do provide a broader possibility for women to surmount the potentially disruptive effect of pregnancy on their careers. The existence of a right to return for all women, even though it is only after 14 weeks, must be a substantial step forward. Where that new right can be advantageously combined with contractual rights which offer a more realistic period of maternity leave, the effect will be still greater. Yet it is possible that what many women would really like is the type of career breaks lasting up to two, three or even five years, which some banks and other service organisations offer, but which are not generally available in other organisations. Financial protection during a much shorter period of maternity leave goes some way towards meeting the needs of those contemplating an unbroken career; it does not affect the position of those who would like a longer period at home with their children before returning to work and attempting to resume their career. The new laws strike a balance between the needs of women who want a family and a career, and the needs of employers for continuity of service. Perhaps in a few years that balance will be struck at a different point.

INDEX